The Female Experience

THE AMERICAN HERITAGE SERIES

The American Heritage Series

under the general editorship of
ALFRED F. YOUNG *and* LEONARD W. LEVY

The Female Experience

An American Documentary

GERDA LERNER

THE BOBBS-MERRILL COMPANY, INC.
INDIANAPOLIS

*in memory of
three remarkable women,
my friends and teachers:*

*my mother, Ilona Kronstein, b. Neumann, artist
Viola Brothers Shore, writer
Melissa Lewis Richter, scientist and educator*

The Bobbs-Merrill Company, Inc.
4300 West 62nd Street
Indianapolis, Indiana 46268

First Edition
First Printing 1977

Library of Congress Cataloging in Publication Data
Main entry under title:

The Female experience.

(The American heritage series; no. 90)
Bibliography: p.
Includes index.
1. Women—United States—Social conditions—Sources. 2. Women—
United States—History—Sources. I. Lerner, Gerda, 1920–
HQ1410.F45   301.41′2′0973   76–40258
ISBN 0–672–51555–5
ISBN 0–672–61248–8 pbk.

Contents

Foreword

The American Heritage Series has pioneered in the publishing of volumes on groups long relegated to second-class status in historical study as well as in American life. *The Female Experience* is another such volume and in our opinion will become a landmark in its field.

The focus of the book is what it has meant to be a woman in America—how women have passed through the life cycle from youth to death, how women have moved out into male-dominated society, and how they have defined themselves, while developing various forms of feminist consciousness. Those familiar with the literature will recognize that this is the richest collection of rare materials on these themes to be assembled in one volume. Over half the documents are taken from manuscripts that have never been published; another quarter are from memoirs, diaries, and printed sources found only in research libraries.

The writing of women's history is passing through several stages. Some scholars continue to emphasize the "contributions" of women which were left out of standard accounts; others deal with once-famous women leaders; still others are concerned with the organized movements for woman's rights. Such approaches, valuable as they may be, are usually based on assumptions of what is important taken from the values of a male-dominated society—and from the values of the elites at that. By contrast, Professor Lerner has hammered out a set of conceptions that in effect provides a new framework for the study of women's history in the United States. She has shifted the emphasis to the experiences of ordinary women and to a wide range of ideas expressed outside formal organizations, and she has avoided using the traditional "periods" of political history by which U.S. history is conventionally studied. In the general introduction and the chapter introductions she furnishes commentary that not only knits together the sources, but also suggests the themes by which women's history can be further analyzed. The total effect is stunning—so much so as to make one wonder what American history may eventually look like once we are able to reconstruct the history of all the groups that have been "left out." In ignoring them, it is very clear, we have distorted our history as a whole.

The volume is the work of many years of research and reflection by a scholar recognized for her command of women's history in the context of American history. Her scholarly interests in nineteenth-century social history, and in abolitionism and black history in particular, were shown most recently in *Black Women in White America: A Documentary History* (1972). She brings to historical scholarship the sensitivity to individuals she has shown as a creative writer of short stories, poems, and a novel. The result of this combination of talents is a book satisfying at many levels, one both analytical and provocative and at the same time rich with the moving, often poignant, experiences of human beings.

This book is one of a series created to provide the essential primary sources of the American experience, especially of American thought. The American Heritage Series constitutes a documentary library of United States history, filling a need long felt among scholars, students, libraries, and general readers for authoritative collections of original materials. Some volumes illuminate the thought of significant individuals, such as James Madison or John Marshall; some deal with movements, such as the Antifederalist or the Populist; others are organized around special themes, such as Puritan political thought or American Catholic thought on social questions. Many volumes take up the large number of subjects traditionally studied in American history for which surprisingly there are no documentary anthologies; others pioneer in introducing new subjects of increasing importance to scholars and to the contemporary world. The series aspires to maintain the high standards demanded of contemporary editing, providing authentic texts, intelligently and unobtrusively edited. It also has the distinction of presenting pieces of substantial length which give the full character and flavor of the original. The American Heritage Series is, we believe, the most comprehensive and authoritative of its kind.

Alfred F. Young
Leonard W. Levy

Acknowledgments

A work of this kind, which rests on finding unknown or rare sources difficult of access, depends on the facilities of many archives and libraries. I am greatly obliged to the following for giving me permission to use their manuscript collections: The American Antiquarian Society; the William L. Clements Library, University of Michigan; the Henry E. Huntington Library; Manuscript Division, Library of Congress; the Minnesota Historical Society Library; the Social Welfare History Archives Center, University of Minnesota; the Newberry Library; the New York Historical Society; the Schlesinger Library on the History of Women in America; the Sophia Smith Collection, Women's History Archive, Smith College; the Tuskegee Archives, Tuskegee Institute; and the Western Reserve Historical Society Library. The advice and assistance offered by archivists and librarians in each of these institutions have been invaluable.

My special thanks go to Miriam Y. Holden, whose superb private collection on the history of women has, over many years, been a source of inspiration and information to me and to two generations of scholars.

The names of those who called my attention to certain documents are mentioned in the text, but I would like here to record my gratitude to my professor colleagues Linda Kerber, University of Iowa, Iowa City; Barbara Fassler, Central University of Iowa, Pella; Kirk Jeffrey, Carleton College, Northfield, Minn.; Gretchen Kreuter, Macalester College, St. Paul, Minn.; Mari Jo Buhle, Brown University, Providence, R.I.; and to my research assistants and former students Anne Hoblitzelle and Dolores Janiewski.

My sincere thanks to professors Joan Kelly-Gadol, City University of New York; Alice Kessler-Harris, Hofstra University; and Joyce Riegelhaupt and Amy Swerdlow, Sarah Lawrence College, and to Virginia Brodine, for their perceptive readings and helpful criticism. I greatly appreciate the support and attention given this work by the educational and trade editors of the Bobbs-Merrill Company and would like to express my thanks to Carol Ann Stevens for her careful and caring copy editing of the manuscript. The technical aspects of my task were greatly lightened by the able assistance and precision of Carole Dascani.

I am grateful above all to Professor Alfred F. Young, general co-editor of this series, whose confidence in this book and its author sustained me through difficult periods. His scholarly knowledge, wide editorial experience, sensitivity, and deep concern with making sources on women's history widely available made his advice particularly valuable. I appreciate his keen critical ability and his openness to new interpretations, from which I have benefited greatly in preparing this book.

Gerda Lerner

Sarah Lawrence College
Bronxville, N.Y.

Notes

In the interest of preserving the authenticity of the documents, grammar and spelling have been retained in their original form, even when such form may seem quaint, erroneous, or offensive to the modern reader. The only changes are slight alterations in punctuation where these seemed necessary for clarity. Cuts and ellipses have been made in such a way as not to affect the content, intent, and tone of the original documents. Rare changes in the order of paragraphs are noted in the text.

* * *

The terms of reference by which Blacks have referred to themselves have changed in the course of history. In recognition of the emotional and symbolic significance of the choice of a name, which is part of self-definition for individuals as well as for groups, usage in this volume follows the spirit of the documents. The terms I have used when referring to the documents are those which were generallly accepted in a given period by the group under discussion. Thus "Negro," "Afro-American," and "Black" appear throughout. When the word "Black" means "Negro," I have capitalized it when used as a noun, but not as an adjective. Should the use of the word "Black" for "Negro" persist, it will undoubtedly be capitalized in the adjectival form, but such usage is still rare.

A similar wide range of usage with sensitive connotations concerns the terms "ladies" and "women." Here I use "ladies" to designate members of the leisured or upper classes, and "women" to refer to all others.

G. L.

Introduction

Women's experience encompasses all that is human; they share—and always have shared—the world equally with men. Equally in the sense that half, at least, of all the world's experience has been theirs, half of the world's work and much of its products. In one sense, then, to document the experience of women would mean documenting all of history: they have always been of it, in it, and making it. But their history has been a special kind, distorted and alienated because it has been refracted doubly—through the lens of man's records and observations; through the application to it of male values. What we know of the past experience of women has come to us largely through the reflections of men; how we see and interpret what we know about women has been shaped for us through a value system defined by men. Instead, the question prompting the writing and editing of this book is: what would history be like if it were seen through the eyes of women and ordered by values they define?

The problem of organizing a work of this kind is essentially that of finding a new framework for conceptualizing the history of women. To begin with, until very recently, historical scholarship has largely ignored the history of women and the female point of view in reconstructing the past. It considered those activities which men have engaged in to have been significant to historical development, while the activities of women were considered to have been marginal and insignificant. In short, a male-oriented conceptual framework has dominated the questions by which the past of humankind has been organized. Even historians working

in women's history at first worked under the assumption that
women were a "marginal minority" and that women's history was no more than a collection of "missing persons and
facts." But women are neither marginal nor a minority. They
are and always have been at least half of all Americans; they
are distributed through all classes and categories of U.S.
society. Therefore, any effort to make of women's history a
sort of supplement to U.S. history and to fit it into the traditional categories can only be an inadequate substitute for
the challenging task of reconstructing the female past and
analyzing it by concepts appropriate to it. Historians of
women's history, seeing the need to go beyond "contribution history" have increasingly turned to primary sources
for the female point of view and for a record of the female
experience. This is an essential first step toward writing a
new history which will with true equality reflect the dual
nature of humankind—its male and female vision.

It is obviously impossible to reconstruct in one volume
the manifold and varied experiences of millions of women.

Instead, what has been attempted here is to give a selec-
tive composite picture of the female past, assembled so as to
tell a story and help the reader to share some of the experiences, concerns, fears, and hopes of American women.

I have sought, in editing this volume, to make the documentary selections as representative as the available
sources would permit, reflecting variations as to age, economic class, race, religion, and ethnicity. I learned to appreciate the difficulty of such an undertaking in my earlier
work *Black Women in White America: A Documentary History* (1972), which revealed many complex variations of historical experience among women of different races. How
was one to select out of the richness of the past of black
women a few items for inclusion in a volume which would
be "representative" of the history of black women in America? Concerning women of other minority groups there was
the opposite problem. Source material by American Indian
or Chicana women is quite difficult to find due to the in-

herent bias of manuscript collections which favor white middle-class women and those connected with the struggle for educational opportunities and with the woman's suffrage movement. Even so, despite inevitable and regrettable omissions, this collection contains many documents concerning working women, immigrants, Blacks, and women on the frontier.

More than half of the documents in this volume have never been printed before and are derived from manuscript sources. A third more come from rare books or from old periodicals, which are not generally accessible. While twentieth-century documents, in particular those of the current woman's movement, have not been neglected, I have followed the principle of omitting well known and readily accessible documents, regardless of their importance. This was done in order to make room for the kind of sources which are usually unavailable to the general reader.

This book presents documents left by American women, commenting on themselves and each other, on their environment, on the men around them. Some look at ideas, values, and social institutions from the woman's point of view; others complain, protest, and seek solutions. They trace the slow process by which women emancipated themselves from the male-dominated, male-defined world in which they live.

The first step toward emancipation is self-consciousness, becoming aware of a distortion, a wrong: what women have been taught about the world, what they see reflected in art, literature, philosophy, and religion is not quite appropriate to them. It perfectly fits man, woman's "other." In here reversing the phrase by which Simone de Beauvoir defines woman as man's "other," I intend to indicate that there comes a moment in woman's self-perception, when she begins to see man as "the other." It is this moment when her feminist self-consciousness begins.

Next comes a questioning of tradition, often followed by tentative steps in new directions: Anne Hutchinson holding weekly meetings for men and women in which *she*, not the male clergy, comments on the Bible; Frances Wright daring to assert woman's freedom of sexual choice; Margaret Sanger discovering in one dramatic moment that societally enforced motherhood was a wrong no longer to be tolerated.

Then comes a reaching out toward other women, the slow painstaking search for sisterhood: sewing circles and female clubs; women workers organizing themselves; woman's rights conventions; the building of mass movements of women.

Out of such communality and collectivity emerges feminist consciousness—a set of ideas which not only challenges patriarchal values and assumptions, but attempts to substitute for them a feminist system of ideas and values. This process of creating feminist consciousness has something, but by no means everything, to do with the quest for woman's rights, equality, and justice—it has a great deal to do with the search for autonomy. Autonomy means women defining themselves and the values by which they will live, and beginning to think of institutional arrangements which will order their environment in line with their needs. It means to some the evolution of practical programs, to others the reforming of existing social arrangements, to still others the building of new institutions. Autonomy means moving out from a world in which one is born to marginality, to a past without meaning, and a future determined by others—into a world in which one acts and chooses, aware of a meaningful past and free to shape one's future.

History has always been distorted by presenting to us mostly that which men have observed and men have ordered. This documentary American history is designed to view the past from an entirely new perspective. It constitutes a self-conscious effort to represent the other—the female—side of the world.

In considering the proper framework for conceptualizing women's history, periodization poses a problem. The periods in which basic changes occur in society and which historians commonly regard as turning points, are not necessarily the same for men and women. This is not surprising when we consider that the traditional time frame in history has been derived from political history. For example, neither during or after the American Revolution nor in the age of Jackson did women share in the broadening out of opportunities and in the political democratization experienced by men. On the contrary, women in both periods experienced status loss and a restriction of their choices as to education or vocation, and had new restraints imposed upon their sexuality, at least by prescription. Thus, the traditional political and military chronology is largely irrelevant to the history of women. In this volume I have sought, instead, to order the female past from within its own consciousness.

The topics proceed from the personal to the institutional, from self and family to group and society, and constitute an attempt at a new ordering of historical categories to make them more appropriate to the experience of women. Part I traces the life stages of women and with them turning points in individual lives. It centers on the family. Part II deals with the major aspects of women's experiences in male-defined institutions, such as the workplace, the school, the trade union, government. It illustrates the ways in which women have adapted to such institutions and have transformed them to their own needs. Part III traces the development of feminist consciousness in its various stages: defiance of traditional roles; definition of sisterhood; the search for new structures; and, finally, the expression of feminist ideology.

Readers wishing to follow this progression may proceed in chapter order, but each chapter is also designed to be read on its own. Chapter introductions, together with the headnotes above the documents, will help to place the documents in their context.

Is it justifiable to speak of a female historical experience different from that of men? To find an answer to this basic question it is useful to examine the life cycles and the turn-

ing points in individual lives of men and women of the past.
Are there significant differences in childhood, education,
maturity? Are social expectations different for boys and
girls? Taking full cognizance of the wide range of variations,
are there any universals by which we can define the female
past? Source material for answering such questions, insofar
as they pertain to women, can be found in Part I.

There are basic differences in the way boys and girls experience the world, and, more importantly, in the social
roles they are trained to fulfill. From childhood on the talents and drives of girls were channeled in directions different from those of boys. For boys, the family was the place
from which one sprang and to which one returned for comfort and support, but the field of action was the larger world
of wilderness, adventure, industry, labor, and politics. For
girls, the family was to be the world, their field of action
the domestic circle. *He* was to express himself in his work
and, through it and social action, was to help to transform
his environment; *her* individual growth and choices were
restricted to lead her to express herself through love, wife-
hood, and motherhood—through the support and nurture of
others, who would act for her. The way in which these
gender-differentiated patterns would find expression would
change in the course of historical development; the differences in the function assigned to the sexes might widen or
narrow, but the fact of different sex-role indoctrination
remained.

Life was experienced at a different rhythm by men and
women. For a boy, education was directed toward a vocational or professional goal, and his life ideally moved upward and outward in a straight line until it reached a
plateau of fulfillment; the girl's education was sporadic and
often interrupted; it did not lead to the fulfillment of her life
role, but rather competed with it. Her development was
dependent on her relationship to others and was often determined by them; it moved in wavelike, circuitous motion. In
the boy's case, the life crises were connected to vocational

goals: separation from the family for purposes of greater educational opportunity; success or failures in achievement and career; economic decisions or setbacks. For the girl such crises were more closely connected to distinct stages in her biological life: transition from childhood to adolescence and then to marriage which meant, in the past, confinement and loss of freedom, and greater restraint rather than the broadening out which it meant for the boy. Love and marriage for her implied a shifting of domesticity from one household to another, and the onset of her serious responsibilities: childbirth, childrearing, and the nurture of the family. Finally came the crisis of widowhood and bereavement which could mean, depending on her economic circumstances, increasing freedom and autonomy or a difficult struggle for economic survival.

In every society people are assigned specific roles and indoctrinated to perform to the expectations and values of their society. But for women this has always meant social indoctrination to a value system which imposed upon them restrictions on the range of their choices greater than those imposed on men. It has meant that women have been trained to fit into institutions shaped, determined, and ruled by men and that their own definitions of selfhood and fulfillment have remained subordinate to patriarchal concepts.

Women often participated in their own subordination by internalizing the ideology and values which oppressed them and by passing those on to their children. Yet they were not passive victims, but always involved themselves actively in the world in their own way. The history of women is the history of their on-going functioning *on their own terms* in a male-defined world. It is also the history of their finding their own consciousness. Starting upon a stage defined by their life cycle, they rebelled against and defied societal indoctrination, developed their own definition of community, and built their own female culture.

In the following pages, beginning with Part II, women

are seen as they functioned within the major institutions of American life. Of these, for women the family came first and loomed largest; next came the workplace, the school, finally government. Since American institutions were decisively affected by industrialization and its consequences, it may be useful here to present as a background for the documents a brief overview of the impact on women of major economic developments in the American past.

Seventeenth-century settlers, like later immigrants, brought European patriarchal values and institutions with them, transplanting them to the new world. The patriarchal tradition confined women to the family, but in the American colonies a shortage of labor, a shortage of women, frontier conditions, and the economic demands of a preindustrial society gave women relatively greater mobility, higher status, and greater independence than what prevailed in other countries. The many occupations in which colonial women can be found and the relative freedom of widows and spinsters to engage in commerce and to trade and conduct business have all been noted by historians. Colonial women enjoyed better living conditions, better health, and higher status than their European counterparts. Lower-class girls, in particular, benefited from the favorable sex ratio which enabled them to secure marriages without dowries and to share in the general upward mobility possible in a frontier society with large and accessible regions of free land. Still, the family structure and the institutions of colonial America remained patriarchal. Women derived their status in society from their fathers and later their husbands. At all times, their work was subordinate to and in the service of the family and, if it was not farm work, was usually complementary to or a continuation of their fathers' or their husbands' work.

In an agricultural economy the family was a self-supporting economic unit in which each individual—from small child to aged parent—made an essential and respected economic contribution. Distribution of work proceeded along gender lines, but the distinctions were easily blurred. The family shared jobs, hardships, and pleasures and intermingled in daily activity and work. For women, these conditions provided benefits, such as their gaining the respect given naturally to those contributing essential economic services, and their acquiring the sense of accomplishment and self-respect which comes to those skilled in a variety of functions.

Women lived in close daily contact with their men, their children, their relatives, and their neighbors of different age groups. If, as historians have noted, they complained more bitterly of isolation and loneliness under frontier settlement conditions than did the men, they also acted to overcome these conditions, which were imposed by environment and economic need. The point here is that in later periods of development, the isolation of women within their homes was caused not by environmental and economic necessities, but by societal strictures. This had a decisive and negative effect on the status and self-perceptions of women.

By the second decade of the nineteenth century, industrialization and urbanization had brought decisive changes in the family and in the status of the women of the Eastern seaboard states.* Class differences and changes in residence, occupation, and in sex ratio similarly altered the position of women.

Starting with preindustrial society, the family began to lose its unified economic function. Men's work had moved out of the home, leading to a separation of economic function along sex lines and with it, to a redefinition of gender roles. Man, the breadwinner, working outside the home and bringing not bread but cash into the home, had entered the

---

* It should be noted that economic development in the United States roughly proceeds in an east-west direction, paralleling the movement of the frontier. It is thus possible to observe frontier conditions in the West, industrializing society in the Midwest, and fully developed industrial society in the East at the same time. Generalizations made about women in the Eastern seaboard states can therefore be extended to hold for women in the West at a later time period.

marketplace as an active and valued participant in its function. Woman, continuing to work in the home as she always had, was now separated from those activities most valued by a society which measured value in cash. Work in the home, not being paid for in cash, was obviously devalued. More importantly, as the focus of economic activity shifted from the home to the marketplace and the business world, woman, by her continuing association with and confinement to the "domestic sphere," became herself gradually devalued. Like the slave, she became inferior not only by enslavement, but by the fact of being a creature one *could* enslave. Woman became inferior in her own eyes and those of society, by not participating fully in the work of the new society. By her unpaid labor in the home her inferior status was constantly reinforced.

In colonial society, marriage and motherhood had been the expected life pattern for women, but marriage and fatherhood had been equally expected of men. In industrial society, sex role expectations shifted slightly, but decisively: fatherhood became a socially approved and desirable option which implied a man's successful performance in labor or business, so that he might provide for his family. For women, marriage and motherhood remained the single societally approved career. Work and business, the world of men, had become physically separated from domestic work and motherhood, the world of women.

Industrialization sharpened class distinctions among women. Middle-class women began to enjoy the benefits of their fathers' and husbands' increasing wealth, in the form of more leisure from household drudgery and greater educational opportunities. By becoming themselves employers of lower-class women, who relieved them of household chores and child care burdens, they became "ladies." The "lady" became the embodiment of her father's or husband's success in direct proportion to her distance from work, inside and outside the home; she became herself an ornament, a

symbol. Women of all classes accepted her as an ideal toward which they should aspire.

From its beginnings American industry required and
used the labor power of lower-class women to support its
growth, but for them entry into industry did not mean an
improvement in their status and a first step toward upward
mobility. Working women added work outside the home to
their home and child care responsibilities; for them industrialization meant a double burden. They entered industry
at wages far below those of men and in unskilled job
categories which did not lead to advancement. Since they
had been trained to regard their assignment to the domestic
sphere as "God-given and natural," they felt guilty for working and regarded their work as only temporary. This, in
turn, became a welcome excuse for their employers, who
shared these cultural assumptions, for paying them lower
wages than men. As "temporary labor" they required only
"pin money" and were kept from advancing their skills and
earning capacity. Thus, work designated as "woman's
work" became characterized by poor pay, low status, no
security. It was, in fact, quite similar to unpaid housework,
regardless of whether it was done in hospitals, laundries, or
factories. Technological changes and the shift of such jobs
from one location to another little affected the essential nature of the work. Even women's advance into white-collar
and middle-range jobs, such as clerical and retail sales
work, only attached the stigma of "woman's work" to these
modern service occupations.

Ideology, cultural values, and psychological pressure
served to reinforce the subordination of women during the
nineteenth century. Industrialization opened economic opportunities to middle-class men and liberalized the access
of lower-class men to economic and political power, but
women did not participate in this advance.

For middle-class women, their exclusion from access to
equal education opportunities and the professionalization of

occupations formerly open to them, plus their indoctrination to the role of the lady, actually meant a lowering of status and a narrowing of opportunities.

During the industrializing period, professional work depended on training and licensing. Since women were excluded from institutions of higher learning, they gradually lost the small foothold they had earlier had in professional and semi-professional occupations. Their disappearance from these occupations reinforced the idea that they were unsuited to such work. In a nation in which seventy years earlier midwifery was an entirely female profession, pioneers like Elizabeth Blackwell and Ann Preston would in the 1850s have to engage in serious public debate as to whether women were morally and constitutionally fitted for medicine and nursing. By then, professional male doctors had taken over obstetrical care of the upper classes and only the poor relied on midwives. Such experiences and the visible fact of the easier access of lower-class men to political institutions, were perceived by upper- and middle-class women as evidence of a widening gap between all men and themselves.

For lower-class women, an improvement in the actual conditions of their lives would come only through unionization, political organization, and protective legislation. Their acceptance of the myth of the lady had a retarding effect on unionization. For all women, industrialization and its accompanying ideology brought a lowering of status and a shrinking of opportunities.

Yet, industrialization also had an opposite effect on women. Educational discrimination based on sex had always been an important factor in perpetuating the subordination of women. Quite naturally, women had expressed their discontent by insisting on the right and opportunity to learn and to teach. The needs and demands of industrial society opened such educational opportunities to a small group of women; they in turn aspired to greater opportunities and organized to assert their demands. They insisted upon entry into the professions and when faced with innumerable obstacles, began to organize their separate female institutions: colleges, professional schools, hospitals, and so on. In the process, there evolved a "new woman," the economically independent, well-educated professional, whose feminist consciousness found expression in the demands for rights and in the organization of female pressure groups.

In addition to their participation in the economic life of society, women have shaped history through community-building and participation in politics. American women built community life as members of families, as carriers of cultural and religious values, and as founders and supporters of organizations and institutions. So far, historians have taken notice mostly of the first of these functions and of the organizational work of women only insofar as they "contributed" to social reforms. Women's political work has been recognized only as it pertains to woman's rights and woman suffrage.

Historical interpretation of the community-building work of women is urgently needed. The voluminous national and local records which document the network of community institutions founded and maintained by women are available. They are so rich that a representative selection of only the most interesting documents would fill several volumes. Yet their pattern and meaning, which may very well be central to understanding the history of American communities, are not revealed in isolated citations. They must be studied in context and against the traditional record of institution-building, which focuses on the activities of men. The research and monographic work which form the essential groundwork for such interpretation, have yet to be done. For this reason it would be premature to try to summarize this important facet of women's past in a separate chapter. The documents in this volume pertaining to women's organizational activities are merely intended to highlight some aspects of this work and to serve as an introduction to the reader.

The importance of the struggle for woman suffrage is undeniable and can be readily documented through accessible sources, but it is impossible to understand the integral involvement of American women in every aspect of the nation's life, if their political activity is so narrowly defined. The documents represented here focus on hitherto neglected political activities of women and bear evidence to their broad range and variety throughout the nineteenth century.

The involvement of American women in the important events of American history—the political and electoral crises, the wars, expansion, diplomacy—is overshadowed by the fact of the exclusion of women from political power throughout three hundred years of the nation's life. Thus women, half of the nation and many times a majority, are cast in the marginal role of a powerless minority—acted upon, but not acting. That this impression of the female past is a distortion should become clear to readers of this volume. It is premature to attempt a critical evaluation or synthesis of the role women played in the building of American society. It is not premature to suggest that the exclusion of women from all those institutions that make essential decisions for the nation, is in itself an important aspect of the nation's past. In short, what needs to be explained in the future is not why women were so little evident in American history as currently recorded, but why and how patriarchal values affected that history.

The emergence of feminist consciousness as a historical phenomenon is an essential part of the history of women.

The steps by which women moved toward self-respect, self-definition, a recognition of their true position, and a sense of sisterhood, are tentative and varied and have occurred throughout our history. Their documentation in Part III is designed to delineate definitions, outline stages of a developmental process, and give a sense of their flow. From defiance of norms, to the search for autonomous values, to a challenging acceptance of deviance—this has been the road along which women have traveled.

Throughout history women have defied traditional roles, at times explicitly, at other times simply by expressing their individuality to its fullest. The creation of new roles for women includes the development of the professional woman, the political leader, the executive, as well as the anonymous working woman, the club woman, the trade unionist. These types, thrown up by history, are created in the process of changing social activities, but they also are the elements which help to create a new feminist consciousness.

By indoctrination, training, and practical experience women learned to accept and internalize the beliefs which would keep them "adjusted" to living in subordinate status in a patriarchal world. The final brick in the wall enclosing woman within the garden of domesticity was her horror and fear of deviance. The threat of female deviance pervades the culture; it is personified in the popular symbols of the witch, the bitch, the de-sexed female, the castrating woman. History casts her up in the distorted image of Anne Hutchinson, Mary Dyer, and the mostly female victims of the witch hunts; the caricature of Fanny Wright and the spinster symbol Susan B. Anthony; crazy Carrie Nation with her hatchet; bomb-throwing Emma Goldman; and the twentieth-century equivalent of the deviant stereotype, the dyke. It was the threat of such deviance which kept women in line ideologically and emotionally and fettered them psychologically. Women were split away from one another not only by class and race, but by arbitrary standards of purity and propriety. As long as the woman's movement participated in this ideological bind by stressing the "respectability" of its members in terms of their competence as wives and mothers and by separating its activities from those of "radicals," it could not completely envision the liberation of women nor could it create the conditions for such liberation.

The process of creating feminist consciousness and a theory of female emancipation is still underway. The challenges of present-day American women are grounded in past experience, in the buried and neglected female past. Women have always made history as much as men have, not "contributed" to it, only they did not know what they had made nor did they have the tools for interpreting their own experience. What is new at this time is that women are now fully claiming their past and shaping the tools by which to interpret it. To this endeavor, it is hoped, this volume will make a modest contribution.

The Female Experience

I
The Female Life Cycle

CHAPTER ONE

Childhood

The selections in this chapter illustrate childhood experiences of nineteenth-century women, focusing particularly on sex role indoctrination and crises in the girl's life. Many of the incidents included are representative of childhood experiences at different periods: Louisa May Alcott's diary account of her indoctrination to patience and self-abnegation in the nineteenth century might just as validly describe colonial childrearing practices; the transition from wilderness freedom to "civilized" constraint described by Frances Willard can be considered typical of frontier life, regardless of period.

For American boys the world was theirs to explore, to tame, to conquer; for girls the home was to be the world. For American boys the development of a strong individuality and strong will was a necessary value, preparing them for their life roles. For girls the subduing of the will, the acceptance of self-abnegation, and the development of excessive altruism were the desired educational goals. Fathers as different as the educational radical Bronson Alcott, the upper-class conservative George Palmer Putnam, and the anonymous fathers or the masters of the slave girls all strove to mold their daughters into this pattern. Interestingly, mothers as different as the reformer Martha Wright, the quiet, domestic mother of Frances Willard, and the anonymous mother of Rose Schneiderman, who toiled in a sweatshop to support her orphaned children, participated in this indoctrination, which seemed to them to be in the best interest of their daughters. To an extent they failed: Louisa May Alcott, through writing, emancipated herself and made an independent life of her own; Mary Putnam became a leading professional woman; Frances Willard and Rose

Schneiderman organized large groups of women for social better-
ment and feminist goals. But if these outstanding women were
able to transcend their upbringing, legions of women of lesser
talent, opportunity, or character strength accepted the roles to
which they had been trained and expressed their dissatisfaction
and unhappiness variously. There is no doubt that many women
also found comfort and satisfaction in filling their expected roles
and considered whatever tensions and difficulties they experienced as merely personal problems.

The historical role of mothers and the relationships of mothers
and daughters is a large subject, which deserves study and
analysis. In the selections in this chapter one can discern a variety
of ways in which mothers made their influence felt. Fathers
demanded, persuaded, forbade, and dictated; mothers tended to
rule more by example, at times by quiet intercession. The slave
mother used every form of resistance open to her to defend her
children and enable her to stay with them. This included
accommodation, if it was in the long-range interest of the family
(see document 2). Abba May Alcott mediated between father and
daughter but persisted by gentle pressure to uphold her daughter's
demand for a room of her own. Martha Wright's words preached
accommodation; her conduct exemplified independence and self-
assertion. The capable mother of Frances Willard took a strong
hand in enforcing societally approved standards on her resistant
daughter, who accepted conformity out of love for her mother. The
message girls received from their mothers was often ambivalent:
the mothers' words and teaching taught one kind of lesson; the
mothers' lives another.

The crises in the girl's life would come when her aspirations
came into clash with parental standards—a situation common to
children of both sexes. But with girls, the issue was often directly
connected with their gender. Mary Putnam's desire to be absent
from home and, later, to become a doctor, would have been considered praiseworthy and acceptable, had she been a boy. Mary
Livermore's childish spirit of adventure, which led her to run away
from home, was a more serious failing in a girl than in a boy. The
crisis in Frances Willard's life was brought on by the departure of a
brother to college, while she was left behind—a situation reported
with considerable frequency in the biographies of outstanding
women. Rose Schneiderman did not offer introspective comments

on her similar fate, but records the bare outlines, leaving us to draw our own conclusions.

A girl's childhood would bring the usual joys, strains, and stresses, but more frequently than the boy she would experience growing up as a loss, a confinement, a decrease of freedom.

Louisa May Alcott (1832–1888)

1. Training the girl to patience

Louisa May Alcott was one of the most popular authors of the nineteenth century, best remembered for her *Little Women* (1868–1869) and *Little Men* (1871). As did many children of her time, she kept a diary not so much for purposes of self-expression, but as a means of self-improvement. The daughter of the educational innovator and Transcendentalist Bronson Alcott, she was the subject of her father's unorthodox educational experiments, some of which are recorded in her diary. Her father's influence was pervasive in her life. Bronson Alcott believed in treating children kindly and respecting their reason, considering them to be not damned, but blessed. In view of such theories his relentless effort at instilling in his daughter self-discipline and self-abnegation through guilt are remarkable. Children of the time reared by less idealistic and visionary parents were subject to much more cruel discipline, but the direction of their education was the same: girls were to acquire patience, self-discipline, and the virtues of obedience. In the case of Alcott's own family such training was particularly inappropriate since Alcott rarely provided for his family, leaving the burden of economic and practical responsibilities to his wife, Abba May, and his second daughter, Louisa.

Louisa May Alcott's diary together with her letters and the comments she added later in life enable us to trace the training of a young girl in unusual detail. The items here cited date from age six to early adolescence, when she began to contribute to the upkeep of the family by teaching school. She kept the diary as an instrument for self-improvement at the suggestion of her father. Occasionally, her parents read her entries and commented upon them, sometimes in writing.

The symbolic and practical significance for this budding writer of the "room of her own" is noteworthy, as is her resolve to "really" improve not because of the guilt instilled by the father but in order to "be a help and comfort . . . to my dear mother."

Ednah D. Cheney, ed., *Louisa May Alcott, Diary and Letters* (Boston: Roberts Bros., 1889), pp. 30, 42–43, 46–48.

Active exercise was my delight, from the time when a child of six I drove my hoop around the [Boston] Common without stopping, to the days when I did my twenty miles in five hours and went to a party in the evening.

I always thought I must have been a deer or a horse in some former state, because it was such a joy to run. No boy could be my friend till I had beaten him in a race, and no girl if she refused to climb trees, leap fences, and be a tomboy.

My wise mother, anxious to give me a strong body to support a lively brain, turned me loose in the country and let me run wild, learning of Nature what no books can teach, and being led,—as those who truly love her seldom fail to be,—

"Through Nature up to Nature's God."

A Sample of our Lessons.

"What virtues do you wish more of?" asks Mr. L. [Louisa's father]. I answer:—

Patience,	Love,	Silence,
Obedience,	Generosity,	Perseverance,
Industry,	Respect,	Self-denial.

"What vices less of?"

Idleness,	Wilfulness,	Vanity,
Impatience,	Impudence,	Pride,
Selfishness,	Activity,	Love of cats.

Mr. L.	L. [Louisa]
SOCRATES.	ALCIBIADES.

How can you get what you need? By trying.
How do you try? By resolution and perseverance.
How gain love? By gentleness.

What is gentleness? Kindness, patience, and care for other people's feelings.

Who has it? Father and Anna.

Who means to have it? Louisa, if she can.

(She never got it.—L.M.A.)

Write a sentence about anything. "I hope it will rain; the garden needs it."

What are the elements of hope? Expectation, desire, faith.

What are the elements in wish? Desire.

What is the difference between faith and hope? "Faith can believe without seeing; hope is not sure, but tries to have faith when it desires."

. . .

What are the most valuable kinds of self-denial? Appetite, temper.

How is self-denial of temper known? If I control my temper, I am respectful and gentle, and every one sees it.

What is the result of this self-denial? Every one loves me, and I am happy.

Why use self-denial? For the good of myself and others.

How shall we learn this self-denial? By resolving, and then trying *hard*.

What then do you mean to do? To resolve and try.

(Here the record of these lessons end, and poor little Alcibiades went to work and tried till fifty, but without any very great success, in spite of all the help Socrates and Plato gave her.—L.M.A.)

DEAREST MOTHER,—I have tried to be more contented, and I think I have been more so. I have been thinking about my little room, which I suppose I never shall have. I should want to be there about all the time, and I should go there and sing and think.

> But I'll be contented
> With what I have got;

> Of folly repented,
> Then sweet is my lot.

From your trying daughter,

LOUY.

MY DEAR LOUISA,—Your note gave me so much delight that I cannot close my eyes without first thanking you, dear, for making me so happy, and blessing God who gave you this tender love for your mother.

I have observed all day your patience with baby, your obedience to me, and your kindness to all.

Go on "trying," my child; God will give you strength and courage, and help you fill each day with words and deeds of love. I shall lay this on your pillow, put a warm kiss on your lips, and say a little prayer over you in your sleep.

MOTHER.

MY LOUY,—I was grieved at your selfish behavior this morning, but also greatly pleased to find you bore so meekly Father's reproof for it. That is the way, dear; if you find you are wrong, take the discipline sweetly, and do so no more. It is not to be expected that children should always do right; but oh, how lovely to see a child penitent and patient when the passion is over. . . .

HILLSIDE, CONCORD

DEAR,—I am glad you put your heart in the right place; for I am sure all true strength comes from above. Continue to feel that God is *near* you, dear child, and He never will forsake you in a weak moment. Write me always when you feel that I can help you; for, though God is near, Mother never forgets you, and your refuge is her arms.

Patience, dear, will give us content, if nothing else. Be assured the little room you long for will come, if it is necessary to your peace and well-being. Till then try to be happy with the good things you have. They are many,—more perhaps than we deserve, after our frequent complaints and discontent.

Be cheerful, my Louy, and all will be gayer for your laugh, and all good and lovely things will be given to you when you deserve them.

I am a busy woman, but never can forget the calls of my children.

MOTHER.

DEAREST,—I am sure you have lived very near to God *to-day*, you have been so good and happy. Let each day be like this, and life will become a sweet song for you and all who love you,—none so much as your

MOTHER.

Thirteen Years Old.

Fruitlands.

March, 1846,—I have at last got the little room I have wanted so long, and am very happy with it. It does me good to be alone, and mother has made it very pretty and neat for me. My work-basket and desk are by the window, and my closet is full of dried herbs that smell very nice. The door that opens into the garden will be very pretty in summer, and I can run off to the woods when I like.

I have made a plan for my life, as I am in my teens, and no more a child. I am old for my age, and don't care much for girl's things. People think I'm wild and queer; but mother understands and helps me. I have not told any one about my plan; but I'm going to *be* good. I've made so many resolutions, and written sad notes, and cried over my sins, and it doesn't seem to do any good! Now I'm going to *work really*, for I feel a true desire to improve, and be a help and comfort, not a care and sorrow, to my dear mother.

2. Childhood in slavery

Children's experiences in slavery could vary as widely as did those of free children, but slave children were more apt than free children to be physically abused, to face separation from one or both of their parents, and to be set to work on some tedious repetitious labor. Unlike white children, they were destined to receive no formal schooling or education, although some of them were trained and taught rudimentary skills by their parents or older siblings.

Sex role indoctrination among slaves was negligible, since both boys and girls were trained to become unpaid laborers and body servants without much regard for sex differences. Boys as well as girls might be set to work in the kitchen, the nursery, or in the fields.

The two reminiscences of former slaves, collected and recorded in an early twentieth-century oral history project at Fisk University under the guidance of black sociologist Charles Johnson, are vivid accounts of childhood in slavery. They offer evidence of the affection between slave parents and their children, of the subtle daily resistance of slaves, and of the strong anger felt by slaves against their oppressors: the mother who would not allow her child to be beaten; the father who killed the overseer; the small child contriving to drop the baby on the floor so she could play. These belie many of the facile generalizations of family disorganization and of slaves adjusted to accepting their condition complacently.

Narrative of Martha Harrison

They had cradles for the little nigger babies, and long before the War I was big enough to rock them babies. . . .

I didn't do nothing but play and pick up chips for old Aunt Fanny. She fed us. They had these round wooden bowls, and Aunt Fanny would take that and pour the licker

Ophelia Settle Egypt, J. Masuoka, Charles S. Johnson, "Unwritten History of Slaves; Autobiographical Accounts of Negro Ex-Slaves," Social Science Source Documents No. 1 (Nashville, Tenn.: Fisk University, Social Science Institute, 1946), pp.113–117, 276–279.

in it, and put bread in it for the chillen to eat. It was a great big bowl, big as that dish pan there. That's what we had for dinner, and milk and bread for supper. Mistress would say, "Go pick up some chips for old Aunt Fan to put on the lid," and I would run and break out to get the chips first, 'cause I was crazy about white bread, and when we all got back with the chips, Mistress would give us some white bread, but she would make me wait till they all got there. I liked it 'cause mammy 'nem didn't get white bread but once a week—that was Sunday, and the rest of the time they had just corn bread or shorts. I was so foolish! When she died [Mistress] it liked to killed me; I just cried and cried, and mammy say, "What's the matter with you, gal?" I said, "Ole Miss is dead, and I won't get no more white bread." She said, "Shet your mouth, gal." I thought when she died she carried all the white bread with her. Folks was saying, "Look at that po little nigger crying 'bout her Mistress," but I wasn't crying 'bout mistress, I was crying 'cause the white bread was gone. . . .

I couldn't tell you how many niggers he [her master] did have; he had so many and his wife had so many. The place was full; times sho' was hard, sho' as you born. Chillen was just as lousy as pigs. They had these combs that was just like cards you "card" cotton with, and they would comb your head with them. That wouldn't get the lice out, but it would make it feel better. They had to use larkspur to get 'em out; that would always get lice out of your head. But there wasn't no chillen would get sick before the War. I reckon the lice musta kept 'em healthy. . . .

Lawd, the times we did have. I know that when the War got over and we got free they put me in the field to work. I never went to school a day in my life; what I learned to read, I learned myself. My children all went to school, though. . . .

[The] overseer . . . went to my father one morning and said, "Bob, I'm gonna whip you this morning." Daddy said, "I ain't done nothing," and he said, "I know it, I'm gonna whip you to keep you from doing nothing," and he hit him with that cowhide—you know it would cut the blood out of you with every lick if they hit you hard—and daddy was chopping cotton, so he just took up his hoe and chopped right down on that man's head and knocked his brains out. Yes'm, it killed him, but they didn't put colored folks in jail then, so when old Charlie Merrill, the nigger trader, come along they sold my daddy to him, and he carried him way down in Mississippi. Ole Merrill would buy all the time, buy and sell niggers just like hogs. They sold him Aunt Phoebe's little baby that was just toddling long, and Uncle Dick—that was my mammy's brother.

The way they would whip you was like they done my oldest sister. They tied her, and they had a place just like they're gonna barbecue a hog, and they would strip you and tie you and lay you down. . . . Old Aunt Fanny had told marster that my sister wouldn't keep her dress clean, and that's what they was whipping her 'bout. So they had her down in the cellar whipping her, and I was real little. I couldn't say "Big Sis," but I went and told Mammy. "Old Marster's got 'Big Jim' down there in the cellar beating her," and mammy got out of bed and went in there and throwed Aunt Fan out the kitchen door, and they had to stop whipping Big Sis and come and see about Aunt Fan. You see, she would tell things on the others, trying to keep from getting whipped herself. I seed mistress crack her many a time over the head with a broom, and I'd be so scared she was gonna crack me, but she never did hit me, 'cept slap me when I'd turn the babies over. I'd get tired and make like I was sleep, and would ease the cradle over and throw the baby out. I never would throw mammy's out, though. Old Miss would be setting there just knitting and watching the babies; they had a horn and every woman could tell when it was time to come and nurse her baby by the way they would blow the horn. The white folks was crazy 'bout their nigger babies, 'cause that's where they got their profit. . . . When I'd get tired, I would just ease that baby over and Mistress

would slap me so hard; I didn't know a hand could hurt so
bad, but I'd take the slap and get to go out to play. She
would slap me hard and say, "Git on out of here and stay till
you wake up," and that was just what I wanted, 'cause I'd
play then. . . .

My husband never did like for me to work; he used to ask
me how come I work when he was doing all he could to give
me what I wanted. "Looks like you don't 'preciate what I'm
trying to do for you." But I'd say, "Yes, I do, honey, I jest
help you 'cause I don't want you to break down. If you put a
load on one horse it will pull him down, but two horses can
pull it jest as easy." . . .

Narrative of an Anonymous Ex-Slave

I know I was born in slavery, and I know they was awful
mean. I was born in 1855, and the War started in '61. My
white folks was awful bad and mean. I'm telling you what I
know; they was mean; they beat us till the blood run down
our legs. . . . My mother was the mother of fourteen chillen, but some died and she had seven chillen that was her
grandchillen. Their mother was the one that did the
weaving.

[Whipped about what?] First one devilment and then
another. You know chillen get into mischief, and they get
whipped for it. I often told my mother time after time that I
didn't blame old mistress for whipping us, but she didn't
need to kill us; she coulda just whipped us. We didn't have
on but one piece [of clothing] winter nor summer, and she
would pull it over our head and whip us till the blood run
down, and we dasn't to holler. I can't remember now like I
can back yonder; but I can remember that just as plain as
day. We stayed there a year after freedom 'cause we didn't
have sense enough to know we was free. My mother took
care of the chillen and washing and ironing, and she took
me with her to wash socks and handkerchiefs. They used to
keep her hired out 'cause she wouldn't let her (mistress)

whip her; so they hired her out, and finally sold her. But she come back 'cause they said she only had two chillen and she was sound, and they found out that she had had fourteen chillen, and when she was a girl she had knocked her toe out of place, and she was a little cripple; so they had to take her back. You know if you sold stock and it wasn't sound like you said it was, you would have to take it back; so that's the way they did. I seen Mistress come in there with a bucket of water to slosh on my mother, and mother grabbed the bucket and threw it on her, and the old woman hollered murder and all the chillen come running in with sticks and things; then the old woman said she wasn't mad, she was just happy in her soul. One of the boys took the stick he had and hit me a lick or two, but they wouldn't let him hurt me; and he wouldn't touch mother.

You know that old woman was mean. When she was dying she said she was all right, and I said to mother, "Yes, she is all right; all right for hell." Mother said I ought to forgive, but I can't forgive her, the way she used to beat us. . . . Mother said when she was sold she had a baby in her arms, and her other boy next to the baby was standing by the fence crying. When she come back, she had me. I was her baby. My father was a Bailey, but mother and father separated before I was born. . . . He and mother just got mad in a quarrel and separated. He tried to get her back and the white folks tried to get her to take him back, but she wouldn't do it, 'cause he drawed back to hit her with a chair, and he'd never done that before. He woulda hit her too if her brother hadn't been there and stopped him.

Mother was put on the block three times after that; and they couldn't sell her. They tried to bid her off for a dime, but nobody would give it. I don't know why they wouldn't but I just know nobody would. . . .

No'm, we didn't have plenty to eat. We had bean soup, cabbage soup, and milk, with mush or bread in it. The chillen never did get no meat. The grown folks got a little meat, 'cause they had to work; but we didn't. Once a man brought

some old hog heads and pieces of fresh meat like that to old
mistress in a barrel, to make soap with, and the things was
just floating on top; and she got mad 'cause the grown folks
[slaves] wouldn't eat it. She give it to us chillen, and 'course
we was glad to get it, 'cause it was meat, and we eat it till it
made us sick, and they couldn't give us any more. Mr.
———— [man who had given meat] came by and found out
what she had done, and he said, "I just brought that meat
here 'cause I thought you might want it to make soap. I
didn't know you was going to make nobody eat it. I
wouldn't give it to my dogs." You know she was mean.
When I heared she was dead I couldn't help but laugh, and
I was grown then and had a child. . . .

Marse Jack Barbee, he was so good to we chillen. He
jerked her off of us many a time, and he'd say, "Plague take
you, you trying to kill that little baby." If he found any of
the old rawhides she'd use, he'd cut 'em up and take 'em out
to the woodpile and burn 'em. Then she'd go to them old
sprouts in the yard. Sometimes I'd rather it been the
cowhide, 'cause sometimes the sprouts would have thorns
on 'em.

My aunt, she'd slip meat skins through the crack to us
chillen till that hole would get right greasy. She had a little
hole in the floor that she could use; and we would go down
to the orchard and broil them or cook 'em some way. We'd
put the little ones in the henhouse, through the hole they
left for the hens; and they'd come out with an apron full of
eggs, and we'd take them out to the woods and cook 'em
some way; and we would steal chickens too. Me and sister
Lottie was the biggest ones in the bunch, and we was real
little. The white chillen would help us eat 'em too, and they
would go to the house and get salt, you know.

[When mistress would whip her]. I'd squally and squall,
and she'd shake me, and tell me to hush; then I'd just jump.
I had to do something. I'd go round back of the chimney and
cry easy. My mother never did whip me over twice, and I
would mind her; I was 'fraid of her, and I always did what

she told me. She was part Indian, you know. I said to her after freedom, "It's funny you wouldn't let mistress whip you and yet you let her whip us chillen all the time." She said, "If I'd started that they woulda sent me away and I never woulda seen you no more."

MARY PUTNAM JACOBI, M.D. (1842–1906)

3. You owe more to your mother and the younger children than you do to any other plans

The early letter of Mary Putnam, who later would become the foremost woman physician of her time, gives a fine instance of the manner in which a spirited and intellectually talented girl was trained to conform with the ideals of "proper" female behavior. Raised in middle-class comfort and given a good education, the girl early decided on a medical career, but in the absence of first-rate medical schools willing to admit women, decided to earn a degree at the New York College of Pharmacy. It was to this decision that her father spoke in his letter to her, characteristically taking for granted the higher claims of domestic duties upon her. That he was liberal enough to offer her a financial reward for the usually unpaid housekeeping services he wished her to perform, may have been as much a tribute to her earlier assertiveness as to his generosity. At any rate, the appeal was typical, although Mary Putnam, after briefly delaying her education, continued with extraordinary persistence to attend college. She earned her pharmaceutical degree in 1863, and went on to earn an M.D. at the Woman's Medical College of Pennsylvania in 1864. After surmounting many difficulties she gained admission to the École de Medicine in Paris, which had never before admitted a woman. She earned her M.D. from that institution in 1871.

Characteristically, she interrupted her studies twice, once to nurse a sick brother in a Louisiana army camp during the Civil

Ruth Putnam, ed., *Life and Letters of Mary Putnam Jacobi* (New York: G. P. Putnam's Sons, 1925), pp. 48–51, 60–61.

War, once to nurse a sick sister who was one of the teachers of freedmen at Port Royal, S.C. After her graduation she established a medical practice in New York, was very active in medical organizations and in furthering the advancement of professional women, wrote more than a hundred medical papers, and lectured frequently.

Her father learned to make the best of her "deviance" although he expressed his fears for her frankly. "Don't let yourself be absorbed . . . in that branch of animal kingdom ordinarily called strong minded women!" he urged his daughter while she was a medical student. "I do hope and trust you will preserve your feminine character. . . . Be a lady from the dotting of your i's to the color of your ribbons—and if you must be a doctor . . . be an attractive and agreeable one. . . ." Mary Putnam took his advice insofar as remaining ladylike was concerned, but her primary commitment in life was to her professional career.

MARY CORINNA PUTNAM TO MARY SWIFT [1858]

[Discussion of an invitation.]

In the first place, I should like you to know that my whole existence is governed by abstract ideas. For instance, there is an abstract general idea extant, of a father coming home regularly tired at night, (from the plough, I believe the usual legend runs,) and being solaced by the brilliant yet touching performance of a sweet only daughter upon the piano, in a manner that calls tears to his eyes, as he remembers the dreams of his youth when that blooming girl in white muslin was a charming cherub in the cradle. Consequently, to carry out this ideal, although my father is very seldom tired, and certainly never ploughs, although he is not particularly fond of music and my performance is so far from either brilliant or touching that I suspect he is entirely indifferent to it . . . I "practise" in accordance, as I said before, with this ideal. For a similar reason, when Nurse goes out, I am supposed to take care of the children, not because they don't take care of themselves perfectly well, but because there is another ideal of an amiable sister that I am supposed to be feebly endeavoring to imitate. Also, although all my brothers and sisters, certainly Edith and Haven, have always been much more decorous and well behaved children than my unlucky self, it has been studiously impressed on my infant mind ever since the time when, unhappy wight that I was, I found myself at five years old the "eldest" of a growing family, by aunts and all sorts of relations, that I must set an angelic example to these same younger urchins, and steadily give myself the task of improving by precept and practice their morals and manners. I can't say that I ever did it, but the principle is the same, that the ideal must be preserved regardless of fact.

Now do you see how all this applies to the matter in question? Two or three weeks ago, Mother was taken ill during the night, and rather alarmed the family, except myself, who was sound asleep all the time (how could I help it?) One of my aunts . . . was staying with us, and she urged me in the most solemn manner the next morning, after mother had quite recovered, to always *sleep* in the house henceforward, to which proposition I rather rashly assented—Hence, a variety of useless resolutions etc. Now as, if I go to the Bible class, I could not return before the time Mother goes to bed, and as, if I stayed in town, I could come home Saturday by the time she was up in the morning, I really do not think that the difference of my presence or absence will amount to so much. But still, you see, this same Ideal *may* interfere, and . . . you need not expect me with any degree of certainty. . . .

GEORGE PALMER PUTNAM TO MARY CORINNA PUTNAM
FEBY. 13, 1861

My dear Minnie—

I want you to think over one or two questions—and I write them down so that you may do so *quietly,* and not too quickly make up your mind pugnaciously, on any pre-arranged plans and arguments, however (to yourself) clear and decisive they may be.

First, may be premised, *all* that you possibly imagine, and *more* than you would claim, in full appreciation on my part, of the disinterested and important character of the plans you have adopted, and of your *intrinsic* ability to carry them out with credit to yourself and usefulness to a great many others. *But,* I want you to consider—

1.   Whether the claims of *home* and your mother are not at present *superior,* even to those disinterested and worthy plans—and

2.   What possible evil can result from your *suspending* those medical studies, entirely, except general reading at home, for the space of two years? Or rather,—why would it not be *better* for *you* as well as *us* that you should do so?

I will not stop to write out all the reasons and pros and cons which are suggested in this connection. "A word to the wise" (?)—I only want you carefully, deliberately, and conscientiously to consider and *weigh* all you *know* I *might* say, to *persuade* you to this postponement. I have no idea of exercising any authority or imposing any command. *You* don't need any—and you *ought* not to need any. You may say, perhaps, that you offered to submit to a *veto* before you *began*—and that it is too late now—and not just or fair &c. &c. I remember all this—But it is never too late to recede from unwise assent—or at least, it is better to re-trace one's steps if the *right* path or the best one is on the other side of the fence. *I* think it *highly* desirable that you should be at home *chiefly* during the next two years and especially during this present year. I really and deliberately think that you owe more to your mother and the younger children than you do to anyone else or to any other plans of enterprise, however worthy and important. I think you may be of *immense* use in relieving and cheering your mother and that she will *need* your aid at home—and that you may benefit the young children and aid generally in *systematizing* home and rendering it cheerful and happy—and that, for the next two years, this is quite as important, and *more* obligatory than any other claims.

I don't ask you to give up your plans—or lose the advantage of all you have done—but only to *suspend them,* for this time so far as they take you from home. You would, of course, continue at Miss Gibson's* and you could doubtless do a good deal of studying at home.

But the active attendance on medical lectures and lessons should be *postponed,* and you would be all the better prepared for those things two years hence. Your being at home would save me an actual expense of $250 a year. I will cheerfully place that sum to your credit in the Savings Bank at the end of each year and that will be fairly *earned* for your own purposes beyond. Consider all this my dear Minnie, and give a cheerful Yes to

Your affectionate Father.

MARTHA COFFIN WRIGHT TO ELLEN WRIGHT

4. A mother advises her daughter

Martha Coffin Wright, the sister of the well-known abolitionist and woman's rights advocate Lucretia Mott, was one of five women who planned and convened the first woman's rights convention at Seneca Falls, New York, in 1848. A birthright Quaker and a life-long abolitionist, she held advanced ideas about the equality of women, which found expression in the education of her daughter largely in terms of training the girl to self-reliance and economic independence. On the other hand her advice about propriety and behavior toward young men is quite traditional. In this respect Martha Wright is typical of the female reformers of her time, who held radical social ideas, participated in radical and reform activities, but maintained traditional attitudes toward

Letters of Martha Coffin Pelham Wright, Garrison Family Papers. Courtesy of the Sophia Smith Collection (Women's History Archive), Smith College, Northampton, Mass. I am indebted to my former student, Anne L. Hoblitzelle, for the research and some of the interpretations of this material.

* A girls' school where M.C.P. was teaching classes—ED.

domesticity and the duties of wives and mothers. Fifteen-year-old Ellen Wright was at the time of the correspondence a student at Theodore Weld's educationally innovative Eagleswood School at Raritan Bay Union, a cooperative association in New Jersey. Despite her vows of celibacy, she later married a son of the abolitionist William Lloyd Garrison (see pp. 50–52). The extensive correspondence between mother and daughter is marked by mutual respect, intimacy, affection, and the mother's self-assured commonsense attitude.

Auburn, Feb. 8 1855

. . . How does it happen that her engagement compels you to re-iterate your vow of perpetual celibacy—'tis a very wise resolution, unless you shd. chance in ten or a dozen years from now to meet some one worthy enough for you and in the meantime I would suggest to you a higher aim than riding on horseback and visiting all over, with the doubtful prospect of an inheritance from that imaginary Croesus who is destined to make you his heir—Find out if you can, what occupation your genius best fits you for, qualify yourself for that by earnest study and effort and resolve to be dependent on no one for the means of enjoyment— Why should it not be just as much a girl's study as a boy's, how she can best secure her own independence—Apropos I suppose that you have heard that Lucy Stone really is engaged to be married—Having shown her ability to take care of herself and earned something of her own, and having reached an age when she was capable of judging intelligently of the character of the one she has chosen, she is ready now to show her capability for "tread'n paths that's thorny"—The path matrimonial not being invariably strewn with marry golds and heart's ease. . . .

Auburn, Sept. 1st, 1855

My dear Ellen,

I was sorry for you to feel so much at Anna's not coming—She wanted to come, but her parents were unwilling to have her away from them so long—perhaps they were afraid such an accident would occur as did at Burlington the other day, when so many were killed, and nearly every person on the train wounded. It would have been very pleasant to have Anna, but as it cannot be, it is not right for you to make yourself uncomfortable about it; you will have to learn to bear disappointments more philosophically. You will find plenty of real griefs to shed tears over, without attaching so much importance to trifling ones. . . . I hope you have remembered the caution I gave you at parting—In your intercourse with gentlemen, you must remember that you are no longer a little girl, and that demonstrations of regard that were admissible a few years ago, may now be misconstrued—marks of affection that are perfectly proper toward an old and tried friend like Mr. Wood, would be unwise and out of place toward the acquaintance of a few days or weeks. In the exercise of a proper and womanly decorum, there is no danger of *your* becoming constrained & artificial, because you have good sense to guide you. I say this now, fearing that among so many strangers, and away from your mother, you may find somebody as "splendid" as Mr. Higginson, but who might not be equally worthy of the *homage* you rendered to him—You don't know how uneasy I felt at leaving you, the evening we came away. . . .

A*UBURN*, J*AN*. 19*TH* '56

My dear little daughter,

. . . Your resolution to diminish the number of your correspondents will avail little, if you make an exception in favor of each one who writes to you. Now I think it would be far wiser for you to wait till young Mr. Hallowell has finished his education, before you renew a correspondence that did so little credit to his scholarship, or to his tact I wd. add, if it wd. not seem severe; but in truth I thought his letters somewhat lacking in courtesy, & it seemed to me that there cd. not be a better leaving off place, than his last one furnished. Eddy Robinson is a good little boy, so far as we know, but his letters are rather too frequent, and you had better not reply so promptly as to call for another quite so soon—I was sorry to hear that he smoked. . . .

Auburn, Jan. 13th 1856

My darling child,

You don't know how glad I was to find . . . that you had resolved not to with-hold your confidence from your mother. I have read your secret thoughts, many a time, with a mother's penetration, and longed that you should be willing to confide in me. . . . It was the deep disappointments that I felt at your continued reserve, and no feeling of unkindness, that made me say to you as a warning, rather than a reproach, that the time would come when you would need a mother's sympathy, and have no mother to bestow it. You say "spare your sarcasm"—could you believe that I should return your confidence by sarcasm? . . . I trust that, as you grow older, you will yourself see the danger of cultivating the affections at the expense of the reason. . . .

Let me beg you to garner up your affections, henceforth, until you are old enough to judge wisely, where they may be worthily bestowed, and then to beware how you proffer too freely, and without proper maidenly reserve, a regard that should never "unsought, be won", and thus compromise yourself, and make for yourself disappointments, sorrow, & regrets.

A sincere and proper regard for *one*, should make you true to that one, and preserve you from accepting attentions from all; but while you are so young, you ought not to allow yourself to dwell, as you have done, on this theme, but resolutely fortify yourself against an unwise indulgence of the affections. This longing for demonstrations of love, can never be gratified, except transiently, the *devotion* of the lover, seldom survives the bridal, but where the wife has

cultivated those qualities which will command lasting regard & esteem, there comes a quiet happiness, far more
enduring. Ignorance of this fact, has made shipwreck of the
happiness of many a wife.

You have marked out for yourself a course in life, for
which the indulgence of the kind of feeling I allude to,
would completely disqualify you; if you would, by your
own example, prove the equality of men & women, throw
aside, resolutely and at once, all sentimental novel reading,
and by severe mental and physical training, qualify yourself
for that cause. Prove your ability to make your own way in
the world, and then, when a suitable time comes, if you
chance to find any one with whom you can go happily thro'
life, as Lucy Stone thinks she has done, you will be old
enough to make a wise choice—if there comes no such opportunity, let your mind be so disciplined, that in the steady
performance of your duties, whatever they may be, and an
earnest desire to promote the happiness of others, you may
secure your own.

Do not fear, my dear Ellen that your confidence will be
betrayed, and indulge no misgivings as to the course you
have pursued—adhere steadily to the principles I have always endeavored to inculcate, and trust implicity to

Your ever affectionate
Mother

MARY A. LIVERMORE (1820–1905)

5. In fear of hell and damnation

Mary Livermore, journalist, Civil War nurse, suffrage leader, and
reform lecturer, describes dramatically in her autobiography the
dread and fear instilled in her by her father's Calvinist educational

Mary A. Livermore, *The Story of My Life* (Hartford, Conn.: A. D. Worth-
ington & Co., 1897), pp. 40–49, 52–56, 60–63.

principles. While the stern religiosity of her upbringing may have
been somewhat extreme even by the standards of her day, other
prominent nineteenth-century women, such as Sarah Grimké and
Catharine Beecher, similarly found their emancipation through
deep religious struggle. The way in which the boisterous, irrepres-
sibly active girl turns into the anxiety-filled, morbidly pious young
woman is quite characteristic. Expressions of personal unworthi-
ness, fear of damnation, certainty of having sinned despite all the
outward signs of a blameless life—these are all themes which
recur frequently in the diaries and the correspondence of women
of that period. To what extent girls were more prone to such reactions than boys is difficult to determine. One can surmise that boys,
even though subject to the same training and indoctrination, were
more easily diverted from it by their active life away from home.
The burden of fear for the salvation of children who died young
certainly fell more heavily on the mothers and sisters who nursed
them and cared for them daily. It tended to reinforce the ever-
pervasive feeling of guilt of the women: perhaps more ardent
prayer during pregnancy, a little more zealous nursing during illness, or more effort in behalf of their religious indoctrination might
have saved these babes. . . . Many a mother recorded tearfully or
rebelliously in her diary how she wrestled with such thoughts and
feelings.

   In a later selection from Mary Livermore's autobiography (document 31), we can find description of the way in which she emancipated herself from this childhood heritage.

   My mother was of medium height and size, much smaller
than my father physically, and in delicate health until middle life. . . . My father was positive, and regarded himself
as the head of his house and the master of his family, and
was never backward in declaring this as his divinely appointed position. My mother never disputed it, nor even
discussed it, and yet no man was ever more completely
under the control of another than was he under that of my
mother. Her word, and even her wishes, if he could ascertain them, were a law to him. And I have heard him say that
he always consulted her in every important matter that came

before him. "Bless the united heads of this family!" was the unchanged formula he uttered at family prayers, which were never omitted night or morning. My father and mother were alternately subjects and rulers in their home, and, as in many other instances, they never knew it.

My father accepted the Calvinistic faith in its entirety and severity as it was taught and believed a hundred years ago. He expounded it in his family with voluminous speech and tremendous power, until I was steeped in it. Before I was ten years old I had the whole system at my tongue's end, and could restate it and dovetail it together like a theological expert. This faith dominated my early life, and has affected me more or less during all the years that have followed. . . .

I was the fourth in a family of six children, two boys and four girls, and was born on Salem Street, at the North End of Boston, on the 19th of December, 1820. . . .

The three children who preceded my birth died during their first year. They were delicate, and lacked vitality for continued existence. There was great anxiety, therefore, when I was born, lest I might be as feeble as they were. But a few months dispelled that anxiety. I was never ill, but grew up physically strong, escaping completely out of babyhood into young girlhood, at the age of two years. Another sort of problem confronted my parents when I appeared. How could the superabundant energy and activity of this romping baby girl be controlled and wisely directed? I was so busy and mischievous that my mother gladly accepted the relief of an infant school, conducted by a motherly woman just across the street. I vaguely remember it,—a large, airy chamber, where were a dozen children of my age, of whom I was very fond, with a garden in the rear into which we were turned loose most of the time, when the weather permitted, for we were only taught to sing and to play.

If the teacher left us alone a moment, some evil genius prompted me to open the gate, no matter how it was fastened, and then to run down the street like a deer. One or two of my tiny companions would sometimes essay to follow me, but I generally outran them, and they went back to the play-ground. When my annoying propensity was discovered, my father trained the house-dog, Hector by name, to follow me, and he would for a short distance; but if I was off for too long a tramp he would return without me. Then there was a scare. . . . The town crier was summoned, who was always successful. . . . As he went through the streets, ringing his ponderous bell to attract attention, he would shout in stentorian tones, "Child lost! Child lost!" which would speedily draw a crowd around him to hear the story and to aid in the search. . . . I rejoiced in his bell and his stentorian cries, and was as eager to find him as he was to discover me. We marched home together, a very happy couple,—he, because the lost one was found, and I, because I had the company of his noisy bell. . . .

As soon as we were able to walk we were taken to church . . . The Sundays of my childhood were not enjoyable days, they were observed with such unnecessary rigor. All work was tabooed on that day, even cooking, winter and summer. The food was cooked the day before. We rose early, and we children were prepared for the morning Sunday school at nine o'clock. The churches were not sufficiently warmed for the winter, and, in many instances, not warmed at all, and so a foot-stove was taken by one of us, which the sexton filled with live coals. We took turns in warming our feet upon it, and then were half frozen. The Sunday school ended at half-past ten, when we adjourned from the vestry to the church. A sounding-board overhung the pulpit, which was small and circular and seemingly suspended in the air, for the posts that upheld it and the narrow, spiral stairway which conducted to it were inclosed by curtains. I thought the minister, when he passed inside these curtains, rose in the air, very much as a bird soars from the ground, until he came to the level where he could be seen by the people.

The minister was Rev. Francis Wayland, afterwards President of Brown University. . . .

The choir sang without instrumental accompaniment, the chorister starting the tune with a pitch-pipe. The prayers were half an hour long, and the hymns contained six or eight stanzas. During the sermon that followed, I gave myself up to all kinds of mental occupation to while away the time, for there was very little of the hour's discourse that I could comprehend. I would count the people; then count the men and women separately, to ascertain the number of each. I imagined little stories; speculated on the lives of some of my playmates about me, and wished with all my heart and soul that God loved us more, so that we could have more happiness in this life and a better chance hereafter. When the church service was over we hurried home to the cold dinner. . . .

We were not allowed to read a story-book, not the religious newspaper, not a missionary magazine, or to look into a school-book. It was Sunday, and the Bible was the only book proper for Sunday reading. At two o'clock we hurried back to the second session of the Sundayschool, then again to afternoon service in the church, and after that came an interminable prayer-meeting in the body of the house, to which all remained who could,—the children always included. This prayer-meeting lasted until dark in the winter and until very nearly suppertime in summer. It was my great dread. The prayers and addresses were rarely delivered in an audible tone of voice, but were yet echoed and re-echoed through the building. The intense stillness without deepened solemnly, and the darkness crept into the nooks and corners of the church till the place seemed ghostly, and I saw specters everywhere. Trembling with fright I would cling to my father, and insist that he should put his arm around me and hold my hand tightly in his.

Sunday evening was devoted to the religious instruction of the children at home. Of this my father took charge, while

my mother in company with friends or neighbors attended
service at one of the churches in the near vicinity. First
came the catechism, through which we went every Sunday
evening, my father occasionally enforcing a precept or ex-
pounding an obscure point. If that catechism is lost,
hopelessly, I can at any time reproduce it, question and
answer, *verbatim et literatim*, for it is burned into my memory forever. Then followed the Bible reading, in which we
all took part, and after this a plain, practical talk from my
father concerning the salvation of our souls and the dangers
under which we lived while unconverted. This never affected my sisters as it did me. I was sometimes shaken to the
very center of my being, and often expressed to my father,
even when very young, what I frequently felt,—a bitter regret that I had ever been born. There were times when I
envied the cat that purred at the fireside, or the dog that
slept on the doorstep. They could be happy, for they had no
souls to be saved or lost. . . .

When I was between seven and eight years old, I was
taken to my mother's chamber one wintry March morning to
welcome a newly-arrived sister. I bent down to kiss the
plump, rosy, sleeping baby. Then the thought flashed
through me, "What if she is not elected to be saved, and is
lost!" I could not keep back the tears, and burying my face
in the pillow I wept aloud. A great rush of affection welled
up within me at the sight of the little one, and an infinite
feeling of pity overcame me as I thought what her doom
might be. "Oh, mother," I cried, "don't lets keep the baby;
let's send her back to God! What if she doesn't grow up to be
a Christian, and is lost!" "We will pray," said my father,
"that God will make her a Christian, and we will try to train
her so that she will become one." But the doctrine of election had been thoroughly taught me, and I was not comforted by that promise. "But, father, if she is not elected to
be saved, how can she be? Do send her back to God! Tell
him we don't want any more babies in this house."

I could not be comforted, and in my sore anxiety added a

new petition to my morning and evening prayer, that God would take the little sister back to heaven before she was seven years old. I had somehow settled on the age of seven as the period when God holds children responsible for their lives. Ah, if my childish petition had been granted, how much of comfort would now be missing from my life! For that sister and myself are to-day the sole survivors of my father's family, and are journeying together to the foot of the hill, as we begin its ascent on the other side,—housemates, members of the same family, living under one roof.

The connection of this life with the next, as I heard it expounded in sermons and at conference meetings, brought me immitigable distress and saddened my childhood. I became morbid and anxious, with nights of wakefulness and days of solitary weeping. When any of my kindred, acquaintances, or playmates passed into death I immediately followed them in my imagination, trying to settle their probable fate. Where had they gone? Generally they were lost. There was no hope that they would ever be ransomed, and unless the same doom overtook me, as I greatly feared it would, I should never see them again throughout eternity. I was devoured with immense concern for all whom I loved, and while I did not regard myself as a Christian, I prayed earnestly and anxiously for those who were dear to me, and who were, as the phrase was, "out of the ark of safety." Night after night I have wakened my father and mother from their sleep, and insisted upon their rising to pray for the salvation of my younger sisters. My mental distress forbade me to sleep, and I could not bear my trouble alone. When my father would remonstrate, and ask, "Is there not danger that you may also be lost? Have you made your peace with God?" I would reply, "No, I expect to be lost, but I don't care if they are saved; I am strong and healthy, and can bear it, but they are so small and delicate they cannot. They *must* be saved, father!"

Under the teaching and influence of both parents, my pastor, Sunday-school teacher, and others, I passed through almost every phase of religious experience during the first fifteen years of my life. My mother tried to comfort me in the despair that sometimes overtook me because there was so little hope for the majority of the world. . . . But I had much less faith in her knowledge of these matters than in that of my father. He was my prophet, priest, and king, and I never doubted that he was correct. I always went to him for the solution of problems that puzzled me, the explanation of difficult texts of scripture, and the anxieties that robbed me of a child's happiness. . . .

FRANCES E. WILLARD (1839–1898)

6. From "Frank" to "Frances"

Frances E. Willard, later to become the leader and long-time president of the largest organization of U.S. women, the Women's Christian Temperance Union, had an unusually happy and free childhood. Frank, as she was then called, grew up on an isolated farm in the Wisconsin Territory. She and her sister Mary shared entirely the life and activities of their brother, Oliver. But Frank had to discover at puberty, that her life was to be run quite differently from her brother's. The shock and force of this experience, which probably occurred in the lives of many women, has seldom been so accurately described as here. The two traumatic experiences she recalls in retrospect undoubtedly reflect the feminist perspective of her adult life. One can speculate whether it was these experiences that caused her feminism or whether her unfettered development during her early childhood enabled her later to aspire and achieve. That farm girl crying "long and loud" when she finds that by putting on long skirts she "can never jump over a fence again, as long as I live," was crying for every woman of her day. Not until the clothing revolution of the early 1920s freed women's bodies, if not their minds, would women be free to jump over fences in adult life, if they so chose.

Frances E. Willard, *Glimpses of Fifty Years: The Autobiography of an American Woman* (Chicago: H. J. Smith & Co., 1889; reprint ed., New York: Source Book Press, 1970), pp. 25–26, 41–43, 62–63, 69–70.

. . . Mother did not talk to us as girls, but simply as human beings, and it never occurred to me that I ought to "know house-work" and do it. Mary took to it kindly by nature; I did not, and each one had her way. Mother never said, "You must cook, you must sweep, you must sew," but she studied what we liked to do and kept us at it with no trying at all. There never was a busier girl than I and what I did was mostly useful. I knew all the carpenter's tools and handled them: made carts and sleds, cross-guns and whip-handles; indeed, all the toys that were used at Forest Home we children manufactured. But a needle and a dishcloth I could not abide—chiefly, perhaps, because I was bound to live out-of-doors. . . .

We girls were fitted out with bags of corn, of beans, onion, turnip or beet seed, which we tied around our waists, as, taking hoe in hand we helped do the planting, not as work, but "just for fun" leaving off whenever we grew tired. We . . . had our own little garden beds of flowers and vegetables, and thought no blossoms ever were so fair or dishes so toothsome as those raised by our own hands. . . . I had a seat in the tall black oak near the front gate, where I could read and write quite hidden from view. I had a box with lid and hinges, fastened beside me, where I kept my sketches and books, whence the "general public" was warned off by the words painted in large, black letters on a board nailed to the tree below: "THE EAGLES'S NEST, BEWARE!" Mary had her own smaller tree near by, similarly fitted up.

Oliver thought all this was very well, but he liked to sit betimes on the roof of the house, in the deep shade, or to climb the steeple on the big barn, by the four flights of stairs, and "view the landscape o'er," a proceeding in which his sisters, not to be outdone, frequently imitated him. Indeed, Oliver was our forerunner in most of our outdoor-ish-ness. . . . One spring Oliver had a freak of walking on stilts; when, behold, up went his sisters on stilts as high as his and came stalking after him. He spun a top; out came two others. He played marbles with the Hodge boys; down went the girls and learned the mysteries of "mibs" and "alleys" and the rest of it. He played "quoits" with horseshoes; so did they. He played "prisoner's-base" with the boys; they started the same game immediately. He climbed trees; they followed after. He had a cross-gun; they got him and Loren to help fit them out in the same way, and I painted in capitals along the side of mine its name, "Defiance," while Mary put on hers, plain "Bang Up!" After awhile he had a real gun and shot muskrats, teal, and once a long-legged loon. We fired the gun by "special permit," with mother looking on, but were forbidden to go hunting and didn't care to, anyway. Once however, Oliver "dared" me to walk around the pasture ahead of him and his double-barreled gun when it was loaded and both triggers lifted. This I did, which was most foolhardy, and we two "ne'er-do-wells," whose secret no one knew but Mary, came home to find her watching at the gate with tear-stained face, and felt so ashamed of ourselves that we never repeated the sin—for it was nothing less. Oliver was famous at milking cows; his sisters learned the art, sitting beside him on three-legged stools, but never carried it to such perfection as he, for they were very fond of milk and he could send a stream straight into their mouths, which was greater fun than merely playing a tuneful tattoo into a tin pail, so they never reached distinction in the latter art. They did, however, train the cat to sit on the cow's back through milking time. Oliver could harness a horse in just about three minutes; his sisters learned to do the same, and knew what "hames" and "tugs" and "holdbacks" were, as well as "fetlock" "hock" and "pastern."

There were just four things he liked that we were not allowed to share—hunting, boating, riding on horseback and "going swimming." But at this distance it looks to this narrator as if hunting was what he would better not have done at all, and for the rest, it was a pity that "our folks" were so afraid "the two forest nymphs" might drown, that they didn't let them learn how not to—which boating and swimming lessons would have helped teach; and as for horseback-riding, it is one of the most noble sports on earth for men and women both. We proved it so when (after the calf-taming episode) it was permitted us, by the intercession of our mother, who had been a fine rider in her younger years. . . .

It is good for boys and girls to know the same things, so that the former shall not feel and act so overwise. A boy whose sister knows all about the harness, the boat, the gymnastic exercise, will be far more modest, genial and pleasant to have about. He will cease to be a tease and learn how to be a comrade, and this is a great gain to him, his sister, and his wife that is to be. . . .

The first great break in our lives was when Oliver went to Beloit, fourteen miles down the river, to finish his preparatory studies and enter college. He had rarely spent an evening away from home in all his life until he was eighteen. Busy with books and papers "around the evening lamp," sometimes "running a (writing) race" with me, going into the dining-room to teach Mike and other "farm hands" to read and write, cipher and spell, busy with his chores and sports and farm work, Oliver, with his perpetual good humor, was a tremendous institution to have about and the shadow was heavy when he first started out from dear old Forest Home into the world. . . .

Father and he mounted the big wagon, stored with bed, stove, etc., for his room, and that precious new trunk; crack went the whip, round rolled the wheels, and Oliver was gone for aye!

"Does God want families to be broken up this way?" was my query, as I watched them from the front piazza until my brother's waving handkerchief was lost to view. "I don't believe He does, and it would be far better for Oliver and for me, too, if we had gone together."

"Or, better still, if we could all go together, and you three children still live on at home, until you had homes of your own," said mother gently as we three women folks, feeling dreadfully left behind, wiped our eyes and went in to help Bridget clear away the dinner dishes. . . .

No girl went through a harder experience than I, when my free, out-of-door life had to cease, and the long skirts and clubbed-up hair spiked with hair-pins had to be endured. The half of that down-heartedness has never been told and never can be. I always believed that if I had been let alone and allowed as a woman, what I had had as a girl, a free life in the country, where a human being might grow, body and soul, as a tree grows, I would have been "ten times more of a person" every way. Mine was a nature hard to tame, and I cried long and loud when I found I could never again race and range about with freedom. I had delighted in my short hair and nice round hat, or comfortable "Shaker bonnet," but now I was to be "choked with ribbons" when I went into the open air the rest of my days. Something like the following was the "state of mind" that I revealed to my journal about this time:

> This is my birthday and the date of my martyrdom. Mother insists that at last I *must* have my hair "done up woman-fashion." She says she can hardly forgive herself for letting me "run wild" so long. We've had a great time over it all, and here I sit like another Samson "shorn of my strength." That figure won't do, though, for the greatest trouble with me is that I never shall be shorn again. My "back" hair is twisted up like a corkscrew; I carry eighteen hair-pins; my head aches miserably; my feet are entangled in the skirt of my hateful new gown. I can never jump over a fence again, so long as I live. As for chasing the sheep, down in the shady pasture, it's out of the question, and to climb to my "Eagle's-nest" seat in the big burr-oak would ruin this new frock beyond repair. Altogether, I recognize the fact that my "occupation's gone."

Something else that had already happened, helped to stir up my spirit into a mighty unrest. This is the story as I told it to my journal:

This is election day and my brother is twenty-one years old. How proud he seemed as he dressed up in his best Sunday clothes and drove off in the big wagon with father and the hired men to vote for John C. Fremont, like the sensible "Free-soiler" that he is. My sister and I stood at the window and looked out after them. Somehow, I felt a lump in my throat, and then I could n't see their wagon any more, things got so blurred. I turned to Mary, and she, dear little innocent, seemed wonderfully sober, too. I said, "Wouldn't you like to vote as well as Oliver? Don't you and I love the country just as well as he, and doesn't the country need our ballots?" Then she looked scared, but answered, in a minute, " 'Course we do, and 'course we ought,—but don't you go ahead and say so, for then we would be called strong-minded."

These two great changes in my uneventful life made me so distressed in heart that I had half a mind to run away. But the trouble was, I had n't the faintest idea where to run to. Across the river, near Colonel Burdick's, lived Silas Hayner and several of his brothers, on their nice prairie farms. Sometimes Emily Scoville, Hannah Hayner, or some other of the active young women, would come over to help mother when there was more work than usual; and with Hannah, especially, I had fellowship because like myself, she was venturesome in disposition; could row a boat or fire a gun, and liked to be always out-of-doors. She was older than I, and entered into all my plans. So we two foolish creatures planned to borrow father's revolver and go off on a wild-goose chase, crossing the river in a canoe and launching out to seek our fortunes. But the best part of the story is that we were never so silly as to take a step beyond the old home-roof, contenting ourselves with talking the matter over in girlish phrase, and very soon perceiving how mean and ungrateful such an act would be. Indeed, I told Mary and mother all about it, after a little while, and that ended the only really "wild" plan that I ever made, except another, not unlike it, in my first months at Evanston, which was also nothing but a plan.

"You must go to school, my child, and take a course of study; I wish it might be to Oberlin"—this was my mother's quiet comment on the confession. "Your mind is active; you are fond of books and thoughts, as well as of outdoors; we must provide them for you to make up for the loss of your girlish good times;" so, without any scolding, this Roman matron got her daughter's aspirations into another channel. . . .

ROSE SCHNEIDERMAN (1882–1972)

7. The childhood of an immigrant working girl

Rose Schneiderman, women's trade union organizer and leader, recounts her poverty-blighted childhood in New York's Lower East side ghetto. It is interesting to note that the burden of housework and care of the younger siblings fell on the girl, even though there was an older brother and that the one child to receive a college education, even at free City College, was the boy. This is quite in keeping with the usual pattern of girls' education being deferred in favor of that of boys, and the earnings of sisters supporting the education of their brothers. On the other hand, it should be noted that when Rose's mother has to make arrangements for the care of her children in order to be able to work, the boys are sent to an orphanage while one girl goes to an aunt, and the other, the oldest girl, stays with the mother. Thus, even under hardship conditions, girls are "protected."

Rose Schneiderman's experience illustrates that of the millions of child workers who shuttled back and forth between premature domestic drudgery and underpaid factory labor, trying to snatch bits of schooling whenever the family could afford to spare their services.

In another biographical account (document 58), Rose Schneiderman tells of her awakening trade union consciousness and mili-

Rose Schneiderman, "A Cap Maker's Story," *The Independent* LVIII, no. 2943 (April 27, 1905): 935–936.

tancy. As a trade union organizer for the Ladies' Garment Workers Union and president of the National Women's Trade Union League, she was one of the most influential and inspiring women of her day.

A Cap Maker's Story

My name is Rose Schneiderman, and I was born in some small city of Russian Poland. I don't know the name of the city, and have no memory of that part of my childhood. When I was about five years of age my parents brought me to this country and we settled in New York.

So my earliest recollections are of living in a crowded street among the East Side Jews, for we also are Jews.

My father got work as a tailor, and we lived in two rooms on Eldridge Street, and did very well, though not so well as in Russia, because mother and father both earned money, and here father alone earned the money, while mother attended to the house. There were then two other children besides me, a boy of three and one of five.

I went to school until I was nine years old, enjoying it thoroughly and making great progress, but then my father died of brain fever and mother was left with three children and another one coming. So I had to stay at home to help her and she went out to look for work.

A month later the baby was born, and mother got work in a fur house, earning about $6 a week and afterward $8 a week, for she was clever and steady.

I was the house worker, preparing the meals and looking after the other children—the baby, a little girl of six years, and a boy of nine. I managed very well, tho the meals were not very elaborate. I could cook simple things like porridge, coffee and eggs, and mother used to prepare the meat before she went away in the morning, so that all I had to do was to put it in the pan at night. . . .

. . . I was a serious child, and cared little for children's play, and I knew nothing about the country, so it was not so bad for me as it might have been for another. . . .

Mother was absent from half-past seven o'clock in the morning till half-past six o'clock in the evening.

I was finally released by my little sister being taken by an aunt, and the two boys going to the Hebrew Orphan Asylum, which is a splendid institution, and turns out good men. One of these brothers is now a student in the City College, and the other is a page in the Stock Exchange.

When the other children were sent away mother was able to send me back to school, and I stayed in this school (Houston Street Grammar) till I had reached the Sixth Grammar Grade.

Then I had to leave in order to help support the family. I got a place in Hearn's as cash girl, and after working there three weeks changed to Ridley's, where I remained for two and·a half years. I finally left because the pay was so very poor and there did not seem to be any chance of advancement, and a friend told me that I could do better making caps.

So I got a place in the factory of Hein & Fox. The hours were from 8 a.m. to 6 p.m., and we made all sorts of linings—or, rather, we stitched in the linings—golf caps, yachting caps, etc. It was piece work, and we received from 3½ cents to 10 cents a dozen, according [!] to the different grades. By working hard we could make an average of about $5 a week. We would have made more but had to provide our own machines, which cost us $45, we paying for them on the installment plan. We paid $5 down and $1 a month after that.

I learned the business in about two months, and then made as much as the others, and was consequently doing quite well when the factory burned down, destroying all our machines—150 of them. This was very hard on the girls who had paid for their machines. It was not so bad for me, as I had only paid a little of what I owed.

The bosses got $500,000 insurance, so I heard, but they never gave the girls a cent to help them bear their losses. I think they might have given them $10, anyway.

Soon work went on again in four lofts, and a little later I became assistant sample maker. This is a position which, tho coveted by many, pays better in glory than in cash. It was still piece work, and tho the pay per dozen was better the work demanded was of a higher quality, and one could not rush through samples as through the other caps. So I still could average only about $5 per week. . . .

CHAPTER TWO

Marriage, Motherhood, and the Single State

From the vantage point of the twentieth-century "liberated woman" the position of nineteenth-century feminists in regard to marriage and sexual mores appears paradoxical and ambiguous. How was it possible, for women who petitioned and lectured in public and who braved the opprobrium of their contemporaries and attended women's rights conventions, to do so in the name of improving the marriage relation and upgrading motherhood? How was it possible for such women to staunchly defend domesticity and to construct an ideology of woman's moral superiority based on her chaste distaste for sexuality?

This paradox is more easily grasped when we begin to think of the function of the marriage institution and the way in which it defined women's status in the society.

Throughout much of the world and most of historical time, marriages were concluded not so much for the benefit of the individual partners as for the benefit of families and of the community. Sons as well as daughters were expected to and did in fact subordinate their own interests to those of the family. In colonial America, however, the ready availability of land and the shortage of women tended to break down traditional marriage arrangements even before the advent of industrialization. For men, especially the more adventuresome, this meant that it was easier than in European societies to free themselves from parental constraints and to set up independent households. For women, it meant a certain amount of freedom in the choice of a husband. It also meant that a girl's lack of inherited property or dowry did not automatically consign her to spinsterhood. Similarly, the relative leniency of colonial courts in recognizing prenuptial contracts and the property rights of married women (within the constraints of a patriarchal society) made the status of colonial wives relatively better than that of their European counterparts. However, for American women from the time of the settlement, marriage was their chief mode of gaining economic support; in fact, it was their most important occupation.

Until the late nineteenth century, a young girl had only two possible reasons for leaving the home of her family of birth: marriage and the death of her parents. If the former, she exchanged service and subservient status within one male-headed family unit (the home of her father) for that of another (the home of her husband). An unmarried daughter frequently lived in the home of a married brother or sister, there, too, occupying the subservient role deemed appropriate for her. She did not, practically, have the choice of living as a single woman with another woman or alone, unless she wanted to give up her good reputation. It was always difficult for an independent woman to earn a living sufficient for self-support. Until well into the twentieth century educational discrimination effectively closed most of the professions to women. For the uneducated, unskilled and service jobs were the only means to earning a living. Wage differentials based on sex served to turn any job held by women into an inferior job. The predominant values of the society held that the home was the proper sphere for women and domesticity and motherhood their natural occupations.

In case any spirited girl might, despite these discouraging prospects, still contemplate a life of independence and single blessedness, she was frightened by the horrid examples of female "deviance." Mary Wollstonecraft, Frances Wright, Fanny Kemble, all gifted intellectuals and assertive women of achievement, had personal lives beset by dishonor, disgrace, divorce. On the other end of the economic scale there was the working girl, in whom a desire for entertainment and independence "inevitably" led to adventure, illegitimate childbirth, finally prostitution. Popular fiction, sermons, and moral tracts propounded these stereotypes, which served to prop up the ideology of domesticity. No wonder marriage seemed the best possible solution to most girls.

Marriage brought change; marriage brought hope. The girl could leave the home of her parents and start building a family of

her own. True, the law made her subordinate to her husband in all
things and deprived her of possible future earnings and property
unless secured by prenuptial contract. Most brides gave little
thought to such matters. If the law gave the husband the right to
the wife's services and the power over her person, even the right to
chastise her physically—that is, beat her—most brides must have
felt confident that their ability to please their husband was sufficient protection. Yet those who had more experience in the world
and had had occasion to observe the lives of married women at
close range often expressed anxiety and doubts in anticipation of
their marriage.

The rather pathetic letter Harriet Beecher Stowe wrote to her
girlfriend on the eve of her marriage gives expression to such ambiguous feelings. It illuminates the psychological stress imposed
upon women by their restricted roles.

In preindustrial society traditional marriage arrangements persisted, as they did much later among certain immigrant groups.
Like so many other customs and values brought from Europe,
these were modified and adapted to the American environment.
Eliza Lucas's saucy response concerning her father's choice of a
marriage partner for her bespeaks the self-confidence of a wealthy,
well-educated girl who since age seventeen had managed her
father's extensive plantations in his absence. The account of Rose
Cohen some 150 years later illustrates the subtle pressure exerted
on a girl by the hopes and expectations of her parents. Her timidity
and feelings of guilt in breaking off her engagement, which contrast so greatly with the attitude of Eliza Lucas, are not so much the
result of a different personality as the reflection of a different economic position. Rose Cohen, growing up amid great poverty in the
ghetto, has a sharp realization of the limited choices before her and
of the serious consequences to herself and her family of her rejec-
tion of a suitor with a business of his own.

Married women living on farms and on the frontier fared better.
They enjoyed the respect and freedom of those doing work essential to the support of the family. Sharing work with their men and
acquiring competence in a wide variety of skills gave such women
the independence of spirit and the self-confidence which their ur-
banized daughters and granddaughters would lack. But in individual cases there were disadvantages to the close daily association
with fathers and husbands, especially if the men were domineer-

ing and exercised their authority oppressively. Jane Swisshelm and the "anonymous farmer's wife," writing sixty years after her, offer lively descriptions of what this meant in terms of daily restraints and frustrations. The shortage of labor and the favorable sex ratio set a natural limit to the extent of such oppression, as can be seen by the frequency of American wives "running away" and abandoning husbands with whom they were dissatisfied.

There were, of course, many happy marriages. Some of the best were what we would today call "emancipated marriages," made by reformers who entered upon the marriage relationship with a conscious desire to avoid the pitfalls of male dominance and female subordination. The marriage of Angelina Grimké and the antislavery organizer Theodore Weld, that of feminist Lucy Stone and the abolitionist Henry Blackwell, that of the Quakers Lucretia Coffin and James Mott are well known examples of partnerships in radical and reform activity within the framework of traditional marriages. The correspondence of Marius and Emily Robinson during the first year of their marriage offers an unusually good example of the love, devotion, and mutual respect needed to combine radical activity with marriage.

Until the beginning of the twentieth century, marriage for most couples meant parenthood. Demographic studies show a steady decline in the length of the childbearing and childrearing periods of married women, due to a decrease in fertility rates and changes in marriage patterns. The figures for three groups of wives compared are*

| | Wives born | | |
	Before 1786 (Quakers only)	1880–1889	1920–1929
Childbearing period	17.4 years	11.3	9.7
Childrearing period	39.7	34.6	31.2
Duration of marriage	30.4	35.4	43.6

* Robert V. Wells, "Demographic Changes and the Life Cycles of American Families," *The Journal of Interdisciplinary History* II, no. 2 (Autumn 1971): 282. Colonial data based on a study of 276 Quaker families. Since Quakers tended to have fewer children than the rest of the American population, the figures would tend to understate the length of the childbearing and childrearing periods.

Wells's data also show that before 1810, marriages were likely to terminate with the death of one partner while there were small children in the home; after 1910 a couple might expect to have less than one year of marriage together without the presence of young children. Only in the middle of the twentieth century could parents realistically expect to have a period of old age together without childrearing responsibilities.

Thus, the concept of marriage as a partnership of husband and wife was exceptional throughout most of our history, and did not reflect the actuality of people's lives. For women, motherhood was the reality, and while most of them expressed pleasure and pride in their children, only a few women could contemplate childbirth without fear and dread. Most of them had been witness to the suffering of women in childbirth and had experienced the death of young mothers or of infants in their family. Pregnancy, as Sarah Grimké and many others observed, was not a period of joyful anticipation, but often a time of anxiety and fear. The hardships of pioneer life, poverty, primitive conditions, and the demands of large families made it difficult for mothers to get proper rest before and after childbirth (see document 12). Absence of obstetrical care for most women, except the urban well-to-do, and frequent pregnancies and miscarriages manifested themselves in women's "complaints" and ailments. These were generally considered the normal lot of women, regarded indifferently by the medical profession and treated by women with a large variety of home remedies and ineffective nostrums. The rise of the health movement of the nineteenth century with its homeopathic remedies, water cures, and dress and diet reforms is a manifestation of the felt need of large groups of women for improved health care.

Yet women loved their babies, cared for them tenderly, and enjoyed motherhood (see document 14). It was only enforced, inevitable motherhood that came to be perceived as an evil. As women had done throughout history, American women cast around for methods to prevent unwanted pregnancies and, in desperation, resorted to abortions.

In an age in which effective birth control knowledge and technology were available only to an exceptional few, the prevention of too-frequent pregnancies was practically possible only through limiting intercourse or through the practice of coitus interruptus. Both were practices over which women could not exert independent control; they could only hope to convince their husbands to cooperate. A commonly practiced and ancient form of birth control was the long nursing of infants, a fallible method at best. One can suspect that it was more effective by preventing intercourse—if the husband respected such restraint as functional, in the best interest of mother and baby, and as "natural"—than it was as a biological method of preventing conception, if intercourse had taken place. For most women there was an inevitable connection between sexual intercourse and pregnancy. The much-discussed "Victorianism" and prudery of nineteenth-century women was, for them, simply functional: for most women, the perils, travails, and hardships of frequent pregnancies far outweighed the benefits and pleasures of sexual intercourse. Abstinence within marriage was the easiest and—from the point of view of women—most desirable way of limiting childbearing. Even tacit acceptance of a husband's infidelities seemed to many women preferable to the small pleasures and large penalties of marital sex.

Given these constraints upon the freedom of choice of women, it is understandable that the most advanced female thinkers of pre-Civil War society saw sexual activity in negative terms and considered it the chief obstacle to the elevation of the status of women. Margaret Fuller had in her erudite book, *Woman in the Nineteenth Century*, evoked the image of Victoria Virginia, the deliberately chaste, emancipated woman. Lucy Stone, in an interestingly frank discussion of marital sex with her brothers, advocates the early feminist ideal of deliberate sexual restraint in marriage. It is noteworthy that her argument is feminist, that is, such restraint is necessary for "the health of a woman." Sarah Grimké, in her essay "Marriage" expounds similar views. This sentiment is frequently echoed by early feminists and one can conjecture that it represented an open acknowledgment of views held by less feminist-minded women. The steady drop in the birth rate in the nineteenth century has been seen by some historians as a sign of an increase in the "domestic power" of women. Since it is difficult to visualize women actually enforcing sexual abstinence upon reluctant husbands, it seems more reasonable to assume that the increasing expense of educating children as well as other economic considerations persuaded husbands to control marital sex. More indicative of the feminist inclinations of women is the increasing number of unmarried women. In the later decades of the century greater numbers of educated women deliberately chose to remain single. Their spirit was anticipated and felicitously expressed earlier in the century by Louisa May Alcott, who wrote on the occasion of her sister's marriage, "I'd rather be a free spinster, and paddle my own canoe." The ambiguous consequences of such a decision are expressed in the diary of another early career woman, the writer Catharine Sedgwick.

The inevitable connection between sexual activity and childbearing could only be severed at a time when advanced medical knowledge and technology made birth control information readily available to the majority of women (in the early decades of the twentieth century). Until such a time, the notion of regarding sexuality as low and degrading must have had great appeal for many women who otherwise did not sympathize with feminist ideas. Conversely, the idealization of woman as "morally superior" because of her supposedly lower level of interest in sexual activity and her, consequently, greater "spirituality," may have served a useful political function. Far from being a paradoxical ideological position for feminists to take, it may have been a practical and popular stance. Popular among women, that is. The final selection in this section, Margaret Sanger's account of the case of Sadie Sachs, explains why.

8.   Engagements

Eliza Lucas Pinckney (1722-1793)

Eliza Lucas Pinckney, the carefully tutored daughter of the royal governor of Antigua, at age seventeen took over the full management of her father's plantations in South Carolina. During his absence she conducted a series of agricultural experiments, which resulted in the development of a marketable indigo seed that soon would become the second largest export staple of the Carolinas. After turning down the marriage candidates selected for her by her father, she later married the older Charles Pinckney, a widower. They had four children, two of whom became leaders of the American Revolution. Widowed at age thirty-six, she resumed the management of her plantations, reared her grandchildren, whose mother had died, and carried on a large correspondence and many intellectual interests until her old age.

1740

Hond. Sir

Your letter by way of Philadelphia which I duly received was an additional proof of that paternal tenderness which I have always Experienced from the most Indulgent of Parents from my Cradle to this time, and the subject of it is of the utmost importance to my peace and happiness.

As you propose Mr. L. to me I am sorry I can't have Sentiments favourable enough of him to take time to think on the Subject, as your Indulgence to me will ever add weight to the duty that obliges me to consult what best pleases you, for so much Generosity on your part claims all my Obedience, but as I know 'tis my happiness you consult [I] must beg the favour of you to pay my thanks to the old Gentleman for his Generosity and favourable sentiments of me and let

Eliza Lucas to Colonel Lucas, *The Letterbook of Eliza Lucas Pinckney, 1739–1762*, ed. Elise Pinckney, with Marvin R. Zahniser (Chapel Hill: Univ. of North Carolina Press, 1972), pp. 5–6. Reprinted by permission of the South Carolina Historical Society.

him know my thoughts on the affair in such civil terms as you know much better than any I can dictate; and beg leave to say to you that the riches of Peru and Chili if he had them put together could not purchase a sufficient Esteem for him to make him my husband.

As to the other gentleman you mention, Mr. Walsh, you know, Sir, I have so slight a knowledge of him I can form no judgment of him, and a Case of such consiquence [!] requires the Nicest distinction of humours and Sentiments. But give me leave to assure you, my dear Sir, that a single life is my only Choice and if it were not as I am yet but Eighteen, hope you will [put] aside the thoughts of my marrying yet these 2 or 3 years at least.

You are so good to say you have too great an Opinion of my prudence to think I would entertain an indiscreet passion for any one, and I hope heaven will always direct me that I may never disapoint [!] you; and what indeed could induce me to make a secret of my Inclination to my best friend, as I am well aware you would not disaprove [!] it to make me a Sacrifice to Wealth, and I am as certain I would indulge no passion that had not your aprobation [!], as I truly am

Dr. Sir, Your most dutiful & affecte. Daughter

E. Lucas

Ellen Wright Garrison (1840–1931)

Ellen Wright, the 24-year-old daughter of Martha Coffin Wright (see document 4 for mother-daughter correspondence) informs her parents of her engagement to William Lloyd Garrison Jr., son of the abolitionist leader and editor of *The Liberator,* who was an old friend and long-time associate of the Coffin-Wright family. Characteristically, the joyous and accepting reply on behalf of both parents, is written by Martha Coffin Wright.

Letters of Martha Coffin Pelham Wright, Garrison Family Papers. Courtesy of the Sophia Smith Collection (Women's History Archive), Smith College, Northampton, Mass.

ELLEN WRIGHT TO MARTHA COFFIN WRIGHT
BOSTON, FEB. 17TH, '64

My beloved Father and Mother—

I wish I knew how to tell you what for two days past, I
have been longing to tell you—that William Garrison has
asked me to marry him, & that I have promised to—I wish I
knew of your full consent, and satisfaction, it is all I need.
Sister is not yet ecstatic. She still holds her opinion about
the Altar fires, but it is because she does not know this brave
strong man, so eager to do what is right, at whatever cost.

I know *you* will be as happy as I desire; if there were any
reason to think otherwise, my peace would be greatly disturbed, for I long to make my offering of a son in law, to you,
as acceptable, and excellent, as my dear sisters have done
before me. Do not fancy that I have acted impulsively, or
blindly in this, nor that I do not strive to appreciate how
serious and irrevocable the step is. For a long time I have
been thinking of it, and I have tried to use my judgment
instead of my feelings. There is now no conflict in my mind,
& as far as I hear that you are gratified, you to whom I owe
everything & whom I love and revere with my whole heart,
I shall be forever at rest—

I dont want it to be generally known quite yet—Of course
Dix Place will have to be informed, and our Eliza & the
boys—I shall write a little note to Mrs. Hall & Lucy & that is
all. I have told Anna & Dick, as in duty bound, also *Mr.
Pierce,* which also seemed a duty—Please do not send it to
Phila. for I want to get a little accustomed to it first. William
made Fanny his immediate confidante & she came up yesterday, bringing me the sweetest welcome—They are all so
cordial & noble, I am certain to be well cared for & I shall
do my best to deserve their esteem. I pray that Dr. Taylor
will make me well and strong, so that I can hurry home &
learn to keep house—

I grudge now every moment of time I am obliged to be
away from home—

> *Goodbye my dear Parents—*
> *Your loving daughter Ellen W.*

MARTHA COFFIN WRIGHT TO ELLEN WRIGHT

My darling child—

We were taken entirely by surprise, by W. L. G.'s letter
which reached us at Eliza's on Friday—It was unexpected
to me, because I supposed he was "as ever, fraternally
yours"—and I felt somewhat at a loss how to answer it—We
can very sincerely welcome a son whose record stands so
fair as his, but it is no small thing to relinquish to another,
our last little daughter—We could not read your sweet and
tender letter unmoved nor without much solicitude, but you
have not decided hastily and it wd. be far from our wish to
interpose any objections in a matter in which we have always been disposed to leave your judgment entirely
unfettered—knowing that whatever promoted your happiness, would ensure ours—

The priceless worth of such a character, as his has been
described to us, by those who know him well, you have
done well to recognize. I trust that his prospects for the
future are such as to warrant you in giving up a home which
secures to you at least all the essentials for comfort—

The kind and loving welcome accorded to you by his
family is gratifying to us, and must be very pleasing to you,
and we can receive him with equal tenderness, not only on
acct. of his own moral worth, but because he is the son of
one whom we have so long regarded with reverence—

I hope that a few weeks at Dr. Taylor's will so strengthen
you that you will be able to come home sooner than you
anticipated . . . I feel very impatient to be with you. . . .

> *Most affectionately*
> *Your Mother*

Rose Cohen—c. 1895

The incidents described by Rose Cohen, an immigrant sweat-shop worker, are quite typical for that time and group. The girl's guilt feelings in rejecting the suitor selected by her parents and her strong sense of responsibility for causing her parents grief are symptomatic of the traditional sex role indoctrination of immigrant girls. It is noteworthy that the only way in which she can justify her decision is by the determination to stay single—a good illustration of the way nineteenth-century women defined their choices.

In the scene preceding the selection below her mother has sent sixteen-year-old Ruth to shop for sugar in an unfamiliar grocery store some distance away, where a young man waits on her.

. . . About two days later my mother asked me hesitatingly and without looking at me, "Well, what do you think of that young man?"

I looked at her in surprise. "What young man?" I asked.

"The young man from the grocery store on Broome Street," she said.

"I did not think of him. Why?"

Then with great earnestness mother explained to me that the young man was a possible suitor and a very desirable one, that he was getting an excellent living out of the store and that he very much wished to become "further acquainted," and, a meeting had already been arranged for Saturday. . . .

He came . . . accompanied by a middle-aged man who introduced himself as "the oldest uncle." I shrank behind my mother. . . . Father and the uncle sat at the table opposite each other and at once began a lively conversation to which the rest of us sat and listened respectfully.

When I felt more at ease I observed the young man. I felt as if I had known him a long time. It seemed quite natural that he should sit with his neck shrunk into his collar and keep his hat on like the two older men and be quite as old-fashioned as they were. . . .

Rose Cohen, *Out of the Shadow* (New York: George H. Doran Co., 1918), pp. 200–207, 224–227.

"Tell me," the uncle asked in his frank blunt way, glancing at me and then looking at my father, "why do you want to marry off that girl? She is so young, and not at all homely. What is the haste?" There was a tone of suspicion in his voice as if he feared a bad bargain.

There was a buzzing in my ears and I wanted to run away. Indistinctly I heard my parents answer something and at the same time I suddenly saw the young man standing before me and asking: "Will you come for a 'walk with me?" I rose quickly, went into the bedroom and stood with my face pressed against the clothes hanging on the wall. Then I came out dressed in my childish hat and coat and we went out. . . . He told me that he had three uncles. I recall these words spoken confidently but piously. "My uncles are all espoused and with the help of God they are making a living." . . .

That evening and the next day my parents looked quietly excited and expectant. The next night, while we were at supper, a message came from the matchmaker saying that the young man and his family were "pleased" and would be happy at an "alliance."

Father was so pleased at the news that his face became quite radiant. . . . "A girl without a cent to her name," he said, quite lost in wonder. Mother too looked pleased. . . .

"And what do you say, Rahel?" [father] asked. . . .

Somehow I had never quite realised that this question would really be put to me and that I would have to answer it. . . . "Well," father said in an easy tone, as if he were quite sure of the outcome, "there is plenty of time. Think it over." . . .

The matchmaker came in during the morning, he came in the afternoon and again at night when father was home. He would sit for hours singing the young man's praise,—his wealth, his business abilities and his character. . . .

When next father asked me, "Well, what do you say?" I trembled. "I have not decided yet," I told him quietly. . . .

"Do you want to see him again?" he asked.

I said: "No."

He thought for a moment. "I don't see what you want," he said. "He is a nice quiet young man and the main thing, he is not a wage earner. The smallest business man is worth ten workingmen. Tell me definitely to-morrow night. We cannot keep the people waiting for an answer any longer. This is not child's play, you know." When father was out of hearing mother added sadly, by way of help perhaps, "It is true that you are young, but you see, father is poor and you are not strong!"

I went into the bedroom and wept with my face buried in the pillows. "Why did I have to decide this? I had never been allowed to decide the smallest thing before—the shape of my shoes, the length of my dress."

The next evening I could not bear to face father. I saw that I must answer him definitely and I did not know what to answer. When it grew dark it occurred to me to go out into the street. I could always think more clearly in the air and while walking. . . .

"Father is poor and I am not strong." These words had impressed themselves on my mind. . . .

"It is clear then," I thought, "that I must marry. And if I did not marry this young man whom could I marry? A tailor?" At the thought of a tailor the young man rose in my estimation. I also saw an advantage in that he was a grocer. "My people could live near and get things at cost price, bread, butter, sugar, potatoes. It will be a great help." But on the other hand I could not picture myself living with the strange young man and his mother. I knew now that he had a mother; she was blind. He was her only son and she would live with him then as now.

It struck me how similar my fate was to my mother's. She too had married an only son, and his mother had been blind. . . . I realized that I was neither so good nor so patient as my mother. . . . But, if I did not marry this young man, what then? . . .

When I reached home supper was already half over. I sat

down at the foot of the table and mother gave me my soup. . . . I knew that there was one thought in every mind. My heart beat as if it would burst. . . .

At last I heard father lay down his spoon and push his chair away from the table a little.

"Well," he asked . . . "what have you decided?" It grew so still, even the breathing seemed to have stopped. And in this stillness I heard myself say, "Yes."

I did not look up. I knew that every face had grown brighter. It was pleasant to know that I was the cause. I had been nothing but a sorrow for so long.

The next day was Friday and Israel kept his store closed in the evening. He came to our house about seven o'clock and showed us two little tickets which were still unfamiliar to my family and myself. "These are for the theatre," he said, "for to-night." . . . We walked to the theatre in silence. Indeed we were never anything else but silent. This was the second time I was out alone with him. The first time had been when we went to get the ring. Then, I merely felt awkward when walking with him. But now I felt nervous and miserable. The silence oppressed me and as we walked along, his sleeve, as if by design, kept coming in contact with mine, and I kept edging away, but very slowly so as not to hurt his feelings. . . . In our seats in the balcony it was the same way. He was very attentive but chiefly with looks, and his elbow was on the arm of my seat. I pressed into the farthest corner and . . . could think of nothing but how to keep clear. . . .

The walk home was again a silent one through the streets now almost deserted. I remember how glad I was when I caught sight of our tenement. . . . I felt that I ought to say something but could not think what. So I said good night and turned to go when he called "Ruth!"* His voice sounded so muffled. . . . He came and stood near me. "I want one kiss," he said. I felt panic-stricken.

* The character in Rose Cohen's autobiography is called "Ruth" or "Rahel" (Yiddish).

"Oh, I couldn't!" I said, "I couldn't possibly. Indeed I couldn't!"

"But, we are engaged now," he said in a hurt tone as if he felt he were within his rights. Then it was . . . that it flashed through my mind what married life may mean with a person for whom one does not care. . . . "I couldn't possibly. I am sorry . . ."

In the morning when mother came into the front room . . . she cried out, "My God, how you look! Do you feel sick?" . . .

"I am not sick," I said. Then I broke down. I told her that I could not marry Israel. I clung to her and begged her not to blame me. She spoke tenderly and tried to quiet me. The children gathered around the couch and father came in. I expected he would upbraid me. But he was as tender as mother who stood with her arms tight around me. "Hush! Hush!" he said, "if you feel so unhappy you need not marry him."

"And won't I be forced?" I asked.

"You won't be forced."

"Can no one force me?"

There were tears in his eyes. "No one can force you."

Still I kept asking it over and over again and laughed and cried hysterically. . . .

[Israel] came about one o'clock. . . . Soon I heard my mother say . . . "Ruth does not feel well." . . . I called to mother and asked her to tell Israel that I wanted to talk to him. . . . He came and leaned up against the door post. . . . Suddenly I burst out that I did not want to get married and wept bitterly with my head in the pillow. I said I was sorry for the unpleasantness and the trouble but I would not get married. I would never marry at all. "But why?" he asked finally. His voice sounded as if he did not take me seriously. A moment before I had decided not to tell him, to spare him the hurt. Now when I saw he did not take me seriously there was only one thought in my mind, to be free of the engagement. So I said, "Because I do not love you." "Oh," he said, in a matter of course tone, "you will love me after we are married." And then he gave me many instances of his uncles and his aunts and his mother. I was in despair. How could I impress it upon him that for me this thing was impossible? . . .

"Listen," I said, "last night you wanted to kiss me." I could see that he felt a little guilty. "That was all right," I said. "I can imagine that if I loved you it would have made me happy. But as it is, the very thought of it drives me mad."

Even in that light I could see that his face changed colour and he stepped back and leaned heavily against the door. . . . I took the little ring from under the pillow and pressed it into his hand. "Now go," I begged him. "I am so sorry, but please go, go!" And he went, and I sat and watched him; his step was unsteady and his back more bent than usual, he looked like an old man.

Harriet Beecher Stowe (1811–1896)

Harriet Beecher, on the eve of her marriage to Calvin Ellis Stowe, confides her fears and anxieties to her good friend Georgiana May. Raised in the shadow of her father, the eminent and overbearing Congregational minister Lyman Beecher, and that of her perfectionist older sister Catharine, Harriet was a withdrawn, dreamy girl, struggling against "morbid feelings." Her marriage at twenty-four to Calvin Stowe, a widowed professor of biblical literature at Lane Theological Seminary, an institution of which her father was then president, was a sensible rather than a romantic choice. The marriage in which she bore seven children, much illness, respectable poverty, and a host of tribulations with a spirit of Christian sacrifice, was the center of her life. When, like so many wives before her, she took up the pen to supplement her husband's inadequate earnings, she did it for the sake of the family. Typically, she hid her "scribblings" in her sewing basket, working on them secretly when the room was empty, and resuming her "proper occupation" of darning and mending when anyone was present. The author of *Uncle Tom's Cabin*, the "little lady" whom

Harriet Beecher Stowe to Georgiana May. In *Life and Letters of Harriet Beecher Stowe*, ed. Annie Fields (Boston: Houghton Mifflin, 1898), p. 91.

President Lincoln metaphorically and gallantly credited with having started the Civil War, found wealth, fame, and self-fulfillment through her writings. But she never transcended the traditional concepts of wife and motherhood.

HARRIET BEECHER TO GEORGIANA MAY/JAN. 6, 1836

"Well, my dear G., about half an hour more and your old friend, and companion, school mate, sister, etc. will cease to be Hatty Beecher, and change to nobody knows who. My dear, you are engaged, and pledged in a year or 2 to encounter a similar fate, and do you wish to know how you shall feel? Well, my dear, I have been dreading and dreading the time, and lying awake all last week wondering how I should live through this overwhelming crisis, and lo! it has come, and I feel *nothing at all. . . .*"

MARIUS AND EMILY ROBINSON

9. An emancipated marriage

Marius Robinson was one of the students at Lane Theological Seminary who, in 1835, under the leadership of Theodore Weld, began to put his antislavery principles into practice by teaching and organizing in the free black community of Cincinnati. As part of their work the students staffed several schools for colored children, enlisting the aid of some women volunteers. One of these was Emily Rakestraw of Newgarden, Ohio, who defied her parents in order to do this work. The students' activities embarrassed the administration of the seminary, then headed by the Rev. Lyman Beecher, who threatened to expel two of the student leaders. Instead the students walked out, set up their own classes, and later helped to establish Oberlin College, where most of them finished their studies. Some, like Marius Robinson, spent one or more years "abolitionizing" Ohio.

Marius Robinson papers. Courtesy of the Western Reserve Historical Society, Cleveland, Ohio.

Emily Rakestraw and Marius Robinson were married in November 1836, which caused her parents to disavow her. The correspondence between them begins a few months after their marriage, when the young husband went on an extended speaking and organizing tour. Mob attacks, like the one he describes in his letter, frequently met the young antislavery agitators, who suffered a great deal of hardship in their radical missionary work. The pain and anxiety suffered by the young bride, as she awaited news of him, was only slightly mitigated by the continuation of her school teaching. As the letters indicate, his lecturing brought him to his wife's hometown and led to a reconciliation with her family.

The couple's separation was more prolonged than they had expected—it lasted almost ten months and culminated in Marius Robinson being tarred and feathered by a mob in June 1837, and injured so severely he suffered the aftereffects for ten years. In 1840, he became editor of the Salem *Anti-Slavery Bugle.* He and his wife continued their antislavery work until their deaths.

WILMINGTON, DECEMBER 31, 1836

My very dear wife:

I love to write this word "wife." It is a little word but full of meaning. Perhaps it is in part for its exclusiveness I love it. No one else can call you by it. It is my prerogative alone. And here you know I may be exclusive without selfishness, and I will try to be. I meant to have sent this from Xenia. But I am on the wing and time and opportunity for writing do not always come together. . . . Here the people seemed right glad to meet me. It is my old battleground. I find the little leaven I was enabled to throw into the lump here last summer is fast leavening the whole mass. . . .

Your husband, Marius

CONCORD, JAN. 5, 1837

Dear Wife:

It is now half past twelve at night but I must give a word. This thing of being married and going away from home and spending two long weeks without even a line or word from my wife is not so comfortable. Ask Hopkins if he thinks it would be. After all, I am not so much of a stoick or a philosopher as I thought for I have some humanity about me after all. I get along very well while I am lecturing, begging or even riding in this cold weather, but when night comes and I meet, as I have done tonight, a happy friend with his most cheerful, lovely wife around their own hearth, then comes over me the desolation of loneliness. I feel—do you know how? I can tell you at any rate, its influence is such that it requires a constant effort to keep from the incivility and rudeness of absolute inattention to the kindness of friends and the fascination of thoroughly intelligent abolition society. My spirit is away, communing with Emily's. Memory recalls her form and features—imagination decks them with a smile and clothes her tongue with words of love. Then again I think of you jaded and weary with the vexations and toils of the day—your spirits dried up with the exhaustion of teaching, and then I want to be with you. When you feel your usedupness, you can lounge upon me, and I can try to inspirit and help you. But adieu to these musings. God and humanity bleeding and suffering demand our services *apart,* and though we may, and ought, to feel the separation, yet we must not confer with flesh and blood. But cheerfully do the will of our kind Father above. Don't think I am unhappy, discontented, or in a murmuring mood because I have written as above—far from it. . . . The Lord have you in his keeping—dearest.

M.

P.S. I wish I could get hold of you wife and I would give you a most affectionate bite. Would you not reciprocate it? I dare say you would with womanish interest . . .

CINCINNATI, 13TH JAN. 1837

Emily Robinson to Marius Robinson

Well, my dear husband, I am glad, right glad that your storephilosophy waxes feeble. Tis almost a nulity, is it not?

Now, methinks I see M. screw up his mouth and say, this is rather womanish. I confess my womanish nature, never had much relish for that kind of stoicism with which you and Augustus* thought to fortify your hearts. Depend upon it children you were at war with nature when you essayed to do it. I got your kind letter yesterday. You were good and kind indeed to write so soon. I long much to have another letter but did not feel worthy the favor yet. . . .

I think I feel about our Separation just as you do, no other than the cause of the fatherless and widows can reconcile me to it. I only hope and pray that we may have health and strength to labor long in this cause so near and dear to us both that if permitted to labor together we may feel grateful and thankful for the privilege, or if apart—due recognition to the will of Him who decrees it. . . . Flora assists in my school now. We are not equal to one whole woman both of us here. Slight sore throats and slight coughs, just enough to make us feel peevish when perplexities multiply too fast. . . .

11 o'clock. I must go to bed. The Lord bless you and guard your slumbers. Good night. . . .

Love, Emily

PUTNAM, JAN. 13, 1837

My dearest [*wife*]:

. . . Sister P. has just informed me that Bro. W[attles] has been thro' Columbiana. That *our* parents manifested no desire to hear from you, and said they never wished to see you. This is the substance of the whole. I cannot give particulars. Now what shall I say my dear? I would cast this burden from your heart if I knew how. But a miserable comforter I am. I dont know how to go about it. But this much at any rate we learn: that we must look alone to God. Look to him. . . .

Much love to all, and especially to your own dear self.

From your devoted husband, Marius

---

* Augustus Wattles, a fellow abolitionist agent.

Cincinnati, 23 Jan. 1837

Beloved [husband]:

My heart was gladened this evening, when I came in from school by finding 2 letters on the table for me. One was from my friend Coal in Fallston, Pa., the other from your dear self. Do you guess which I read first? Yes, well I did, and who will wonder? My M. is my only beloved and I have a right to be partial to him, and I will be so, my parents have cast me off in the fullness of bitterness, grief, reproach, and scorn, my sisters and other friends whom I have loved too dearly, and still too fondly remember, love me less and care less for me than they did in by-gone days and who I say again can wonder that heart and affection cling to my husband as the first, best and dearest, and then the thought that he will not chide me for loving him better than any other earthly mould is so pleasurable. . . .

My dear, if you have no business with the Society at New Garden dont go there; it will certainly be better for you not to go to my father's. I wish it was not your duty to go into that section now. The thought of your going there fills my breast with trouble. If they treat you as I fear they will I shall cease to love them and cease to be happy. . . . But never mind it—go on and do your duty, and may the Lord sustain you in it. He is all wise, leave the consequences to Him. I do not know that I can write to you at New Lisbon. I do not feel like it. Now, if I do, let no one read my letter, but I must insist upon it, that you give me a faithful record of whatever you hear or see about my family concerning ourselves. Is this unfair? Perhaps I am not fit to judge but I think I could do the same for you. But if the task is too much for you, bid my sister R. do it. Chide her for her long silence with her pen, surely she is not doing as she would be done by.

My dear, kind husband. You are so good and faithful about writing; will you write from Steubenville, write from any place and as often as you can. I wrote you as soon as I received your letter from Columbus, and in time for it to get

to Putnam two or three days before you did. I have also
written to you at Mt. Vernon. . . .

Our school is still increasing. We have nearly as many as
we can stow in that little room; you can imagine how I feel,
and you may laugh at me too beside that I cannot write
about anybody or anything but myself.

Dear heart, may the Lord be with you in everything that
you do and strive to do for the good of your fellow creatures,
heavenly favor and wisdom to know your duty and heavenly
strength to perform it be ever yours.

With increased affection I am
Your wife

GRANVILLE, JAN. 25, 1837

Dear Wife:

Since I wrote you a week since I have been upon the
go-go-go. Have spoken ten times, been mobbed thrice, once
most rousingly. On Saturday last I went to Hartford in this
county. Stopped at the tavern and found it full of men who
had come to mob me. I talked with them some, got my
dinner and at two o'clock the bell rung. I went and found a
respectable number of decent orderly intelligent people
commingled with about 20 white savages. I kept talking
amidst great confusion for about three quarters of an hour
when I found myself unable to be heard and told them if
any *one* of them would speak I would give way but we
could not all talk at once. One of them commenced an oration when the audience moved an adjournment to a private
house. Then we formed a [abolition] society of about 40
members. The mob swearing we should never have a society. We then appointed another meeting for the evening.
When we were disturbed as before. Whenever I commenced speaking they commenced singing and thus alternated for some time until finally we adjourned to the
schoolhouse for a prayer meeting. I was told by the leader
that I could not speak in Hartford. I replied that I would try

it next Monday at one o'clock. . . . Monday morning the ruffians began to assemble, only, having been warned out the day previous, every one with his cudgel in his hand. About 300 of them were assembled by eleven o'clock. The veriest savages I ever saw. At the hour of meeting a fearless, noble band of women assembled but we were delayed in commencing and the women went to praying that the Lord would make the wrath of men to praise him. The meeting-house was on the opposite side of the Square of the town. The mob was in the vicinity of the house where I was, when I made my appearance they commenced their ribaldry and shouts, pushing each other upon me, etc. They then made a rush ahead of me for the house. I finally got in, took my stand on the seat of the pulpit and made an effort to be heard. Succeeded in pronouncing one sentence so as to be heard and then confusion, curses, cries of drag him out, kill him, etc., accompanied with brandishing of clubs succeeded. Finally their Captain General got as near to me as he could and with his club raised proposed terms to me. They were that in twenty minutes I should leave town never to return or lecture there again. . . . I [told] them that I was an American citizen and could not so far forget my duty and my rights as such as to render obedience to their direction. By this time I had opened the door of the room thinking that a retreat to the open air would give me a better field for action. One of the mobocrats in obedience to the cry, drag him out, aided me in my design, as he seized me by the left arm and pulled away with all his might to drag me from the pulpit. . . . I finally got out of doors. About a half dozen of the men had hold of me in the public square for a half hour. A man has just called for me—it is most sundown and I must go five miles and lecture tonight. Suffice it to say that the Lord delivered me out of their hands and that evening I lectured four miles distant and formed a society. Farewell, dear wife. The Lord is my protection. Have no fears on my account.

Your Husband, Marius.

Roscoe, Jan. 29, 1837

My dear Wife:

. . . I wish you could have seen that noble band of friends both men and women that stood by the truth in that hour of peril. You had their sympathies and prayers on that occasion as well as myself. One woman climbed into the meetinghouse at the window, when I was hemmed in by the mob in the pulpit, determined to see what was going on and if possible to aid in my rescue. . . .

Oh, my dear wife, I have wanted more than ever to see you since I received that letter. If I could not dry your tears I could at least shed others in painful and yet sweet communion with your own. I trust the Lord may ere long permit us to live and work together. This separation requires more of that ingredient called self-denial than I was ever before called to exercise. I fear you are running yourself down too fast. How is it? Dont work beyond your strength. Your measure of duty is not the amount of labor you see to be performed. But the amount of strength you have for its performance. This may and should be all employed, but not more. Since you have been in Cincinnati you have taxed your constitution beyond its power of endurance. . . .

My love, the time seems long—long ere I can expect to see you. Dont be anxious about me because I have been mobbed. You see the Lord has not suffered the wicked to hurt me and he will still be my shield and buckler. . . . Much love to you my dear, dear wife

from Your Marius

[Emily Robinson responds to the news of her husband's mobbing by urging him to have strength and faith.]

Feb. 4, 1837

. . . The time does seem long since you left. I have been lonely since, very sorrowful sometimes and sometimes comfortable. . . . But I am happier now than I was some time ago. I regret many things that happened during last year but do not feel the least remorse for *us*.

[Marius Robinson continued lecturing in Harrison and Jefferson counties, encountering no opposition. He complained about not receiving any mail from her for four weeks.]

GILFORD, FEB. *16, 1837*

Dear Wife:

Look up cheerily, gratefully and glad dear wife. The crisis has come and past and all is well or at any rate much better than our fears. The night before last I spent under the roof of your father. They received and treated me with kindness and attention. But I will begin and recount particulars. Monday night lectured in the Hicksite meetinghouse in Salem. A crowded house. Tuesday morning Candace came with me to this place. . . . Elizabeth came out to me at my horse and gave vent to the pentup ardor of her heart by a thorough sisterly embrace. She is a noblehearted girl. I love her for your sake and her own. They did not invite me into the house till your father came. He was at the stable. He received me with no particular favor or otherwise. Invited me in. Mother seemed about *so*. Much more cordial than I expected. William was not at home. Milton would not see me, at all. His wife seemed kindly in her feelings. After supper I went to the schoolhouse where an appointment had been made for me. . . . The audience was a perfect jam. Many could not obtain admittance and many who were in, stood up. Returned after meeting. Considerable sociability, about health, cousins, and matters and things in general. In the morning before I left I had some conversation with Father about the relation we sustained to each other. I told him, in substance, that there was perhaps some difference in opinion between us, and that of course as honest men we must each act in such method as our views of truth and duty should dictate. But that this difference should make no diminution on my part of affection or respect. And that I should ever esteem it my duty and my highest pleasure ever to entertain those feelings and pursue that course of conduct which my relation to him demanded. He cordially reciprocated these sentiments. Said that altho he regretted our haste, yet as we were now man and wife all he wished was our highest happiness. He repeatedly urged me to make his house my home while I was in the neighborhood and added a special invitation to return there tonight. And what was to me a most grateful evidence of kind feeling on his part, he proposed to write you a letter. To this proposition I added a word of encouragement. Parental affection will yet triumph, my dear E. If we nurture it properly and give it time to operate. It has already done much, and their feelings towards both you and me are different from what they were a few weeks since. . . . I hope to make some further advances in their confidence. . . . Father, Mother, sisters, all look with great interest to your visit here next spring. . . .

Fare you well, my dear, dear wife

Marius

ATWATER, FEB. 21, 1837

Well, my dear Emily:

Here I am with a room to myself today for the first time since I left home. . . . I wish you would come and sit down beside me and let me whisper in your ear some curious things I want to say. I dont like to poke them at you with the point of my pen. So if you dont come you shant have them. . . . I hope you feel happier since you heard from me at N.G. You see, it all worked well. Had I arrived there some four or five weeks earlier my reception would perhaps have been quite different. But time and affection for you had so operated upon the good sense of your father as to produce a material change in his feelings and purposes. My lecturing too in the neighborhood produced at least no unfavorable impression on his mind. . . . After meeting I went to

Father's. He received me with far greater apparent cordiality and kindness than before. . . . *Our* parents were both urgent in their solicitations that when you visit them in the spring I shall by all means accompany you. Thus I left them all I think much better friends to myself than I found them, and with much less alienation of feeling towards you. For this result my dear E. we must and will feel most ardent gratitude to God. Now, dry your tears—trust in the Lord and do good and he will direct our way in love and mercy. . . .

You ask when I shall be at home? I dont know. Just as soon as I can. Perhaps five weeks. It may be longer, and again it may be shorter, for the attraction, like that of gravitation increases in power as I near its center. However I will try to check my momentum before I get home so as not to dash you all to pieces. You say I must feel no anxiety about your health. Now would not you be sorry if I felt none? I cant help feeling it. I dont want to help feeling it so long as you have that "slight cough." Take care of that my dear. . . . And now wife wont you lay aside your despondency. Be happy and cheerful. One cause of grief is I hope now removed. Have confidence that all will be and let your mind be staid in perfect peace because you trust in Him who is mighty to save and strong to deliver.

Adieu my most precious one. More and more are you beloved daily by

Your Husband, Marius

JANE SWISSHELM (1815–1884)

10.   In woman's sphere and out of it

Jane Grey Cannon Swisshelm was born in Pittsburgh, Pa., then a frontier town. Her father died when she was eight years old, and

Jane Swisshelm, *Half a Century* (Chicago: Jansen, McClurg & Co., 1880), pp. 47–50, 113–114.

Jane had to help her mother to support the family by lacemaking and schoolteaching. At twenty she married James Swisshelm, a devout Methodist with a domineering mother. Her efforts to fit into her husband's narrow definition of "woman's sphere," which she describes in the passage below, soon faltered. She could not forever repress her independent spirit. After a stormy marriage, during which she ran a corsetmaking business and then took up a journalistic career, she finally left her husband in 1857 and took her only daughter to St. Cloud, Minn. Later her husband divorced her for desertion. In St. Cloud she became the owner and editor of the *St. Cloud Visiter*, which she ran as a vigorous and controversial antislavery paper. Jane Swisshelm soon became a force in local politics, earning the enmity of the Democratic boss, Sylvanus B. Lowry, by exposing his proslavery record. He paid some men to destroy her press and convened a public rally with the express purpose of forcing the troublesome editor to leave town. Jane Swisshelm took up the challenge. At the meeting, she announced that she had made her will and that a friend of hers was in attendance with a pistol and orders to "shoot her square through the brain, if there was no other way of preventing her from falling into the hands of the mob." Her defiant courage won over the crowd; they even collected money to replace her press. Mrs. Swisshelm promptly renewed her denunciation of Lowry, who then brought a $10,000 libel suit against her. Since she had no money for a long court fight, she settled by signing a pledge that the *St. Cloud Visiter* would never refer to Mr. Lowry again. She kept her word. The next week she stopped publication of the *St. Cloud Visiter* and appeared with a new paper, *The Democrat*, in which she repeated all her charges against Lowry and stated, "We have pledged our honor that the paper we edit will discuss any subject we have in mind to discuss." She was never bothered again by either politician or mob, and continued to delight her readers by her savage and irrepressible comments.

During all my girlhood I saw no pictures, no art gallery, no studio, but had learned to feel great contempt for my own efforts at picture-making. A traveling artist stopped in Wilkinsburg and painted some portraits; we visited his studio, and a new world opened to me. Up to that time painting had seemed as inaccessible as the moon—a sublimity I no more thought of reaching than a star; but when I saw a portrait on the easel, a palette of paints and some brushes, I was at home in a new world. . . .

Bard, the wagon-maker, made me a stretcher, and with a yard of unbleached muslin, some tacks and white lead, I made a canvas. In the shop were white lead, lampblack, king's yellow and red lead, with oil and turpentine. I watched Bard mix paints, and concluded I wanted brown. Years before, I heard of brown umber, so I got umber and some brushes and began my husband's portrait. I hid it when he was there or I heard any one coming, and once blistered it badly trying to dry it before the fire, so that it was a very rough work; but it was a portrait, a daub, a likeness, and the hand was his hand and no other. The figure was correct, and the position in the chair, and, from the moment I began it, I felt I had found my vocation. . . . I forgot God, and did not know it; forgot philosophy, and did not care to remember it; but alas! I forgot to get Bard's dinner, and, although I forgot to be hungry, I had no reason to suppose he did. He would willingly have gone hungry, rather than give any one trouble; but I had neglected a duty. Not only once did I do this, but again and again, the fire went out or the bread ran over in the pans, while I painted and dreamed.

My conscience began to trouble me. Housekeeping was "woman's sphere," although I had never then heard the words, for no woman had gotten out of it to be hounded back; but I knew my place and scorned to leave it. I tried to think I could paint without neglect of duty. It did not occur to me that painting was a duty for a married woman! Had the passion seized me before marriage, no other love could have come between me and art; but I felt that it was too late, as my life was already devoted to another object— housekeeping.

It was a hard struggle. I tried to compromise, but experience soon deprived me of that hope, for to paint was to be oblivious of all other things. In my doubt, I met one of those newspaper paragraphs with which men are wont to pelt women into subjection: "A man does not marry an artist, but a housekeeper." This fitted my case, and my doom was sealed.

I put away my brushes; resolutely crucified my divine gift, and while it hung writhing on the cross, spent my best years and powers cooking cabbage. . . .

Friends have tried to comfort me by the assurance that my life-work has been better done by the pen than it could have been with the pencil, but this cannot be. I have never cared for literary fame . . . and never could be so occupied with it as to forget a domestic duty. . . .

Where are the pictures I should have given to the world? . . . Is that Christianity which has so long said to one-half of the race, "Thou shalt not use any gift of the Creator, if it be not approved by thy brother; and unto man, not God, thou shalt ever turn and ask, 'What wilt thou have me to do?' "

It was not only my art-love which must be sacrificed to my duty as a wife, but my literary tastes must go with it. "The husband is the head of the wife." To be head, he must be superior. An uncultivated husband could not be the superior of a cultivated wife. I knew from the first that his education had been limited, but thought the defect would be easily remedied as he had good abilities, but I discovered he had no love for books. His spiritual guides derided human learning and depended on inspiration. My knowledge stood in the way of my salvation, and I must be that odious thing—a superior wife—or stop my progress, for to be and appear were the same thing. I must be the mate of the man I had chosen; and if he would not come to my level, I must go to his. So I gave up study, and for years did not read one page in any book save the Bible. . . .

[Jane Swisshelm began a career in journalism.]

My paper was a six column weekly, with a small Roman

letter head, my motto, "Speak unto the children of Israel that they go forward." . . .

It was quite an insignificant looking sheet, but no sooner did the American eagle catch sight of it, than he swooned and fell off his perch. Democratic roosters straightened out their necks and ran screaming with terror. Whig coons scampered up trees and barked furiously. The world was falling and every one had "heard it, saw it, and felt it."

It appeared that on some inauspicious morning each one of three-fourths of the secular editors from Maine to Georgia had gone to his office suspecting nothing, when from some corner of his exchange list there sprang upon him such a horror as he had little thought to see.

A woman had started a political paper! A woman! Could he believe his eyes? A woman! Instantly he sprang to his feet and clutched his pantaloons, shouted to the assistant editor, when he, too, read and grasped frantically at his cassimeres, called to the reporters and pressmen and typos and devils, who all rushed in, heard the news, seized their nether garments and joined in the general chorus, "My breeches! oh, my breeches!" Here was a woman resolved to steal their pantaloons, their trousers, and when these were gone they might cry "Ye have taken away my gods, and what have I more?" The imminence of the peril called for prompt action, and with one accord they shouted, "On to the breach, in defense of our breeches! Repel the invader or fill the trenches with our noble dead." . . .

George D. Prentiss took up the cry, and gave the world a two-third column leader on it, stating explicitly, "She is a man all but the pantaloons." I wrote to him asking a copy of the article, but received no answer, when I replied in rhyme to suit his case:

> Perhaps you have been busy
> Horsewhipping Sal or Lizzie
> Stealing some poor man's baby,
> Selling its mother, may-be.
> You say—and you are witty—

That I—and, tis a pity—
Of manhood lack but dress;
But you lack manliness,
A body clean and new,
A soul within it, too.
Nature must change her plan
Ere you can be a man.

This turned the tide of battle. One editor said, "Brother
George, beware of sister Jane." Another, "Prentiss has
found his match." He made no reply, and it was not long
until I thought the pantaloon argument was dropped
forever.

11. Runaway wives

In a frontier society, it was not overly difficult for a man to break up
an unhappy marriage by leaving town and making a new start,
perhaps under a new identity, in another community. The frequency of bigamy and desertion charges in petitions for divorce
attests to the relative ease with which this means of ending a
marriage was used. Interestingly, women also availed themselves
of this method. The need for female workers and the oversupply of
males in the population put women in colonial America in a
somewhat more favorable position than women of a later period to
use this method of last resort. While marriage was, by colonial law,
considered a civil contract, it was a contract between two unequal
partners. The wife had to render service, the husband support—in
this respect the contract resembled an indenture. This is reflected
in the practice of husbands who advertised their runaway wives
among announcements for runaway servants or lost horses. The
purpose of such advertisements was to protect the husband against
any debts his wife might run up, but such public notices also
served as a way of shaming or punishing an unfaithful or disgruntled wife and discouraging others from her support. As can be seen
in the following selections, wives did not hesitate to respond in
kind.

[A]

Whereas Elizabeth Perkins, Wife to me the Subscriber, of the Township of Willingburg and County of Burlington hath not only eloped from my Bed and Board, but otherwise behaves in a very unbecoming manner toward me; and as I am apprehensive from what I have already experienced, she may endeavor to run me in Debt, I am obliged to take this public Method to forewarn all Persons from trusting her on my Account, as I am determined I will not pay a single Farthing of her contracting from the Date hereof. And I hope no Person will encourage her on such Occasions, as it may be a Prejudice to me, and will render them liable to Prosecution.

Pennsylvania Chronicle, *August 10–17, 1767.*

Joseph Perkins

Joseph Perkins, of the township of Willingborough, and county of Burlington, my graceless husband, having maliciously advertised to the world, that I have eloped from his bed and board, run him in debt, and otherwise behaved in an unbecoming manner towards him, I am obliged to take this method solemnly to declare, that those charges against me have not the least foundation in truth, which can be easily made to appear; and were entirely occasioned by my refusing to assign over to him the little interest I have, that he might squander it away in disorderly company, as he hath done the greatest part of his own, and my declining to entertain and encourage the infamous guests he frequently brought to his house, where, amidst the most notorious scenes and disorder, I often met with treatment, which would have shocked a savage of the Ohio, which at last obliged me to fly to my mother's house in this city, which I unfortunately left, as the only sanctuary I could expect to find from his persecutions. There being a greater probability of his running me in debt, than my injuring him in that manner, I desire that no person may trust him from any expectation that I will pay his debts, for I have determined never to pay a Farthing of his contracting from the date hereof.

Pennsylvania Chronicle, *August 18–25, 1767.*

Elizabeth Perkins,
Philadelphia

[B]

TAKE NOTICE

And beware of that swindler JESSE DOUGHERTY, who married me in November last, and some time after marriage informed me that he had another wife alive, and before I recovered, the villain left me, and took one of my best horses—one of my neighbors was so good as to follow him and take the horse from him and bring him back. The said Dougherty is about forty years of age, five feet ten inches high, round shouldered, thick lips, complexion and hair dark, grey eyes, remarkably ugly and ill-natured, and very fond of ardent spirits, and by profession a notorious liar. This is therefore to warn all widows to beware of the swindler, as all he wants is their property, and they may go to the devil for him after he gets that. Also, all persons are forewarned from trading with the said Dougherty, with the expectation of receiving pay from my property, as I consider the marriage contract *null* and *void* agreeable to law; you will therefore pay no attention to any lies he may tell you of his property in this country. The said Dougherty has a number of wives living, perhaps eight or ten, (the number not positively known,) and will no doubt, if he can get them, have eight or ten more. I believe that is the way he makes his living.

Livingston County, Kentucky, Sept. 5, 1817.   Mary Dodd

Reprinted from the *Kentucky Reporter* in Henry Fearon, *Sketches of America* (London, 1818), as cited in E. A. Dexter, *Career Women of America, 1776–1840* (Francestown, N.H.: Marshall Jones Co., 1950), p. 197.

12. Motherhood in the Minnesota territory

This anonymous account of the birth of the tenth baby of a pioneer farmwife is quite typical of the less dramatic stories of the frontier. Indian attacks, the hardships of extreme weather, drought, freezes, storms, accidents treated without benefit of doctors—these were the dramatic moments. Year in, year out, there was hard work and the simple interdependence of the self-sufficient family. The women, separated from their families of origin, depended on other women, living sometimes a considerable distance away, for support and friendship in times of need. The priorities were quite clear: the stock had to be seen to, the men had to be fed. One woman reported that on the day on which she gave birth to her child she got up early, "baked six loaves of bread. Made a kettle of mush and have now a suet pudding and beef boiling. . . . I have managed to put my clothes away and set my house in order. . . . Nine o'clock p.m. was delivered of another son." The unnamed Minnesota mother in the selection below was not very different from the other anonymous women who settled the West. She gave birth to her child, one hopes quickly and without much fuss, then sat up in bed and peeled potatoes for the threshing crew.

. . . My Grandmother, a pretty young girl, fourteen years her husband's junior, bidding goodbye forever to her own family and with three little boys ages four years, twenty months and a new baby, it seems like a tremendous undertaking.

Both Benjamin and Lydia left comfortable homes. Ben had a good farm in Lancaster County, Penn. But this fever to go West had taken hold of him. . . .

Grandmother and her little boys had to live with settlers until her house was built. Every man helped build and soon

Kathryn Stoner Hicks Moody, "Territorial Days in Minnesota," unpublished manuscript, pp. 10–12, 15. Papers of the Minnesota Historical Society, St. Paul. Used courtesy of Kathryn H. Moody. I am indebted to Gretchen Kreuter of Minneapolis for calling this item to my attention.

she had what was considered a good house with a floor unit, windows, and even an upstairs. But I wonder how it compared with the home she had left in Pennsylvania? Perhaps by this time she had seen enough of how other pioneers lived and had been living without a home for so long that any home where she could assemble her family and belongings seemed acceptable. . . .

The winters were long and severe. Grandmother would go for months without seeing anyone but her own husband and children. And about every two years she had a new baby to add to the family. In all grandmother had ten children in a period of twenty-four years—seven boys all of whom lived to manhood, and three daughters. One named Fanny died when she was nine years old of what was called "belly ache." Fanny had eaten choke cherries and drunk cream and was doubled up with pain. This was their only death until grandfather died in 1889 at the age of 72. . . .

Midwives had most of the maternity cases that the neighboring women did not attend. My grandmother had all her babies without the help of a doctor and never had an anesthetic.

When one was ill, mothers took care of the nursing and if they failed, grandmothers were called in. Doctors were few and far between and were only called as a last resort. The pioneers had lived many years without professional advice. . . .

Many of the men were hard on their families. After all what could a woman do if she did not like her lot? There was no place to go, no one to turn to—her husband was master. . . .

August 6, 1876 was a very warm day and this was the day the threshers arrived at the Stoner farm. Early that morning grandmother surprised the family by giving birth to a baby boy.

I said surprised the family! This sounds impossible, doesn't it? Yet her older daughter Mary, then about eighteen years old was surprised and greatly annoyed because she felt her mother had had enough children. She left home for the day—leaving all the work to fall on someone else.

This baby was grandmother's tenth child. She was forty-five years old and this was her last baby. . . .

But the men had to be fed and grandmother sat up in bed and peeled potatoes for the crew. Lydia showed her pioneer spirit in that she met the emergency in spite of all she had been through that morning.

FANNY WRIGHT

13. A difficult childbirth

Martha Coffin Wright (1806–1878) in a letter to her daughter Ellen (1840–1931) here describes the difficult delivery of her daughter-in-law, Fanny, the wife of Ellen's brother Frank. The baby, to be named Mabel, was the couple's first child. Eliza, mentioned in the letter, may have been Fanny's mother or she may have been Martha Wright's older sister. Harriet Bogart was most likely a nurse hired for the lying-in period. At the time of the writing of this letter Ellen herself was the mother of two children. She later gave birth to three more. (See also documents 4, 8, 14, 19.)

Auburn/Oct 31st 1869

. . . at 6 P.M. we sent for them, and Fanny was so much worse that I got her into her room. From that time she had pretty severe pain at short intervals and Eliza came up to spend the night. We tho't the baby would be born in 2 or 3 hours, and I guess the Dr. (Horatio) tho't so too, for he did not go away, but read in the parlor, and rested a couple of hours in Frank's room. About 12 we called him, as there was little intermission in her pains, and from that time till 3:10

Martha Coffin Wright to Ellen Wright Garrison, letters of Martha Coffin Pelham Wright, Garrison Family Papers. Courtesy of the Sophia Smith Collection (Women's History Archive), Smith College, Northampton, Mass.

P.M. she suffered dreadfully with ineffectual forcing
pains—Horatio's strength was giving out, and he sent for his
father and instruments. The old Dr. soon got here, but
thought it best to get along without them. I asked him to
give her ether, and Frank was anxious she should take it, but
she preferred not to take it, and said the Dr. would not give
it to her when he cut a needle out of her foot, fearing for her
lungs. They did however give her a little, wh. may have
relaxed the muscles a little but it seemed as if the baby
never cd be born alive. It was too distressing to see her
torture, & Frank was entirely overcome, & had to go to his
room. Your father hurried away as soon as he had eaten his
dinner, saying he could not stay in the house. Eliza sat with
him at dinner, & Harriet went down to get something.
Frank ate nothing. . . .

Fanny bore her sufferings with wonderful heroism and
seemed somewhat reconciled when all was over, & her
pretty little blackhaired Mabel by her side. I never saw so
much hair—large dark eyes & a round face—Harriet Bogart
does nicely & Fanny likes her. I have just made a bright
little fire in her room. Frank nailed a comfort over each
window in the corner & we moved the bedstead along. She
is doing very well, today she sd. Frank said she never
should have another. "Te he", sd Miss Bogart "I've heard
people say that afore". I could not get her suffering out of
my mind for hours. She is so quiet and sensible that I trust
now she will get along. . . .

MARTHA COFFIN WRIGHT

14. Why don't I wean him?

Martha Coffin Wright, at the time this letter was written, was forty
years old. Frank was her sixth child, nearly two years old. Charles,
her last child, was born two years later, and lived only a year.

Martha Coffin Wright to Lucretia Coffin Mott, ibid.

DEC. 14, 1845—AUBURN

. . . All night I heard it pattering against the windows and it was so comfortable to know I had not to be out in it, but had only to turn and go to sleep when Frank would let me, the little nuisance! "Why don't I wean him?" Because it seems so cruel these dismal long nights, and if it didn't I couldn't summon resolution, it is so much easier to nurse him and poke him back into his crib, than to "sit up on ends" as they say here and fight with him an hour and run the risk of waking Willy overhead. I always dread weaning the poor little botherations, they take so much comfort in nursing. . . .

LUCY STONE (1818–1893), FRANCIS, WILLIAM BOWMAN, LUTHER AND SARAH STONE

15. A feminist debates marital restraint with her brothers and sister

Lucy Stone, who would later become one of the leaders of the woman's rights movement and one of its leading public figures as a journalist and lecturer, was a student at Oberlin College in 1846. She had just come to the decision that she would dedicate her life to lecturing for abolition and woman's rights and had anxiously asked her father's opinion of this, in her day, daring and outrageous decision. Of her six siblings, only two brothers offered encouragement, while her parents, sisters, and sisters-in-law tried their best to dissuade her. In a letter, which is not preserved, she apparently also raised the question of birth control for the sake of women's health. The replies of her brothers and sister, which fortunately have been preserved, provide us with an unusually frank discussion of sex and birth control among members of a New England farm family. Lucy Stone's argument echoed the views of the most

Blackwell Family Papers (1846, 1847), Manuscript Division, Library of Congress, Washington, D.C.

radical communitarian reformers of her day: the health and well-being of mothers was jeopardized by too-frequent childbirths and it was incumbent upon the male to exercise self-restraint. The casual and matter-of-fact way in which the brothers debate this issue with their sister and, by inference, with their wives, shows them to have been untouched by notions of Victorian prudery and indicates that such discussions must have occurred at other times among the young people.

Lucy Stone, then still pledged determinedly to spinsterhood for the sake of upholding her feminist principles, later married the abolitionist Henry Blackwell and had one child. The couple deliberately set out to make an emancipated marriage which would allow the wife full freedom for a public career, and celebrated their wedding by signing a contract, in which the husband renounced all legal rights to his wife's services and property and in which the wife contracted to keep her maiden name.

The debate between the brothers and sisters continued, apparently, for some time. It is fascinating that, in 1847, after citing his own wife's good health and—rather casually—announcing the birth of his last child, brother Francis reports the illness and expected death of a friend's wife. "She has a child about eight weeks old," he writes, seemingly unconscious of the way in which he is bolstering sister Lucy's argument with this explanation.

SARAH AND WILLIAM BOWMAN STONE TO LUCY STONE
NOVEMBER 28, 1846

My dear sister,

. . . I don't know as I was very much surprised at the content of your letter. I have *half-believed* for a long time that you were preparing for a public speaker, though I hoped I might be mistaken. Not that I think it wrong in itself, but because I think it an employment a great many grades *below,* what I believe my *only* and *dearly loved sister* qualified to engage in. I don't hardly know what you mean by "laboring for the restoration and salvation of our sex" but I conclude you mean a salvation from some thralldom imposed by man. Now my sister I don't believe woman is groaning under half so heavy a yoke of bondage as you imagine. I am sure I do not feel burdened by anything man has laid upon me, be sure I can't vote, but what care I for that, I *would* not if I could. I know there is a distinction made in the wages of males and females when they perform the same labor, this I think is unjust, and it is the only thing in which woman is oppressed, that I know of, but women have no one to blame, but themselves in this matter. If as a general thing they had qualified themselves, as men have they would command the same price, but they have not, and the few who have are obliged to suffer on that account. I think my sister if you would spend the remainder of your life in *educating* our sex, you would do a *far greater* good than you will if you spend your *noble energies* in forever *hurling* "back the insults and indignities that men heap upon us." This I am sure you can never do "by the grace of God" for it is entirely contrary to his spirit and teachings. My sister commit your ways unto the Lord, and he will direct your steps.

With regard to the note you enclosed, I think there is much of truth in it, though I don't see how it can be called adultery. I was talking with mother once against it and she argued for it by the passage "To avoid fornication let every man have his own wife" for nobody ever committed fornication for the sake of offspring. I don't think married women are any paler than unmarried ones, they are not as far as my observation and *experience* extend. Husband don't [!] like your idea of running away from temptation, he thinks there is more virtue in resisting. He says, if to avoid temptation they must refrain from sleeping with their wives, they must also cease to look upon them to avoid lust. . . .

Your sister, Sarah

Dear Sis—

Though we had just written to you Sarah thought she could not delay writing as soon as she received yours. You see from what she has written how your labors will be regarded by those for whose rights you design to toil. I think that those who are sighing for deliverance from bondage have a stronger claim upon our efforts than those who hug their chains. I think you should do that which you think to be your duty. No one can be truly happy who neglects to do what he feels he ought [This is in response to her announced decision to become a public lecturer]. . . .

In relation to the subject of moral reform among married people, I think with Sarah that there is some truth in your views. I think that whatever is injurious to health is wrong and I have no doubt that many do injure themselves by excess. Perhaps you would be a better judge of the matter if you were married. I think that husbands and wives are to sleep together and that nothing is wrong which is the necessary result of so doing. God has joined them together and nothing should separate them from the same bed, especially on cold winter nights. Write soon. Yours in love,

W. B. Stone

Luther Stone to Lucy Stone/*December 2, 1846*

Sister Lucy

. . . I felt much pleasure to receive so long a letter from you. . . . For several days past I have been unwell, this being the first sickness I have had since in Oberlin. Today I feel much better and what little strength I have shall be wasted in writing to you. First. Our wife is in the best of health, and family prospect the same as when in Oberlin. It takes some time for Northern *Seed* to become acclimated to Southern soil. It don't grow the first year. In answer to your inquiry about sexual intercourse I shall say in brief that God made the whole of man for his own glory. All the organs he has given to man are to be used with reference to this glory. Our Generative organs should never be used except for propagation & we should always be able to ask God's blessing to follow their use. Nine tenths of all the half grown men and of all the invalids, and men of ½ minds have become what they are by their own or their fathers indulgence in the Beast-like use of their generative organs. But I am not yet through. *Lucy I Think It As Great A Sin To Not Suffer These Organs To Be Used At All As To Use Them To Much. . . .*

We have no news to write. All was well at home when we last heard from there. Frank was looking for another Baby. A. Howland was married to Miss Adaline Henshaw. When I commenced writing I thought I would write a long letter but the flesh won't hold out to day. So I will let Phebe finish. I am very much better today than I have been but I am so weak I can't write more.

Yours truly, Luther

Francis Stone to Lucy Stone/*June 6, 1847*

Very dear sister,

As a line from home is always acceptable to you, and as I have some things that I wish to say, I thought I would scribble a little and send it along by male [!], and first of all you will wish to know how we all do. Father and mother have gone to meeting, of course they are all well, except father has a lame back just now, I am well and strong to work, and enough of it to do, we have a boy from Ware Village helping us this summer, he is not the best of help, but we get along. . . . [Various items of family news follows.] You spoke of not writing for commencement unless you could read your own composition, as you think it would be a sacrifice of principle we think you do right in not writing.* As to the course you intend to persue after you get through, you know I have no objections to women lecturing, but the question of women's rights is rather a lean one is it not; But

* A reference to the fact that Lucy Stone had been selected by her classmates at Oberlin to read her commencement essay at graduation. By custom, only male students read their own essays, while the work of female students was read by a male professor. Lucy refused to submit an essay unless she could read it herself and was joined in this feminist protest by several of the students, both male and female.—ED.

you must decide *that* for yourself, The question of Human
rights is in my estimation a good one. Mr. Kent is quite out
of health this spring and summer he is not able to do any
thing, Elijah Clap lives with his mother. John Clap has
cried his wife down because she refuses his bed and
board, . . . Emeline & Nancy were at our house the other
day, I suppose they came to see our baby. O; I have not told
you that we have got another baby, a fine fat one born the 7
of May weighed about 8 lbs, weighed 10¼ this day, they all
say that it looks like me, we dont call her quite as handsom
[!] as the other one was, but she looks well enough, Some
think as you do that it is having them rather to [!] fast but
Mrs. Foot says that it is not a mite to [!] quick. This waiting
three years Sis, as you intimate is all nonsense. Have them
as fast as you can if you can take care of them, and if you
cant, trust Providence and obey the command given to our
first parents to multiply and replenish the Earth and subdue
it. Were all to follow the example of Mrs. Weld* and the
advice of your self, when think you would the wilderness
and the solitary place in the natural world bud and blossom
as the rose? Your own good sense will answer never. Beasts
of prey, and venomous serpents would increas upon man
until he would be destroyed from the earth and there would
be none to till the ground. Nor is this all. Are you thankful,
do you rejoice that God has given you an existence on the
earth? I answer for you yes. Then think of the multitudes
that have lived and that will live who would never have had
an existence, had the generations past, and the generations
yet to come acted as you advise. You spoke of cohabiting
only fore [!] the sake of children, I would like to now [!]

---

* The reference is to Angelina Grimké Weld, the well-known antislavery
and woman's rights lecturer, whose example was apparently cited by Lucy
Stone in her letter. Angelina Grimké Weld had, indeed, at the time of this
writing had three children, the last two spaced three years apart. Since
Lucy Stone, who admired Angelina Grimké Weld as a model of the female
reformer, did not then know the Welds personally, she must have been
ignorant of the fact that Mrs. Weld had given birth to her first child in 1839,
another in 1840 and then had suffered a miscarriage before the birth of her
third child in 1844.—ED.

what advice you would give to Back Ellis and his wife & to those who are like them? I would ask still further for what do you take your regular meals each day; do you eat that you may live, or do you eat because you are hungary [!], so then I suppose individuals do not cohabit fore the sake of children only, but because they want to. You speak of injuring the health of the woman and therefore it must be wrong, now my dear, do you not know that it injures the health of a woman, fore a time at least, to have a child if it is only once in three years, it may impair her health for life, what then is it wrong? I will just say here that my wife is as well now I presume as Mrs. W. is after she has gone three years and then had one. There is much more that might be said but I can not with pen and ink. Our little babe we call Rhoda, wife sends love and so do I lots of it. Harriet can nurse this babe.

F. Stone

P.S. It is thought that George Cutter's wife can't live long. She has a child about eight weeks old. . . .

SARAH M. GRIMKÉ (1792–1873)

16. Marriage

Sarah Moore Grimké, daughter of a South Carolina planter, who together with her sister Angelina Emily Grimké Weld pioneered in asserting woman's rights and advancing woman's status within the abolition movement, was one of the earliest feminist writers in the United States. Her *Letters on the Equality of the Sexes and the Condition of Woman* (1838) developed the first full-fledged argument for the rights of women written by an American woman. Sarah Grimké's other theoretical contributions to this subject remain scattered among her letters, diaries, and notebooks.

Sarah M. Grimké, "Marriage" and "Sisters of Charity," Miscellaneous Essays, Weld-Grimké Papers. Courtesy of the William L. Clements Library, Univ. of Michigan, Ann Arbor.

In the period 1852–1857 Sarah Grimké attempted to write a
major work, of which the two excerpts below are a part, in which
she hoped to detail the disabilities under which the women of her
day suffered, with particular emphasis on the law. She felt she
needed more education than she had acquired by sporadic reading
and, at the age of sixty-one, made inquiries about entering law
school. Her efforts were met with discouragement since women
were not admitted to law schools, and she finally abandoned the
project.

The essay "Marriage," of which the major part is here published,
offers the modern reader an unusually clear insight into the way
nineteenth-century feminists linked sexuality with the subjugation
of women. Sarah Grimké argued that unwanted pregnancies and
economic dependence were the chief causes of women's oppression in marriage, and mentioned the double standard and the existence of prostitution as intrinsically connected with these evils. In
her earlier work she had presented a well-documented biblical and
natural rights argument for the emancipation of women, advocat-
ing education and equal rights before the law as the chief remedies. This was similar to the Wollstonecraft argument, with which
she was familiar. But Sarah Grimké had earlier shown an acute
awareness of the pernicious influence of what we would today call
sex role indoctrination and had vigorously stressed the need for
women to build self-confidence. In the fragmentary essay "Sisters
of Charity," she had strongly argued for "self-reliance" and self-
definition for women. In "Marriage" she raised a demand for
women's control over their own bodies, a concept which puts her
far in advance of feminist thinkers of her day. That she could con-
ceptualize such a demand only in terms of voluntary chastity is a
reflection of her upbringing and makes her representative of her
time and place. (See also document 87).

Sarah Grimké's writings suffer from her heavy, complex style
and from her uncritical acceptance of scientific and pseudoscien-
tific theories popular in her day. Her fate defines the difficulties
and frustrations of nineteenth-century women intellectuals. Although quite well-educated for a woman of the Southern planter
class, she had never had the benefit of a systematic classical education. Her own reading had been profoundest in theology, Bible
study, and the law and only sporadic and superficial in other fields.
The education denied her, the inevitable burdens of service to

others imposed by her upbringing and indoctrination, the loneliness of decades of pioneering, all these speak out of the fragments before us.

Yet, Sarah Grimké managed intellectually to transcend these limitations, though in her life she acted out the traditional role of the spinster living in her married sister's household and carrying a good deal of its domestic burdens. In these fragmentary notes, she went beyond the legal rights argument and her own oft-repeated argument for educated womanhood, and moved on to discuss sexuality, the acceptance of male values, lack of control by women over their own bodies, and lack of autonomy as the root causes oppressing women.

At the age of seventy-nine, Sarah Grimké trudged through the Massachusetts countryside selling copies of John Stuart Mill's essay, *Subjection of Women.* Her own bold argument, which urged women to advance their condition for their own sakes, not only for the sake of better marriages and a better society, was closer to twentieth-century feminism than was Mill's celebrated essay.

From the essay "Marriage"

In the summer of 1855 the *New York Times* professing to give a history of the rise and progress of what is called "Free Love" identified it with the Woman's Rights movement. This writer says, "The Woman's Rights movement leads directly and rapidly in the same direction, viz. to Free Love, that extreme section of it we mean which claims to rest upon the absolute and indefeasible right of woman to equality in all respects with man and to a complete sovereignty over her own person and conduct."

This exposition of the *principles* of the Woman's Rights movement I heartily accept. We do claim the absolute and indefeasible right of woman to an equality in all respects with man and to a complete sovereignty over her own person and conduct. Human rights are *not* based upon sex, color, capacity or condition. They are universal, inalienable and eternal, and none but despots will deny to woman that supreme sovereignty over her own person and conduct which Law concedes to man.

The conclusion that this writer draws from this equality of rights, viz., that this "movement leads directly and rapidly to the principles of 'Free Love'," or that a claim for Woman's rights "nullifies the very idea of marriage as anything more than a partnership at will" I utterly deny. Man is acknowledged to have rightfully supreme sovereignty over *his own* person and conduct, and yet, who believes that this nullifies marriage, making it, in *his* case, a mere partnership at will. Why then should it be so in the case of woman? Is *she* less worthy of being trusted with this right than he? Let the 20,000 prostitutes of New York whose virtue is often bought by *married* men answer. Is *her* heart more inconstant and less penetrated than his by the love of children? Even if experience had not taught us otherwise, the nature of the two beings would determine the question. . . . Is it not wonderful that woman has endured so long and so patiently the hidden wrongs which man has inflicted upon her in the marriage relation, & all because her heart so cleaves to her children & to home and to *one* love, that she silently buries her sorrows & immolates herself rather than surrender her heart's dearest treasures.

Let us examine these assertions calmly, reverently, for we are treading upon holy ground: all *rights* are *holy*. Let us first look at the effect upon the marriage relation of the hitherto acknowledged principle that man had rights superior to woman. Has it not subordinated her to his passions? Has she not been continually forced into a motherhood which she abhorred, because she knew that her children were *not* the offspring of love but of lust? Has she not in unnumbered instances felt in the deepest recesses of her soul, that she was used to minister to Passion, not voluntarily to receive from her husband the chaste expression of his *love?* Has she not, too often, when thus compelled to receive the germ *she could not welcome,* refused to retain & nourish into life the babe, which she felt was not the fruit of a pure connubial love?

Ponder well the effects upon woman of the *assumed*

superiority of rights in the stronger sex, that sex too in which the constitutional element of sex has far greater strength. Look too at the effect upon children, who are the product of such *one-sided rights*—puny, sickly, ill-organized & unbalanced—bearing about in body & mind the marks of their unholy origin.

And yet the Times is horror-struck at the idea of woman's claiming "*A supreme sovereignty over her own person & conduct.*" Is it not time that she should? Has not man proved himself unworthy of the power which he assumes over her person & conduct? How I ask has he protected & cherished her? Let her faded youth, her shatter'd constitution, her unharmonious offspring, her withered heart & *his* withered intellect answer these questions. Is it not time then that she asked for "a redress of grievances" & a recognition of that *equality of rights* which alone can save her?

Let us now look at the results of such a recognition. A right on the part of woman to decide *when* she shall become a mother, how often & under what circumstances. Surely as upon her alone devolves the necessity of nurturing unto the fulness of life the being within her & after it is born, of nursing & tending it thro' helpless infancy & capricious childhood, often under the pressure of miserable health; she *ought* to have the right of controlling all preliminaries. If man had all these burdens to bear, would not *he* declare that common sense & common justice confer this right upon him.

An eminent physician of Boston once remarked that if in the economy of nature, the sexes alternated in giving birth to children no family would ever have more than three, the husband bearing one and the wife two. But the *right* to decide this matter has been almost wholly denied to woman. How often is she forced into an untimely motherhood which compels her to wean her babe, thus depriving it of that nutriment provided by nature as the most bland & fitting, during the period of dentition. Thousands of deaths from this cause, in infancy, are attributed by superstition &

ignorance to the dispensations of Divine Providence. How many thousands, too, of miscarriages are forced upon woman by the fact that man lives down that law of his being which would protect her from such terrible consequences just as animal instinct protects the female among brutes. To save woman from legalized licentiousness is then one of the reasons why we plead for *equality of rights.*

No one can fail to see that this condition of things results from several causes:

1st   Ignorance of those physical laws which every man & woman *ought* to know before marriage, the knowledge of which has been withheld from the young, under a false & fatal idea of delicacy. Many a man ruins his own health & that of his wife and his children too, thro' ignorance. A diffusion of knowledge respecting these laws would resolve existing evils.

2nd   A false conception in man & woman of *his* nature & necessities. The great truth that the most concentrated fluid of the body has an office to perform in the production of *great tho'ts & original ideas,* as well as in the reproduction of the species is known to few & too little appreciated by all. The prodigal waste of this by legalized licentiousness has dwarfed the intellect of man. . . .

3rd   The fact that many legal marriages are not love marriages. In a pure, true relation between the sexes, no difficulties can ever arise, but a willing recognition of each other's rights & mutual wants, naturally & spontaneously resulting in voluntary motherhood, a joyful appreciation of the blessedness of parentage, the birth of healthy, comely children & a beautiful home.

But it may be asked, what is to be done in cases of uncongenial marriages. Are not such men & women to follow their attractions outside of the legal relation. I unhesitatingly answer no! Where two persons have established a false marriage relation, *they are bound to abide by the consequences* of the mistake they have made. Perhaps they did love each other, but a nearer intimacy has frozen this love or changed it into disgust. Or theirs may have been a marriage of convenience or one for the sake of obtaining a house, a fortune, a position in life: or it may have been a mere act of obedience to parents, or of gratitude, or a means of canceling a monied obligation. Multiform are the *unworthy* motives which seduce men & women into this sacred relation. In all these cases, let them abide the consequences of their own perversion of marriage in exchanging personal chastity for the pride of life, vanity in dress, position or a house to live in without that *love* which alone can make that house a *home*.

In some cases, it may be duty for the parties to separate, but let both keep themselves pure, so long as both are living. Let them accept the discipline thus afforded, and spiritual strength and growth will be their reward.

The Doctrine that human beings are to follow their attractions, which lies at the base of that miscalled "Free Love" system, is fraught with infinite danger. We are too low down to listen for one moment to its syren voice. . . .

Let me then exculpate "the woman's rights movement," from the charge of "tending directly and rapidly to the Free Love system, & nullifying the very idea of Marriage as anything more than a partnership at will." On the contrary our great desire is to purify & exalt the marriage relation & destroy *all* licentiousness. To every unhappy couple we say again, bear in quiet home seclusion, the heart withering consequences of your own mistakes. You owe this to yourselves, to your children, to society. Keep yourselves pure from that desecration of the marriage relation, which brings children into the world who have not upon their brows the seals of love & chastity. If you cannot live thus purely together & separation becomes necessary, let no temporary or permanent relation be formed by either party during the life of the other. . . .

In marriage is the origin of life. In the union of the sexes exists a creative energy which is found nowhere else. Human nature tends to the uses of all the faculties with which it is endowed, and desire is strong in proportion to the greatness of the result which flows from its exercise. Hence the creative is stronger than any other faculty, birth being the *great* fact of our existence here, & its *legitimate* exercise is the natural result of the purest & most unselfish love, the spontaneous giving away of oneself to the only loved one & the receiving of that other to ourselves in return. Marriage is a necessity of our being, because of our halfness. Every man and woman feels a profound want, which no father nor mother, no sister nor brother can fill. An indescribable longing for, & yearning after a perfect absorbing of its interests, feeling & being itself into one kindred spirit. The man feels within him a lack of the feminine element, the woman the lack of the masculine, each possessing enough of the other's nature to appreciate it & seek its fulness, each in the other. Each has a deep awareness of incompleteness without the other . . . & seek[s] that divinity in her & in him, with whom they would companion for life. *This divinity* is the only true basis of union, out of it alone, grow these holy affinities which bind soul to soul, not only in a temporal relation but in an eternal marriage.

Full well do multitudes of human beings know in bitterness of soul, that the empty ceremony of a priest and connubial relations do *not* constitute marriage. Many a woman (I call her not *wife*) loathes the unhallowed connection she has formed & would gladly welcome death as a deliverer from that polluted prison house, which the world *miscalls* her *home*. A revolting experience has forced upon her the conviction that she is a legal prostitute, a chattel personal, a tool that is used, a mere convenience—and too late does she learn that they who desecrate the marriage relation sin against their own bodies & their own souls, for no crime carries with it such physical suffering or so deep a sense of *self* degradation. . . . Man seems to feel that Marriage gives him the control of Woman's person just as the Law gives him the control of her property. Thus are her most sacred rights destroyed by that very act, which, under the laws of Nature should enlarge, establish & protect them. In marriage is the origin of Life—in it woman finds herself endowed with a creative, energy she never possessed before, in it new aspirations take possession of her, an indescribable longing after motherhood as the felt climax of her being. She joyfully gives herself away, that she may receive the germ of a new being, and true to nature, would fain retire within herself & absorb & expend all her energies in the development of this precious germ. But alas! How few are permitted, unmolested to pursue that end, which for the time being, has become the great object of life. How often is she compelled by various considerations to yield to the *unnatural* embraces of her husband, and thus to endanger the very existence of her embryo babe. How often is it sacrificed to the ungoverned passion of its own father & the health of the mother seriously impaired. Every unnatural process is deleterious, hence abortions are destructive to the constitution and many women are broken down in the prime of life by them alone, and their haggard countenances too plainly reveal their secret sorrows. A lady once said to me I have but one child, but I have had 12 miscarriages—another had 4 children and 15 abortions. And why I would ask this untimely casting of her fruit? Do the beasts of the field miscarry? Why not? *They* are governed by instinct. Are the *brutes* safe during the period of gestation whilst *Woman* is not?

. . . Again—look at the burdens imposed upon her by the care of many children following in quick succession. How can any mother do her duty to her family, if in 8 years she have 6 children. Look at the unnatural tug upon her constitution, her night watches, her sore vexations and trials & causes nameless & numberless, that wear away her life. If men had to alternate with their wives, the duties of the nursery, fewer & further between would be its inmates. . . .

O! how many women who have entered the marriage relation in all purity and innocence, expecting to realize in it the completion of their own halfness, the rounding out of their own being, the blending of their holiest instincts with those of a kindred spirit, have too soon discovered that they were unpaid housekeepers & nurses, & still worse, chattels personal to be used & abused at the will of a master, & all in a cold matter of course way. O! the agony of realizing that personal & pecuniary independence are annihilated by that "Law which makes the husband and wife one & that one is the husband." How many so called wives, rise in the morning oppressed with a sense of degradation from the fact that their chastity has been violated, their holiest instincts disregarded, and themselves humbled under an oppressive sense of their own pollution, and that, too, a thousand times harder to bear, because so called husband has been the perpetrator of the unnatural crime. . . .

Who does not see that Men must grow out of that nondevelopment in which they now are, before they will have ears to hear or hearts to love the truth on this subject, and that to Woman must be conceded an *equality of rights* thro' out the circle of human relations, before she can be emancipated from that worst of all slaveries—slavery to the passions of Man.

And this equality cannot—will not be conceded until she too grows out of that stratum of development in which she now is. Her imperfect education unfits her for acquiring that pecuniary independence which would lift her above the temptation to marry for a home. Dependence subjects her too often to be duped *in* the marriage relation as well as out of it. And the great work to be done now for woman by woman, is to impress her with the necessity of pecuniary independence, each working out that independence according to her taste and ability. Now they work under great disadvantages and can obtain a mere pittance. But be not discouraged sisters—Is not a dinner of herbs and simple apparel such as you can provide, infinitely better than sumptuous fare, costly attire, elegant furniture and equipage received in exchange for *freedom* & *personal purity.*

They must yearn to be *women* rather than fine statues to be draped in satins & lawns—elegant automatons grac[ing] a drawing room, or pretty play things to be toyed with by respectable rakes or heartless dandies under the guise of lovers and husbands. . . .

In all great changes thro' which Society passes in her upward progress, there seem to be periods of interregnum, when the old usage has died out before the new one was ready to be inaugurated in its place. . . .

Let the old contract system remain, until that new & divine form of spirit union, shall have gently undermined its hold upon society, pushing it gradually off & taking its place in the hearts & lives of all who are prepared to welcome it in purity & love. . . .

From the Essay "Sisters of Charity"

The laws respecting married women are one of the greatest outrages that has been perpetrated against God and humanity—To couple the highest and holiest institution, an institution connected . . . with the noblest aspirations of our being, an institution designed above all others to bring the sexes into harmony, to educate not only the married pair but their offspring to a more exalted life—to couple such an institution on the one side with injustice and oppression and on the other with the loss of self-respect, independence and degradation is an insult . . . to the divinity he has conferred upon man which has no parallel. Unless marriage become a grand and holy institution, unless birth be invested with the consecration of the Divine Presence it is in vain to expect domestic felicity. . . .

I feel deeply, strongly because I have seen the terrible effect of these laws on noble minded women even where the husbands did all in their power to annul them. It was impossible not to feel that their rights were ignored and that they enjoyed the privileges they had, not by right, but by courtesy. The laws respecting women are a blasphemy against God. . . . The law which gives women the right

before marriage to make the most important far reaching
contract which a human being can make and then by legal
enactment proclaims her incapable of the most common
business contracts is too absurd to need any comment. Is
there anything to hope for the world under the existing
laws? Why hold we to these dead symbols of barbarism?
We need laws now inspired by the vitality of the present
era—laws bounding with the life blood of advancing civilization. If we would go on from glory to glory as a nation—let
us not borrow or reenact the laws of a barbarous age, but
. . . invest woman with the halo which omnipotence designs for her brow. What an unwise man said of books, viz.
that it would be better for the world if every book was destroyed may be said of the laws respecting woman. If every
one of these enactments were obliterated the world would
be the better for it. . . .

MARGARET SANGER (1880–1966)

17. The story of Sadie Sachs

Margaret (Higgins) Sanger learned early in life to associate poverty and large families. She later wrote, "Mother bore eleven children. She died at forty-eight. My father lived until he was eighty."
Margaret Higgins left home early and became a trained nurse. At
the end of her training she fell in love with and married William
Sanger, an architect, and for the next twelve years devoted herself
to being a housewife and mother. She had three children whom
she raised in an atmosphere of warmth and happiness. When they
were old enough to be in school she returned to the job of a public
health nurse in the slums of New York. She wrote,

> My own motherhood was joyous, loving, happy. I wanted to
> share these joys with other women. . . . Since the birth of my
> first child I had realized the importance of spacing babies, but

Margaret Sanger, *An Autobiography* (New York: W. W. Norton and Co.,
1938), pp. 86–92. Reprinted courtesy of Grant Sanger, M.D.

only a few months before had I fully grasped the significant fact that a powerful law denied and prevented mothers from obtaining knowledge to properly space their families.

It was during this period of her life that the event described below took place. It proved to be decisive in causing Margaret Sanger to devote the rest of her life to making reliable contraceptive information available to women. In order to do so, she had to circumvent and later defy the federal and New York obscenity laws, travel abroad to amass scientific family planning information, face a jail term, and create a social movement. Birth control—a phrase she coined—became her personal crusade.

After years of pioneering for a cause to which she was fanatically devoted and which most social reformers considered of secondary importance, public support and interest grew rapidly after 1920. Passage of a law permitting physicians to give birth control information in cases where maternal health might be impaired by childbearing, spurred organizational effort and in 1925 the movement became international. Mrs. Sanger had the satisfaction of seeing the dissemination of birth control information by doctors legalized in the United States in 1937.

Margaret Sanger has been honored as a social reformer, yet her significance as a theorist of women's emancipation has yet to be fully appreciated. It was she who insisted that the crucial need for women lay not so much in the ballot and in the winning of legal rights as in their gaining control over their reproduction. It was she who dedicated her life to enabling women to sever the inevitable link between sexuality and childbearing. She did so in the name of "joyous voluntary motherhood," but her work challenged the ancient patriarchal assumption that women's sexuality and motherhood were a fit subject for legislative action. Singlehandedly, and facing the disapproval of her contemporaries, Margaret Sanger gave women a means for their emancipation which far outweighed all other reforms in its impact: the concept that they have a right to control their own bodies and the practical knowledge with which to do so.

During these years in New York . . . more and more my calls began to come from the Lower East Side, as though I were being magnetically drawn there by some force outside my control. I hated the wretchedness and hopelessness of the poor, and never experienced that satisfaction in working among them that so many noble women have found. My concern for my patients was now quite different from my earlier hospital attitude. I could see that much was wrong with them that did not appear in the physiological or medical diagnosis. A woman in childbirth was not merely a woman in childbirth. My expanded outlook included a view of her background, her potentialities as a human being, the kind of children she was bearing, and what was going to happen to them. . . .

As soon as the neighbors learned that a nurse was in the building they came in a friendly way to visit, often carrying fruit, jellies, or gefüllter fish made after a cherished recipe. It was infinitely pathetic to me that they, so poor themselves, should bring me food. Later they drifted in again with the excuse of getting the plate, and sat down for a nice talk; there was no hurry. Always back of the little gift was the question, "I am pregnant (or my daughter, or my sister is). Tell me something to keep from having another baby. We cannot afford another yet."

I tried to explain the only two methods I had ever heard of among the middle classes, both of which were invariably brushed aside as unacceptable. They were of no certain avail to the wife because they placed the burden of responsibility solely upon the husband—a burden which he seldom assumed. What she was seeking was self-protection she could herself use, and there was none. . . .

Pregnancy was a chronic condition among the women of this class. Suggestions as to what to do for a girl who was "in trouble" or a married woman who was "caught" passed from mouth to mouth—herb teas, turpentine, steaming, rolling downstairs, inserting slippery elm, knitting needles, shoe-hooks. When they had word of a new remedy they hurried to the drugstore, and if the clerk were inclined to be friendly he might say, "Oh, that won't help you, but here's something that may." The younger druggists usually refused to give advice because, if it were to be known, they would come under the law; midwives were even more fearful. The doomed women implored me to reveal the "secret" rich people had, offering to pay me extra to tell them; many really believed I was holding back information for money. They asked everybody and tried anything, but nothing did them any good. On Saturday nights I have seen groups of from fifty to one hundred with their shawls over their heads waiting outside the office of a five-dollar abortionist.

Each time I returned to this district, which was becoming a recurrent nightmare, I used to hear that Mrs. Cohen "had been carried to a hospital, but had never come back," or that Mrs. Kelly "had sent the children to a neighbor and had put her head into the gas oven." Day after day such tales were poured into my ears—a baby born dead, great relief—the death of an older child, sorrow but again relief of a sort—the story told a thousand times of death from abortion and children going into institutions. I shuddered with horror as I listened to the details and studied the reasons back of them—destitution linked with excessive childbearing. The waste of life seemed utterly senseless. . . .

I knew the women personally. They were living, breathing, human beings, with hopes, fears, and aspirations like my own, yet their weary, misshapen bodies "always ailing, never failing," were destined to be thrown on the scrap heap before they were thirty-five. I could not escape from the facts of their wretchedness; neither was I able to see any way out. My own cozy and comfortable family existence was becoming a reproach to me.

Then one stifling mid-July day of 1912 I was summoned to a Grand Street tenement. My patient was a small, slight Russian Jewess, about twenty-eight years old, of the special cast of feature to which suffering lends a madonna-like expression. The cramped three-room apartment was in a sorry state of turmoil. Jake Sachs, a truck driver scarcely older than his wife, had come home to find the three children crying and her unconscious from the effects of a self-induced abortion. He had called the nearest doctor, who in turn had sent for me. Jake's earnings were trifling, and most of them had gone to keep the none-too-strong children clean and properly fed. But his wife's ingenuity had helped them to save a little, and this he was glad to spend on a nurse rather than have her go to a hospital.

The doctor and I settled ourselves to the task of fighting the septicemia. Never had I worked so fast, never so concentratedly. . . .

Jake was more kind and thoughtful than many of the husbands I had encountered. He loved his children, and had always helped his wife wash and dress them. He had brought water up and carried garbage down before he left in the morning, and did as much as he could for me while he anxiously watched her progress.

After a fortnight Mrs. Sachs' recovery was in sight. . . . As I was preparing to leave the fragile patient to take up her difficult life once more, she finally voiced her fears, "Another baby will finish me, I suppose?"

"It's too early to talk about that," I temporized.

But when the doctor came to make his last call, I drew him aside. "Mrs. Sachs is terribly worried about having another baby."

"She well may be," replied the doctor, and then he stood before her and said, "Any more such capers, young woman, and there'll be no need to send for me."

"I know, doctor," she replied timidly, "but," and she hesitated as though it took all her courage to say it, "what can I do to prevent it?"

The doctor was a kindly man, and he had worked hard to save her, but such incidents had become so familiar to him that he had long since lost whatever delicacy he might once have had. He laughed good-naturedly. "You want to have your cake and eat it too, do you? Well, it can't be done."

Then picking up his hat and bag to depart he said, "Tell Jake to sleep on the roof."

I glanced quickly to Mrs. Sachs. Even through my sudden tears I could see stamped on her face an expression of absolute despair. We simply looked at each other, saying no word until the door had closed behind the doctor. Then she lifted her thin, blue-veined hands and clasped them beseechingly. "He can't understand. He's only a man. But you do, don't you? Please tell me the secret, and I'll never breathe it to a soul. *Please!*"

What was I to do? I could not speak the conventionally comforting phrases which would be of no comfort. Instead, I made her as physically easy as I could and promised to come back in a few days to talk with her again. . . .

Night after night the wistful image of Mrs. Sachs appeared before me. I made all sorts of excuses to myself for not going back. I was busy on other cases; I really did not know what to say to her or how to convince her of my own ignorance; I was helpless to avert such monstrous atrocities. Time rolled by and I did nothing.

The telephone rang one evening three months later, and Jake Sachs' agitated voice begged me to come at once; his wife was sick again and from the same cause. For a wild moment I thought of sending someone else, but actually, of course, I hurried into my uniform, caught up my bag, and started out. All the way I longed for a subway wreck, an explosion, anything to keep me from having to enter that home again. But nothing happened, even to delay me. I turned into the dingy doorway and climbed the familiar stairs once more. The children were there, young little things.

Mrs. Sachs was in a coma and died within ten minutes. I folded her still hands across her breast, remembering how they had pleaded with me, begging so humbly for the knowledge which was her right. I drew a sheet over her pallid face. Jake was sobbing, running his hands through his hair and pulling it out like an insane person. Over and over again he wailed, "My God! My God! My God!"

I left him pacing desperately back and forth, and for hours I myself walked and walked and walked through the hushed streets. When I finally arrived home and let myself quietly in, all the household was sleeping. I looked out my window and down upon the dimly lighted city. Its pains and griefs crowded in upon me, a moving picture rolled before my eyes with photographic clearness: women writhing in travail to bring forth little babies; the babies themselves naked and hungry, wrapped in newspaper to keep them from the cold; six-year-old children with pinched, pale, wrinkled faces, old in concentrated wretchedness, pushed into gray and fetid cellars, crouching on stone floors, their small scrawny hands scuttling through rags, making lamp shades, artificial flowers; white coffins, black coffins, coffins, coffins interminably passing in never-ending succession. The scenes piled one upon another on another. I could bear it no longer.

As I stood there the darkness faded. The sun came up and threw its reflection over the house tops. It was the dawn of a new day in my life also. The doubt and questioning, the experimenting and trying, were now to be put behind me. I knew I could not go back merely to keeping people alive.

I went to bed, knowing that no matter what it might cost, I was finished with palliatives and superficial cures; I was resolved to seek out the root of evil, to do something to change the destiny of mothers whose miseries were vast as the sky.

CATHARINE M. SEDGWICK (1789–1867)

18. On spinsterhood

Catharine Maria Sedgwick, the most popular woman novelist before Harriet Beecher Stowe, supported herself by writing romantic historical novels, moral tracts, and tales for magazines. She is best known for *Hope Leslie* (1827), a vividly narrated novel of life in

Mary E. Dewey, ed., *Life and Letters of Catharine M. Sedgwick* (New York: Harper, 1871).

seventeenth-century Massachusetts. Her diary entries below offer a frank appraisal of voluntary spinsterhood—she had, as she states, several opportunities to accept offers of marriage—which reflect her pleasant and varied social life at Lenox, Mass., as well as her inevitable sense of deprivation at being single in a marriage-oriented society. In Sedgwick's last novel, *Married or Single* (1857), she returned to the theme with the stated purpose of lessening "the stigma placed on the term, old maid."

Journal

New York, May 18, 1828. Again the spring is here, the season of life and loveliness, the beautiful emblem of our resurrection unto life eternal. . . . I will not say, with the ungracious poet, that I turn from what Spring brings to what she can not bring, but alas! I find there is no longer that capacity for swelling, springing, brightening joy that I once felt. . . . Hope now seems to turn from me; and if I now and then catch some glimpses of her averted face, she looks so serious, so admonitory, that I almost believe that her sister Experience, with an eye of apprehension, and lips that never smile, has taken her place. All is not right with me, I know. I still build on sandy foundations; I still hope for perfection, where perfection is not given. The best sources of earthly happiness are not within my grasp—those of contentment I have neglected. I have suffered for the whole winter a sort of mental paralysis, and at times I have feared the disease extended to my affections. It is difficult for one who began life as I did, the primary object of affection to many, to come by degrees to be first to none, and still to have my love remain in its entire strength, and craving such returns as have no substitute. How absurd, how groundless your complaints! would have a dozen voices exclaim, if I ever ventured to *make* this complaint. I do not. Each one has his own point of sight. Others are not conscious—at least I believe they are not—of any diminution in their affections for me, but others have taken my place, naturally and of right, I allow it. It is the necessity of a solitary condition, an unnatural state. He who gave us our nature has set the solitary in families, and has, by an array of motives, secured this sweet social compact to his children. From my own experience I would not advise anyone to remain unmarried, for my experience has been a singularly happy one. My feelings have never been embittered by those slights and taunts that the repulsive and neglected have to endure; there has been no period of my life to the present moment when I might not have allied myself respectably, and to those sincerely attached to me, if I would. I have always felt myself to be an object of attention, respect, and regard, and, though not *first* to any, I am, like Themistocles, *second* to a great many. My fortune is not adequate to an independent establishment, but it is ample for ease to myself and liberality to others. In the families of all my brothers I have an agreeable home. My sisters are all kind and affectionate to me, my brothers generous and invariably kind; their children all love me. My dear Kate, my adopted child, is, though far from perfect even in my doting eyes, yet such as to perfectly satisfy me, if I did not crave perfection for one I so tenderly love. I have troops of friends, some devotedly attached to me, and yet the result of all this very happy experience is that there is no equivalent for those blessings which Providence has placed first, and ordained that they should be purchased at the dearest sacrifice. I have not set this down in a spirit of repining, but it is well, I think, honestly to expose our own feelings—they may serve for examples or beacons. While I live I do not mean this shall be read, and after, my individual experience may perhaps benefit some one of all my tribe. I ought, I know, to be grateful and humble, and I do hope, through the grace of God, to rise more above the world, to attain a higher and happier state of feeling, to order my house for that better world where self may lose something of its engrossing power. . . .

New York, December 17, 1835. More than a fortnight has elapsed since I came to this city—a fortnight of my short remainder of life passed away without exertion and without fruit. I have been met by every one with congratulations about my book, which has, I think, proved more generally acceptable than anything I have before written. My *author* existence has always seemed something accidental, extraneous, and independent of my inner self. My books have been a pleasant occupation and excitement in my life. The notice, and friends, or acquaintance they have procured me, have relieved me from the danger of ennui and blue devils, that are most apt to infest a single person. But they constitute no portion of my happiness—that is, of such as I derive from the dearest relations of life. When I feel that my writings have made any one happier or better, I feel an emotion of gratitude to Him who has made me the medium of any blessing to my fellow-creatures. And I do feel that I am but the instrument.

CHAPTER THREE
Just a Housewife

If there is one universal fact about women, it is that until very recently the overwhelming majority of them have been engaged in domestic food preparation, maintenance of the home and clothing, and, in families with children, childrearing. Single, married, or divorced, and regardless of whether she holds a paid job or not, a woman is a housewife, at least part of her life. Whatever her station or position, unless she is wealthy enough to hire another woman to do her housework, she is a housewife. Even the wealthiest women with staffs of servants or slaves, had responsibility for managing their households. Yet, curiously, the subject has received little historical or analytical attention, even from feminists.

The job description has changed relatively little over the course of 250 years. Work previously done by hand is now done with the aid of machines; many jobs formerly performed in the home are now done out of it, requiring the modern housewife to spend more time in fetching, carrying, and ordering than in making the product itself. Of all the occupations and services provided by the society, this occupation has been least affected by technological change and modernization. Its function has changed, but its essential characteristics have not: it is an unpaid, repetitious job performed by one woman in the service of one or more adults and children. While essential work and indispensable services are rendered, the job holds low status, is not counted as part of the Gross National Product (GNP), and confers no rights or fringe benefits upon the worker. In a self-sufficient farming economy, the housewife had access to some cash income through marketing surplus products. In a money economy it is the only job offering no pay but, like indentured servitude, support in exchange for services.

While the job of the housewife has changed relatively little, her status has altered depending on historical development. In preindustrial society, the work of the housewife was an essential part of the family economy and provided family subsistence just as much as the work of the men in the family. Thus the economic contribution of the housewife was functional, essential, and therefore highly regarded by herself and others. With much of health care and education centered in the home, she also made an indispensable cultural contribution to the society.

Modernization, a sex-based division of labor, the transfer of production outside the home, and the institution of a cash economy, changed the function of the housewife. As the family has shifted from being a unit of production to being a unit of consumption, so has the housewife changed from being primarily a producer and processor of goods to being primarily a consumer. The educational and health service functions have been transferred out of the home into the hands of professionals, incidentally often women, who invest these professions with the stigma of low status and low pay. Yet the modern housewife (as documents 21 and 25 illustrate) spends nearly as much time in pursuit of domestic activities as did her predecessor two hundred years earlier. If there are children in the home, she must be available around the clock, except for the hours when they are in school.

The home, once at the center of the economy, has become a place deliberately outside of it, a retreat, a refueling station to which the family members return periodically for spiritual, physical, and psychological sustenance. Such sustenance depends to a large extent on the services of the housewife-mother. These are the services which are "labors of love" and intangible of definition and which supposedly are their own reward. The mass media, especially women's magazines, have sought to upgrade the status of the housewife by calling her a "home maker" and stressing her creativity—from decorating to gourmet cooking—her opportunities for self-expression—hobbies, gardening, crewelwork—and her freedom of choice—between one brand of soap powder and another. There is no question that these factors for many women outweigh the lack of economic compensation. But in a modern society, in which value is expressed in money terms, the housewife has become an anachronism. In an economic context it must be observed that with the smaller size of U.S. families, the modern housewife's increasingly skilled services now benefit fewer people than formerly. The gap between the efficiency of mechanized mass production and the relative inefficiency of the housewife has widened, with the direct result of loss of status for her. Regardless of compensatory terminology, her own self-esteem has diminished with her loss of status. This is symbolized by the self-effacing and factually erroneous answer to the question "Do you work?" given by countless modern women: "No, I'm just a housewife."

The housewife does, indeed work. What is the value of her work in economic terms? Economists of the Chase Manhattan Bank of New York have recently calculated that the thirty million American women, who do not work outside of the home and who list their occupations as "housewives," are each doing unpaid work worth $257.53 a week on the current labor market.* The work they do includes twelve different skill categories. Each of the services the housewife performs becomes a legitimate paid occupation when performed by men in the marketplace, from cooking and sewing to window washing and floor cleaning. Computing the average housewife's work in terms of hourly wages needed to replace her, the Chase Manhattan economists calculate that each housewife performs a job worth $13,391 a year. The aggregate of housewives' services amounts to $250 billion a year, which would be a sizeable portion of the GNP, if it were included in it. That these staggering sums are a conservative estimate is indicated by the fact that they do not include the childrearing services rendered by housewives, nor do they include the housework of those women who work outside of the home, but who are also part-time housewives. Another way to visualize the complexity of her job is to calculate how many paid employees of varying skills it takes to replace the work of a single housewife. The figure runs from three to five. Judging from descriptions of the activities of nineteenth-century housewives (see documents 23 and 24), it would appear that housewives in the past produced even more and covered an even wider range of skills.

Who pays the housewife's support? Who benefits from her unpaid labor?

At first glance it seems obvious that the husband or male family head (in the case of unmarried women) pays the housewife's sup-

---

* Sylvia Porter, "What's A Wife Worth?" *New York Post Magazine*, July 13, 1966, p. 2. Also, updated figures in Ann Crittenden Scott, "The Value of Housework—For Love or Money," *Ms.* I, no. 1 (July 1972): 56–59.

port in exchange for her services. Apologists for the institution have explained that this represents an even exchange of bartered services for upkeep, but the figures just cited would tend to disprove this argument. Charlotte Perkins Gilman pointed out* that were there any rational relationship between the labor performed by the housewife and the amount of financial support she receives, the poorest housewife would be the most amply rewarded, and the richest housewife, the least. Since the exact opposite is the case, this argument can be disregarded.

Another explanation offered focuses on the "home making" aspects of the housewife's work. Thorstein Veblen has much earlier pointed to the upper-class household as a place in which the wealth of male family members is conspicuously displayed by the luxury of the home furnishings, clothing, and jewelry, and by the idleness of the women.† The rise of modern "consumerism" has spread to the lower classes this use of the home as a place in which to display the status of the breadwinner. The ability to acquire and show off the material goods deemed indispensable for respectability is one of the required skills of the housewife. The respect accruing to her from this as well as from the achievements of her children, are her supposed intangible rewards. Such an interpretation sees the housewife as essentially self-employed, a volunteer working for "love" and for the respect gained through the achievements of her family members.

Since all occupations, in addition to cash payments also offer intangible rewards, such an explanation sidesteps rational economic analysis. It does highlight the benefits to the husband and to members of the family derived from the housewife's work and thus calls attention to the peculiar way in which the occupation seems to be institutionalized within the family. Some of the major theoretical discussions of the subject by modern feminists have focused on this view. By simplifying the economic relationship of husband and wife, this interpretation makes it appear that the husband is the sole beneficiary of the housewife's unpaid labor. He exploits her and has a vested interest in maintaining her in this occupa-

---

* Charlotte Perkins Gilman, *Women and Economics* (1898; reprint ed., Harper & Row, 1966).

† Thorstein Veblen, *The Theory of the Leisure Class* (1899; reprint ed., New York: Mentor, 1962).

tion.* Thus the question "Who does the dishes?" becomes not only emotionally charged, but a politically dynamic issue.

While there is some merit to this approach, it essentially over-simplifies and disregards the way in which family function and structure differ in different classes of society. It makes it appear that the oppression of the housewife and her economic exploitation are primarily institutionalized in the family, and this has led some feminists to demand the destruction of the family or its reorganiza-tion as the basic solution to the problems of women.

It is partially true that the male family head benefits from the housewife's work. So do the children, the husband's employer, and the major economic institutions of the society. As Mary Inman has pointed out in "In Woman's Defense," employers assume that their male workers have the unpaid services of a housewife avail-able to them.† If they did not, businesses would either have to incur increased expense to provide food, clothing, and laundry for their employees or would have to increase wages sufficiently for such services to be paid for by the worker. If the work of house-wives were to be treated as other work is, in terms of Social Secu-rity benefits, pensions, vacations, and health insurance, every in-stitution of the economy would be affected. Alternately, if every man, woman, and child were to take care of the equivalent of his own personal service, untold hours would have to be deducted from production and recreational pursuits.

Since "occupation housewife" is gender-linked—by definition, a housewife is a woman and every woman is also a housewife—it obviously is central to any analysis of the position of women in society. Thus, proposed programs for improvement of the status of women depend to a large extent on the analysis made regarding the housewife. Classical Marxism, especially in the works of En-gels, Bebel, and Lenin, offers one such theory, which has been very important as the basis of political programs. According to this analysis the domestic work of women is an archaic remnant of

* Cf. Pat Mainardi, "The Politics of Housework," in *Sisterhood Is Pow-erful*, ed. Robin Morgan (New York: Vintage, 1970); and Meredith Tax, "Woman and her Mind: The Story of Daily Life," in *Female Liberation: History and Current Politics*, ed. Roberta Salper (New York: Knopf, 1972).

† For more recent Marxist interpretations along similar lines, see Jean Gardiner, "The Role of Domestic Labour," *New Left Review* 89 (Jan.–Feb. 1975): 47–58, and bibliography.

feudal economic relations under the conditions of advanced capitalism, and socialists advocate its replacement by socialized domestic support services. The experience of socialism in the Soviet Union has shown that institutionalizing child care, mass feeding, and establishing commercial laundering has not abolished the position of the housewife. In the absence of changes in the basic family structure, it has remained an occupation curiously resistant to change and social engineering.

In societies where collective living and housing conditions were institutionalized, such as in Israel or in Communist China, the jobs formerly done by individual housewives for individual families are still being carried out by women, but now for the benefit of larger numbers of people. These efforts at modernizing and socializing housework bear an interesting resemblance to the somewhat utopian proposals of an American feminist, who was influenced by early socialist theory. In 1898 Charlotte Perkins Gilman (in "A Modest Proposal . . .") spelled out her own version of what such support services might be in the American setting. The approach she advocates has been approximated in some of the social welfare institutions of the Scandinavian countries. There, especially in Sweden, large-scale experiments in redefining family roles and in attacking sex role indoctrination of children are now underway. Possibly this approach and the multifaceted approach to changing the status of women taken in some of the newly socialist societies, will in the long run sufficiently erode the position of the housewife to supplant this occupation permanently.

In the very recent past, due largely to the impact of the feminist movement, there are some trends toward changing the functioning of the modern American family through sharing of work and a redefinition of roles, in order to upgrade the position of women within the family. Whether these relatively minor changes will permanently affect the occupation and the status of women in the society, remains to be seen.

What can be learned from a historical survey of "women as housewife" is an understanding of the connection between the subordination of women in general and their work as housewives. As long as housework is by definition woman's work and unpaid work at that, an exchange of services for economic support, all the work of women will be downgraded. The low status of the housewife reinforces the low status of the woman worker and of the woman professional and excuses any discrimination against her in the job market, by the assumption that her main and primary work is as a housewife. The existence of "occupation housewife" as the major female occupation assures the subordinate status of women not just in the family, but in every institution of society.

19. The practicing housewife

In a letter to her sister Lucretia Mott, Martha Coffin Wright describes some of the ordinary tasks of the housewife of her day. A patient woman of great equanimity, she managed to deal with the most vexatious situations with gentle good humor and common sense. Even so, she admitted, at age forty-one, that she had done her share of housework and would gladly give it up, if she had "an independent fortune."

AUBURN, FEB. 7TH, 1847

. . . How sorry I feel for Phebe Gibbons . . . poor child, I pity her to have to learn how to make candles &c. as much as I pity myself for having had to—and yet there is a pleasure in achieving it when you know you must. In making candles we have three moulds which make 32 candles in all which expedites the process, tho' it takes ten times longer to mould than to dip them, but they are so much neater that it compensates one for the labor. February is the best time. We have a very large tin coffee pot on purpose to melt the tallow in—taking care only to melt it, not let it get hot. As to soap we make it with but little trouble—Keep a leach always set and boil out our soap grease as soon as we have half a gallon of grease collected, and strain it into a barrel. When the barrel is half full, pour on strong lye as fast as you can get it—stirring it often, or whenever you add to it—it soon becomes soap, without any further trouble. For keeping eggs we buy 20 dozen in the spring when they are 6 d. a dozen, pack them carefully in a large stone pot and pour on

Martha Coffin Wright to Lucretia Coffin Mott, Letters of Martha Coffin Pelham Wright, Garrison Family Papers. Courtesy of the Sophia Smith Collection (Women's History Archive), Smith College, Northampton, Mass.

a pail full of water in which we have dissolved a pint of salt
and a pint of unslacked lime. We are going to part with all
our hens this spring, they are so troublesome in the garden
and it costs as much to feed them as to buy eggs. At Sarah's
their hens don't lay at all in winter, but we buy liver occasionally for ours and they lay from one to five eggs a day. I
forgot to say in speaking of soap, that we save every particle
of grease & bones, and collect a great deal of grease from the
latter—but it seems hardly necessary to write all this for
Phebe, when probably all her neighbors could tell her much
better than I can write it—I know one thing—let me once
get an independent fortune, and I will gladly impart all the
valuable information I possess on such subjects, but as to
practising—I believe I have done it my share. . . .

JANE SWISSHELM (1815–1884)

20. Woman's work and man's supremacy

In her newspaper, *The St. Cloud Visiter* (she insisted on this archaic spelling), Jane Swisshelm ran a column of comments and
advice in response to readers' letters. In 1853, she published a
collection of these columns in book form. *Letters to Country Girls*
brought her sharp, satirical comments to a national readership and
helped to spread her journalistic reputation.

Jane Swisshelm was an ardent abolitionist and worked as a nurse
during the Civil War. Her feminism found expression in her newspaper columns in her advocacy of self-reliance and educated
womanhood, in her defense of the property rights of women and,
belatedly, in her advocacy of woman suffrage. She always went her
own way, did not participate in organizational activities, and was
the prototype of the self-made woman.

Jane Swisshelm, *Letters to Country Girls* (New York: J. C. Riker, 1853), pp.
75–81.

I am puzzled this week. Anniss asks me to "say something about those rich old farmers who make their wives work out in the fields, and leave their babies in the fence corners for the snakes to eat." She goes on to describe how the women, "after working in the fields until meal time, come home, cook, milk and churn, while the men lounge around and rest."

This is a very bad case, but a very common one, of the masculine-superiority fever which has converted so many millions of men into ruffians. I understand the disease very well, and can cure it easily when I have access to the patient, and can get my prescriptions administered. . . .

These old fellows do not take the Visiter! I am too much out of "woman's sphere" to be tolerated in their august presence. No one has access to them but preachers and political stump speakers. They see no paper but a religious or political one. The former never speaks about woman, except to lecture her about her *duties*—her obligation to *obey* her husband—her vocation to forget herself and live only for the welfare of her liege lord and some particular church. The latter never speaks about woman or her interests a bit more than if such a creature never existed. The laws and policy they are discussing set her down midway between men and monkeys. She has no vote to solicit, no offices to confer, but is a kind of appendage to her master. Of course the ignorant boor gets a vast opinion of his own importance, as it is continually held up to view by church and state; and it cannot be wondered at that he *practises* what our divines, statesmen, philosophers, and poets teach. . . .
He applies a common sense rule to the common principle, and argues "if Sallie has no right to hold office in church or state—if she is to submit to me in all things, to keep silence in churches, and learn from me at home, of course I must be wiser than she, and better too. The Constitution puts her down with "niggers" and ingins, or a little below 'em. She is heaven's "last best gift to man," an' mighty useful one can make her! She can make hay as well as I can—then cook the

victuals while I'm restin', and raise some sons and darters in the meantime to take care uv me when I get old! Tell ye, there isn't a horse on the place I wouldn't rather lose nor Sallie!" So he puts his wife into "a woman's place," and keeps her there. . . . It is very well known that thousands nay, millions of women in this country are condemned to the most menial drudgery, such as men would scorn to engage in, and that for one-fourth wages; that thousands of women toil at avocations which public opinion pretends to assign to men. They plough, harrow, reap, dig, make hay, rake, bind grain, thrash, chop wood, milk, churn, do any thing that is hard work, physical labor, and who says any thing against it? But let one presume to use her mental powers—let her aspire to turn editor, public speaker, doctor, lawyer—take up any profession or avocation which is deemed honorable and requires talent, and O! bring the Cologne, get a cambric kerchief and a feather fan, unloose his corsets and take off his cravat! What a fainting fit Mr. Propriety has taken! Just to think that "one of the deah creathures," the heavenly angels, should forsake the spheres—woman's sphere—to mix with the wicked strife of this wicked world! . . .

The efficient remedy for this class of evils is education; an equal education! . . . If you wish to maintain your proper position in society, to command the respect of your friends now, and husbands and children in future, you should read, read—think, study, try to be wise, to know your own places and keep them, your own duties and do them. You should try to understand every thing you see and hear; to act and judge for yourselves; to remember you each have a soul of your own to account for;—a mind of your own to improve. When you once get these ideas fixed, and learn to act upon them, no man or set of men, no laws, customs, or combination of them can seriously oppress you. Ignorance, folly, and levity, are more or less essential to the character of a slave. If women knew their rights, and proper places, we would never hear of men "making their wives" do this, that, or the other.

21. Female trials

This item by an anonymous lady in the Ohio abolitionist newspaper, *Anti-Slavery Bugle*, reveals in curiously contemporary terms the complaints of the middle-class housewife.

. . . Shall I give a short sketch of domestic life *as it is?* . . . My neighbor, Mr. Benson, is a lawyer by profession and is what the world calls a respectable man. His income is small but he married a lady who was able to furnish the house handsomely, and they have some hope of property in reversion. Mrs. B. was educated in modern times and somewhat fashionably; . . . it is Monday morning and this speaks of "unutterable things" to a New England wife who has been married a dozen years.—Mr. Benson has had his breakfast in season—has kissed the children and gone to the office where the boy has a good fire—the books and papers are all in order, and Mr. B. sits down to answer a few agreeable demands upon his time, which will eventually turn to cash. He goes home to his dinner punctually at one o'clock—it is ready for him—he takes it quietly, perhaps—frolics ten minutes with the baby, and then hurries back to the office. At the hour for tea he goes home—everything is cheerful. . . .

But how has it been with Mrs. Benson through the day? She has an ill-natured girl in the kitchen who will do half the work only, at nine shillings per week. Monday morning! Eight o'clock—four children must be ready for school— Mrs. B. must sponge their faces—see that books, slates, pencils, papers, pocket handkerchiefs . . . are all in order—and now the baby's crying—the fire is low—it is time Sally

Letter to the Editor by "Cleo Dora," *Anti-Slavery Bugle*, no. 55, August 21, 1846.

should begin to wash—the parlor, the chambers, the breakfast things are all waiting. Well! A song to the baby who lies kicking in the cradle—a smile to smooth ruffled Sally with all the energy that mind and body can summon, things are "straightened out." . . . It is almost dinner time. By some accident the joint of meat is frozen—company calls—Mr. Benson forgot to gather eggs on Saturday—Mrs. B. must do the next best way. The bell rings twelve—the door opens and in rush the children from school. John has torn his pantaloons—Mary must have some money then to get a new thimble, she has just lost hers—William has cut his finger with a piece of glass and is calling loudly for his mother.

Poor Mrs. Benson endeavors to keep cheerful and look delighted in the hubbub; and now that dinner by her efforts alone is on the table; her husband comes in and perhaps wonders the "pie is not a little better warmed" and with this comment, and a smile *on the baby,* he is off til it is time for tea—I forbear to finish the day, Mr. Editor, though only say the afternoon is made up of little trials too small to mention, large enough to try the faith and patience of all the patriarchs.

Yes, sir, the wife has surely borne the burden and heat of the day—her limbs are wearied, her whole energy of mind and body exhausted, and she is exhorted to "welcome her husband with a smile." *She does it,* for in woman love is stronger than death. I would ask, should not Mr. Benson give his wife a smile? What has he done to lighten her cares through the day? How is it? In nine cases out of ten after sitting idle for an hour he wishes Mrs. B would put all those noisy children to bed—he should be glad to have her tell David to go to the Post Office for letters and papers. At length, when halfway between sleeping and waking he looks at his pale, exhausted *helpmeet* and exclaims "Well, wife, you begin to look a little fatigued." Mr. Editor . . . I pray you be more just and now and then exhort husbands to do their parts.

CATHARINE ESTHER BEECHER (1800–1878)

22. Words of comfort for a discouraged housekeeper

In this chapter from her popular *Domestic Receipt Book*, which was a sequel to her earlier *A Treatise on Domestic Economy**, Catharine Beecher addressed herself to the baffled and often resentful housewife of her day, offering reassurance and expert advice. Her response to the bewilderment of American housewives who, due to increased mobility, found themselves living far removed from the support provided by accustomed familial ties, was to offer systematic, standardized instruction in all aspects of modern housekeeping. It was also to give them a sense of heightened gratification and self-esteem by thinking of their work as an important social function (they were "homemakers" and moulders of the national and Christian character), and one which they could do with competence and skill. The spectacular success of these books and their numerous revised editions are a tribute to her shrewd appraisal of a felt need. By systematizing and modernizing housework into a "domestic science" and by turning the household drudge into a respected homemaker, Catharine Beecher set the tone for the twentieth-century mass media approach to the housewife. She deflected the housewife's anger at her individual frustrating position from erupting against either her husband or against the institutions of society.

Her own lifework as educator and writer was dedicated to improving the status of women, not through political feminism, of which she disapproved, but through self-discipline, education, and moral leadership. She romanticized domesticity, saw women as the saviors of society, and sought to elevate their personal influence over the men in their family and over their children into a mission of moral leadership and Christian redemption. An out-

Catharine Beecher, *Miss Beecher's Domestic Receipt Book . . .* (New York: Harper & Bros., 1846), pp. 276–280.

* Catharine Beecher, *Treatise on Domestic Economy for the Use of Young Ladies at Home and at School* (Boston: T. H. Webb & Co., 1843).

standing career woman of her day—founder of educational institutions, teacher and successful author—she remained single, economically self-supporting, and independent-minded. Her feminism expressed itself in her discussing late in life the desirability of unmarried women living together and founding Christian homes and settlement houses, in which to adopt needy children and live in female-headed family units. Yet her major intellectual contribution consisted of elaborating an apologetic rationale, which would keep women contented with their domestic role and housewifely occupation and which sought to make the home the only "proper" sphere for most women.

There is no doubt of the fact, that American housekeepers have far greater trials and difficulties to meet than those of any other nation. . . .

Perhaps you find yourself encompassed by such sort of trials as these. Your house is inconvenient, or destitute of those facilities for doing work well which you need, and you cannot command the means to supply these deficiencies. Your domestics are so imperfectly qualified that they never can do anything *just right*, unless you stand by and attend to everything yourself, and you cannot be present in parlor, nursery, and kitchen all at once. . . .

And perhaps your children are sickly, and rob you of rest by night, or your health is so poor that you feel no energy, or spirits to make exertions. . . . And then, perhaps, you lose your patience and your temper, and blame others, and others blame you, and so everything seems to be in a snarl.

Now the first thing to be said for your comfort is, that you *really have* great trials to meet; trials that entitle you to pity and sympathy, while it is the fault of others more than your own, that you are in this very painful and difficult situation. You have been as cruelly treated as the Israelites were by Pharoah, when he demanded bricks without furnishing the means to make them.

You are like a young, inexperienced lad, who is required to superintend all the complicated machinery of a manufactory, which he never was trained to understand, and on penalty of losing reputation, health, and all he values most.

Neither your parents, teachers, or husband have *trained* you for the place you fill, nor furnished you with the knowledge or assistance needed to enable you to meet all the complicated and untried duties of your lot. . . .

The next word of comfort is, the assurance that you *can* do *every one* of your duties, and do them well, and the following is the method by which you can do it. In the first place, make up your mind that it never is your *duty* to do anything more than you *can*, or in any better manner than *the best you can*. And whenever you have done the best you can, you have done *well*, and that is all that man *should* require, and certainly all that your Heavenly Father *does* require.

The next thing is, for you to make out an inventory of all the things that *need* to be done, in your whole establishment. Then calculate what things you find you *cannot* do, and strike them off the list, as what are not among your *duties*. Of those that remain, select a certain number that you think you can do *exactly as they need to be done*, and among these be sure that you put the making of *good bread*. This every housekeeper *can* do, if she will only determine to do it.

Make a selection of certain things that you will *persevere* in having done *as well as they can be done*, and let these be only so many as you feel sure you can succeed in attempting. . . .

By this course, you will have the comfort of feeling that in *some* respects you are as good a housekeeper as you can be, while there will be a cheering progress in gaining on all that portion of your affairs, that are left at loose ends. You will be able to measure a gradual advance, and be encouraged by success. Many housekeepers fail entirely, by expecting to do *everything well at first*, when neither their knowledge or strength is adequate, and so they fail everywhere, and finally give up in despair.

Are you not only a housekeeper, but a *mother?* Oh, sacred
and beautiful name! how many cares and responsibilities
are associated with it! . . . You are training young minds
whose plastic texture will receive and retain every impression you make, who will imitate your feelings, tastes, habits,
and opinions, and who will transmit what they receive from
you to their children, to pass again to the next generation,
and then to the next, until a *whole nation* will have received
its character and destiny from your hands! No imperial
queen ever stood in a more sublime and responsible position than you now occupy. . . .

Remember, then, that you have a Father in heaven, who
sympathizes in all your cares, pities your griefs, makes al-
lowances for your defects, and is endeavoring by trials, as
well as by blessings, to fit you for the right fulfilment of your
high and holy calling.

LYDIA MARIA CHILD (1802–1880)

23. Employments in 1864

Lydia Maria Child, a successful editor and the author of twenty-
one books, earned her living by her pen. Married to a gentle and
ineffectual man who seldom made a living, but who offered her
moral support, she was childless and lived in great simplicity in
Wayland, Mass. Her diary contains an entry for 1864, in which she
meticulously summarizes all her activities. It illustrates convincingly how great a share of a woman's life was taken up by domestic
occupations, even under the most favorable circumstances. The
way in which it is constructed—intellectual activities above,
domestic activities below, and the dramatic discrepancy in the
quantity of these two sets of activities—makes its own comment. It
is an ironic and somewhat bitter comment, which this sixty-two-

Lydia Maria Child Papers, Anti-Slavery Collection. Courtesy of the Cornell University Library, Ithaca, N.Y. I am indebted for this item to Prof.
Kirk Jeffrey, Carleton College, Northfield, Minn.

year-old author of a two-volume history of women offers regarding
her own way of life.

> Wrote 235 letters.
> Wrote 6 articles for newspapers.
> Wrote 47 autograph articles for Fairs.
> Wrote my Will.
> Corrected Proofs for Sunset book.
> Read aloud 6 pamplets and 21 volumes.
> Read to myself 7 volumes.
>
> Made 25 needle books for Freedwomen.
> 2 Bivouac caps for soldiers.
> Knit 2 pair of hospital socks.
> Gathered and made peck of pickles for hospitals.
> Knit 1 pair of socks for David.
> Knit and made up 2 pairs of suspenders for D.
> Knit six baby shirts for friends.
> Knit 1 large Affghan [!] & made the fringe.
> Made 1 spectacle case for David.
> Made 1 Door mat.
> Made 1 lined woollen cape.
> Made 3 pair of corsets.
> > 2 shirts for D.
> > 1 Chemise.
> > 2 flannel shirts for D.
> Cut and made three gowns.
> 1 shirt with waist.
> 1 thick cotton petticoat.
> 1 quilted petticoat.
> made 1 silk gown.
> Cut and made 1 Sac for myself.
> Made double woollen dressing-gown for D.
> 1 pair of carpet-slippers for D.
> made 4 towels.
> 3 large lined curtains. 3 small ditto.
> 4 pillow cases.
> New collars & wristbands to 6 shirts.

1 night cap.

1 pair of summer pantaloons.

Made a starred crib quilt, and quilted it; one fortnights
    work.

———————

Spent 4 days collecting and sorting papers & pamphlets
    scattered by the fire.*

Mended five pair of drawers.

Mended 70 pair of stockings.

Cooked 360 dinners.

Cooked 362 breakfasts.

Swept and dusted sitting-room & kitchen 350 times.

Filled lamps 362 times.

Swept and dusted chamber & stairs 40 times.

Besides innumerable jobs too small to be mentioned,
    preserved half a peck of barberries.

Made 5 visits to aged women.

Tended upon invalid friend two days.

Made one day's visit to Medford and 3 visits to Boston; 2
    of them for one day, the other for two days.

Made 7 calls upon neighbors.

Cut and dried half a peck of dried apples.

24.   The life of an Illinois farmer's wife

This article, submitted anonymously, appeared in *The Independent*, a cultural reform journal, as part of a series of "personal
confessions" by members of the "industrial classes." The author
states in her full account, which is here excerpted, that she entered
a correspondence school and wished to begin a literary career. In a
headnote, the publishers mention that an earlier, more "literary"
version of this article was rejected by them, and that they urged the

"One Farmer's Wife," *The Independent* LVIII, no. 2932 (February 9,
1905): 294–298.

   * The fire occurred in the summer of 1863. It damaged several rooms in
the Childs's Wayland home.

woman instead to write a "truthful narrative," in which she would "tell everything." The account quoted below was the result. From what we know of the life of farm women and the length of their working day, there is no reason to think it is not typical of many farm women. What distinguishes it is only the author's restlessness and resentment at her thwarted intellectual aspirations.

I have been a farmer's wife . . . for thirteen years. . . .

I was an apt student at school and before I was eighteen I had earned a teacher's certificate of the second grade and would gladly have remained in school a few more years, but I had, unwittingly, agreed to marry the man who is now my husband, and tho I begged to be released, his will was so much the stronger that I was unable to free myself without wounding a loving heart, and could not find it in my heart to do so. . . .

I always had a passion for reading; during girlhood it was along educational lines; in young womanhood it was for love stories, which remained ungratified because my father thought it sinful to read stories of any kind, and especially love stories.

Later, when I was married, I borrowed everything I could find in the line of novels and stories, and read them by stealth still, for my husband thought it a willful waste of time to read anything and that it showed a lack of love for him if I would rather read than to talk to him when I had a few moments of leisure, and, in order to avoid giving offense and still gratify my desire, I would only read when he was not at the house, thereby greatly curtailing my already too limited reading hours. . . .

It is only during the last three years that I have had the news to read, for my husband is so very penurious that he would never consent to subscribing for papers of any kind and that old habit of avoiding that which would give offense was so fixed that I did not dare to break it.

The addition of two children to our family never altered or interfered with the established order of things to any appreciable extent. My strenuous outdoor life agreed with me, and even when my children were born I was splendidly prepared for the ordeal and made rapid recovery. . . .

While the children were babies they were left at the house, and when they were larger they would go with me to my work; now they are large enough to help a little during the summer and to go to school in winter; . . .

Any bright morning in the latter part of May I am out of bed at four o'clock; next, after I have dressed and combed my hair, I start a fire in the kitchen stove, . . . sweep the floors and then cook breakfast.

While the other members of the family are eating breakfast I strain away the morning's milk (for my husband milks the cows while I get breakfast), and fill my husband's dinnerpail, for he will go to work on our other farm for the day.

By this time it is half-past five o'clock, my husband is gone to his work, and the stock loudly pleading to be turned into the pastures. The younger cattle, a half-dozen steers, are left in the pasture at night, and I now drive the two cows a half-quarter mile and turn them in with the others, come back, and then there's a horse in the barn that belongs in a field where there is no water, which I take to a spring quite a distance from the barn; bring it back and turn it into a field with the sheep, a dozen in number, which are housed at night.

The young calves are then turned out into the warm sunshine, and the stock hogs, which are kept in a pen, are clamoring for feed, and I carry a pailful of swill to them, and hasten to the house and turn out the chickens and put out feed and water for them, and it is, perhaps, 6:30 a.m.

I have not eaten breakfast yet, but that can wait; I make the beds next and straighten things up in the living room, for I dislike to have the early morning caller find my house topsy-turvy. When this is done I go to the kitchen, which also serves as a dining room, and uncover the table, and take a mouthful of food occasionally as I pass to and fro at my work until my appetite is appeased.

By the time the work is done in the kitchen it is about 7:15 a.m., and the cool morning hours have flown, and no hoeing done in the garden yet, and the children's toilet has to be attended to and churning has to be done.

Finally the children are washed and churning done, and it is eight o'clock, and the sun getting hot, but no matter, weeds die quickly when cut down in the heat of the day, and I use the hoe to a good advantage until the dinner hour, which is 11:30 a.m. We come in, and I comb my hair, and put fresh flowers in it, and eat a cold dinner, put out feed and water for the chickens; set a hen, perhaps, sweep the floors again; sit down and rest and read a few moments, and it is nearly one o'clock, and I sweep the door yard while I am waiting for the clock to strike the hour.

I make and sow a flower bed, dig around some shrubbery, and go back to the garden to hoe until time to do the chores at night. . . .

I hoe in the garden till four o'clock; then I go into the house and get supper . . . when supper is all ready it is set aside, and I pull a few hundred plants of tomato, sweet potato or cabbage for transplanting . . . I then go after the horse, water him, and put him in the barn; call the sheep and house them, and go after the cows and milk them, feed the hogs, put down hay for three horses, and put oats and corn in their troughs, and set those plants and come in and fasten up the chickens. . . . It is 8 o'clock p.m.; my husband has come home, and we are eating supper; when we are through eating I make the beds ready, and the children and their father go to bed, and I wash the dishes and get things in shape to get breakfast quickly next morning. . . .

All the time that I have been going about this work I have been thinking of things I have read . . . and of other things which I have a desire to read, but cannot hope to while the present condition exists.

As a natural consequence there are daily, numerous instances of absentmindedness on my part; many things left

undone. . . . My husband never fails to remind me that it is
caused by my reading so much; that I would get along much
better if I should never see a book or paper. . . .

I use an old fashioned churn, and the process of churning
occupies from thirty minutes to three hours, according to
the condition of the cream, and I always read something
while churning. . . .

I suppose it is impossible for a woman to do her best at
everything which she would like to do, but I really would
like to. . . . When the work for the day is over, or at least
the most pressing part of it, and the family are all asleep and
no one to forbid it, I spend a few hours writing or
reading. . . .

HERMA L. SNIDER

25. A modern housewife's lament

During 1960–1961, *Redbook* Magazine ran a series of articles,
"Why Young Mothers Feel Trapped," in which young mothers
described their lives and problems. The women writing these autobiographical stories usually enumerated complaints quite similar to those discussed by housewives of an earlier day and each
told how she had solved her problem. All the solutions were
characterized by the woman seeking a better "adjustment" to her
situation, finding some temporary escape (as in the story below) or
finding a better, more efficient way of doing her housework and
childrearing. The predominance of this viewpoint probably reflected the editorial selection by the magazine staff and is, as such,
an indication of popular thinking during the period. It was coming
out of the constraints of such ideas that Betty Friedan, herself a
writer for *Redbook* and other women's magazines, would in 1963
write her epitaph to this ideology, the highly influential *The
Feminine Mystique.* Friedan's challenge to her contemporaries

Herma L. Snider, "I Stopped Feeling Sorry for Myself," *Redbook* 115, no.
5 (December 1960): 32, 33, 104. Reprinted courtesy of *Redbook.*

was the bold assertion that the "problem that has no name," the
malaise of middle-class women, was a societal not an individual
problem and required for its solution changes in the society and its
values, rather than changes within the individual family.

I grew up on a farm in Michigan, surrounded by 11 brothers
and sisters and countless other relatives and friends. My
world was full of people and companionship and talk. Ten
years after my marriage it was a very different world.
Cemented to my house by three young children, there were
days in which I saw no adult human being except the
milkman as he made his deliveries and spoke to none from
the time my husband left in the morning until he returned
at night.

My husband is a young pharmacist in his mid-30s. He is
gifted in his work, dedicated to his ideals and a good husband and father. . . .

I pride myself upon being a woman of average intelligence and understanding. During my high-school and college days I had dreams of a career in journalism. . . . But
after my marriage these dreams were abandoned.

At first I rather enjoyed the routine of cooking and cleaning. Inclined to be a perfectionist in anything I undertook, I
was proud of my ability to keep my floors gleaming and my
closets in good order. Then my three children arrived in
rapid succession and I found myself riding on a whirling
merry-go-round, vainly attempting to keep a level head in a
topsy-turvy world filled with baby bottles, sterilizers, dia-
pers, formulas, vaporizers, aspirins and vitamin pills. With
my morale sagging even lower than my tired stomach muscles I managed to cook, bake, iron, scrub, shop, clean and
wash: I flopped into bed at night like a wilting lettuce leaf,
only to be rudely awakened at all hours by the urgent wail
of a hungry baby.

How I survived those hectic years, I do not know. . . .
The only consolation I could give myself each night was the
knowledge that my children were one day older. I looked

forward to the day when they would be toilet-trained, to the day when they would be in school, to the mythical, wonderful, ever-approaching, never-arriving day when I would have "a little time to myself."

The culmination of all this discontent came when my husband accepted an offer of a position in Nevada, far from our friends and family and everything I had ever known or loved. Actually I did not protest too much about this move, for I felt that it might be my salvation. Perhaps in a new home, in new surroundings, with new friends and a new background, I would develop a fresh outlook on life. I recognize this now as wishful thinking. . . .

I quickly found myself in the same old rut, existing on cigarettes and cleanser fumes, up to my elbows in dishwater, up to my armpits in the incessant demands of home and community. . . .

I developed a host of ailments: headaches, nausea, dishpan hands, matronly bulge (despite a loss of appetite) and housemaid's knee. I screeched at my children in a voice that rivaled a hog caller at the peak of condition, swilled three pots of coffee a day and nagged my husband incessantly.

Meanwhile, the mind that I thought I had camphored away refused to stay put. It yearned for a chance to flex its muscles on something besides the grocery bills and the perpetual "why?" of three small boys. . . .

I yearned for a full, satisfying life and I felt that the world was passing me by. Each night as I tucked my sons into bed, I thanked God that they would grow up to be *men*, that they would be able to teach, write, heal, advise, travel or do anything else they chose. Not for them the endless tasks of clearing up, picking up, cleaning up, cheering up, washing up, hanging up, sewing up, mopping up and all the other ups and downs of household work which I found so difficult to accept.

At last I became the phantom of the doctor's office with my weekly list of ailments. The doctor examined me thoroughly and finally informed me that I was suffering from "nerves."

"My God," I said bluntly, "I could have told you that. Even my nerves have nerves."

"I have a prescription for you," he told me after he had listened to my impressive array of symptoms. "I want you to go out and get yourself a job."

I was appalled. How could I work? I had a big house to care for, three children to rear and a weekly laundry that attained the height of Pike's Peak. Besides, my husband had a good position and an adequate salary. I had never thought it right for a woman to hold a job when it was unnecessary. Not only that but I was unprepared, unskilled. I could set a mean dinner table, but I had forgotten how to type, I couldn't figure percentages and the multiplication table was beyond my abilities. . . .

[But] I had reached the point where a glass of spilled milk could send me into a rage. . . . Quietly, desperately, I walked outside the world of skinned knees and macaroni casseroles and found myself a job as a cashier in a local hotel.

It wasn't easy. I made mistakes, but luckily I had found a patient employer who smiled at my fears and helped me gain confidence in my ability. Daily I struggled with my feeling of guilt at leaving my children with a baby sitter for a few hours each day. I imagined all sorts of disasters overtaking them while I was away. I drove home from work and I had to muster courage to turn into the drive, so frightened had I become of what I would find when I arrived. I worried about my husband too. Suppose he wasn't eating enough? Suppose he became tired of me and turned to another woman? Suppose? . . .

I was a tired, inefficient, unorganized woman who could not possibly handle two jobs. I hired a girl to help with the cleaning, sent the laundry out, and then discovered that my expenses overpowered my meager salary. Talking it over with my husband and with my employer solved the problem. I began to work three days of the week. In this way I could work with a clear conscience and still have time for my housework and my family.

My cashier's job is not the glamorous career I once dreamed of. And I know that it can be said that my solution is not a solution at all, merely an escape. But it seems to me that when the demands of children and household threaten to suffocate you, an escape *is* a solution, although perhaps just a temporary one. . . .

A part-time job whereby I swap some of the drudgery and confinement of housework for the refreshing free air of the adult world may be only an escape, but for me it is also a solution.

If I can spend a few hours away from the children, I can enjoy them and allow them to enjoy me for the rest of the day.

If I can find time to write this, then I don't resent the pile of ironing. . . .

The ultimate solution, if there is one, will have to come later, when the children are a little older, when I understand better exactly what it is that I want, or perhaps when I learn to accept some of the things that I have been battering my head against. But for the time being I know that as long as I am not confined to the premises, my house is a home instead of the place I once dubbed my "chintz prison."

26. The working mother keeps house

The reformer and journalist Lillie B. Chace Wyman wrote a story on working and living conditions among factory workers, designed to create opinion favorable to passage of the ten-hour law. As an

Lillie B. Chace Wyman, "Studies of Factory Life: Among the Women," *Atlantic Monthly* 62, no. 371 (September 1888): 321.

early journalistic exposé it vividly describes the conditions which led reformers to work for several decades for passage of maximum hours and minimum wages legislation. From the vantage point of modern women, who take such protection for granted but chafe at those aspects of it which have been used to discriminate against women in employment, it is sometimes difficult to understand that protective legislation has had a special and positive significance for working women. Women laboring eleven or more hours a day in a factory and then returning home to bake bread, prepare food, and handwash the laundry for their children, had good reason to think that protective labor legislation was "splendid, the best thing as ever happened."

Homely but pathetic was the rejoicing of a hard-worked Irish widow over the ten-hour law. She had been the mother of thirteen or fourteen children, but most of them died; and last of all, her husband, a handsome man, whom she seemed to consider a being quite superior to herself, died, after a protracted illness. He did the housework long after he could not do other labor, so that she might be the chief wage-earner of the family. After his death, she said: "I fretted a deal for him,—I could not help it. I know he had been sick a long time, but you miss a person just the same if they have been sick; an' he was such a clean man about the house, kept it so neat when he was able to be about."

In a worldly way she manages very well without him. She and a grown girl and two young lads work in the mill. Two younger children profess to guard the house, and sometimes go to school. The daughter takes books occasionally from the village library, and she has read The Scarlet Letter and even the Blithedale Romance. . . . The mother found the ten-hour law a great help. "Why," said she, "the extra quarter of an hour at noon gives me time to mix my bread; an' then when I comes home at night, at six o'clock, it is ready to put in the pans, an' I can do that while Katie sets the table; an' after supper, an' the dishes are washed, I can bake; an' then I am through, an' ready to go to bed, mebbe afore it's quite nine o'clock. Oh, it's splendid, the best thing as ever

'appened. I used to be up till 'way into the night, bakin',
after my day's work in the mill was done."

She probably was glad of the Saturday half-holiday, because it gave her a good chance to do her washing. Holidays,
to women like her, mean little but the time to do some
different kind of work from that by which they earn their
living. Her boy rejoiced in healthy fashion. "Saturdays,"
says he, "when you are let out at one o'clock, you don't feel
as if you'd been at work at all."

THERESA MALKIEL (1874–?)

27. The housewife and the eight-hour day

Socialist organizer Theresa Malkiel, in one of her regular newspaper columns selected below, tried to enlist the support of socialist
working men in behalf of their wives and sisters. She asks the men
for sympathy and help to the housewife "in small things" and
expects some limit to her working hours "in time." She assumes
that whatever gains are to be made by housewives will be granted
them by their benevolent husbands. This reasoning seems curiously moderate, coming from a feminist Socialist who spent most
of her life organizing women's activities within the Socialist party
and who would in 1917 lead one of the biggest campaigns in suffrage
history for the passage of the New York State suffrage amendment.
Within the ranks of the Socialist party, she worked to promote the
woman's cause by forming separate women's organizations, which
raised demands of special interest to women within the party and
tried to enlist women outside the movement to the socialist cause.

Her moderate approach toward male Socialists reflects the level
at which the "woman question" was discussed within this radical
organization. For most Socialists this meant focusing on the woman
worker and her position in industry. They regarded the housewife

Theresa Malkiel, "The Housewife and the Eight-Hour Day," Chicago
Daily Socialist, April 29, 1910. From the Labadie collection.

as a secondary, often socially backward element. The appeal to male workers was to "enlighten" their wives and help to organize working women in the interest of strengthening the socialist movement. The long-range program called for the abolition of housework and the liberation of women through entry into paid productive work. Thus the housewife, who was notoriously difficult to organize, was not regarded as worth organizing.

The demands of women in their own right received relatively little attention. The contrast between Malkiel's moderate exhortative approach toward her male comrades and her militant feminist efforts in public, reflected an unresolved conflict within the socialist movement. Should socialist women help to organize women workers in support of revolutionary changes in the general society and hope that these would also advance the position of women, or should they concentrate on organizing *all* women, including housewives, focusing on the special interests of women?

Over two decades have passed since the socialists assembled in international congress first demanded the eight-hour work day. . . . Today, man's work is done long before the sun is down but woman's work is still never done. Her life is still one continual—broom, washtub and pot, pot, needle and tub. She is still a stranger to shorter hours and better pay. On the contrary, the rapid growth of monopolies and the increased cost of living tend to make the house-wives lot harder than ever. She can't afford to buy bread nowadays. It is entirely above her means. So she must bake it herself. Ready-made clothing costs so much that the submissive house-wife spends her evening in making up new, and more often in patching the old, wearing apparels. Meat is being sold at the rate of gold, and she is compelled to use her whole skill and ingenuity to make some other palatable. . . . The wage-earning man and woman realize that their suffering and hardship cannot be done away with under a capitalist regime, that we need a complete change of our social structure before we can hope to have justice done for the working class. But each man and woman at their trade are, as a rule, eager to buy the latest appliances in the line of tools in order to lighten their burden. And what is more, they will not hesitate to spend their last dollar to do so. The carpenter will not take the expense into consideration when he is about to buy the new sort of chisel that is to help him in his work. The painter will seek the best brush, the cutter the sharpest knife, all with the excuse that their bread and butter depends on it.

But the patient house-wife will never dream of buying a fireless cooker, a vacuum cleaner, an automatic washing machine, an electric dishwasher, or an electric attachment to her sewing machine. It never enters her mind that over-time work should by rights be shared with husband and wife, and yet—her welfare depends upon the small things, for they would in time help her to reach some hour limit.

. . . It is therefore only proper that the celebration of the eight-hour work day be made at the same time a universal protest against the house-wife's double oppression against her shameful servitude, for ought not the socialist and the union man who strive with all their might to gain a reduction of hours for the wage-earning population consider the injustice to the average house-wife who is fairly drooping under the weight of her heavy burden?

MARY INMAN

28. In woman's defense

The writer of this obscure pamphlet of the 1940s, which contains reprints of her articles in the *Daily People's World*, offers an un-usual theoretical approach to the discussion of the work of the housewife. Her general theoretical framework is the Marxist approach to the "woman question" (see introduction to this chapter, p. 112). But Inman, who elsewhere describes the outmoded nature

Mary Inman, "In Woman's Defense," (Los Angeles: Committee to Organize the Advancement of Women, 1940), pp. 142–146, 149, 170–173.

of housework in traditional Marxist terms, becomes quite original and controversial in her answer to the question, who benefits from the labor of the housewife? Inman's answer is, big business or all the employers of male workers. Inman thus continues the discussion of the problem posed by socialist theory regarding women, which was earlier discussed by Malkiel: should only working women be organized around working-class issues or should all women, including housewives, be organized around women's issues. Inman's analysis leads her to argue for the unity of working men and women against the bosses, giving primacy to organizing workers of both sexes around general revolutionary issues while simultaneously stressing the need for separate organization of housewives around women's issues. Her argument also merits attention because it anticipates a theoretical position taken by some contemporary radical feminists in Italy, which has aroused a good deal of interest among contemporary U.S. feminists.*

The Housewife's Role in Social Production

One very striking peculiarity of certain trends of theory about woman and what is called woman's work, is that this work has been described and then elsewhere, generally apart from it, broad generalizations have been made referring to woman's subjugation being a part of the system of the exploitation of human labor, but these two things have not been adequately connected.

It is somewhat as if the woods were described and in a separate section the trees were also described but the whole matter was left in such a disconnected shape that neither seemed to have any relation to the other; the trees did not appear to be in the woods and the woods were not a collectivity of trees. . . .

Let us illustrate the point further: The work of a cook in a logging camp is a necessary part of the production of lumber. The services of all the cooks in all the camps, restaurants and eating places wherever productive workers are

---

* Mariarosa Della Costa, "Women and the Subversion of the Community," *Radical America* 6, no. 1 (Jan.–Feb. 1972). See also *Radical America* 7, nos. 4–5 (July–Oct. 1973).

fed, are a necessary part of production. And for the same reason, the work of the cooks in the homes of productive workers is also, at present, a necessary part of production.

The labor of a woman, who cooks for her husband, who is making tires in the Firestone plant in Southgate, California, is essentially as much a part of the production of automobile tires as the cooks and waitresses in the cafes where Firestone workers eat. . . .

The labor of workers in the laundries who wash clothing for productive workers is necessary to the system of production. Maids and porters who sweep the floors, make the beds and tidy the rooms in boarding houses or camps where productive workers sleep and rest, so that they may prepare themselves to return to work the next day, are a necessary link in the productive process.

And in the same way, the labor of housewives in the homes of productive workers who perform the services of keeping clothing washed and beds and floors clean, is also an indispensable part of production. . . .

The housewife does not cook eight or nine hours like the camp cook, nor wash and iron a stated number of hours like the laundry worker, nor make beds for certain hours like the maid in the hotel or rooming house, nor teach and nurse and feed children, future productive workers, a stated number of hours like teachers and workers in nurseries and schools, but she does perform all these tasks, and more, for unlimited and unstated hours every day, every week, and every month for years.

If the man cook in the lumber camp could be held to a subordinate economic position, directly under another worker and required to work, not nine hours, but an indefinite number, from ten to twelve, or more, and be paid nothing directly but have to get his keep from the little extra given the worker over him, and then be scornfully referred to as being "kept," it is easy to see that his employer would be further enriched by the decreased status and lengthened hours of the cook.

And it is some such manner that the collective owners of industry, the Hearsts, Rockefellers, Mellons, du Ponts, Fords and Morgans benefit by the cheap labor of the collective housewives and their resultant economic and social degradation. Besides, the wife's dependence is a means of binding the man too, and of reaching through the parents their subject children.

And what shall we say of the housework middle class women performed under developing capitalism, cleaning, cooking, ironing, scrubbing and washing clothes and dishes? We must consider the work of most of these women as being necessary to the system of production and distribution also. . . .

Housewives of both the middle and working classes helped create this wealth that is America today, and part of it belongs to them by right of toil. . . .

"DO I NOT KEEP YOU?"

To do hard toil, and useful work, yet be branded as dependent, labeled "kept," "supported," nothing in the world is as galling as this. The worker engaged directly in industry is robbed of part of the product of his toil, but at least he is given credit for being self supporting. But the housewife is more completely robbed, being also robbed of part of the value of her toil, and robbed of credit for doing useful labor in relation to social production, for her work is commonly considered to be merely a labor of love for her intimate little group and to have no value apart from her immediate family. . . .

Nor is the housewives' relation to social production the only part of the process that has been distorted, but, because the husbands of 22 million women stand in relation to their wives and the owners of industry as go-betweens supplying workshops in the form of "homes" where these women toil, the husband's role has been confused as that of the owner himself.

How absurd to call the majority of these men the owners

of anything when they do not own their jobs in production, and their very bread is the private property of another.

The law makes it mandatory on the husband to "support" the woman in this workshop, and their children. And while the "support" the husband gives his wife must come out of production, and the owners of the means of production are not unaware of her existence, and while they also know that children must be raised if the supply of labor and soldiers is to remain adequate to their needs, yet the working man who is the support of his family is not secure in this amount.

Its inclusion in his pay check is not something he can take for granted and dismiss. It is instead something he must struggle desperately for, and a great many fail to get it at all and others are paid this amount only part of the time. . . .

We come then to see the social importance of 22 million housewives' work, and its present day relation to the production of commodities. And we see how erroneous is the belief that the housewife became unimportant to the system of production when the home mainly ceases to be the place of production it once was. We say mainly, and not entirely, because the most valuable of all commodities is still produced there: Labor Power.

We see that although the work these women do is socially useful and the subsistence they receive in payment of it comes out of production, that they have access to this work only by personal invitation based on a sex relationship, and that if a woman fails to receive an invitation to marry she is denied this work. . . .

The "solution" offered by capitalism's spokesmen is a most transparent fraud: they tell the unemployed housewives to go into industry, and the unemployed industrial women workers to marry and become housewives. . . .

[Inman continues to discuss the outmoded nature of housework, arguing that it is inefficient that on any evening 100,000 women in individual homes cook 100,000 meals for their families, when the work could more efficiently be performed on a mass scale. She calls for a reorganization of the work of housewives, for socialization of domestic services and of child care. She continues:]

The majority of women have, together with the majority of men, general problems as members of society, relating to such issues as building strong trade unions; resistance to reactionary political measures; resistance to reduced living standards through wage cuts and increased living costs; and the necessity of having adequate new housing constructed.

Women have general problems as women, such as "the necessity to struggle against the ideology of female bondage," and against the subservient doctrines preached to them through most of the women's magazines and the general press. . . .

Women have special problems as women, because of economic groupings, or levels of political awareness.

Most important of all, the housewife must be given credit for performing, in the home, work that is indispensable to the present method of machine production. . . .

[Inman continues with an argument for the unity of interests of working class men and women and concludes:]

We can find no decisive factor in the present economic arrangement, of the family's dependence on the man, that should cause the average man to desire a subservient economic and cultural status for women.

It certainly is against his interests, and against his wife's interests, too. For the principal fact remains, that she is held to economic dependence, and an out-of-date method of performing socially useful work, which is reached only by personal invitation.

CHARLOTTE PERKINS GILMAN (1860–1935)

29. A modest proposal for freeing women from housework

Charlotte Perkins Gilman, a widely-acclaimed and influential author and lecturer, was one of the foremost feminist theoreticians in

Charlotte Perkins Gilman, *Women and Economics* (1898; reprint ed., Harper & Row, 1966), pp. 225, 237, 239–243, 246–247.

America. Widely read in natural and social science, she believed that the principles of evolutionary biology guaranteed the progressive improvement of the human race, provided outmoded social institutions did not stand in the way of progress. Arguing that male dominance had stifled the personal growth of women and created significant feminine inferiority, she advocated the emancipation of women as a necessary precondition for the improvement of society. She developed a sharp and original critique of motherhood and housekeeping as institutionalized in the United States. In her highly successful book, *Women and Economics*, she argued that economic dependency, based on the performance of unpaid housework in exchange for marital services, was at the root of women's inferiority. Only the fullest development of female talents, physical strength, will power, self-discipline, and economic independence would enable women to achieve first equality, then the superiority which she believed was implicit in their biological endowment.

Gilman was influenced by Marxian socialist thought, but rejected "the narrow and rigid determinism" of Marx, favoring instead a "socialism of the early humanitarian kind," such as the one of Edward Bellamy. She was acclaimed by suffragists, participated in some of their congresses and lectured under their auspices, but had serious intellectual differences with them. Gilman approved of woman suffrage, but did not consider it central to winning equality for women. Drastic changes in the family, in sex mores, and in social organization were more essential requirements she believed.

Although she was unconventional in her own life and recognized her inability to function in the traditional housewife and mother role, she did not see any contradiction between a woman's function as wife and mother and her full development as an independent human being. Once society adopted more rational means of childrearing and housekeeping, women would be able to combine motherhood and work as men combined fatherhood and work. Gilman defined the emancipated woman of the twentieth century as "a mother economically free, a world-servant instead of a house-servant; a mother knowing the world and living in it."

Her incisive critique of the housewife as an institution remains her most important theoretical contribution. The specific remedies for altering the position of the housewife-mother which she advocated are summarized in the selection below taken from her book, *Women and Economics.*

As a natural consequence of our division of labor on sex-lines, giving to woman the home and to man the world in which to work, we have come to have a dense prejudice in favor of the essential womanliness of the home duties, as opposed to the essential manliness of every other kind of work. We have assumed that the preparation and serving of food and the removal of dirt, the nutritive and excretive processes of the family, are feminine functions; and we have also assumed that these processes must go on in what we call the home, which is the external expression of the family. . . .

[But] the human race is not well nourished by making the process of feeding it a sex-function. The selection and preparation of food should be in the hands of trained experts. And woman should stand beside man as the comrade of his soul, not the servant of his body.

This will require large changes in our method of living. . . . While we treat cooking as a sex-function common to all women and eating as a family function not otherwise rightly accomplished, we can develope no farther. . . .

There was a time when kings and lords retained their private poets to praise and entertain them; but the poet is not truly great until he sings for the world. So the art of cooking can never be lifted to its true place as a human need and a social function by private service. Such an arrangement of our lives and of our houses as will allow cooking to become a profession is the only way in which to free this great art from its present limitations. It should be a reputable, well-paid profession, wherein those women or those men who were adapted to this form of labor could become cooks, as they would become composers or carpenters. . . .

That we have found it convenient in early stages of civilization to do our cooking at home proves no more than the allied fact that we have also found it convenient in such stages to do our weaving and spinning at home, our soap and candle making, our butchering and pickling, our baking and washing.

As society develops, its functions specialize; and the reason why this great race-function of cooking has been so retarded in its natural growth is that the economic dependence of women has kept them back from their share in human progress. When women stand free as economic agents, they will lift and free their arrested functions, to the much better fulfilment of their duties as wives and mothers and to the vast improvement in health and happiness of the human race. . . .

If there should be built and opened in any of our large cities today a commodious and well-served apartment house for professional women with families, it would be filled at once. The apartments would be without kitchens; but there would be a kitchen belonging to the house from which meals could be served to the families in their rooms or in a common dining-room, as preferred. It would be a home where the cleaning was done by efficient workers, not hired separately by the families, but engaged by the manager of the establishment; and a roofgarden, day nursery, and kindergarten, under well-trained professional nurses and teachers, would insure proper care of the children. The demand for such provision is increasing daily, and must soon be met, not by a boarding-house or a lodging-house, a hotel, a restaurant, or any makeshift patching together of these; but by a permanent provision for the needs of women and children, of family privacy with collective advantage. This must be offered on a business basis to prove a substantial business success; and it will so prove, for it is a growing social need. . . .

In suburban homes this purpose could be accomplished much better by a grouping of adjacent houses, each distinct and having its own yard, but all kitchenless, and connected by covered ways with the eating-house. . . .

Many women would continue to prefer the very kinds of work which they are doing now, in the new and higher methods of execution. Even cleaning, rightly understood and practised, is a useful, and therefore honorable profession. It has been amusing heretofore to see how this least desirable of labors has been so innocently held to be woman's natural duty. It is woman, the dainty, the beautiful, the beloved wife and revered mother, who has by common consent been expected to do the chamber-work and scullery work of the world. All that is basest and foulest she in the last instance must handle and remove. Grease, ashes, dust, foul linen, and sooty ironware,—among these her days must pass. As we socialize our functions, this passes from her hands into those of man. The city's cleaning is his work. And even in our houses the professional cleaner is more and more frequently a man.

The organization of household industries will simplify and centralize its cleaning processes, allowing of many mechanical conveniences and the application of scientific skill and thoroughness. We shall be cleaner than we ever were before. There will be less work to do, and far better means of doing it. The daily needs of a well-plumbed house could be met easily by each individual in his or her own room or by one who liked to do such work; and the labor less frequently required would be furnished by an expert, who would clean one home after another with the swift skill of training and experience. The home would cease to be to us a workshop or a museum, and would become far more the personal expression of its occupants—the place of peace and rest, of love and privacy—than it can be in its present condition of arrested industrial development. And woman will fill her place in those industries with far better results than are now provided by her ceaseless struggles, her conscientious devotion, her pathetic ignorance and inefficiency.

CHAPTER FOUR
Old Age, Sickness, and Death

Until the early twentieth century, when the care of the sick and the dying was institutionalized in hospitals in the United States, the experience of death and sickness was a commonplace aspect of family life. Calvinist religion reinforced this familiarity by deliberately urging a preoccupation with one's fate after death. The theme of the fear of death and damnation was used as a means of educating and indoctrinating the young and reforming the sinner. If Americans of an earlier period were able to meet the physical aspects of sickness and death with greater equanimity than their modern counterparts, they seem to have labored under far greater psychic stress over the spiritual aspects. Since so much of the actual care of the sick fell on the women, this relationship to death and illness forms an important part of the historical experience of women.

It is difficult to determine with any accuracy in what way the experience of death differed for men and women of the past. There were some obvious contrasts: men experienced death by seeking it out or confronting it alone or in a predominantly male context: on sea voyages, in Indian fighting, in wars. Women encountered death in the home or went out to bring home their wounded and dying men (see p. 170) during wartime. One of the significant differences between the life experiences of frontier women and those in well-settled regions relates to the frontier woman's direct encounter with death and her ability to stand up to it "like a man."

In the following pages there are first person accounts of the various ways in which women experienced death: the death of a mother, of a young sibling; of a woman in childbirth, of an infant; the death of a husband at war. There are expressions of gentleness, of patient nurturing of the feeble and helpless, of quiet acceptance of the help of female relatives or neighbor women. "Sister . . . sat up with X during the night. . . ." "Fanny has come down to help out. . . ." There was a community of suffering, while suffering was accepted as a normal part of living.

Women of the past were reticent in their correspondence and did not often speak freely of their feelings. Possibly, they were educated to think less of self, more of others. One is struck by the dry, matter-of-fact tone of many of their accounts. If we want to understand how women in the past felt about themselves, we have to draw on material from other sources. One such source is the woman's page in nineteenth-century newspapers, which often featured a column of poetry written by women. The frequency with which poems concerning the death of children appear indicates that this was a theme close to the heart of female readers and writers. The theme of death also recurs in embroidery samplers and needlepoint paintings: the gravestone, the weeping willow, the girl's figure kneeling by the tomb.

There was, of course, one particularly female mode of the death experience: in pregnancies, abortions, and during and after childbirth. Fear and dread of childbirth was one theme openly expressed in female diaries and in correspondence among women friends or between husbands and wives. One can only guess at the effect upon the psychology of women exerted by the inevitable connection between sexual activity and consequent pregnancy, at a time when it was much more likely for a woman to die in childbirth than it was for a man to die violently in war. In the centuries before soldiers were drafted, a man meeting death on the battlefield or in Indian warfare usually had made a choice in the matter. Women's way of death, like women's lives, was cast in a passive mold. Even as late as the twentieth century, women like Sadie Sachs (see document 17) had pregnancy and consequent death forced upon them; their fate, not their choice based on deliberate risk. This subject has so far received inadequate attention by historians. Part of it may be due to the paucity of "hard" data. Statistics are quite unreliable when it comes to maternal deaths—unless a woman died actually in childbirth, her death would be listed as caused by a "fever" or some other complication, even if it occurred as a direct result of childbearing (such as death during pregnancy or by failed abortions).

The subordination of women in patriarchal society found expression not only in their lives, but also in their deaths. Gravestones invariably listed husbands first, women second and referred to the woman, regardless of her other achievements, in terms of her marital status. The "memorial" or "memoir" to a departed wife is a specific literary genre which developed in a society based on female assignment to the home. As long as it was considered proper that a woman's name should appear in print only on the occasion of her wedding and on the occasion of her death, the publication of a memoir was the single public recognition afforded many women. Such documents are an interesting source for historians of women. In them the women appear curiously alike— stereotyped embodiments of domestic virtues, praised for their modesty, prudence, and dedication to husband, children, and church. These memoirs often speak more strongly of what men wished to remember of women than they do of the lives of women. Yet from time to time, a dynamic and arresting personality emerges from the formula. We are fortunate to be able to include such a memoir in this selection, a memorial to Salome Lincoln, a female preacher.

Women's experience in nursing the sick was perhaps less poignant, but certainly more frequent than their experience of death. The societal dictum that women primarily were responsible for the care of sick and enfeebled family members probably had a more far-reaching effect on women's psychology and on their life pattern than any other single factor. It certainly served, more than did exhortation and custom, to tie women closely to the home. It is not surprising that it was women who were responsible for turning nursing into a profession after the Civil War. There had been a similar development in charity and social welfare work, which at first had been carried out on a personal, "visiting neighbor" basis. With urbanization, class differentiation, frequent economic crises, and the proliferation of poverty, care of the indigent was no longer possible on this personal basis. Thus, beginning in the early decades of the nineteenth century, women were instrumental in setting up charitable organizations. Their work gradually led to the founding of almshouses, orphanages, and old age homes (see document 38 on organized charity). They transformed a domestic function into a public service, creating institutions and new professions in the process.

In this chapter, a small sampling of women's social welfare activity must stand for yet another vast unexplored region of the female past.

30. The death of an aged Quaker woman

The deathbed scene described below is quite typical of the American death ritual prevalent from colonial times to the late nineteenth century. The dying woman, Eliza Coffin Yarnall, having been nursed at home for a prolonged period by her female relatives, was surrounded by her nearest relatives and some close neighbors. The family, in attendance for some time before the death, has come from different parts of the state, lodging in the homes of nearby relatives and expecting to stay through the funeral and the opening of the will. Death came without much medical interference, the doctor in attendance confining himself to the prescription of soothing medication, sometimes painkillers, and daily reassurance to the bereaved family. His skill was mainly sought for predicting the time of death, since it was assumed that he could do little to postpone its coming. The fact of the impending death was quite openly discussed with the dying person, who displayed an attitude of resignation and submission to God's will. Prayers for salvation and acceptance in heaven eased the minds of the dying and of the family. It is noteworthy that women in the family seemed to be in charge during such periods. The sentence, "The sons were very lovely and attentive to every wish of their sisters—remaining to meals often," indicates unusual sensitivity and deference on the part of male family members.

Descriptions of deathbed scenes, which occur unhappily with great frequency in family correspondences, usually dwell on the resigned, patient suffering of the dying person and her acceptance of her fate. Proper spiritual preparation for death and practical disposition of one's earthly goods were virtues to be cultivated and were considered worth recording. Such an attitude must have eased the fear of the dying person as well as the grief of the survivors. To modern observers the social nature of death is striking—the dying were up to their last breath involved in life, the family, the practical aspects of their own situation.

Martha Coffin Wright to Ellen Wright Garrison, Letters of Martha Coffin Pelham Wright, Garrison Family Papers. Courtesy of the Sophia Smith Collection (Women's History Archive), Smith College, Northampton, Mass.

In the particular case of the death of seventy-nine-year-old Eliza Yarnall, which her sister Martha Wright describes in a family letter, the following family members are mentioned as being present: Lucretia [Mott], the dying woman's older sister; Martha, her younger sister; her married daughter Sarah and Sarah's son Ellis; her unmarried daughter Rebecca; two nieces, Marianna and Anna Brown; several of these with other children, with their husbands and wives.

The speed with which the sale of house and furnishings follows upon the death of the mother speaks of the need of the unmarried daughter to find a home with another of her relatives. It may also indicate a desire to share the work and worry of the sale of a home and of the distribution of its proceeds with other family members while they were still present during the period after the funeral.

Martha Coffin Wright to her daughter, Ellen Wright Garrison / *Roadside, Feb. 11th [1870]*

My dear Ellen,

It seems a month since my last letter to you, telling of dear sister Eliza's illness, & you have heard of her death on Friday afternoon, 4th. We had little hope of her recovery; she had had such a wasting cough, for a year—Her children had felt much anxiety on her acct. When I wrote you, she seemed a little better, but the next morning she was not so well, & the Dr. said that if there was anything to be attended to, it should be done then, as that was probably her last clear day. Anna Brown was telegraphed for, & word sent out to Sister L. who had gone out, to spend that day at home. She came in, at once, and saw quite a change, as we all did—her breathing was shorter, & her mind a little wandering, tho' at the same time she met all with a pleasant smile & welcome. She couldn't keep her eyes open, but often opened them, & coughed less than she had, being so much weaker—she turned often & sd. "I am so tired." She was gentle & lovely all the time, saying very little—enquiring often for Anna Brown & Marianna, asking if 'the travellers had arrived' & saying Anna cd. sleep with me & Walter with

Ellis Brown. On Thursday she said to Rebecca, ask Aunt Lucretia to stay, & told her what pillow to put on the bed—she asked often after Sister L. when she was out of sight. All the children (sons & daughters) were collected Thursday evening, & she did not seem surprised to see them. She asked Sarah what the Dr. sd. & she told her he tho't her very sick—she sd. "I think he considers me sicker than I am. Life has not been to me, for some time, what it once was, but I cannot say that I didn't wish to live—there are some things to be done"—I told her never mind, they would be done. I told her she knew my opinion—she smiled—said I know what *thee says* is thy opinion. The others some of them came to the bed, & she said to Elly Brown, "Thee hasn't been with us long, but it has been a great pleasure to us to have thee."—This was on Thursday evening. . . . Friday morning she continued to grow weaker—was catching at imaginary things, & occasionally brushing dust from the bed . . . The Dr. tho't she would live thro' the day . . . Between 4 & 5 she stopped breathing—without any seeming suffering. All her children were at her bedside, some summoned hastily & one or two, arriving just in time. Anna Brown got there just too late—she felt dreadfully, that she cd. not have got there when she cd. have recognized her. Sister L. sd. no one cd. tell the loss it was to her. Rebecca feels keenly the loss in every way—she says no one knows what it is to her, to have no home—She will go to Sarah's & the house & furniture will be sold, soon as possible. Ellis read the will a few hours after we returned from the funeral (Laurel Hill). All in the house left to Rebecca—all other property equally divided—She told Rebecca where to find her will. I seldom left her during her illness, & was very thankful to have been with her from the first. Her peculiar characteristics, neatness & extreme precision were shown thro' out. She liked her Doctor. He has attended her & Becky for the last year. He gave but little medicine, & kept her strength by stimulants, as long as he cd. "What next?" she wd. say, when Rebecca wd. go to her with anything—she disliked her spoonful of

medicine, every two hours, but was not sick at her stomach
at all—I could not bear to leave the girls, after the funeral, &
remained till yesterday night, spending two days with
Marianna, Sister L. meeting me there & spending the nights
with me. . . . Sister E. was placed in ice till Monday—she
was like a wax image of Sister L.—not a bit like herself—a
white cashmere robe & thin cap & muslin handkerchief
such as she wore, & the little silk shawl. Margt. Yarnall &
her sister Anne brot. beautiful flowers, & a white rose &
placed on her pillow & breast. The sons were very lovely &
attentive to every wish of their sisters—remaining to meals
often—I looked some for yr. father before the funeral. . . .
He returned in time to receive my letter mentioning Sister
Eliza's illness, & after resting a day or two at home he
reached Phila. Tuesday night & went to the Continental, not
knowing of her death. . . . He met me at Marianna's on
Wednesday, & we spent that & the next night at Sister Eliza's, he aiding them in such law questions as they had to
ask. . . . I left her at 3 p.m.—went back to Sister E's & got
my things & left the dear, bereaved daughters to make their
plans & arrange their prices for a private sale. Sarah spends
her days there, & was there to wait on her mother nights
thro' the lask wk. —I shall go in again, on Monday. . . .

MARY A. LIVERMORE

31.   The death of a younger sister

The author of this narrative, who earlier has described the oppressive effect on her of her father's stern Calvinist upbringing (see
document 5), here tells of the death of her sister, Rachel. The
torment of anxiety concerning the eternal fate of the dead child,
which weighed heavily on the grief-stricken family, has seldom
been so vividly described as in this account. It provoked a crisis in

Mary A. Livermore, *The Story of My Life* (Hartford, Conn.: A. D. Worth-
ington & Co., 1897), pp. 130–131, 133–142.

the narrator's life, as similar events had in the lives of other nineteenth-century feminists (cf. Catharine Beecher, Sarah Grimké). It led Mary Livermore to search for knowledge in her own way, to equip herself to refute the religious leadership of her minister and especially of her father, and to construct a more hopeful and humanist theology, in which she could believe. It is most interesting to see the way in which the mother, who in all matters deferred to her husband, persisted in her own interpretation of predestination and election. This kind of silent rebellion concerning religion on the part of a generally meek and submissive woman is described rather frequently in early autobiographies and correspondences.

My sister Rachel, next in age to myself, and three years younger, was a delicate child from birth. It was only by the most untiring care and watchfulness that she lived through infancy to young girlhood. . . .

Always pale, with large brown eyes, her oval face framed in her hair like spun sunshine, gentle, and always sweet-tempered, my sister Rachel exerted a perpetual influence for good in our family circle. . . . We grew up together, occupying the same room, after the birth of a still younger sister, and such was the imperative need of my care, and of supplementing her weakness with my strength, that my relation to her was far more motherly than sisterly. . . . During the last two years of her life she suffered extremely from curvature of the spine. The treatment prescribed for the disease caused her more suffering than she was able to bear. To rest on an inclined plane for hours of every day, supported by a strap under the arms to prevent slipping, and another under the chin, while heavy weights were attached to the ankles, for the straightening of the spinal column, was unbearable torture to the delicate child. Everything was done to tone up her system, and to build up her general health, but she failed and faded visibly before our eyes, and yet so sweetly and uncomplainingly that we were hardly aware of her increasing weakness. . . .

One afternoon she asked me to bring my books to her

chamber, and to study by her bedside. I did as she desired, but there was no chance for study. She was in a mood for talk. Her eyes were exceedingly brilliant, and her cheeks glowed with a vivid flush. She talked incessantly, and of everything while we sat together. I brought her sewing-table and writing-desk to her bedside, and all the small treasures she had accumulated in her short life. She apportioned them all among her kindred and friends, and wrote on each gift the name of the person to whom she bequeathed it, anf left all in my charge. . . .

A premonition of impending sorrow came over me. If my sister was standing on the verge of the other world, I must know if she feared death, or if she anticipated it with hope. . . .

"My dear sister, you are not afraid to die? You are sure God will receive you, and will welcome you?" She swept my face with her preternaturally bright eyes. . . .

"No, Mary, I am not afraid. God will take care of me, even better than you have done! If I die," she continued after a moment's hesitation, "be sure to tell Papa that I cannot remember once to have omitted my prayers, night or morning, in all my life, and that I read the Bible regularly just as he has planned it. And tell Mamma to forgive me if I spoke fretfully when we drove to Dorchester last week, for I was very ill for a few moments, and didn't want her to know it." . . .

In an hour we were summoned to her bedside, for she was battling for her life with a cruel assault of pain that was unendurable. Two physicians were called, and both arrived at the same moment, but before they were able even to make a diagnosis of her case, she had passed into unconsciousness, and was gone.

. . . My father gathered us around our sister's bedside, and we knelt together, while he poured out to God the anguish of our common bereavement, in a language that was burdened with sorrow. He implored our heavenly

Father to give us in our own soul the witness of her happiness in the unknown world whither she had gone. He entreated that we might have a spirit of resignation to the great affliction, and not murmur or fault the Divine Providence, when he who gave the beloved one had, in his own good time, taken her away.

I listened as if my soul's salvation depended on the act of hearing. Not one word was uttered of assurance that all was well with the dear sister; not one intimation that she had entered into a larger, nobler, and happier life. Flung out of existence into the dark, a delicate, white-souled child, who had never in the stern discipline of her father's house suffered punishment; . . . who was, in the family, the perpetual Messiah, forever winning us over to that which was right and good,—and now,—where was she? I could not endure the despairing thoughts that enwrapped me like a pall, and when my father had uttered the "Amen" which closed his prayer, involuntarily I broke into a petition myself:

"Our Father! our beloved daughter and sister cometh to Thee! Open thine arms to receive her with divine compassion, and fatherly tenderness. . . . Receive her, O God, . . . and enfold her in thy compassionate love!"

My mother, who knelt beside me, enclosed me with her arm, and held me tightly. I had voiced her feelings, as I had my own. My father made no comments, but remained on his knees sobbing, till my unusual prayer was ended. . . .

The funeral services were as desolate and devoid of comfort as they could be. It was esteemed the proper thing to make them so, in those days. Black, black, everywhere,—no flowers,—no uplifting music,—no helpful words of faith, hope, or blessedness. The tendency of the service was towards instruction, and warning to the young. They were liable to be overtaken by sudden death, and, if unprepared for it, how sad their doom! With solemnity and discordance, they sang a dismal hymn of warning, beside the open coffin of the whitest-souled being I have ever known, on whose glorified face there rested at that very moment, a beatific and smiling content.

I had now reached a crisis in my life. Happiness and I had parted company forever, unless in some certain and assured manner I could be convinced that my sister Rachel was not among the lost. My father was plunged into despair as deep and dark as my own, but he besought heaven if all was well with his child, to give him internal evidence of the fact, and came, in course of time, to believe her one of the "redeemed." There was no such easy way for me out of my mental trouble. I must know how it was, and how could I know? If my sister were lost, then I would follow her, and share with her the eternal anathema of banishment from heaven. And in the half-frenzied conversations I held with our large-hearted, generous, and liberal minister, Dr. Neale, I repeatedly asserted this. . . .

He entreated me not to rebel against God's will, but to accept the inevitable. "Make your own calling and election sure," was his advice, "and be content to leave your sister in the hands of a God who is too good to be unkind, and too wise to be mistaken." It was not advice that I needed, but light in my mental darkness, and rest and peace. I had not an acquaintance who was liberal in religious thought,—not one who was what was called an "unbeliever,"—and I knew of not one book, or periodical that taught a different theology, or philosophy of life, from that in which I had been instructed. "Who would be free themselves must strike the blow." And I now began a re-reading of the New Testament, marking all passages which were relied on as teaching "the eternal punishment of the finally impenitent,"—and also those which seemed to refute such a doctrine, and, to my surprise, found the latter many times more numerous than the former.

My mother alone was able to comfort me. Broken-hearted herself at the loss of a child whose well-being from birth had lain upon her heart, and whose delicacy of physique had required more than usual tender and watchful affection, she rejected the idea that Rachel was lost. "Does God command us to be better than He is?" she would inquire, when assailed because of her "unsoundness of faith," as many called it. . . . "If my daughter has failed of heaven, then there is no hope for any one who has ever lived." When reminded that "mere morality" could not save a human being, my mother replied, "Morality is practical good living, and is a part of religion, and those whose lives are noble and helpful to the world show themselves to be followers of Christ, and are Christians."

No amount of theological disputation removed her from her anchorage, and to the day of her death, quiet woman as she was, my mother never hesitated to avow her belief that religion is love to God and love to man; and that it is not possible for God, whose very nature is love, to send into life any creature, knowing that eternal torment awaits him. An infinite fiend might do this, but never an infinite God. I finally decided to read for myself the New Testament in the original. In the disputations and controversies of that time, much was said concerning the incorrect translations of words and phrases of the New Testament, and at last I determined to acquire a sufficient knowledge of Greek to enable me to read the book in the language in which it was written. I succeeded in securing the services of a tutor who was a college graduate, but at that time an ex-minister, who had retired from his profession on account of ill health. Quietly and almost secretly, I began my work with him. I had studied Greek before, and already knew a little of the language. My teacher was not of the best, and could not give me the time and instruction for which I had stipulated. But the earnestness of my purpose held me steadily to my work, through all hindrances and obstructions. And when I had finished this task of months, to which I had set myself, I closed the New Testament with the firm conviction that the doctrine of endless punishment is not taught in its pages. . . .

I found the gospels and epistles luminous with love and good-will, with compassion and forgiveness, with pity and mercy, and at times my spirits became buoyant at the divine tenderness that glorified the printed page, as I slowly read it in the original. I hardly dared breathe it to myself, for I supposed I was the only person in the world who doubted the accepted belief. I lacked confidence in myself and in my own judgment, and knowing what a host of scholars were arrayed on the other side, and that their views had been held for centuries, I was afraid I was not competent to judge, and was not much happier than before. . . .

32. The death of a mother after childbirth

It is a rare family correspondence in nineteenth-century America that does not contain at least one account of the death of a mother in or after childbirth. Since women were usually in attendance upon sick family members, it must have been unusual for a girl to grow to womanhood without having witnessed at least one such death. The psychological effect on women of these experiences can be surmised from the frequency with which they speak of their fears of childbirth.

Nothing further is known about the writer of the letter and the young mother. This particular death occurred late in the century and in a sizable town. This is probably why there were three physicians in attendance holding a medical consultation. This fact renders the account atypical. If the event had occurred earlier in the century or in a rural setting, the woman would have been more typically attended by relatives and a midwife, with a physician, at best, called in at the very end.

Mary R. Lewis to Mary Holywell Everett, Everett Family Papers, Newberry Library, Chicago. Courtesy of the Newberry Library and Roberts Everett.

MARY R. LEWIS TO HER COUSIN, MARY H. EVERETT, *UTICA, N.Y. OCT. 21, 1870*

I thought I would wait a few days before answering your kind letter, for which, and your trouble, I thank you. I waited so as to tell you how smart our dear Sarah was getting, but all our hopes centered in her are blasted. She left us last night about 9 o'clock. Poor Alex, I think I have never known a paralell [!] case, almost everybody has a parents home to go to, a child or some home tie, but he has lost his all in losing her. He was entirely unprepared for such a blow as indeed we all were. We shall miss her much, and every day. . . .

The baby was born last week, Wednesday. The same afternoon I called to see her just before going to Remsen, she was looking real bright and comfortable. The next Monday afternoon I called on my way home from Remsen, found her comfortable but she said she had had a terrible time since I had been gone. The next day a flood of water, seemingly scalding hot, would pass from her involuntarily, so burning she would scream every time it would pass. Was much better then, although the flow of bloody water had not ceased. Tuesday morning I found her comfortable and bright, at 2 p.m. I went down to sit with her while the nurse had a nap. She told me the Dr. said it would be a long time before she would be able to go up and down stairs much. Alex had been measuring the bedroom out of the back parlor & the bed would go in nicely, the washstand in a little pantry from that & the bureau would do very well in the back parlor so everything would be convenient, said she "I am well repaid for all the care I took of Alex while he was sick. He is just as devoted *as anybody can be.* . . ." The Dr. told her she might sit up on Friday, and today there her body lies just where she laid while telling me so. She turned a little pale about her nose and mouth twice while I sat there . . . The next day 2 p.m. found her much worse and considered in great danger. At 7 p.m. had another consultation (Drs. Gardiner & Watson) thought her symptoms decidedly better than a few hours before. Such a change as those words wrought in Alex voice you can hardly imagine. The next morning Morris Child came to say Sarah was *very much* worse, there was hardly the least hope for us now, he said. From that time she lay in a stupor, excepting when aroused, mind wandered in spells. Alex would touch her cheek and speak, she knew him every time until the next morning at 9, then he was almost frantic, he "never spoke to her before but what she would answer," he said. He stood over her and said "you saved my life but *I can't* save yours." He is more composed today by spells, and . . . willing to trust the Saviour and receive his strength but "does not know how."

Thomas came home Wednesday night, I am thankful he is with us now. The funeral is to be tomorrow, Saturday, at 1 o'clock. She is to be buried at Cassville. Love to you from your cousin.

SALOME LINCOLN (1807–1841)

33.   Memorial to a female preacher

In keeping with the "Memorial" genre as it was applied to women, the memorial for Salome Lincoln describes her appearance only to stress her modesty and neatness. It describes her character only by stressing her reserve (a primary female virtue) and her gentleness. The author, obviously self-conscious about his controversial subject, begins the memoir with a lengthy apology to the reader, in which he tries to counter all the arguments prevalent against women speaking in public. Since the remarkable achievement of Salome Lincoln was precisely her work as a female preacher, the memorialist is in the uneasy position of celebrating the memory of the departed by apologizing for her life.

Almond H. Davis, *The Female Preacher, or Memoir of Salome Lincoln, Afterwards the Wife of Elder Junia S. Mowry* (Providence, R.I.: Elder J. S. Mowry, 1843), pp. 2, 12, 16–17, 29–33, 36–37, 40, 42–44, 141–142, 148–151, 153, 161.

Otherwise, the author of the memorial, Almond H. Davis, follows the genre faithfully: the feminine virtues of the dead woman are stressed, her dedication to religion and duty is reported, her credentials for her public life are justified by citing numerous endorsements from important men in her behalf. (Only one sample of such an endorsement has been included in the excerpt below.) The proper memorials for a woman required a listing of her wifely and motherly virtues, her acceptance of the will of God on the death of her infant, and finally a detailed deathbed scene, in which resignation to God and patient suffering were stressed. Davis followed this pattern, yet despite his efforts at stressing the conventional aspects of her life, Salome Lincoln emerges from the brief volume as a remarkable person.

The account of Salome Lincoln's life revises the commonly held notion (held until the present also by the editor), that the lecture tour of the Grimké sisters in Massachusetts in 1837–1838 represented the first public lecture tour by American-born women. Lincoln's ministry antedated the Grimkés' tour, and her twelve prayer meetings in Boston also exceeded in length the four Boston lectures delivered by Maria Stewart, a black woman. The description in the memoir of the psychological stress experienced by Salome Lincoln before she embarked on her public career parallels the mental state described by Sarah Grimké, as she was trying to prepare herself for the Quaker ministry. Tremendous anxiety and guilt, a conviction that they were being tempted by the devil, and feelings of doubt and worthlessness all spoke to the psychic burden upon the women, who felt deep within them a vocation to the ministry. Sarah Grimké succumbed to the stress, at least for a time, and abandoned her hopes of a ministry. Maria Stewart gave up after four lectures, because of the severe disapproval of her conduct by her circle of acquaintances. It is all the more remarkable that this untutored mill girl persisted, and built a successful public career. Another aspect of Salome Lincoln's public life is revealed in the memoir—her leadership in what appears to be one of the earliest strikes of female mill workers on record (see document 53).

The final paragraphs of the memoir reproduce the epitaph on Salome Lincoln's gravestone, which manages to hide her life as a preacher under the innocuous phrase "a public laborer," and to subsume her vocation under the ascription "the wife of." Her husband of six years gets full title and equal space on her gravestone, although her "public labors of five years" consisted of a pioneering ministry before she met him and extended, according to the memorialist's own testimony, for thirteen years. No matter what a woman might accomplish in life, what she was remembered for in death was being "the wife of. . . ."

APOLOGY FOR THIS WORK. I am aware, that female preaching at the present day, among a large and respectable body of christians, has become very unpopular. But this is no reason why we should keep silent. Many things which are rejected by the world, are undoubtedly approved by God. . . .

OBJECTIONS TO FEMALE PREACHERS: It is advocated with considerable warmth, that woman is acting out of her sphere, when she takes a part in the public congregation. . . . I am now satisfied, that God's ways are not as our ways; and he will choose just such agents to execute his plans, as best subserves his ends. . . .

WOMEN DID PROPHESY, OR PREACH IN THE TIME OF CHRIST AND THE APOSTLES; AND WERE APPROVED. . . .

It was woman that first preached a risen Savior! and shame on that man, who will take advantage of the apostle's meaning, in the fourteenth of Corinthians, by construing it into something he never intended; in order to make her condition still more degraded.

Boston, April 28, 1843   *A. H. Davis*

[Salome Lincoln was born in 1807 in Raynham, Massachusetts, the eldest of six children. She describes her religious conversion at age 15 as follows:]

I had now returned home, and determined that I would seek the Lord at the loss of all things. But the more I sought, the more I saw the wretchedness of my situation. I attended on the preaching of the gospel, but every word was like a thunderbolt to my wounded soul! I felt that I was justly condemned, and despaired of the mercy of God. . . . One day as I retired to a small grove near the house, and sat

down under a large tree to meditate upon my lost condition
without Christ; it seemed to me as though the heavens were
brass, and the earth was iron under my feet. . . . I felt that I
had sinned away the day of grace, and driven the heavenly
messenger from my breast!—While I sat thus meditating; a
thought like this, came to my mind. Has not Christ died for
the very worst of sinners? I cannot be worse than the
worst—perhaps there is yet mercy for *me!* I will cast myself
upon him; and if I die, I will die pleading—I then threw
myself upon my knees, and began to cry:—O, Jesus—If thou
wilt, thou canst make me clean! While praying, it seemed as
though the mountains had rolled away, and I heard these
words:—"I will, be thou clean!" My fears subsided. . . .

O, what glory filled my soul at that moment! I arose, and
every thing looked new around me! Every thing seemed to
praise the Lord! and I longed to tell the whole world, what a
DEAR SAVIOR I had found. I knew then, that he had taken my
feet from the miry clay; and had set them upon the ROCK,
even the *rock* CHRIST JESUS! . . .

[She was baptized on April 8, 1823. However:]

Though Salomé gained so good an evidence of her acceptance with God, . . . we are obliged to record a short
period of her life, after her conversion, when she was without the enjoyment of religion. In speaking of it herself, she
says—"The church began to decline, and I with the rest."

She remained in a backslidden state until sometime in
the year 1825; when she was again reclaimed and brought
back to her first love. This was during a powerful revival of
religion in Raynham and the vicinity where she was then
laboring.

The cause of her backsliding, she attributes to a neglect of
duty. From the time of her conversion, it was deeply impressed upon her mind, that God had something for her to
do as a public laborer in his vineyard. . . .

Her trials of mind, in relation to preaching, as we may
naturally suppose, were severe. Situated as she was in a

community, where female preachers were but little known:—and where the tide of popular favor was turned against them—with but limited means, without many friends to encourage her on,—while the spirit of God, and the convictions of conscience, said, go go!—and on the other hand, Satan, and the world, cried *Woman,*—WOMAN!—it is no wonder, that at the midnight hour, while she wept and prayed till her pillow was wet with tears;* she should sometimes exclaim, "Lord I pray thee, have me excused!"

According to her own relation, her mind was first exercised on the subject of preaching, about the year 1823, soon after she united with the church. In a letter addressed to a friend, she says;—"I was employed in the weaving-room at Taunton.—My mind had often been exercised, in relation to entering the vineyard of the Lord, as a public laborer. But, O, my soul shrunk from the work! I thought I could never move forward; and soon lost the enjoyment of religion."

In another letter she says:—"I felt that it was a great undertaking; and it was with a trembling hand, that I came to the conclusion to give up all, and enter the field. But on making up my mind, I felt the approbation of heaven, and since then, I have been more and more convinced, that these convictions were from the Lord!"

In remarking to a friend, she said, that it did not seen right to her, for a woman to speak in public; and on account of this, like Jonah, she had fled from the presence of the Lord, to get rid of duty. . . .

Salomé not only had the witness of God, and the approval of her own conscience, as an evidence of *her call;* but the hearty cooperation, of several distinguished brethren in the ministry. . . . The following recommendation which she received from Elder Norris,—now the Editor of the Olive Branch,† in 1834, will serve to illustrate the manner in which her labors were regarded.

---

* It is related by her friends, that so great was her anxiety of mind on the subject of preaching, that she would often weep hours, after she had retired—[Davis' note].

† A Paper published in Boston, Mass.—[Davis' note].

BOSTON, AUGUST 13, 1834

TO WHOM IT MAY CONCERN:—As Miss Salome Lincoln, is about to visit the State of Maine, and is a stranger there; I would state, that she is well known to the Christian Public, in this section of the country. She sustains a good moral character, and her connections are among some of the first families in this city, and vicinity. She is also highly respected, as an exemplary christian. She is approved, by a respectable, and in this State numerous class of christians, to help in the gospel ministry.—Many hundreds in this city, and in the neighboring towns have listened to her pulpit instructions, with apparent pleasure and profit.

THOMAS F. NORRIS,
Pastor of the Reformed Methodist Church, Boston

PREACHED HER FIRST SERMON. Sister Lincoln commenced her public labors in the vicinity of her father's, by taking part in prayer and conference meetings. Her first sermon was preached October 17th, 1827—The meeting was held about two miles from her father's residence. She had just returned from a Quarterly Meeting, held at Rochester, Mass.; and in speaking of the meeting she says,

"I started expecting to hear Elder Brett preach. But my mind was uncommonly burdened; and I felt that I should have something to do. As I went up to the door, a little girl met me, and informed me that the preacher had not come. The thought was immediately suggested—he will not come! I felt almost sure of it. I went into the house, and sat down in the kitchen, while the people were assembling in another room. A large number of young persons were present, and not one among them that had ever professed religion. I sat a few moments trembling under the cross: and then fell upon my knees and commenced praying. While in prayer, the power of God was manifested—and the fear of man taken away. I then arose and began to speak. The promise of the Lord was verified—"Open thy mouth wide, and I will fill it."—While I spoke the eyes of the youth were fixed upon me, and many were affected even to tears.

After I sat down, one aged woman arose and spoke a few words of exhortation, setting forth the importance of attending to the duties of religion while in youth. But not feeling my mind freed, I arose again, and spoke a few words, and then dismissed the meeting.

I expected that much would be said in relation to this meeting; but I felt that the Lord approbated me. And if the Lord *is for me,* who can be against me." . . .

[After preaching on several different occasions, Salomé Lincoln became a full-time itinerant preacher in 1830. For the next five years she toured New England, holding twelve revival meetings in Boston and spending almost two years preaching at Martha's Vineyard. In December 1835 she married Elder Junia S. Mowry, a minister of her church. During her married life she preached on various occasions, the last time in 1840, and was active in church conferences and revivals.]

BIRTH AND DEATH OF HER CHILD.—Her first child, Mary Elizabeth, was born Nov. 2, 1837, but she was not blessed with its society long, as God in his providence saw fit soon after to take it to himself. God's ways are mysterious. . . .

This child was never well from birth, and was several times brought so low, that it was thought to be dying. The disease which finally terminated its existence, was the *dropsy,* and after a protracted illness of several months it fell asleep Feb. 5, 1839, leaving its fond parents to mourn its loss.

At the request of Sister Mowry, Elder James McKenzie, Pastor of the Freewill Baptist Church at Newport, R.I., attended the funeral, and preached a discourse from a text selected by herself.

"Is it *well* with *thee?* Is it *well* with thy *husband? Is it well* WITH THE CHILD?—And *she* answered; *It is well.*"—II Kings iv. 26.

She felt the death of her child severely, yet she manifested Christian resignation.—Says Elder McKenzie— "When I entered the room, there was no boisterous emotions of grief, but her looks and language, was expressive of an entire submission to the will of God."

In a letter afterwards written to her devoted friend Elizabeth Liscom, she says:—"The sweet little pratler has gone to the world of spirits, and I shall soon follow!" . . .

[A second child was born while she was already ill with consumption. The memoir continues with this description of her death, four months after the birth of her second child:]

Subsequent to the twentieth of May, 1841, she never left her room, only as she was carried in the arms of her husband; and for about nine weeks previous to her death, she had constant watchers, and every means that could be suggested to the minds of her friends, was resorted to, in order to secure her recovery; but all in vain, as from that time she rapidly declined. . . .

LAST HOURS AND DEATH.—A few days before her death, Elder Joseph Whittemore, from Tiverton, called to see her. He says—"She appeared to know me, and would converse rational about the people of Tiverton. She expressed a *strong desire* for the prosperity of the church there; and when asked in relation to her own feelings, she said she was sensible, she should never get well, and felt *resigned* to the will of God. She also remarked, that in prospect of death, she felt more calm than she ever expected; although if it was the will of God, she should like to regain her health; but not so much on her own account, as on the account of her husband and child." . . .

During the last few hours of her life, she seemed to lie almost entirely senseless, and in so great a bodily distress, that her groans were heard in the street; and at the same time, she was in a state of mental *aberration.* Her *bodily suffering* during this period was doubtless *beyond conception,* and it would not be surprising if under these circumstances, she often appeared indifferent, as to her situation. She remained in this state until about *four o'clock* Wednesday afternoon, July 21, 1841, *when she departed this life to be with* JESUS.

She is now free from pain and sorrow—her trials are at an

end, and she is reaping a rich reward for all her toils, in the *Kingdom of Heaven!* . . .

Among a large circle of *relatives* and *friends,* Mrs. Mowry left one child; then *four months* old—a bright black eyed little girl! Though possessing naturally a delicate constitution, yet by the tender care of her parent and guardian, she may live many years, to follow in the footsteps of her mother,—an ornament in society—a pillar in the church, and useful to all around her! . . .

Mrs. Mowry was buried near her child, in the yard a few rods north of the Stone meeting-house belonging to the Freewill Baptists in Tiverton. The grave is situated in the southern part of the yard, near the gate. It is marked by two white marble slabs, on which is inscribed the following appropriate words:—

In memory

of

SALOME MOWRY,

the wife of

ELDER JUNIA S. MOWRY,

Who died July 21, 1841, in the 34th year of her age.
She spent more than five years as a public laborer
in various places; mostly in the south-
eastern part of Massachusetts.

MARY A. DENNISON

34. The death of a husband at war

Another kind of death has been experienced by many women: that of their sons, brothers, and husbands at war. Because wars have been relatively infrequent in American history, although violent deaths have not, this particular experience fell heavily only upon certain generations of women. The Civil War generation bore more than its share.

Severance Family Papers, Used courtesy of the Western Reserve Historical Society, Cleveland, Ohio.

This poem written by Mary Dennison was copied in a "Memory Book" kept in the 1860s by an Illinois farm woman, in which she collected poems by various authors. It was found in a family correspondence together with several other such albums kept by Mary Long. Several of those "Memory Books" are filled with poems about death and home and friendship, each written in different handwriting by one of her friends. Mary Long appended a note to many of these poems, telling what had become of the friend who wrote it. It is striking to note how many of her friends died within a twenty-year period.

The poem below, purporting to be written in an Irish dialect, although without literary distinction, is of considerable interest as a cultural document. The sentimental dramatization of an illiterate wife learning, presumably from the local judge, that her husband has died at the front, is written in the wife's voice. The fact that the soldier is Irish, a member of an ethnic group which was at the time much despised and subject to prejudice, was obviously intended to arouse sympathy for the Irish and extol their patriotism. Mary O'Conner, the wife of the Union volunteer, mentions her worries over the rent and the doctor bills for her sick baby, reflecting the fact that Civil War soldiers received no dependency allotments and not infrequently left their families in great distress. Men went to war; women waited and worried and dreaded the kind of scene Mary O'Conner experienced. When the men were killed in war, not only bereavement but the threat of destitution became the women's reality. Perhaps it was Mary O'Conner's poignant exclamation "O! how will I live and O! where will I go?" which made the poem meaningful to Mary Long, who clipped it from a newspaper and carefully copied it into her "Memory Book."

MARY O'CONNER, THE VOLUNTEER'S WIFE

An' sure I was told to come here to your honor,
    To see if you'd write a few words to me Pat;
He's gone for a soger is Mr. O'Conner,
    With a stripe on his arm and a band on his hat.
An' what'll you tell him? It ought to be easy
    For such as your honor to spake with the man
And say Pat all right and that . . . Daisy
    (The baby your honor) is better agen.

For when he went off, it's so sick was the children,
    She niver held up her blue eyes to his face,
And when I'd be crying, he'd look but the wilder,
    And say would I wish for the country, disgrace?
So he left her in danger, and me sorely greeting,
    To follow the flag with an Irishman's joy.
O! It's often I drame of the great drums a beating,
    And a bullet gone straight to the heart of my boy.
And say will he send me a bit of his money,
    For the rint, and the doctor's bill, due in a week?
Well surely there's tears in your eyelashes, honey,
    Ah! faith I've no right with such freedom to speak.
You're over much trifling—I'll not give you troubles;
    I'll find some one willin';—oh! what can it be?
What's that in the newspaper folded up double?
    Yer honor—don't hide it—but read it to me.
What! Patrick O'Conner?—no, no, it's some other;
    Dead! dead!—no, not him, 'tis a week since gone by;
Dead! dead! why the kiss on the cheek of his mother
    It hasn't had time yet, your honor, to dry.
Don't tell me—it's not him—O God! am I crazy!
    Shot dead!—oh! for love of sweet heaven say no;
And what'll I do in the world with poor Daisy?
    O! how will I live and O! where will I go?
The room is so dark—I'm not seein' your honor;
    I think I'll go home;—and a sob quick and dry
Came sharp from the bosom of Mary O'Conner,
    But never a tear-drop welled up to her eye.

                                              Mary A. Dennison

MARIAN LOUISE MOORE (1813–?)

35. Nursing an aging mother

In her manuscript journal written in Ohio between 1831 and 1860,
Marian Louise Moore records some of the daily events of life on a

Journal of Marian L. Moore, 1831–1860. Used courtesy of the Western
Reserve Historical Society, Cleveland, Ohio.

wilderness homestead, a few wildly dramatic disasters that befell her or her family and, in loving detail, her relationship to her mother and father. It is the mother-daughter relationship which makes this diary so interesting. The mother was apparently a strong-minded, reasonably well-educated woman; the daughter was introspective, given to dramatizing and exaggerating slights and injuries, and was strongly influenced by what she considered the trials and tribulations of her mother's life, toward a simple, religiously expressed feminism (see also document 86).

Marian Louise Moore's mother was the daughter of a wealthy Connecticut farmer who married a man somewhat beneath her station. They moved to Ohio in 1812, where they and their three sons settled in the wilderness in a log cabin. "At night they heard wolves and panthers howling." There the couple had three more children, two daughters and a son. In 1827 the father was appointed postmaster of the new township of Wayne, his wife working as his assistant. The father, who at various times reported dreams of wrestling with lions and who had visions of the devil appearing at his bedside, served as minister of the Methodist Episcopal Church for twenty-six years. His wife inherited a great deal of money and land from her father and managed her property herself, even in advanced old age.

In the following selection from her diary, which is marred by the manuscript's poor condition and the illegibility of key passages, Marian Louise Moore describes the events leading to the death of her mother. Although she repeatedly ascribes her mother's death to advanced old age, illness, and the result of nervous tensions following upon a violent attack by a disgruntled handyman, the daughter manages to blame herself entirely for her mother's death. Excessively guilt-ridden, she belabors this point and returns to it over and over again.

My mother was a female that was much admired and greatly sought after by college bred men, and popular characters on different stations of honor and trust. At one time invited to teach an academy school from which, however, her great bashfulness shrunk from. Another time, received and accepted an invitation to an assembly dance . . . her father called her his beloved child and instructed his daughters to prosper [see to] their own prosperity. If their husbands were good, they would not hurt them and if they were bad, they would have enough. She was also privileged with a good library being kept in her father's house and herself often appointed to receive and present the books and improve much of her time in reading when in school and teaching, as she taught for several years near her father's residence.

My mother . . . used to instruct her children in my father's absence in impressing their young and tender minds in the culture and principles of virtues, and in the culture of a good moral education. . . .

I was born in the year 1813, August the 9th. . . . When 7 years old I was sent to school, about 2 miles to a log school house. In my 8th and 9th years I studied grammar and obtained the prize locket of the school in orthography and other lessons. At 10 I went about 1 mile to a new found school house . . . at 12 years old my schoolmaster came to engage me as a school teacher in Andover district, where he resided. Was kept secret from me, as my mother did not think my judgment good enough. My mother never struck me a blow in her life and my father never did but once or twice to wake me up to study. In returning from school I was frightened by a couple of youth who tried to insult me, and my mother caught one of them and whipped him most severely, and always committed me to the care of some trusty friends thereafter in going and returning from school. . . . We were sent for a season to a school devoted exclusively to young ladies . . . many were the offers of marriage I had. I had an offer of marriage from a traveling minister, corresponding with him whilst on his circuit and by letter correspondence. My sister had offers from wealthy ones, some of which my parents blamed me in opposing, but I had my female views. . . . [After the death of the oldest brother] it looked indisputable that one of us [two sisters] must marry. I was decided I should not, but my sister married a man not wealthy and allowed she had enough of her own, if he was a kind husband. The history of this marriage I supress [!]. . . . My sister lived to be the mother of 5 children. At the birth of the last one, an infant daughter in the year 1851, July 19th, she died living one week from the confinement, aged 33 years.

[Apparently, following upon this Marian Louise Moore had typhoid fever and was ill for four years. The family also suffered a fire and her father had an accident falling from a horse.]

Mr King had borrowed my Mother's horse to go to the funrel [!] of his wife's sister and had left a hired man of her Father's to keep their house. My unsuspecting Mother and myself . . . rested till the latter part of the day, when Mr. King's brother came also and all three of them were drunk. As my Mother and myself were seated to our evening supper one of them rushed in and caught hold of my dress; exposed to their mercy I arose, caught an apron, threw it over me, ran to the other house to tell another one to take care of that one but he was to [!] drunk to understand what I said. . . . I then ran for the woods and back again, not daring to leave my Mother. The third one was out, Ewing on horseback . . . had demanded money of my Mother through the day. I ran again for the young man's Father, praying almost every step that God would take the breath out of the young man's body if he did not let my Mother alone. I would on no account have made such a prayer, only in the defence of life. This young man, whilst I was gone from fifteen to twenty minutes, rode back, hitched his horse in my Mother's dooryard. Whilst she was barring the door to keep him out, he pushed the door back on her, struck her on the forehead, struck her several times, she said, demanding the whole sum for his labour. She had given him five dollars once that day on the urgency of his case, that he was going to be married that evening at four o'clock. She now invited him to her table and drink some coffee and partake of a supper, but gave him no money until her Father came, when she borrowed it of him. . . . This was the prelude to my beloved Mother's death, for she would at times awake from irregular dreams or think someone had been talking to her about various things when they had not, from that time. In the Spring of 1871 in the ninety sixth year of her age . . . she was able to do the same work she had formerly performed. At this time she sold a farm of 100 acres willed to three different heirs: my Brother, Myself and the Grandson, property that came from her Father's house for four thousand dollars, though she retained the most of it, whilst she lived, to herself. . . .

I fear I was the transgressor on my beloved Mother's health. . . . My Mother now being in the ninety seventh year of her age bid fair to have lived four or five years longer for ought I could see . . . if she could have the proper indulgence and peace her age required. . . .

My Mother had a mind capable of acting and enjoying the good or beautiful things of this life, but the thoughts that she must soon leave it kept her meditative and sedate. . . .

In the Spring of the year 1872 . . . she was sick three months, part of the time helpless, typhoid inflamatory rheumatism. . . . This sickness of hers brought more work upon me, washing and other work, when I had more work of my own than I could possibly do well. My dear Mother when in the parroxism [!] of her pain, inhaling into her breath with the great drop standing upon her forehead, would wrestle in prayer . . . I looked on in sympathy, but did not put up one prayer for her recovery . . . He, if he saw fit to ease her, I hoped he had some good purpose. . . . Her medicines did not relieve her as formerly they had; she could set to the table and partake of her meals and even exercise a little. When on the third or fourth day she did not sit up for dinner as usual and at evening called for cold water, I summoned the Doctor immediately. He said it would have been better if he had been called before. She told the Doctor that she thought he would call her sickness a billious [!] fever. And when I look back upon it now, I believe it was riveted in her system: first, her not having the

reasonable quiet her years in life demanded, with the intelligence she possessed from a child and the education and
privileges in which she had been reared—of loving and
being loved. . . . Second the minor things and sicknesses
of which I have before spoken that she had to be subjected
to, and then my insensibility of her danger through all her
sickness that I may say she died a Martyr. I was asked if I
understood giving her her medicine. I did but I did not
understand performing all the unusual labor I did with a
sick patient on my hands. Not a teaspoon was placed to her
lips or work done for her but what I done. . . . From the
first week she could not rise out of her chair or out of her bed
without a considerable lifting, and as often as she was a
mind to get up or lay down in the day I assisted her. Not
more than half a dozen times in all this time did she get up
or rise alone, which I attributed to her weakness . . . I got
her a strengthening plaster. Her limbs swelled, but the Doctor encouraged her of telling her of one of his patients that
had swelled limbs that had got well. And by the Doctor's
permission I painted the house, and I cooked two hundred
weight of apples or more whilst my Mother would sit twice
a day and wipe the dishes. . . . I now told her, Mother I
have got my work done and I ain't going to let you wipe the
dishes anymore. I am going to do everything in my power to
get you well, and I now believe had I or could I have [put
aside] my work from the first and just attended to her and
been sensible that unless she was very carefully attended to
she must lose her life, she would have recovered for my
comfort. . . . Had I been sensible I should have wrestled
in prayer for her. I did pray but not with thought that life or
death depended on it. . . . My Mother had dreams and
would shriek out in them, sometimes so violent that I would
have to raise up and hold her. She said she dreampt that
murderers had hold of her. A number of times she dreamt
it. . . .

[During this period the daughter painted the house, washed all
the windows, and scoured the beams and the floors. It was the

harvesting season, and she picked five barrels of apples and packed five more. Her mother took medicine regularly and was able to sit up and dry the dishes twice a day. The farm work continued during the fall. Twice the mother collapsed and the daughter sent for the doctor.

In the next weeks she had on several occasions to run errands in the nearby village and do shopping. Each time she had to leave her mother alone, and blamed herself for this. Once when she came back the fire was low:]

. . . I told her, Mother you have taken cold, and I won't leave you again. . . .

The winter was now setting in. I did not have the help and kindness shown I had ought to have had at this time, though I performed and did as well as I could as far as I was able. She told the Doctor she must be a burden to me. I told them she was not. . . . I think just after this that I made a mistake in giving her her medicine. . . . I misunderstood the Doctor or the Doctor made the mistake himself. But my Mother appeared to get over this. I thought I would carry six or seven pails of some kind to the hogs every day, do my work, get three meals and take care of my Mother . . .

[The diary becomes quite illegible at this point. What can be gathered from later context is that the mother died shortly after this incident and that the daughter wrestled for the rest of her life with a disproportionate sense of guilt, apparently blaming herself for her mother's death.]

MARY HOLYWELL EVERETT, M.D. (1830–1916)

36. Duty commands you

The remarkable letter below, written by an older male physician to a female physician, illustrates sharply the pervasiveness of

Samuel Lilienthal, M.D. to Mary Holywell Everett, M.D., Everett Family Papers, Newberry Library, Chicago, Ill. Courtesy of the Newberry Library and Roberts Everett.

stereotyped assumptions regarding proper behavior for women. Dr. Mary Holywell Everett, at the time of the correspondence a forty-six year-old woman, was a graduate of the New York Female Medical College and a busy professional with a large practice. From other correspondence it is obvious that Dr. Lilienthal respected her as a colleague and had been helpful to her in her career. Nevertheless, when she expressed doubts about leaving her patients and her practice in order to nurse her sister, his response was unequivocal. "Even at the risk of losing your practice entirely," he advises her that a higher duty demands her nursing her sister. Such "sacrifice" would not have been demanded of a male physician, in case of the illness of his brother, sister, child, or wife.

How widespread was the assumption that it was a woman's "natural" duty to perform such nursing services for near relatives, can be seen from another letter in Dr. Holywell's correspondence of the same year. In this one, a woman patient of Dr. Holywell comments on her absence in order to help her mother nurse her sister, in the following words: "There seems to be a providence in it all, being that you have no husband, your dear mother has the first claim to you." Husband, child, mother, or sister—it might be debatable who had the first claim, but there was no question that a woman's duty was the domestic care of the sick and the dying. Even a woman physician was not exempt.

SAMUEL LILIENTHAL, M.D. TO MARY HOLYWELL EVERETT, M.D./*New York, Sept. 8, 1876*

My dear girl!

It is really hard to give you advice in the case of your sister. I must confess to very little hope that your poor patient will ever rally much, I rather think, it will be a quiet sinking, till her sweet spirit soars home to our heavenly Father. Even at the risk of losing your practice entirely, duty commands you to remain by the side of your old mother & help her to carry the burden. You will be rewarded for such a sacrifice, my child, but certainly I would not leave your sister yet to the care of strangers. In the treatment I do not see that any change can be made for the present, we must fight symptoms as they appear, only I beg you to keep cool

& steady, there is no necessity to change a well acting remedy for every chance symptom just coming up & then passing off again. I know too well, my dear Mary, the anxiety
we have for those, dearly enshrined in our hearts & how we
try to keep away from them every anguish & every pain & I
beg you therefore not to misunderstand me; I do not blame
you, for it is a fault of all physicians when attending members of their own household. . . . If I can do anything for
you or yours, command my services. With love to all, & the
old one to you,

fraternally yours
S. *Lilienthal*

JANE SWISSHELM

37. From family nursing to volunteer nursing in the Civil War

There were no provisions for the organized care of wounded soldiers prior to the Civil War. The army sometimes employed
slightly wounded soldiers or those unfit for duty due to other disabilities to nurse their wounded comrades. Except for the skilled
nursing by Catholic Sisters of Mercy available in a few urban hospitals only, nursing care was inadequate and unplanned.

On both sides of the Civil War women took the initiative for
organizing the medical supply and the nursing of sick soldiers.

In April 1861, some 3,000 New York women, brought together
through the efforts of Dr. Elizabeth Blackwell, organized the
Woman's Central Association for Relief, which began immediately
to train 100 women as army nurses. The organization also brought
order into the chaos created by the spontaneous enthusiasm of
20,000 aid societies, which had been created by women on both
sides to support their soldiers with food, warm clothing, and medi-

Jane Swisshelm, *Half a Century* (Chicago: Jansen, McClurg & Co., 1880),
pp. 251–253, 274–280, 300–316, 358–359.

cal supplies. In the North, the work of the Woman's Central Association led to the establishment, in 1861, of the U.S. Sanitary Commission. The commission coordinated the care of Union soldiers, staffed and supplied hospitals, and organized transportation for the wounded. It appointed Dorothea Dix, pioneer medical reformer, as superintendent of nurses. Dorothea Dix helped to overcome the resistance of army medical officers, who considered women in "their" hospitals as meddlers and threats, and created a modern nursing service. Scores of women from all walks of life volunteered as nurses, serving under Miss Dix. Included among them were black women, such as Harriet Tubman, Sojourner Truth, and the "contraband" Susie King Taylor. There were women like Jane Swisshelm and Clara Barton, who went their own way and worked alone, at times over Miss Dix's opposition. Clara Barton, after the Civil War, went on to organize the professional training of nurses and establish the International and American Red Cross.

On the Confederate side women also set up hospitals and organized the supplying and nursing of soldiers. In 1862 the Confederacy granted official status to women nurses. In all, at least 3,200 women on both sides gave nursing services during the Civil War. Discrimination and male prejudice dogged their steps; most of them received no pay for their services and many were left in want and ill-health. It took until 1892 before a bill was passed in Congress granting Civil War nurses pensions of $12 a month.

The move from unpaid home nursing to nursing as a profession and a career was made through the efforts of many women and over the opposition of men. Like similar developments in other fields of welfare reform, the newly established profession would retain for many decades the stigma of being a "female occupation"—low status, low pay. Only after decades of professional organization and two more wars, during which the profession advanced in status, would nursing become a career paid sufficiently well to attract men to its ranks.

Jane Swisshelm, in Washington as a self-appointed lobbyist in 1863, volunteered her services as a nurse. She served in hospitals in the capital and later in Fredericksburg, Md. Her vivid descriptions of hospital conditions reveal better than most contemporary accounts the horrors, neglect, indifference, and hostility women encountered in their efforts to help the wounded.

The following scenes took place in Campbell Hospital in Washington, D.C. (See also documents 10 and 20 by Jane Swisshelm.)

About nine o'clock I returned to the man I had come to help, and found that he still slept. . . .

I had sat by him but a few moments when I noticed a green shade on his face. It darkened, and his breathing grew labored—then ceased. I think it was not more than twenty minutes from the time I observed the green tinge until he was gone. I called the nurse, who brought the large man I had seen at the door of the bad ward, and now I knew he was a surgeon, knew also, by the sudden shadow on his face when he saw the corpse, that he was alarmed; and when he had given minute directions for the removal of the bed and its contents, the washing of the floor and sprinkling with chloride of lime, I went close to his side, and said in a low voice:

"Doctor, is not this hospital gangrene?"

He looked down at me, seemed to take my measure, and answered:

"I am very sorry to say, madam, that it is."

"Then you want lemons!"

"We would be glad to have them!"

"Glad to have them?" I repeated, in profound astonishment, "why, you *must* have them!"

He seemed surprised at my earnestness, and set about explaining:

"We sent to the Sanitary Commission last week, and got half a box."

"Sanitary Commission, and half a box of lemons? How many wounded have you?"

"Seven hundred and fifty."

"Seven hundred and fifty wounded men! Hospital gangrene, and half a box of lemons!"

"Well, that was all we could get; Government provides none; but our Chaplain is from Boston—his wife has written to friends there and expects a box next week!"

"To Boston for a box of lemons!"

I went to the head nurse . . . who . . . gave me writing materials, and I wrote a short note to the *New York Tribune:*

"Hospital gangrene has broken out in Washington, and we want lemons! *lemons!* LEMONS! LEMONS! No man or woman in health, has a right to a glass of lemonade until these men have all they need; send us lemons!"

I signed my name and mailed it immediately, and it appeared next morning. That day Schuyler Colfax sent a box to my lodgings, and five dollars in a note, bidding me send to him if more were wanting; but that day lemons began to pour into Washington, and soon, I think, into every hospital in the land. Gov. Andrews sent two hundred boxes to the Surgeon General. I received so many, that at one time there were twenty ladies, several of them with ambulances, distributing those which came to my address, and if there was any more hospital gangrene that season I neither saw nor heard of it.

The officers in Campbell [Hospital] knew of the letter, and were glad of the supplies it brought, but some time passed before they identified the writer as the little sister in the bad ward, who had won the reputation of being the "best wound-dresser in Washington."

[In recognition of her work, the surgeon in charge made an exception to his rule of not permitting women nurses on his staff, and arranged for her to live at the hospital. When Jane Swisshelm refers to "nurses," these are usually male nurses.]

COST OF ORDER

In making molds and rests for mangled limbs, I had large demands for little cushions, and without economy could not get enough. When one just fitted a place I wanted to keep it, and to do this, must have it aired, perhaps washed. To avoid lint dressings, I hunted pieces of soft, table linen, gave to patients pieces to suit, and as the supply was short they would get nurses and surgeons to leave their pieces of linen, after dressing their wounds until I should take charge, and have them cleansed for next time. To do all this, I must use the grass-plats and railings for airing and drying cushions and rags. These plats and railings were for ornament, and there was soon a protest against putting them to "such vile uses." I had gone into the hospital with the stupid notion that its primary object was the care and comfort of the sick and wounded. It was long after that I learned that a vast majority of all benevolent institutions are gotten up to gratify the aesthetic tastes of the public; exhibit the wealth and generosity of the founders, and furnish places for officers. The beneficiaries of the institutions are simply an apology for their existence, and having furnished that apology, the less said about them the better.

The surgeons of Campbell did really want its patients to be happy and get well; but it was a model institution, with a reputation to sustain; was part of a system under general laws, which might not be broken with impunity. There was no law against a man dying for want of sleep from pain caused by a misplaced muscle; but the statutes against litter were as inexorable as those of the Medes and Persians. The Campbell surgeons winked at my litter, until one regular inspection day, when my cushions and rags, clean and unclean, those marked John Smith, and those labeled Tom Brown, were all huddled up and stuffed *en masse* into the pantry closet.

I used to wonder if the Creator has invented a new variety of idiot, and made a lot in order to supply the army with medical inspectors, or, if by some cunning military device, the Surgeon-General had been able to select all those conglomerations of official dignity and asinine stupidity, from the open donkey-market of the world. . . .

One day we had a particularly searching inspection, and next day nurse told me of some four new cases which had been brought in a week before, one of whom the inspectors said was past hope. I found his feet and legs with a crust on them like the shell of a snail; had a piece of rubber cloth laid under them, and with tepid water, a good crash towel, and plenty of rubbing, got down to the skin, which I rubbed well with lard. Then with fresh towels and water at hand, I drew away the sheet in which the patient had rolled his head, and while I washed his head and arms and breast, I talked, and he tried to answer. . . .

When I had done washing and given directions to a nurse to cleanse the balance of his person, I asked if there was anything more I could do for him, when he stammered:

"Not unless you could get me a cup of tea—a cup of good green tea, 'thout any milk or sugar in it. If you do, I'll pay you for it."

"Pay me for it, will you? and how much will you give me—three cents?"

"Oh, I'll give you twenty-five cents."

"Twenty-five cents for a cup of good green tea, without any milk or sugar in it!"

I called the ward to witness the bargain, said I should grow rich at that rate, and hurried off for the tea.

I had a little silver tray and tea-set, with two china cups. Mrs. Gangewer, of the Ohio Aid Society, had sent me a tin tea-kettle and spirit-lamp; folks at a distance had sent plenty of the best tea; and that little tea-tray had become a prominent feature of Campbell long before this poor fellow specified his want. I made the tray unusually attractive that day, and fed him his tea from a spoon, while he admired the tiny pot, out of which, with the aid of the kettle, I could furnish twenty cups of good tea. When I had served all in that ward who wanted tea, the first one took a second cup, and while taking it his skin grew moist, and I knew he was saved from that death of misplaced matter vulgarly called "dirt," to which well-paid medical inspectors had consigned him, while giving their invaluable scientific attention to floor-scrubbing and bed-making, to whitewashing and laundry work.

I doubt if there were a Medical Inspector in the army who was not a first rate judge of the art of folding and ironing a sheet or pillow-slip; of the particular tuck which brought out the outlines of the corners of a mattress, as seen through a counterpane; and of the art and mystery of cleaning a floor. It did seem as if they had all reached office through their great proficiency as cabin-boys.

Next day I went to that ward with my tea-tray; and after learning that that man had been washed once more, asked him if he wanted another cup of tea.

"I'd like to have one," he stammered; "but I didn't pay you for the last one, and I can't find my wallet!"

I saw the debt troubled him, and took this as one more evidence that somewhere there were people who sold hospital stores to sick soldiers. So I took pains to explain that he owed me nothing; that the tea was his—ladies had sent it to me to give to him—and all the pay they wanted was for him to get well, and go home to his mother.

The idea that some one was thinking for him seemed to do him almost as much good as the tea.

I left Campbell next day, but on my first visit found him convalescing, and on the second visit he ran down the ward holding his sides and laughing, and I saw or heard of him no more.

LEARN TO CONTROL PIEMIA

About ten days after I went to Campbell, I was called at midnight to a death-bed. It was a case of flesh-wound in the thigh, and the whole limb was swollen almost to bursting, so cold as to startle by the touch, and almost as transparent as glass. I knew this was piemia and that for it medical science had no cure; but I wanted to warm that cold limb, to call circulation back to that inert mass. The first thought was warm, wet compresses, hot bricks, hot flannel; but the kitchen was locked, and it was little I could do without fire, except to receive and write down his dying messages to parents, and the girl who was waiting to be his wife.

When the surgeon's morning hour came he still lived; and at my suggestion the warm compresses were applied. He said, "they feel so good," and was quite comforted by them, but died about ten o'clock. I was greatly grieved to think he had suffered from cold the last night of life, but how avoid any number of similar occurrences? There was no artificial heat in any of the wards. A basin of warm water was only to be obtained by special favor of the cooks. . . .

[I decided to] lay my trouble before the cooks, who gathered to hear me tell the story of that death . . . and of my sorrow that I could not drive away the cold on that last, sad night.

They all wiped their eyes on their aprons; head cook went to a cupboard, brought a key and handed it to me, saying:

"There, mother, is a key of this kitchen; come in here whenever you please. We will always find room on the ranges for your bricks, and I'll have something nice in the cupboard every night for you and the nurses."

This proved to be the key to the situation, and after I received that bit of metal from cook, there was not one death from piemia in any ward where I was free to work, although I have had as many, I think, as sixty men struck with the premonitory chill, in one night. I concluded that "piemia" was French for neglect, and that the antidote was warmth, nourishing food, stimulants, friction, fresh air and cheerfulness, and did not hesitate to say that if death wanted to get a man out of my hands, he must send some other agent than piemia. I do not believe in the medical theory concerning it; do not believe pus ever gets into the veins, or that there is any poison about it, except that of ignorance and indifference on the part of doctors and nurses. . . .

[Later, Jane Swisshelm, over the strenuous objections of Superintendant of Nurses Dorothea Dix, went to the front at Fredericksburg, Md. She asked to be assigned to the "worst place, where there was most need," and found herself in the Old Theater.]

The Old Theater

This building was on Princess Ann street. The basement floor was level with the sidewalk, but the ground sloped upward at the back; so that the yard was higher than the floor. . . .

The mud was running in from the yard. Opposite the door, in a small room, was a pile of knapsacks and blankets; and on them lay two men smoking. To get into the large room, I must step out of the hall mud over one man, and be careful not to step on another. I think it was six rows of men that lay close on the floor, with just room to pass between the feet of each row; they so close in the rows that in most places I must slide one foot before the other to get to their heads.

The floor was very muddy and strewn with *debris,* principally of crackers. There was one hundred and eighty-two men in the building, all desperately wounded. They had been there a week. There were two leather water-buckets, two tin basins, and about every third man had saved his tin-cup or canteen; but no other vessel of any sort, size or description on the premises—no sink or cess-pool or drain. The nurses were not to be found; the men were growing reckless and despairing, but seemed to catch hope as I began to thread my way among them and talk. . . .

I found some of the nurses—cowards who had run away from battle, and now ran from duty—galvanized them into activity, invented substitutes for things that were wanting—making good use of an old knapsack and pocket-knife—and had tears of gratitude for pay.

One man lay near the front door, in a scant flannel shirt and cotton drawers, his left thigh cut off in the middle and the stump supported on the only pillow in the house. It was six by ten inches, stuffed with straw. His head was supported by two bits of board and a pair of very muddy boots. He called me, clutched my dress, and plead:

"Mother, can't you get me a blanket, I'm so cold; I could live if I could get any care!"

I went to the room where the men lay smoking on the blankets; but one of them wearing a surgeon's shoulderstraps, and speaking in a German accent, claimed them as his private property, and positively refused to yield one. The other man was his orderly, and words were useless— they kept their blankets. . . .

After I returned to the large room, I took notice about clothing, and found that most of the men had on their ordinary uniform; some had two blankets, more had one; but full one-third were without any. There was no shadow or pretense of a bed or pillow, not even a handful of straw or hay! . . . [She discovered that the wounded had not had a meat ration and had sustained themselves only by eating hardtack.]

I spoke the first night to Dr. Porter about blankets and straw, or hay for beds, but was assured that none were to be had. Supplies could not reach them since being cut off from their base, and the Provost Marshal, Gen. Patrick, would not permit anything to be taken out of the houses, though many of them were unoccupied, and well supplied with bedding and other necessaries. I thought we ought to get two blankets for those two naked men, if the Government should pay their weight in gold for them; and suggested that the surgeons take what was necessary for the comfort of the men, and give vouchers to the owners. I knew such claims would be honored; would see that they should be; but he said the matter had been settled by the Provost, and nothing more could be done. . . .

On Monday morning I sent for Dr. Porter, and stated the trouble about nurses shirking. He had them all summoned in the front end of the large room, and in presence of the patience, said to them:

"You see this lady? Well, you are to report to her for duty; and if she has any fault to find with you she will report you to the Provost-Marshal!"

I have never seen a set of men look more thoroughly subdued. There were eleven of them, and they all gave me the military salute. The doctor went off, and I set them to work. . . .

When there was so much to be done, I would do the most

needful thing first, and this was ridding the wounds of worms and gangrene, supporting the strength of the men by proper food, and keeping the air as pure as possible. I got our beef into the way of being boiled, and would have some good substantial broth made around it. I went on a foraging expedition—found a coal-scuttle which would do for a slop-pail, and confiscated it, got two bits of board, by which it could be converted into a stool, and so bring the great rest of a change of position to such men as could sit up; had a little drain made with a bit of board for a shovel, and so kept the mud from running in at the side door; melted the tops off some tin cans, and made them into drinking cups; had two of my men confiscate a large tub from a brewery, set it in the vestibule to wash rags for outside covers to wounds, to keep off chill, and had others bring bricks and rubbish mortar from a ruin across the street, to make substitutes for pillows.

I dressed wounds! dressed wounds, and made thorough work of it. In the church was a dispensary, where I could get any washes or medicines I wished, and I do not think I left a worm. Some of them were over half an inch long, with black heads and many feet, but most were maggots. They were often deeply seated, but my syringe would drive them out, and twice a day I followed them up. The black and green places grew smaller and better colored with every dressing. The men grew stronger with plenty of beef and broth and canned milk. I put citric acid and sugar in their apple sauce as a substitute for lemons. I forget how many thigh stumps I had, but I think as many as twelve. . . .

[After the Battle of the Wilderness, Fredericksburg was evacuated, and Jane Swisshelm had to leave on a transport with the wounded.]

Some months after leaving Fredricksburg, I was walking on Pennsylvania Avenue, when the setting sun shone in my face, and a man in uniform stopped me, saying:

"Excuse me! you do not know me, but I know you!"

I turned, looked at him carefully, and said:

"I do not know you!"

"Oh, no! but the last time you saw me, you cut off my beard with your scissors and fed me with a teaspoon. When you left me you did not think you would ever see me again."

"Oh!" I exclaimed joyfully, "you are Dutton."

He laughed, and replied, "That's me. I have just got a furlough and am going home." . . .

This is all I have ever heard from or of the men with whose lives mine was so knit during that terrible time.

I fear that not many survived, and doubt if a dozen of them ever knew me by any other name than that of "Mother."

38. Organized charity

The earliest women's organizations grew out of church work. Women meet weekly in sewing circles and in the so-called "cent societies" in which they contributed one cent a week as dues. Proceeds were used to support missionary work abroad or welfare work at home. From such activities it was only a small step to forming separate welfare and charitable institutions. Quaker women in Pennsylvania pioneered in organizing orphan asylums, free schools for the poor and for black children, and prison aid societies. Other religious denominations did not lag far behind.

The Society for the Relief of Poor Widows with Small Children, formed by Mrs. Isabella Graham and fifteen ladies in New York City in November 1797, was typical of these early charitable organizations. The women organized their charity in a businesslike manner, keeping careful accounts and disbursing funds according to rules and bylaws. Their effort was aimed at helping the "worthy poor" and at creating jobs for poor women. From a modest beginning they expanded steadily. In 1816 they supported 202 women and 500 children. The organization continued well into the twentieth century as "The Society for Relief of Women and Children."

Charitable activity of this kind was organized by women in every community. Document B illustrates this kind of work on the Oregon frontier in the 1870s.

Club activities of black women followed quite similar patterns, as document C illustrates.

The dedication, persistence and organizational talents of tens of thousands of anonymous women in the nation's communities helped to alleviate suffering and provided needed social services long before the political leadership recognized such needs. As the documents here show, women often progressed from charitable and welfare services to setting up orphanages, hospitals, and educational institutions. What is important here is not only the scattered activity of small groups of women, which has remained unnoticed and generally neglected. More important is the suggestion of a developmental pattern of community building, whereby the early infrastructure is created and maintained through the voluntary association of women, who then proceed to institution building. Frequently, such institutions, once established, become "businesses" or are taken over by the community as public institutions. In either case, they are then headed by a man and led by corporate trustees, usually also men. Once institutions have reached that stage, they are noted as "existing" by historians. Thus, the community-sustaining initiative of women remains outside of history, while that of men is noticed and thereby validated. Research into this huge neglected field of local work should yield valuable insights.

[A]

CONSTITUTION

Among the many humane institutions in this city, there is none for the particular assistance of a large class of sufferers, who have peculiar claims on the public beneficence, viz. POOR WIDOWS WITH SMALL CHILDREN.

Commiserating their situation, and persuaded that none can be relieved with happier effect, a number of Ladies have formed, for their exclusive aid, a Society upon the following

Constitution of the Ladies Society, established in New York, for the Relief of Poor Widows with Small Children (New York: James Oram, 1800); *By-Laws and Regulations of the Society for the Relief of Poor Widows with Small Children* (New York: Printed for the Society, J. Seymour, 1811), pp. 5–8. Both used courtesy of the New-York Historical Society.

PLAN

the name of the society SHALL BE, *The Society for the Relief of Poor Widows with Small Children.*

[The details of the Constitution were revised in 1811 as follows:]

BY-LAWS AND REGULATIONS

Every Manager shall insert in a book the name, place of abode, and circumstances of every widow whom she relieves; the ages of her children; and the kind and amount of the relief granted to each family. . . .

Relief shall be given in necessaries, never in money, but by special vote of the Board.

It shall be the duty of the Manager to report to the Board from time to time, such widows under her care as have children of age to be bound to trades, or put out to service.

Every Manager shall confine her expenditures within the sum allowed, except in cases of sickness. . . .

Any poor widow of fair character, having two children under ten years of age, may, on application, be entitled to the attention and bounty of this society.

If any widow be seen begging publicly, either by means of a petition or otherwise, after having been cautioned against it by her Manager; her name shall be erased from the books of the Society.

Any woman applying to the society for relief on account of the supposed death of her husband, must satisfy the Manager that he has not been heard of for twelve months and of the probability of his death. . . .

No widow shall be assisted, who, having a child fit for service, will not consent to its being put out to trade or service to a suitable person, if such can be found, unless special reasons can be given to the contrary.

No widow shall be deprived of, or suspended from receiving, the society's bounty, either by the Directress or Managers, except by vote of the Board.

Relief shall not be granted to any applicant, till she be

visited at her dwelling by one of the Managers, and particular inquiry made into her character and circumstances. Immorality excludes from the patronage of the society.

No widow who possesses property, the interest of which is sufficient to pay her house-rent, shall be entitled to relief from this society.

No widow who sells spirituous liquors shall be relieved by this society.

A widow with one child under ten years of age, and who is charged with an aged parent, entirely incapable of maintaining him or herself, or who has a child having any natural infirmity, so as to prevent it from being put out to a trade or service, shall be assisted. . . .

REPORT

In 1802, the Society had become so respectable, and the blessings disseminated by them so universally acknowledged, that the Legislature constituted them a body corporate, by the name of "The Society for the relief of Poor Widows with Small Children," and in 1803, granted them the privilege of raising by lottery, the sum of 15,000 dollars to meet and alleviate the increased and multiplied miseries occasioned by the Yellow Fever that year.

[In 1804 the Board of Directors, with the aid of the above funds provided by the City of New York through a lottery, purchased a house and established in it a workshop for spinning flax, a tailor shop and sales room, and a school.]

On receiving such a large addition to their Funds, the Society turned their views to an object which had long been the subject of much anxiety, without the means of obtaining relief, viz. the number of children on their books growing up in habits of idleness, and its native consequence, vice.—They had ever been industrious in filling up all the vacancies in the different Charity Schools; and a select

List of Additional Subscribers to the Society for the Relief of Poor Widows with Small Children n.p., 1804.

number of young ladies (an honor to their sex!) had offered their own personal services—engaged in, and succeeded beyond the Society's most sanguine expectations, in teaching 20 girls the arts of reading and sewing; still the number for whom no means was provided, was great.

There are now in different parts of the suburbs, where the poor reside, three schools taught by widows, supported by the Society, and are visited, examined, and the minds of the children stored with religious and moral instruction. . . .

[B]

THE LADIES' RELIEF SOCIETY
PORTLAND, OREGON

March 20, 1867, a little band of women met in the basement of the First Presbyterian Church . . . to consider how best to systematize their efforts for the relief of the poor of Portland. Previous to this the few families needing aid were chiefly those who had crossed the plains, and who had exhausted their little means. When, in the fall, the long trains of emigrant wagons wended their way down through the valleys they were cordially met and their wants relieved. Thirty-two ladies composed the society, which was then organized under the name of the "Ladies' Relief Society." These women represented no one denomination.

For several years the mode of raising funds was by giving various kinds of entertainments, the well remembered amateur concerts, literary festivals, sociables, bazaars and charity balls. These were liberally patronized by all classes of citizens.

In a few years the great number of forsaken and neglected children appealed strongly to the sympathies of the members of the society, and the need of a home where they could be kept and cared for was discussed. A committee was ap-

M. O. Douthit, *The Souvenir of Western Women* (Portland: Anderson & Duniway Co., 1905), pp. 119–120.

pointed to look for a suitable house and also for a matron to take charge of it.

July 8, 1871, a special meeting was called to consider the expediency of purchasing a piece of land and erecting a building. The minutes of that meeting read as follows: "Two lots and a small house across the creek have been offered for sale at $2000, which business men think cheap and desirable for our purpose." It was unanimously voted that the purchase be made.

Since at that time an incorporation composed of women only could not legally hold real estate, some of the leading business men of the city became members of the relief society, and acted as its board of trustees.

In 1880 a block of land in South Portland, on Corbett Street, was donated by Henry Villard, of New York. Through the liberality of friends the handsome and commodious building erected upon it and now occupied as "The Home" was completed in November, 1884, free of debt. Beautiful grounds surround the home. . . .

The home accomodates [!] 100 children. The age limits are, for girls, from 3 to 14 years; for boys, from 3 to 10 years. The nurseries are large and well supplied with beautiful toys and nursery books, showered upon the home by the children of the well-to-do and the rich, who delight to share their numerous gifts with the poor ones who find shelter here.

More than 2000 children have been cared for, many of whom were placed, by adoption, in good families, and have grown up useful members of society.

To fit the girls for self-support, training in domestic science is given insofar as means and circumstances will permit. A systematic domestic training school is hoped for in the near future.

The sick in the home have been attended by physicians of the city gratuitously.

For a few years a donation from the state was given the

home, though for the greater part it has been supported through the efforts of the society and the munificence of the people. . . .

The work of the relief society has not been confined to the maintenance of the home. Until the support by the state was withdrawn and the work of the home had grown into large proportions, the society attended systematically to its first work, ward visiting, thereby keeping in touch with the poor families of the city and ministering to their wants intelligently.

[C]

The following accounts of black women's club activity were typical of those reported to the 1906 convention of the National Association of Colored Women. This organization, founded in 1896, united over 100 local women's clubs. In 1914 it consisted of twenty-eight state federations and 1,000 clubs. Its 1968 membership was 850,000.

Like their white counterparts, black club women were concerned with self- and community improvement, but the greater social needs of their group were reflected in their emphasis on welfare and educational work. The kind of social and welfare services, which were tax supported and communally administered in the white community, were frequently denied to black communities due to race prejudice. Through the initiative and effort of black club women the black community set up its own welfare institutions, which were financed through private contributions of the kind exemplified in these documents.

PHILLIS WHEATLEY HOME ASSOCIATION OF DETROIT

The Phillis Wheatley Home Association of Detroit, Michigan was organized in 1897, the object being the establishment of a home for our aged colored women. In 1897 a few earnest women met . . . and they were without funds but each one contributed her might [!] and the Committee

Mary Margaret Washington Papers, Tuskegee Archives. Courtesy of Tuskegee Institute.

rented a building. Furnishings were solicited . . . applications were received and on our opening day seven old ladies were received in the Phillis Wheatley Home. In 1901 the Phillis Wheatley Home Association was incorporated under the state laws, and seeing the necessity of having a permanent building, we purchased the property at 176 East Elizabeth Street at a cost of $4000, paying $1300 cash. We had [!] at present 12 inmates. . . . We have 24 members, regular meetings are held every Tuesday evening. Cash receipts (from donations for the past two years, 1904–1906) includes $1847. Respectfully submitted, Eliza Wilson, President.

THE ST. LOUIS COLORED ORPHAN HOME
ST. LOUIS, JULY 8, 1906

Dear Sisters and Co-workers for God and the promotion of the welfare of our race. In submitting to you a report of our work we do not intend to weary you with a lengthy report. . . . Today we give you the report of three months labor, which resulted in the hearty cooperation of our people. "Orphans Home Day" free will offerings represent the churches, Sunday schools, secret, benevolent, and social organizations of St. Louis and vicinity. . . . We gave two Day Excursions just one week apart, 25th of June and 2nd of July, and of course we feel very proud to submit the financial report of this effort. Especially because it truly represents race effort, for there is not in this over fifty Dollars contributed by our white friends. We would not have you think they are not generous to our work they are. *But these* are our special Days.

Total [funds raised through these activities]		$1576.00
Paid on Principal	$1000.00	
For carpentry, painting & roofing	164.00	
Special Sewer Tax	200.00	
Total	$1364.00	$1364.00
Balance		$ 212.00

SUMMARY OF FIVE YEARS.

Dec. 1901 we came in possession of property by paying $1200 cash. Have raised and paid during five years on principal $4500. Paid on Interest $930.00. Improvements and repairs $1200.00. Making a total on property $7830. Besides meeting the current expenses of the Home *this* represents the co-operation of *our* people in St. Louis. . . . Yours Sincerely, Interest Note Club, Wardrobe Club and Nursery Club Board of Managers, Mrs. M. L. Harrison Pres.

II

Women in Male-Defined Society

CHAPTER FIVE

The Right to Learn, the Right to Teach, the Right to Think

The problems women faced in acquiring education were threefold: they had to win the right to learn, the right to teach, and the right to think. The right to learn implied both the right of access to educational institutions and the overcoming of institutional practices and structures which prevented the equal education of women. It also meant overcoming society's prejudices against educated women. The right to teach meant access to and equality of status in the various levels of the teaching profession. Frequently, it also meant the setting up of sex-segregated institutions, which became a means for defining and controlling the content and shape of women's education. The right to think depended on winning the other two rights and on raising several generations of women, who had been educated in the male-defined and male-dominated culture. It meant affording such women and others enough time, leisure, institutional support, and cultural prodding to define their goals, problems, and intellectual priorities. Historically, the above progression has defined the chronological development of women's educational emancipation. Comparative studies, by nationality, race, or class, show that this holds true cross-culturally.

The right to learn, for American women, has meant first a struggle against illiteracy—always greater among women than men—then the right of access to all educational levels. In the Eastern seaboard colonies, girls shared the same rudimentary education with boys in dame schools, but were barred from more advanced learning.* In the Southern colonies, elementary education was more a privilege of class than of sex. In the wake of the American Revolution, private academies and seminaries for girls began to offer education through the early teen years, but it was separate and inferior education and was affordable only for the economically privileged (see document 39). The pre-Civil War era saw the demand for female education challenging patriarchal prejudices and institutional restrictions. Arguments in favor of female education began to proliferate and the furtherance of female education became the primary way in which an early feminism found its expression (see documents 40 and 41). The resistance of established institutions led to the formation of a separate system of higher education for girls. Simultaneously, the spread of the common school raised the demand for teachers and with it opened new educational opportunities to women. American communities wanted female teachers regardless of their level of training; women wanted educational opportunities. In struggling for the right to teach, women advanced their claims for equal education.

At the very period when women were exhorted to regard the home as their only proper sphere, communities discovered that women were the natural teachers of youth and could do the job better than men. Women now were preferred for such employment, provided that they worked for one-third of the pay given to men. In the 1840s, the wages of male and female teachers were respectively:

	male	female
Vermont	$12.00/month	$4.75
New York	14.96	6.69
Massachusetts	24.51	9.07

The result was predictable: by 1888, 63 percent of all teachers were women; in the cities alone women were 90 percent of all teachers. Elementary school teaching had become a female profession.

* In New England female literacy remained at 47 percent of the female population until 1800, while male literacy rose to 90 percent as a result of the establishment of common schools. Kenneth A. Lockridge, *Literacy in Colonial New England* (New York: W. W. Norton, 1974), p. 4.

Women teachers were subject also to discriminatory restrictions on their advancement, even after the occupation had become professionalized with the 1857 founding of the National Teachers Association. By 1953 women were 93 percent of the primary school teachers, 60 percent of the secondary school teachers, but less than 25 percent of the professional teachers and staff in higher education. A 1960 census analysis showed that both male and female elementary school teachers were paid wages far below those to which their educational qualifications entitled them (47 percent below in the case of male teachers, 52 percent below in the case of female teachers). The percentage by which the median wage of such teachers related to the average wage of all U.S. male workers was 3 percent above for male teachers, 15 percent below for female teachers. Thus, while both male and female teachers were grossly underpaid, female teachers as late as 1960 were paid far less than men of the same educational qualifications. Despite Susan B. Anthony's eloquent protest and despite one hundred years of organizational effort, sex discrimination was the rule in school teaching* (see document 43).

The fact that prior to the Civil War, of all institutions of higher learning, only Oberlin College admitted women, spurred the formation of women's colleges. The pioneering institution of this kind was Mount Holyoke founded by Mary Lyon in 1837, to be followed in 1865 by Vassar and, in rapid succession, Smith, Wellesley, Bryn Mawr, Barnard, and Radcliffe colleges. Beginning with the land grant colleges in the West, universities increasingly opened their doors to women, first on the college level and then for graduate training as well. In the last decade of the nineteenth century a college-educated elite of American women was clamoring for acceptance in all professions without discrimination.

The establishment of separate women's colleges created a demand for female administrative and executive talent. However, even in women's colleges the majority of teaching and administra-

* Statistical references: Thomas Woody, *A History of Women's Education in the United States*, 2 vols. (New York: Science Press, 1929), I: 492–493; and U.S., Bureau of the Census, *1960 Census of Population*, Subject Report PC(2)-7A, "Occupational Characteristics" (Washington, D.C.: U.S. Govt. Printing Office, 1960), as cited in Barbara Deckard, *The Women's Movement: Political, Socioeconomic, and Psychological Issues* (New York: Harper & Row, 1975), p. 115.

tive jobs were held by men as late as 1972, while in the administration of coeducational colleges women remain a minority to this day.

A 1972 report on the status of women in academe based on 125 reports by academic institutions yielded the following generalizations: 20 percent of all college teachers were women, but their distribution was a function of institutional ranking.* The more prestigious the educational institution, the fewer numbers of women on the faculty. Women comprised 25.6 percent of faculty at two-year colleges, 22.7 percent at four-year colleges, 14.8 percent at universities, and at elite schools their faculty representation drops to 2 percent. Women were discriminated against in pay, promotions, tenure, the granting of fellowships and finally, in appointments to academic administration. In administration the old rule still holds—(1) the higher the position, the fewer the women, and (2) administrative units typically are headed by men and staffed by women (see document 46).

Despite governmental pressure for affirmative action under Title VII of the Civil Rights Act of 1964, the equalization of women's status in higher education is proceeding at a snail's pace. Gains made in the past five years are already being eroded by financial troubles in the academic world and by the decline in enrollment and expected enrollment due to the falling birth rate. Thus, it has been estimated that if upgrading of women in the academic establishment proceeded under affirmative action at the same rate as it has been going, it would take over a hundred years for equalization to be achieved.

Historically, American women have been outsiders, marginal to the educational institutions of the nation. Much of their history in the past 150 years has been a struggle for access and equal opportunity. Marginality and lack of opportunity has been reinforced by psychological indoctrination. Women have been told for centuries that abstract thought is beyond their capacity. From the supposedly "smaller female brain" to the "frail female physique" to the "scientifically proven" lesser capacity of women for abstract reasoning there has been a steady stream of discouragement directed at women. In this respect the analogy between American

* Lora H. Robinson, "Institutional Variation in the Status of Academic Women," in *Academic Women on the Move*, ed. Alice S. Rossi and Ann Calderwood (New York: Russell Sage Foundation, 1973), p. 202 *passim.*

women and minority groups, such as American Blacks, is quite apt. The deleterious effect of extended marginality and indoctrination to inferiority on the overall achievement, self-perception, and motivation of groups of people has been extensively documented and analyzed.* Far too little attention has been given to this pervasive fact in the history of women.

Lastly, the societal assumption that the primary function of all women is childrearing and family nurture has been expressed institutionally in many subtle ways. Scheduling of education, job training, and work has developed so as to fit the male life cycle. It assumes that domestic supporting services are provided by some woman, and it favors the single and childless person. Women who study and work have had to fit into these patterns, whether this meant postponing childbearing or carrying the burden of full-time work plus homemaking. This has meant that woman's time (each day and over the long run) is time which can be interrupted for whatever needs and crises arise. The time of men, their work, study, and thinking time, is respected as private. The metaphor so felicitously used by Virginia Woolf—a woman's greatest need is for a room of her own—expressed not only the need for physical privacy—a place, but more importantly the need for private time.

At first glance it may appear that it requires no social struggle or historical development to exericse one's right to think, a capacity inherent in humanity which cannot be restrained by social conditions. This is certainly true for thought generated by daily living— although thought at that level is also affected by social conditioning. But at the creative and abstract level of mental activity, where theories and systems of theories can be generated, women have been notably deficient—a fact which is not infrequently used to justify their neglect by historians. Women just have not made "important contributions" to the history of ideas.

The achievement of abstract thought and the creation of theories depend on education in the best of the existing tradition and acceptance by a peer group of educated persons who, by means of criticism and interaction, provide "cultural prodding"; and it demands private time. Women, historically, have been denied all of

* Cf. Helen Hacker, "Women as a Minority Group," *Social Forces* 30 (Oct. 1951): 60–69; Ann Sutherland Harris, "The Second Sex in Academe," *AAUP Bulletin* 55, no. 3: 283–295; and Matina S. Horner, "Women's Will to Fail," *Psychology Today* 3 (1969):36–38, 62.

these and, despite a few notable exceptions, women have not attempted to create theories. It is no accident that the few women who have been achieving at this level have done so by sacrificing private and family life.

The data in document 46 substantiate the disproportionately low representation of women in the higher ranks of academe and the persistently low percentage of women recipients of foundation grants. Such discrimination extending over decades, even centuries, must result in a thwarting of creative and intellectual potential and in a loss of female talent.

For women, the most unattainable of the preconditions for abstract thinking has been "cultural prodding," which is institutionalized in the upper reaches of the academic establishment and in such outside equivalents as "think tanks." Only since the development of the modern feminist movement with its turbulent intellectual activity and its network of female support systems, can a few women hope to share in the preconditions for creative thought which male intellectuals of superior talents have long taken for granted. Thus the absence of "great" female minds, of women who build theories and systems of theories based on their own ideas and life experiences and on the cultural heritage of their nation, can be explained as a result of a particular historical deprivation. It should disappear in one or more generations.

39. Education for young ladies

One of the earliest female academies, the Young Ladies' Academy of Philadelphia was the first to be publicly incorporated. Under the direction of John Poor, it opened in Philadelphia on June 4, 1787. Its purpose was to instruct "Young Ladies in Reading, Writing, Arithmetic, English Grammar, Composition, Rhetoric, and Geography." A board of "gentlemen Visitors" supervised its work and every few months gave its pupils a public examination, awarding prizes in "reading, spelling, arithmetic, writing, English grammar, geography." The winners in these categories were awarded "premiums," but during the first year of operations the board "recommended to the parents of the children obtaining premiums, to repay the Principal for the same . . . inasmuch as honor is the object sought after, and not profit."

In June 1789 premiums for "good behavior" were added to the others. In that year the commencement address was given by the Rev. Dr. Sproat, one of the board members. It expresses the attitude of the educators and parents regarding the education of "the fair sex." The tradition-bound indoctrination of the young ladies to "accomplishments" had as its goal "to molify the temper, refine the manners, amuse the fancy, improve the understanding, and strengthen virtue—to lay a foundation for a life of usefulness and happiness here, and if rightly improved, for a blessed immortality hereafter."

Later, a "Gentleman who attended the Commencement" expressed the good of such education poetically: "To form the maiden for th' accomplish'd wife, And fix the basis of a happy life!"

The academy, which attracted students from every state of the Union and from as far as Canada and the West Indies, obviously encouraged its students to accept these educational principles with grace. Several of the valedictories express such agreeable sentiments and are fulsome in their praise of the principal and the

The Rise and Progress of the Young-Ladies' Academy of Philadelphia . . . (Philadelphia: Stewart and Cochran, 1794). I am indebted to Prof. Linda Kerber, Department of History, University of Iowa, for bringing this source to my attention.

teachers. All the more astonishing is the confident and self-consciously feminist expression in the valedictory oration given in June 1792 by Molly Wallace, in which she defends the propriety of women speaking in public.

Her sentiments were echoed in the valedictory oration given by Miss Eliza Laskey the following year, 1793. During that same commencement, the salutatory oration offered by Miss Priscilla Mason not only reiterates the same sentiments, but accuses "our high and mightly lords" of denying women the means of knowledge, and refers to women as a sex doomed "to servile or frivolous employments" for the purpose of degrading their minds so that men "might hold unrivall'd, the power and pre-eminence they had usurped." An increasing awareness of the need to widen the sphere of activity for educated (even slightly educated) women seems to be a direct outgrowth of lowering educational barriers. The same tendency showed up over and over again, as the students in female academies graduated into a world which frustrated their expectations of contributing to the work of society.

Rev. Doctor Sproat

The education of youth in the various branches of useful knowledge, appears to be highly important, by the attention paid to it among all nations in a civilized state. Hence we find all polished nations have been peculiarly careful to found and support seminaries of learning, where the rising generation may be furnished with the best means of instruction, to render them advantageous to themselves, and of public utility in future life. . . . The instruction of female youth, till of late, has not been sufficiently attended to amongst us. . . . The Ladies' Academy, is a new institution in this city. And I cannot but hope, that the plan of female education, now adopted and prosecuted in this excellent seminary, will merit the approbation and patronage of all who wish well to the learning, virtue and piety of the rising fair of this metropolis. The proficiency these delicate pupils have made, in several branches of useful literature, not only displays the fertility of their blooming geniuses, but reflects honor on the abilities, and praise to the attention of their worthy Preceptor and his assistants in their instruction. Accuracy in orthography, a very necessary part of an early education—reading with propriety their native language—an acquaintance with English grammar—writing a neat and beautiful character—a knowledge of figures, with many of their valuable uses—a general knowledge of the different parts of the terraqueous globe—its divisions, inhabitants, and productions—such knowledge of the planets that compose the solar system, and their periodical motions—together with such a sketch of history, as to remark the rise, progress, declension, and final extinction of the most remarkable states, kingdoms and empires—the virtues which contributed to their greatness, and the vices which were productive of their ruin—these are such valuable branches of literature, as are not only ornamental, but in many respects exceedingly advantageous to the rising generation of the fair sex. Let it suffice to say, that such academical improvements, tend to molify the temper, refine the manners, amuse the fancy, improve the understanding, and strengthen virtue—to lay a foundation for a life of usefulness and happiness here, and if rightly improved, for a blessed immortality hereafter. . . .

[The following lines were written by a "GENTLEMAN who attended the Commencement."]

> On the soft accents of the female tongue,
> To rapt attention every nerve was strung.
> While decent confidence, and modest grace,
> Diffus'd a lustre o'er each charming face!
> Delightful talk, t'expand the human mind,
> With virtue, knowledge, sentiment refin'd—
> To teach th'aspiring faculties to soar,
> And the bright realms of science to explore;
> To form the maiden for th'accomplished wife,
> And fix the basis of a happy life!

Miss Molly Wallace

The silent and solemn attention of a respectable audience, has often, at the beginning of discourses intimidated even veterans in the art of public elocution. What then must my situation be, when my sex, my youth and inexperience all conspire to make me tremble at the task which I have undertaken? But the friendly encouragement, which I behold in almost every countenance, enables me to overcome difficulties, that would otherwise be insurmountable. With some, however, it has been made a question, whether we ought *ever* to appear in so public a manner. Our natural timidity, the domestic situation to which, by nature and custom we seem destined, are urged as arguments against what I now have undertaken:—Many sarcastical observations have been handed out against female oratory: But to what do they amount? Do they not plainly inform us, that, because we are females, we ought therefore to be deprived of what is perhaps the most effectual means of acquiring a just, natural and graceful delivery? No one will pretend to deny, that we should be taught to read in the best manner. And if to read, why not to speak? . . .

. . . But yet it may be asked, what, has a female character to do with declamation? That she should harangue at the head of an Army, in the Senate, or before a popular Assembly, is not pretended, neither is it requested that she ought be be an adept in the stormy and contentious eloquence of the bar, or in the abstract and subtle reasoning of the Senate;—we look not for a female Pitt, Cicero, or Demosthenes. . . .

Why is a boy diligently and carefully taught the Latin, the Greek, or the Hebrew language, in which he will seldom have occasion, either to write or converse? Why is he taught to demonstrate the propositions of Euclid, when during his whole life, he will not perhaps make use of one of them? Are we taught to dance merely for the sake of becoming dancers? No, certainly. These things are commonly studied, more on account of the habits, which the learning of them establishes, than on account of any important advantages which the mere knowledge of them can afford. So a young lady, from the exercise of speaking before a properly selected audience, may acquire some valuable habits, which, otherwise she can obtain from no examples, and that no precept can give. But, this exercise can with propriety be performed only before a select audience: a promiscuous and indiscriminate one, for obvious reasons, would be absolutely unsuitable, and should always be carefully avoided. . . .

Miss Priscilla Mason

. . . Respected and very respectable audience; while your presence inspires our tender minds with fear and anxiety, your countenances promise indulgence, and encourage us to proceed. . . .

A female, young and inexperienced, addressing a promiscuous assembly, is a novelty which requires an apology, as some may suppose. I therefore, with submission, beg leave to offer a few thoughts in vindication of female eloquence. . . .

Is a power of speech, and volubility of expression, one of the talents of the orator? Our sex possess it in an eminent degree.

Do personal attractions give charms to eloquence, and force to the orator's arguments? . . . Do tender passions enable the orator to speak in a moving and forcible manner? . . . In all these respects the female orator stands on equal,—nay, on *superior* ground. . . .

Granted it is, that a perfect knowledge of the subject is essential to the accomplish'd Orator. But seldom does it happen, that the abstruse sciences, become the subject of eloquence. And, as to that knowledge which is popular and practical . . . who will say that the female mind is incapable?

Our high and mightly Lords (thanks to their arbitrary constitutions) have denied us the means of knowledge, and then reproached us for the want of it. Being the stronger party, they early seized the sceptre and the sword; with these they gave laws to society; they denied women the advantage of a liberal education; forbid them to exercise their talents on those great occasions, which would serve to improve them. They doom'd the sex to servile or frivolous employments, on purpose to degrade their minds, that they themselves might hold unrivall'd, the power and pre-eminence they had usurped. Happily, a more liberal way of thinking begins to prevail. . . . But supposing now that we possess'd all the talents of the orator, in the highest perfection; where shall we find a theatre for the display of them? The Church, the Bar, and the Senate are shut against us. Who shut them? *Man;* despotic man, first made us incapable of the duty, and then forbid us the exercise. Let us by suit-able education, qualify ourselves for those high departments—they will open before us. They *will*, did I say? They have done it already. Besides several Churches of less importance, a most numerous and respectable Soci-ety, has display'd its impartiality—I had almost said gallen-try [!] in this respect . . . The members of the enlightened and liberal Church, . . . look to the soul, and allow all to teach who are capable of it, be they male or female.

But Paul forbids it! Contemptible little body! The girls laughed at the deformed creature. To be revenged, he de-clares war against the whole sex: advises men not to marry them; and has the insolence to order them to keep silence in the Church—: afraid, I suppose, that they would say some-thing against celibacy, or ridicule the old bachelor.

With respect to the bar, citizens of either sex, have an undoubted right to plead their own cause there. Instances could be given of females being admitted to plead the cause of a friend, a husband, a son; and they have done it with energy and effect. I am assured that there is nothing in our laws or constitutions, to prohibit the licensure of female Attorneys. . . .

Heliogabalus, the Roman Emperor of blessed memory, made his grand-mother a Senator of Rome. He also established a senate of women; appointed his mother President; and committed to them the important business of regulating dress and fashions. . . . It would be worthy the wisdom of Congress, to consider whether a similar institution, established at the seat of our Federal Government, would not be a public benefit. . . . Such a Senate, composed of women most noted for wisdom, learning and taste, delegated from every part of the Union, would give dignity, and independence to our manners; uniformity, and even authority to our fashions. . . .

EMMA HART WILLARD (1787–1870)

40. A plan for improving female education

When, in 1819 Emma Willard presented the New York legislature with a well-reasoned plan for public-supported institutions of higher learning for women, she intended to prove, among other things, that girls were capable of absorbing and utilizing the same academic subjects offered to boys. Although her effort received the approval of Governor DeWitt Clinton, James Monroe, John Adams, and Thomas Jefferson, the New York legislature did not enact it. It granted a charter to her Waterford Academy for Young Ladies, but failed to provide the needed financial support. Emma Willard published her "Plan," saw it widely circulated, and concluded: ". . . when the people shall become convinced of the justice and expediency of placing both sexes more nearly on an equality, with respect to privilege of education, the Legislators will find it in their interest to make the proper provision."[*]

Emma Willard, "An Address to the Public; Particularly to the Members of the Legislature of New York, Proposing A Plan for Improving Female Education," 2d ed. (Middlebury: S. W. Copeland, 1819).

  [*] As cited in Alma Lutz, *Emma Willard: Pioneer Educator of American Women* (Boston: Beacon Press, 1964), p. 38.

Encouraged by the willingness of the town's Common Council to finance the purchase of a suitable building for a female seminary, Emma Willard moved her Waterford School to Troy, N.Y. Troy Female Seminary, founded in 1821, became the pioneering model institution for the higher education of women and for later normal schools for teacher education. Emma Willard's rigorous academic curriculum, combined with practical education in homemaking skills and her insistence on regular tests and public examinations, set standards for quality higher education for girls. Willard's seminary trained over 200 female teachers before any normal schools were established, and her graduates spread far and wide, staffing the nation's public schools.

In the course of her educational career Emma Willard wrote textbooks in geography, history, and science, which were widely used. In later life she assisted Henry Barnard in improving the Connecticut public schools.

Emma Willard was not a supporter of the organized woman's rights movement and, significantly, reasoned in her address to the legislature that women should be given higher education because, as mothers, they would affect the characters of future citizens of the republic. This argument is quite distinct from the feminist argument for improving female education because it would benefit women and implement their right to equality as citizens. Willard is at pains to show that she does not advocate the doctrine that women are "the legitimate children of the legislature" and entitled to "a share of their paternal bounty," which would lead to the "phantoms of a college-learned lady." She assures the legislators that she does not recommend "masculine education" for women. This conservative stance characterized Emma Willard's attitude throughout her career, yet despite it, the students who had benefited from her rigorous training and purposeful moral indoctrination became a moving force for American feminism. Some, like Elizabeth Cady Stanton, would take direct and personal leadership of the woman's movement; others in their role as professionally trained teachers became models for a new definition of womanhood. Still others, disappointed at finding professional opportunities closed to them upon their graduation from the seminary, would advance demands for the admission of women to colleges. The dynamic of her life work and theoretical contribution far exceeded the modest claims advanced by Emma Willard in her Address.

The object of this Address, is to convince the public, that a reform with respect to female education is necessary; that it cannot be effected by individual exertion, but that it requires the aid of the legislature; and further, by shewing the justice, the policy, and the magnanimity of such an undertaking, to persuade that body to endow a seminary for females, as the commencement of such reformation. . . .

DEFECTS IN THE PRESENT MODE OF FEMALE EDUCATION, AND THEIR CAUSES

Civilized nations have long since been convinced that education, as it respects males, will not, like trade, regulate itself; and hence, they have made it a prime object to provide that sex with everything requisite to facilitate their progress in learning: but female education has been left to the mercy of private adventurers; and the consequence has been to our sex, the same, as it would have been to the other, had legislatures left their accommodations, and means of instruction, to chance also.

. . . Male education flourishes, because, from the guardian care of legislatures, the presidencies and professorships of our colleges are some of the highest objects to which the eye of ambition is directed. Not so with female institutions. Preceptresses of these, are dependent on their pupils for support, and are consequently liable to become the victims of their caprice. In such a situation, it is not more desirable to be a preceptress, than it would be to be a parent, invested with the care of children, and responsible for their behaviour, but yet depending on them for subsistence, and destitute of power to enforce their obedience.

Feminine delicacy requires, that girls should be educated chiefly by their own sex. . . . Boarding schools, therefore, whatever may be their defects, furnish the best mode of education provided for females.

Concerning these schools it may be observed:

1. They are temporary institutions, formed by individuals, whose object is present emolument. But they cannot

be expected to be greatly lucrative; therefore, the individuals who establish them, cannot afford to provide suitable accommodations, as to room. At night, the pupils are frequently crowded in their lodging rooms; and during the day they are generally placed together in one apartment, where there is a heterogeneous mixture of different kinds of business, accompanied with so much noise and confusion, as greatly to impede their progress in study.

2.   As individuals cannot afford to provide suitable accommodations as to room, so neither can they afford libraries, and other apparatus, necessary to teach properly the various branches in which they pretend to instruct.

3.   Neither can the individuals who establish these schools afford to provide suitable instruction. It not infrequently happens, that one instructress teaches, at the same time and in the same room, ten or twelve distinct branches. If assistants are provided, such are usually taken as can be procured for a small compensation. . . .

4.   It is impossible, that in these schools such systems should be adopted and enforced, as are requisite for properly classing the pupils. Institutions for young gentlemen are founded by public authority, and are permanent; they are endowed with funds, and their instructors and overseers, are invested with authority to make such laws, as they shall deem most salutary. From their permanency, their laws and rules are well known. With their funds they procure libraries, philosophical apparatus, and other advantages, superior to what can elsewhere be found; and to enjoy these, individuals are placed under their discipline, who would not else be subjected to it. Hence the directors of these institutions can enforce, among other regulations, those which enable them to make a perfect classification of their students. They regulate their qualifications for entrance, the kind and order of their studies, and the period of their remaining at the seminary. Female schools present the reverse of this. Wanting permanency, and dependent on individual patronage, had they the wisdom to make salutary regulations, they could neither enforce nor purchase com-

pliance. The pupils are irregular in their times of entering and leaving school; and they are of various and dissimilar acquirements.

Each scholar . . . thinks she has a right to judge for herself respecting what she is to be taught. . . . Under such disadvantages, a school cannot be classed. . . .

5. It is for the interest of instructresses of boarding schools, to teach their pupils showy accomplishments, rather than those, which are solid and useful. . . .

6. As these schools are private establishments, their preceptresses are not accountable to any particular persons. Any woman has a right to open a school in any place; and no one, either from law or custom can prevent her. . . .

Thus the writer has endeavoured to point out the defects of the present mode of female education; chiefly in order to show, that the great cause of these defects consists in a state of things, in which legislatures, undervaluing the importance of women in society, neglect to provide for their education, and suffer it to become the sport of adventurers for fortune, who may be both ignorant and vicious.

OF THE PRINCIPLES BY WHICH EDUCATION SHOULD BE REGULATED

. . . Education should seek to bring its subjects to the perfection of their moral, intellectual and physical nature: in order, that they may be of the greatest possible use to themselves and others: or, to use a different expression, that they may be the means of the greatest possible happiness of which they are capable, both as to what they enjoy, and what they communicate. . . .

Studies and employments should, therefore, be selected from one or both of the following considerations; either, because they are peculiarly fitted to improve the faculties; or, because they are such, as the pupil will most probably have occasion to practice in future life.

These are the principles, on which systems of male education are founded; but female education has not yet been systematized. Chance and confusion reign here. Not even is youth considered in our sex, as in the other, a season, which should be wholly devoted to improvement. Among families, so rich as to be above labour, the daughters are hurried through the routine of boarding school instruction, and at an early period introduced into the gay world; and, thenceforth, their only object is amusement.—Mark the different treatment, which the sons of these families receive. While their sisters are gliding through the mazes of the midnight dance, they employ the lamp, to treasure up for future use the riches of ancient wisdom; or to gather strength and expansion of the mind, in exploring the wonderful paths of philosophy. When the youth of two sexes has been spent so differently, is it strange . . . that our sex have been considered by the other, as the pampered, wayward babies of society. . . .

It is the duty of a government, to do all in its power to promote the present and future prosperity of the nation. . . . This prosperity will depend on the character of its citizens. The characters of these will be formed by their mothers. . . . If this is the case, then it is the duty of our present legislators to begin now, to form the characters of the next generation, by controlling that of the females, who are to be their mothers. . . .

But should the conclusion be almost admitted, that our sex too are the legitimate children of the legislature; and that it is their duty to afford us a share of their paternal bounty; the phantom of a college-learned lady would be ready to rise up, and destroy every good resolution, which the admission of this truth would naturally produce in our favour.

To shew that it is not a masculine education which is here recommended, and to afford a definite view of the manner in which a female institution might possess the respectability, permanency, and uniformity of operation of those appropriated to males; and yet differ from them, so as to be adapted to that difference of character and duties, to which the softer sex should be formed, is the object of the following imperfect

Sketch of a Female Seminary

. . . **I.** There would be needed a building, with commodious rooms for lodging and recitation, apartments for the reception of apparatus, and for the accommodation of the domestic department.

II. A library, containing books on the various subjects in which the pupils were to receive instruction; musical instruments, some good paintings, to form the taste and serve as models for the execution of those who were to be instructed in that art; maps, globes, and a small collection of philosophical apparatus.

III. A judicious board of trust, competent and desirous to promote its interests, would in a female, as in a male literary institution, be the corner stone of its prosperity. On this board it would depend to provide,

IV. Suitable instruction. . . . 1. Religious and moral. 2. Literary. 3. Domestic. 4. Ornamental. . . .

[There follows a detailed description of the educational content of each of these "branches" of education and an argument for the inclusion of such subjects as natural philosophy and science, subjects not previously taught to girls; "domestic instruction" on a systematic basis; and the inclusion of dancing to promote "grace of motion."]

V. There would be needed, for a female, as well as for a male seminary, a system of laws and regulations, so arranged, that both the instructors and pupils would know their duty; and thus, the whole business move with regularity and uniformity. . . .

Perhaps the term allotted for the routine of study at the seminary, might be three years. The pupils, probably, would not be fitted to enter, till about the age of fourteen.

BENEFITS OF FEMALE SEMINARIES

. . . They would constitute a grade of public education, superior to any yet known in the history of our sex; and through them, the lower grades of female instruction might be controlled. The influence of public seminaries, over these, would operate in two ways; first, by requiring certain qualifications for entrance; and secondly, by furnishing instructresses, initiated in their modes of teaching, and imbued with their maxims.

Female seminaries might be expected to have important and happy effects on common schools in general; and in the manner of operating on these, would probably place the business of teaching children in hands now nearly useless to society; and take it from those, whose services the state wants in many other ways. . . .

1. Females, by having their understandings cultivated, their reasoning powers developed and strengthened, may be expected to act more from the dictates of reason, and less from those of fashion and caprice.

2. With minds thus strengthened . . . they might be expected to acquire juster and more enlarged views of their duty, and stronger and higher motives to its performance.

3. This plan of education, offers all that can be done to preserve female youth from a contempt of useful labour. The pupils would become accustomed to it . . . and it is to be hoped that both from habit and association, they might in future life regard it as respectable.

To this it may be added, that if housewifery could be raised to a regular art, and taught upon philosophical principles, it would become a higher and more interesting occupation. . . .

4. The pupils might be expected to acquire a taste for moral and intellectual pleasures, which would buoy them above a passion for show and parade. . . .

5. By being enlightened in moral philosophy, and in that, which teaches the operations of the mind, females would be enabled to perceive the nature and extent of that influence, which they possess over their children, and the obligation, which this lays them under, to watch the formation of their characters with unceasing vigilance, to become their instructors, to devise plans for their improvement, to weed out the vices from their minds, and to implant and foster the virtues. . . .

In calling my patriotic countrymen, to effect so noble an object, the consideration of national glory, should not be overlooked. . . . Where is that wise and heroic country, which has considered, that our rights are sacred, though we cannot defend them? that tho' a weaker, we are an essential part of the body politic, whose corruption or improvement must affect the whole? . . . History shows not that country. . . . Yet though history lifts not her finger to such an one, anticipation does. She points to a nation, which, having thrown off the shackles of authority and precedent, shrinks not from schemes of improvement, because other nations have never attempted them; but which, in its pride of independence, would rather lead than follow in the march of human improvement. . . . Does not every American exult that this country is his own? And who knows how great and good a race of men may yet arise from the forming hand of mothers, enlightened by the bounty of that beloved country,—to defend her liberties,—to plan her future improvement,—and to raise her to unparalleled glory?

FRANCES WRIGHT (1795–1852)

41. In a daughter they have a human being; in a son the same

Well-educated and wealthy, Frances Wright arrived in America from her native Scotland in 1824, determined to support and improve American democracy. She was a talented writer, a tireless reformer and founder of a short-lived utopian community, who scandalized Americans as much by her behavior as by her unorthodox opinions. She advocated a broad spectrum of reforms: the emancipation of slaves, birth control, liberal divorce laws, sexual freedom, improvements in the status of women, and free public education for all children from age two upward in state-supported

Frances Wright [d'Arusmont], *Course of Popular Lectures with 3 Addresses* (London: James Watson, [1834]), pp. 24–32.

boarding schools. The latter demand won the support of the first
American working-class political party, the briefly successful New
York Workingmen's Association. Frances Wright, after the failure of
her own colony, joined Robert Dale Owen's utopian colony, New
Harmony (Indiana), and for several years became co-editor with
Owen of the *New Harmony Gazette* and the (New York) *Free En-
quirer*. Beginning in 1829, she lectured in Ohio, Pennsylvania,
and New York, arousing some support and much public curiosity,
hostility, and vituperation.

The selections below are drawn from her public lectures, in
which she sought to advance rationalism and the spirit of free inquiry. They were intended to counteract what she considered the
pernicious influence of organized religion and to promote her educational reforms. The equal access of women to education was a
basic tenet of her beliefs. It is interesting to contrast her argument
with that of the more pragmatic and conservative Emma Willard.
Wright based her frankly feminist argument on the assumption that
women as rational beings had an inherent right to self-
improvement and that, as citizens of a democracy, they had an
inherent right to equality in law and condition.

However novel it may appear, I shall venture the assertion,
that, until women assume the place in society which good
sense and good feeling alike assign to them, human improvement must advance but feebly. It is in vain that we
would circumscribe the power of one half of our race, and
that half by far the most important and influential. If they
exert it not for good, they will for evil; if they advance not
knowledge, they will perpetuate ignorance. Let women
stand where they may in the scale of improvement, their
position decides that of the race. Are they cultivated?—so is
society polished and enlightened. Are they ignorant?—so is
it gross and insipid. Are they wise?—so is the human condition prosperous. Are they foolish?—so is it unstable and
unpromising. Are they free?—so is the human character
elevated. Are they enslaved?—so is the whole race degraded. Oh! that we could learn the advantage of just practice and consistent principles! . . .

Your political institutions have taken equality for their basis; your declaration of rights, upon which your institutions rest, sets forth this principle as vital and inviolate. Equality is the soul of liberty; there is, in fact, no liberty without it. . . .

How are men to be secured in *any* rights without instruction; how to be secured in the *equal exercise* of those rights without *equality of instruction?* By instruction understand me to mean knowledge—*just knowledge;* not talent, not genius, not inventive mental powers. These will vary in every human being; but knowledge is the same for every mind, and every mind may and *ought to be* trained to receive it. If then, ye have pledged, at each anniversary of your political independence, your lives, properties, and honor, to the securing [of] your common liberties, ye have pledged your lives, properties, and honor, to the securing of your *common instruction.* . . .

All men are born free and equal! That is: *our moral feelings acknowledge it to be just and proper, that we respect those liberties in others, which we lay claim to for ourselves; and that we permit the free agency of every individual, to any extent which violates not the free agency of his fellow creatures.*

There is but one honest limit to the rights of a sentient being; it is where they touch the rights of another sentient being. Do we exert our own liberties without injury to others—we exert them justly; do we exert them at the expense of others—unjustly. And, in thus doing, we step from the sure platform of liberty upon the uncertain threshold of tyranny. . . .

Who among us but has had occasion to remark the ill-judged, however well-intentioned government of children by their teachers; and, yet more especially, by their parents? In what does this mismanagement originate? In a misconception of the relative position of the parent or guardian, and of the child; in a departure, by the parent from the principle of liberty, in his assumption of rights destructive of those of the child; in his exercise of authority, as by right divine, over the judgment, actions, and person of the child; in his forgetfulness of the character of the child, as a human being, born "free and equal" among his compeers; that is, having equal claims to the exercise and development of all his senses, faculties, and powers, with those who brought him into existence, and with all sentient beings who tread the earth. Were a child thus viewed by his parent, we should not see him, by turns, made a plaything and a slave; we should not see him commanded to believe, but encouraged to reason; we should not see him trembling under the rod, nor shrinking from a frown, but reading the wishes of others in the eye, gathering knowledge wherever he threw his glance, rejoicing in the present hour, and treasuring up sources of enjoyment for future years. . . .

What, then, has the parent to do, if he would conscientiously discharge that most sacred of all duties, that, weightiest of all responsibilities, which ever did or ever will devolve on a human being? . . . He is to encourage in his child a spirit of inquiry, and equally to encourage it in himself. He is never to advance an opinion without showing the facts upon which it is grounded; he is never to assert a fact, without proving it to be a fact. He is not to teach a code of morals, any more than a creed of doctrines; but he is to direct his young charge to observe the consequences of actions on himself and on others; and to judge of the propriety of those actions by their ascertained consequences. He is not to command his feelings any more than his opinions or his actions; but he is to assist him in the analysis of his feelings, in the examination of their nature, their tendencies, their effects. Let him do this, and have no anxiety for the result. . . .

Who, then, shall say, inquiry is good for him and not good for his children? Who shall cast error from himself, and allow it to be grafted on the minds he has called into being? . . . We see men who will aid the instruction of their sons, and condemn only their daughters to ignorance. "Our sons", they say, "will have to exercise political rights, may aspire to public offices, may fill some learned profession, may struggle for wealth and acquire it. It is well that we give them a helping hand; that we assist them to such knowledge as is going, and make them as sharp witted as their neighbours. But for our daughters," they say—if indeed respecting them they say any thing—"for our daughters, little trouble or expense is necessary. They can never *be any thing;* in fact, they *are nothing.* We had best give them up to their mothers, who may take them to Sunday's preaching; and with the aid of a little music, a little dancing, and a few fine gowns, and fit them out for the market of marriage."

Am I severe? It is not my intention. I know that I am honest, and I fear that I am correct. . . . But to such parents, I would observe, that with regard to their sons, as to their daughters, they are about equally mistaken. . . . Let possibilities be what they may in favour of their sons, they have no calculations to make on them. It is not for them to ordain their sons magistrates nor statesmen; nor yet even lawyers, physicians, or merchants. They have only to improve the one character which they receive at the birth. They have only to consider them as *human beings,* and to ensure them the fair and thorough development of all the faculties, physical, mental, and moral, which distinguish their nature. In like manner, as respects their daughters, they have nothing to do with the injustice of laws, nor the absurdities of society. Their duty is plain, evident, decided. In a daughter they have in charge a human being; in a son, the same. Let them train up these *human beings,* under the expanded wings of liberty. Let them seek *for* them and *with* them just knowledge; encouraging, from the cradle upwards, that useful curiosity which will lead them unbidden in the paths of free inquiry; and place them, safe and superior to the storms of life, in the security of well-regulated, self-possessed minds, well-grounded, well-reasoned, conscientious opinions, and self-approved, consistent practice.

I have as yet, in this important matter, addressed myself

only to the reason and moral feelings of my audience; I could speak also to their interests. . . . Were it only in our power to enlighten part of the rising generation, and should the interests of the whole decide our choice of the portion, it were the females, and not the males, we should select.

When, now a twelvemonth since, the friends of liberty and science pointed out to me, in London, the walls of their rising university, I observed, with a smile, that they were beginning at the wrong end. "Raise such an edifice for your young women, and ye have enlightened the nation." It has already been observed, that women, wherever placed, however high or low in the scale of cultivation, hold the destinies of human-kind. Men will ever rise or fall to the level of the other sex; and from some causes in their conformation, we find them, however armed with power or enlightened with knowledge, still held in leading strings even by the least cultivated female. Surely, then, if they knew their interests, they would desire the improvement of those who, if they do not advantage, will injure them; who, if they elevate not their minds and meliorate not their hearts, will debase the one and harden the other. . . . Let them examine the relation in which the two sexes stand, and ever must stand, to each other. Let them perceive, that, mutually dependent, they must ever be giving and receiving, or they must be losing:—receiving or losing in knowledge, in virtue, in enjoyment. Let them perceive how immense the loss, or how immense the gain. Let them not imagine that they know aught of the delights which intercourse with the other sex can give, until they have felt the sympathy of mind with mind, and heart with heart; until they bring into that intercourse every affection, every talent, every confidence, every refinement, every respect. Until power is annihilated on one side, fear and obedience on the other, and both restored to their birthright—equality. Let none think that affection can reign without it; or friendship, or esteem. Jealousies, envyings, suspicions, reserves, deceptions—these are the fruits of inequality. Go, then! and remove the evil first from the minds of women, then from their condition, and then from your laws. Think it no longer indifferent whether the mothers of the rising generation are wise or foolish. Think it not indifferent whether your own companions are ignorant or enlightened. Think it not indifferent whether those who are to form the opinions, sway the habits, decide the destinies, of the species—and that not through their children only, but through their lovers and husbands—are enlightened friends or capricious mistresses, efficient coadjutors or careless servants, reasoning beings or blind followers of superstition.

There is a vulgar persuasion, that the ignorance of women, by favouring their subordination, ensures their utility. It is the same argument employed by the ruling few against the subject many in aristocracies; by the rich against the poor in democracies; by the learned professions against the people in all countries. And let us observe, that if good in one case, it should be good in all; and that, unless you are prepared to admit that you are yourselves less industrious in proportion to your intelligence, you must abandon the position with respect to others. But, in fact, who is it among men that best struggle with difficulties?—the strong-minded or the weak? Who meet with serenity adverse fortune?—the wise or the foolish? Who accommodate themselves to irremediable circumstances? or, when remediable, who control and mould them at will?—the intelligent or the ignorant? Let your answer in your own case, be your answer in that of women. . . .

42. The school marm

School teaching emerged as a female occupation in the early nineteenth century, coincident with the spread of common schools. The nation's enthusiasm for educating every citizen was tempered by the taxpayers' unwillingness to finance such education. The answer was the school "marm"—the low-paid, poorly trained female teacher, who regarded her employment as a stopgap on the road to her main career as housewife and mother.

The following selections describe the life of the school teacher on the Michigan and Minnesota frontiers and in upstate New York. One-room school houses, inadequate heat, few if any books, rote learning, and irregular school attendance due to family demands on the students characterized the country school. For the teacher the work meant long hours, low pay, "boarding out" under often very unsatisfactory living conditions, poor food, and a social life restricted by local notions of propriety. As Susan B. Anthony had foreseen, the status of the entire profession was depressed by the low pay of female teachers.

Anna Howard Shaw *(1847–1919)*

Anna Howard Shaw earned two graduate degrees—the Doctor of Divinity in 1878 and the M.D. in 1886, both from Boston University. Later in life, from 1904 to 1915, she was president of the National American Woman Suffrage Association. In her autobiography, she tells of her arduous childhood on the Michigan frontier and of her struggles for subsistence and for an education. She also describes vividly what it was like to be a "school marm" in a recently settled frontier community.

In 1859 Anna Shaw's father had left his wife and four young children under the care of his oldest son on a newly staked wilderness claim in Michigan, while he returned East to earn money needed to support the family. When the son got ill and had to return East and the mother suffered a mental breakdown, twelve-year old Anna assumed responsibility for the little family. Eighteen months later the father and brother briefly rejoined the family, but his daughter writes: "he was not an addition to our executive staff." A man more interested in reading than planting corn, he spent his time "poring over books," leaving the women in the family to do the best they could. Still, he once berated Anna for "idling away" her time reading, while her mother worked hard. The narrative continues:

Anna Howard Shaw, D.D., M.D., *The Story of a Pioneer* (New York: Harper and Bros., 1915), pp. 44–46, 50–53. Copyright 1915 by Harper & Row, Publishers. Renewed 1943 by Lucy E. Anthony. Reprinted by permission of the publishers.

The injustice of the criticism cut deep; I knew I had done and was doing my share for the family, and already, too, I had begun to feel the call of my career. For some reason I wanted to preach—to talk to people, to tell them things. Just why, just what, I did not yet know—but I had begun to preach in the silent woods, to stand up on stumps and address the unresponsive trees, to feel the stir of aspiration within me.

When my father had finished all he wished to say, I looked at him and answered, quietly, "Father, some day I am going to college."

I can still see his slight, ironical smile. It drove me to a second prediction. I was young enough to measure success by material results, so I added, recklessly:

"And before I die I shall be worth ten thousand dollars!"

The amount staggered me even as it dropped from my lips. It was the largest fortune my imagination could conceive, and in my heart I believed that no woman ever had possessed or would possess so much. So far as I knew, too, no woman had gone to college. But now that I had put my secret hopes into words, I was desperately determined to make those hopes come true. After I became a wage earner I lost my desire to make a fortune, but the college dream grew with the years; and though my college career seemed as remote as the most distant star, I hitched my little wagon to that star and never afterward wholly lost sight of its friendly gleam.

When I was fifteen years old I was offered a situation as a school-teacher. By this time the community was growing around us with the rapidity characteristic of these Western settlements, and we had nearer neighbors whose children needed instruction. I passed an examination before a school-board consisting of three nervous and self-conscious men whose certificate I still hold, and I at once began my professional career on the modest salary of two dollars a week and my board. The school was four miles from my home, so I "boarded round" with the families of my pupils, staying two weeks in each place, and often walking from three to six miles a day to and from my little log school-house in every kind of weather. During the first year I had about fourteen pupils, of varying ages, sizes, and tempera-ments, and there was hardly a book in the school-room ex-cept those I owned. One little girl, I remember, read from an almanac, while a second used a hymn-book.

In winter the school-house was heated by a woodstove, to which the teacher had to give close personal attention. I could not depend on my pupils to make the fires or carry in the fuel; and it was often necessary to fetch the wood my-self, sometimes for long distances through the forest. Again and again, after miles of walking through winter storms, I reached the school-house with my clothing wet through, and in these soaked garments I taught during the day. In "board-ing round" I often found myself in one-room cabins, with bunks at the end and the sole partition a sheet or a blanket, behind which I slept with one or two of the children. It was the custom on these occasions for the man of the house to delicately retire to the barn while we women got to bed, and to disappear again in the morning while we dressed. In some places the meals were so badly cooked that I could not eat them, and often the only food my poor little pupils brought to school for their noonday meal was a piece of bread or a bit of raw pork.

I earned my two dollars a week that year, but I had to wait for my wages until the dog tax was collected in the spring. When the money was thus raised, and the twenty-six dollars for my thirteen weeks of teaching were graciously put into my hands, I went "outside" to the nearest shop and joyously spent almost the entire amount for my first "party dress." . . .

In the near future I had reason to regret the extravagant expenditure of my first earnings. For my second year of teaching, in the same school, I was to receive five dollars a week and to pay my own board. I selected a place two miles and a half from the school-house, and was promptly asked by my host to pay my board in advance. This, he explained, was due to no lack of faith in me; the money would enable him to go "outside" to work, leaving his family well supplied with provisions. I allowed him to go to the school committee and collect my board in advance, at the rate of three dollars a week for the season. When I presented myself at my new boarding-place, however, two days later, I found the house nailed up and deserted; the man and his family had departed with my money, and I was left, as my committeemen sympathetically remarked, "high and dry." There were only two dollars a week coming to me after that, so I walked back and forth between my home and my school, almost four miles, twice a day; and during this enforced exercise there was ample opportunity to reflect on the fleeting joy of riches. . . .

[The Civil War had begun. All the men, including her father and two brothers, enlisted in the Union Army.]

Between those years I was the principal support of our family, and life became a strenuous and tragic affair. . . . We eked out our little income in every way we could, taking as boarders the workers in the logging-camps, making quilts, which we sold, and losing no chance to earn a penny in any legitimate manner. Again my mother did such outside sewing as she could secure, yet with every month of our effort the gulf between our income and our expenses grew wider, and the price of the bare necessities of existence climbed up and up. The largest amount I could earn at teaching was six dollars a week, and our school year included only two terms of thirteen weeks each. It was an incessant struggle to keep our land, to pay our taxes, and to live. Calico was selling at fifty cents a yard. Coffee was one dollar a pound. There were no men left to grind our corn, to get in our crops, or to care for our live stock; and all around us we saw our struggle reflected in the lives of our neighbors. . . .

After Eleanor's death my brother Tom was wounded, and

for months we lived in terror of worse tidings, but he finally recovered. I was walking seven and eight miles a day, and doing extra work before and after school hours, and my health began to fail. Those were years I do not like to look back upon—years in which life had degenerated into a treadmill whose monotony was broken only by the grim messages from the front. . . . It seemed that nothing short of a miracle could lift my feet from their plodding way and set them on the wider path toward which my eyes were turned, but I never lost faith that in some manner the miracle would come to pass. As certainly as I have ever known anything, I *knew* that I was going to college! . . .

Susan B. Anthony (1820–1906)

Susan Brownell Anthony, later to become the foremost organizer and leader of the woman's rights movement, grew up in a Quaker home. Unlike many women of her day, she was encouraged by her father and brothers in her desire for an education. She was taught in a home school established by her father, then in the district school, and finally, for four months, she attended Friends' Seminary near Philadelphia. She had no difficulty obtaining teaching assignments in the schools near her home in upstate New York. To help her father pay his debts, she left home in 1839 to teach at Friends' Seminary in New Rochelle, N.Y. In 1846, she became headmistress of the Female Department at Canajoharie Academy near Rochester.

It was early resentment at the inequality in pay for women teachers, which made her receptive to the feminist ideas of Elizabeth Cady Stanton, whose closest friend and lifelong co-worker she became.

Susan B. Anthony, . . . having been a successful teacher in the State of New York fifteen years of her life, had seen the need of many improvements in the mode of teaching and in the sanitary arrangements of school buildings. . . .

In 1853, the annual [education] convention being held in

Elizabeth Cady Stanton, Susan B. Anthony, and Matilda Joslyn Gage, eds., *History of Woman Suffrage*, 6 vols. (New York: Fowler & Wells, 1881), I: 513–516.

Rochester, her place of residence, Miss Anthony conscientiously attended all the sessions through three entire days. After having listened for hours to a discussion as to the reason why the profession of teacher was not as much respected as that of the lawyer, minister, or doctor, without once, as she thought, touching the kernel of the question, she arose to untie for them the Gordian knot, and said, "Mr. President." If all the witches that had been drowned, burned, and hung in the Old World and the New had suddenly appeared on the platform, threatening vengeance for their wrongs, the officers of that convention could not have been thrown into greater consternation. . . .

At length President Davies, of West Point, in full dress, buff vest, blue coat, gilt buttons, stepped to the front, and said in a tremulous, mocking tone, "What will the lady have?" "I wish, sir, to speak to the question under discussion," Miss Anthony replied. The Professor, more perplexed than before, said: "What is the pleasure of the Convention?" A gentleman moved that she should be heard; another seconded the motion; whereupon a discussion pro and con followed, lasting full half an hour, when a vote of the men only was taken, and permission granted by a small majority; and lucky for her, too, was it, that the thousand women crowding that hall could not vote on the question, for they would have given a solid "no." The president then announced the vote, and said: "The lady can speak."

We can easily imagine the embarrassment under which Miss Anthony arose after that half hour of suspense, and the bitter hostility she noted on every side. However, with a clear, distinct voice, which filled the hall, she said: "It seems to me, gentlemen, that none of you quite comprehend the cause of the disrespect of which you complain. Do you not see that so long as society says a woman is incompetent to be a lawyer, minister, or doctor, but has ample ability to be a teacher, that every man of you who chooses this profession tacitly acknowledges that he has no more brains than a woman? And this, too, is the reason that teaching is a less lucrative profession, as here men must compete with the cheap labor of woman. Would you exalt your profession, exalt those who labor with you. Would you make it more lucrative, increase the salaries of the women engaged in the noble work of educating our future Presidents, Senators, and Congressmen."

This said, Miss Anthony took her seat, amid the profoundest silence, broken at last by three gentlemen, . . . walking down the broad aisle to congratulate the speaker on her pluck and perseverance. . . .

To give the women of to-day some idea of what it cost those who first thrust themselves into these conventions, at the close of the session Miss A. heard women remarking: ". . . I was actually ashamed of my sex." "I felt so mortified I really wished the floor would open and swallow me up." "Who can that creature be?" "She must be a dreadful woman to get up that way and speak in public." . . .

Miss Anthony attended these teachers' conventions from year to year, at Oswego, Utica, Poughkeepsie, Lockport, Syracuse, making the same demands for equal place and pay, until she had the satisfaction to see every right conceded. Women speaking and voting on all questions; appointed on committees, and to prepare reports and addresses, elected officers of the Association, and seated on the platforms. In 1856, she was chairman of a committee herself, to report on the question of co-education; and at Troy, . . . she read her report, which the press pronounced able and conclusive. The President, Mr. Hazeltine, of New York, congratulating Miss Anthony on her address, said: "As much as I am compelled to admire your rhetoric and logic, the matter and manner of your address and its delivery, I would rather follow a daughter of mine to her grave, than to have her deliver such an address before such an assembly." Superintendent Randall, overhearing the President, added: "I should be proud, Madam, if I had a daughter capable of making such an eloquent and finished argument, before this or any assembly of men and women. I congratulate you on your triumphant success. . . ."

43. Teaching the freedmen

No group of teachers worked under more difficult conditions than did the Northern volunteer teachers of the newly freed slaves. During the war this "missionary work" had been organized and financed by Northern abolitionists and church-related groups. The Bureau of Refugees, Freedmen and Abandoned Lands (Freedmen's Bureau), set up by Congress in 1865, consolidated this vast volunteer effort and supplied money for school buildings, leaving the staffing of the schools to philanthropic organizations in the North. Within five years of the end of the war, this vast social experiment saw nearly a quarter of a million black children instructed in over 4,300 schools by 9,000 teachers, 45 percent of them women. There are no figures available on the adult freedmen who received instruction in these schools, but their number must have been considerable. Most of the white women teachers came from the North, most of the black women from the South. The white teachers faced not only the usual hardships of poverty and inadequate pay, but ostracism and hostility from the white Southern communities in which they worked.

In several Southern states Ku Klux Klan terrorism spearheaded the drive to destroy congressional Reconstruction, the Freedmen's Bureau, and the Republican Party in the South. In Mississippi in particular, KKK terror focused on anyone connected with the freedmen's schools. The testimony of Sarah A. Allen describes one instance of the intimidation of a white school teacher. Significantly, she testifies to being roughly treated, but not actually abused. Black teachers fared considerably worse at the hands of KKK bands, suffering whippings, rape, and death. The testimony of the KKK hearings fills thirteen volumes with graphic descriptions of a reign of fear against Blacks and their white allies in Reconstruction. Despite the recommendations of the congressional committee for continuing strong protective measures by the federal government and the retention of federal troops in the Southern states, Republican power was already collapsing. The withdrawal of federal troops in 1867 was only the final blow, ending Reconstruction and the effort to institute democratic government based on a grassroots black and white alliance. The end of Reconstruction doomed the effort at providing equal educational opportunities for black and white children of the South. From then on till well into the middle of the twentieth century, Southern education would, in law and custom, be race-segregated and discriminatory to Blacks.

Miss Mary S. Battey

ANDERSONVILLE, GA., DEC. 1866

. . . Our school begun—*in spite of threatenings from the whites,* and *the consequent fear of the blacks*—with twenty-seven pupils, four only of whom could read, even the simplest words. At the end of six weeks, we have enrolled eighty-five names, with *but fifteen unable to read.* In seven years teaching at the North, I have not seen a parallel to their appetite for learning, and their active progress. Whether this zeal will abate with time, is yet a question. I have a little fear that it may. Meanwhile it is well to "work while the day lasts." Their spirit *now* may be estimated somewhat, when I tell you that three walk a distance of four miles, each morning, to return after the five hours session. Several come three miles, and quite a number from two and two-and-a-half miles.

The night school—taught by Miss Root—numbers about forty, mostly men, earnest, determined, ambitious. One of them walks six miles and returns after the close of school, which is often as late as ten o'clock. One woman walks three miles, as do a number of the men.

On Sabbath mornings, at half-past nine, we open our Sabbath school, which is attended by about fifty men, women and children, who give willing, earnest attention to our instruction. The younger ones are given to the charge of "Uncle Charlie"—a good old negro who wants to do something to help. Miss Root takes the women, and leaves the men to my care. As they are unable to read, we take a text or passage of Scripture, enlarge upon and apply it as well as

Everett Family Papers, Newberry Library, Chicago. Courtesy of the Newberry Library and Roberts Everett.

we are able, answering their questions, correcting erroneous opinions, extending their thoughts. . . .

Lucy Chase

GORDONSVILLE [VA], DECR 14TH '69
Miss Lowell . . .

. . . I am delighted with my school! As I am alone, of
course the school is ungraded, and my classes are many; but
I keep school until half past three; and, very often until four
o'clock, and so I am able to add what I will call intellectual
exercises to the ordinary exercises. I oblige every class to
learn the meaning of all the important words in every-days
reading-lessons; and I am daily gratified by their prompt-
ness and accuracy in defining the words, when they stand in
class. I appoint, every morning, one from each class as inter-
locutor, and I oblige the whole school to listen to all the
definitions; while all who can write, put upon their slates
the words in their own lessons, with the definitions thereof.
Time is demanded for that exercise, but it is indeed well
spent. The children, all of them, enjoy it. Most of them
comprehend it, and their wits are perceptibly quickened by
it. I have one class in the Fr'dm'ns Book which offers an
amazing store of valuable words. I frequently call the attention of the whole school to illustrations of the meaning of
familiar words. I spend a good deal of time in teaching
Arithmetic both Mental and Written. Many of the children
add, subtract, multiply and divide, units, tens, and even
hundreds, with readiness. I spend so much time upon these
exercises that I can mark the improvement, which is rapid. I
have three classes in Geography, and I give, daily, lessons
to the whole school on Maps. All the children can navigate
the Gulfs and Bays of the Globe, and they are now journeying with pleasure through the U.S., halting at the capital

Lucy Chase manuscripts, Chase Family Papers. Courtesy of the American
Antiquarian Society, Worcester, Mass.

cities and sailing on the pleasant rivers. In addition to the defining exercise, of which I have told you, I hear . . . the whole school spell daily from a speller. Pleasant though my task is, I have all the trials that every teacher must have, who—*empty handed*, takes charge of a school that, for three previous winters, has had a rod suspended over it.

Alone, too, I keep a night school. For awhile, I kept it five nights in the week, but generally I have but three night sessions. . . .

Sincerely
LUCY CHASE

Miss Sarah A. Allen

COLUMBUS, MISSISSIPPI, NOVEMBER 11, 1871

WITNESS: MISS SARAH A. ALLEN

QUESTION: Please state your place of residence and occupation to the committee.

ANSWER: Geneseo, Henry County, Illinois. I have no occupation at home. I am teaching here.

QUESTION: State whether you have been engaged in the business of teaching in this county.

ANSWER: In this county I have been teaching a few weeks. . . .

QUESTION: Were you engaged as a teacher of a school outside of Columbus at any time?

ANSWER: If you refer to my teaching school last spring, I taught in Monroe County. I was teaching at Cotton Gin Port, twelve miles northeast of Aberdeen.

QUESTION: Were you teaching a white or colored school?

ANSWER: A colored school.

QUESTION: You may state to the committee whether you

U.S., Congress, *Joint Select Committee to Inquire Into the Condition of Affairs in the Late Insurrectionary States*, 2 vols. (Washington, D.C.: U.S. Govt. Printing Office, 1872), "Mississippi," II: 777–779.

were interrupted by any persons in your business.

ANSWER: I taught six weeks, until I think the 18th of March, when I was told to leave; warned to leave, between 1 and 2 o'clock at night by about fifty men, I think; they were disguised; there were but two that came into my room.

QUESTION: Do you say they came into your room?

ANSWER: Between 1 and 2 o'clock at night I was wakened by a great noise around on the outside of the house. They told me to get up. I went to the window and asked them what they wanted. They said they wanted me to get a light and dress; that they wanted to talk to me; that they would not harm me. I said, "Very well," I would be ready in a few moments. I admitted them. The captain said, "If you will take a seat the lieutenant shall come into the room and the rest shall stay out." The lieutenant came in with a pistol in his hand. He sat down opposite the fire-place. The captain sat in the center of the room. There were eight or ten men stood inside the door, and the porch was full.

QUESTION: What did they say to you?

ANSWER: They asked me my name and occupation, and where I came from, and what I was doing, and who I boarded with, and what my wages were. We talked about an hour on politics, mostly against Colonel Huggins and his whipping. He had been whipped about one week before that. They asked me if I had heard of it and what I thought of it; and also asked if I had heard that other teachers had been sent away, and what I intended to do. I told them it was a very short notice, and I did not know. They said they never gave a warning but once; that I was to understand it so. I told them I did. They said I should leave—I believe the lieutenant told me I should leave—Monday morning. That was Saturday evening, or Saturday night. The captain said he thought that would be rather hard; he would give me till Thursday morning to leave; that probably some one of them would be around. I told them . . . I would go, if it was possible to get away; the roads were very bad. I did not get away until the next Tuesday. . . .

QUESTION: Was there any threat made of what would be the consequence of your continuing to teach school?

ANSWER: No, sir.

QUESTION: Further than the remark that they never gave a second notice?

ANSWER: Yes, sir; that was all.

QUESTION: What did you infer from that?

ANSWER: Well, I supposed that they would, if I should stay and continue, take harsher means. . . .

QUESTION: Did you discontinue your school in consequence of this warning?

ANSWER: Yes, I did.

QUESTION: After you had been teaching about six weeks?

ANSWER: I taught just six weeks.

QUESTION: For how long a term had you been engaged as a teacher?

ANSWER: Four months.

QUESTION: What wages were you receiving per month?

ANSWER: Seventy-five dollars.

QUESTION: Did they say what their motive was for breaking up your school?

ANSWER: Yes. They did not want radicals there in the South; did not want northern people teaching there; they thought the colored people could educate themselves if they needed any education; they advised me to go home again. . . .

QUESTION: The men were all disguised that you saw?

ANSWER: Yes, sir.

QUESTION: Can you give the committee a description of the disguises they wore?

ANSWER: They wore long white robes, a loose mask covered the face, trimmed with scarlet stripes. The lieutenant and captain had long horns on their head, projecting over the forehead; a sort of device in front—some sort of figure in front, and scarlet stripes.

QUESTION: Did you recognize any one of the number?

ANSWER: I did not. . . .

QUESTION: You have not heard of any other visitation in that part of the country except there?

ANSWER: There was a teacher left Smithville the week before I did.

QUESTION: A female teacher?

ANSWER: Yes, sir.

QUESTION: Was she said to be warned off?

ANSWER: She heard they were coming there, and the man she was boarding with, who was one of the school directors, thought it was best for her to leave.

QUESTION: Was she a northern woman?

ANSWER: Yes, sir.

QUESTION: Have you heard of any other schools in Monroe County broken up by the same means?

ANSWER: Yes, sir; nearly all the schools in Monroe County were broken up in that term, with the exception of some in the larger places.

QUESTION: Did these men have anything to say about the heavy taxation to support the common schools?

ANSWER: Yes, sir; that was their principal subject of conversation. The captain talked, as I said, about an hour about the heavy taxation, and against Colonel Huggins's conduct, and politics generally.

QUESTION: Colonel Huggins had been whipped at that time?

ANSWER: Yes, sir. They finally asked me what time it was. I told them I did not know. One of the men stepped up and said it was seventeen minutes past two. . . . I said it was a very unreasonable hour of the night, and I preferred they would not remain, and after a few minutes longer they left. They threatened the colored woman that lived in the house pretty severely; they used strong language to her after they left my room.

QUESTION: What threats did they use towards her?

ANSWER: That radicals should be cleaned out of the country, if they died, every man. They treated me gentlemanly and quietly, but when they went away I concluded that they were savages—demons.

QUESTION: They did not threathen you, I understand?

ANSWER: They yelled like Comanche Indians.

QUESTION: When they went away?

ANSWER: Yes, sir. . . .

QUESTION: Did they advise you to leave because you would not be paid?

ANSWER: No; they advised me to leave because I was a white person teaching a colored school. . . .

EMMA J. WILSON

44.   The cotton gin school house— c. 1895

If white women had to struggle for admission to institutions of learning, facing discrimination by sex, black women, facing dis-

Clement Richardson, ed., *National Cyclopedia of the Colored Race* (Montgomery, Ala.: National Publishing Co., 1919), p. 312.

crimination by race as well, frequently had to struggle to create such institutions from the ground up. The hardships overcome by black boys and girls in their struggle first for education, then for education equal to that of whites, deserve more extended documentation than can be offered here. The story is one of heroic and often spectacular achievement in which, as usual, the contribution of women has been neglected. While the achievement of Booker T. Washington in founding and building up Tuskegee Institute in Alabama has been justly celebrated, that of women who did the same work is hardly known. Thus Lucy Lainey founded Haines Normal Institute in Atlanta, Ga., starting with seventy-five pupils in 1886. By 1940 the school had over one thousand students and was valued at $45,000. Charlotte Hawkins Brown founded Palmer Memorial Institute in Sedalia, N.C., in 1902 and built this finishing school for black girls into one of the leading Southern schools, with fourteen modern buildings and a plant valued at over a million dollars. Nannie Burroughs, under the slogan "We Specialize in the Wholly Impossible," performed a similar feat of entrepreneurship and educational pioneering in her National Training School for Girls in Washington, D.C. In Daytona, Fla., Mary McLeod Bethune literally started a school on a garbage dump in 1904, earning money for beds, groceries, and the packing boxes which served as desks by daily baking pies with her pupils and selling these to railroad workers. Today, Bethune-Cookman College stands as a monument to the organizational genius and indomitable spirit of this great woman.

The work of Emma J. Wilson described below is less spectacular and dramatic, but it is possibly more representative of the work of hundreds of men and women who came out of the Southern Negro colleges such as Tuskegee and Hampton institutes with a missionary zeal for spreading education. The rural school system they built through self-help and community effort was, in the face of racist neglect and economic oppression, a lifeline for survival of the black Southern community. Their work deserves historical attention and recognition.

Mayesville Educational and Industrial Institute is Miss Emma Wilson's monument, her life story. Born in the days bordering on slavery, Miss Wilson early grew eager for an education. In making known her desire to her slave mother, the latter replied, "Why you are crazy, child, you can't go to

school. Only white children go to school." Since this was so
the child did the next best thing. She got three little white
children to teach her. Having learned her alphabet, she got
hold of a speller and began to master the big words. Later
she attended a Mission School taught by Northern women.
From here she enrolled at Scotia Seminary, at Concord,
North Carolina.

When she was planning and praying that she might go to
Scotia, she promised the Lord that she would go to Africa as
a Missionary, if that was His will. Finishing her course at
Scotia, she returned to Mayesville, her birth place, and
"found her Africa at her own door." That is she found her
home village without a Negro school building or any one to
teach. Securing the use of an old abandoned cotton gin
house, she opened school with ten pupils. Books were donated, children paid tuition in eggs, chickens and provisions. However, Miss Wilson did not accept these as her pay.
She had her mother cook these and sell them. The proceeds
she turned in to the work of her cotton gin school house.

In a short time the school outgrew the gin house. Believing in her work, Dr. Mayes, for whom the little town was
named influenced the County Board of Education to grant
her forty-five dollars a year to aid in her work. This she
invested in an Assistant Teacher, and then used for a school
house any building she could secure free of rent charges.
Pupils now began to pour in from the surrounding country.
To meet the increasing demand, Dr. Mayes advised her to
go North and solicit funds.

She started her journey North by asking the minister in
her church for the Sunday night collection. This he granted.
The sum amounted to fifty cents. With this she rode to the
next town where she found a camp meeting. Given the collection here, she raised seventy-five cents. In this way she
made her way North, where she often suffered rebuffs and
extreme hunger. . . . She remained in the North three
years, sending back funds to keep the school going. When
she returned she had money enough to put up a new school
building.

This marked the formal beginning of the Mayesville Institute. From this point it grew in number, in standing, in building, in land, in friends, in money. In 1896 it obtained a charter from the state of South Carolina. . . .

The school is now well equipped and . . . has [in 1919] an enrollment of 500 students. . . . Among the Mechanical and Domestic Arts are taught Carpentry, Shoe-making, Brick-making, Tailoring, Sewing, Cooking, Nursing and House Work. Miss Wilson herself is the founder of the course in brick-making. Having found clay on her farm, she went to Pittsburg and learned brick-making first hand. . . . She has an annual Farmers' Conference, of which she is President. The United States Government has established an Experiment Station here.

RENA RIETVELD VERDUIN (1882–1974)

45. Illinois farm girl debates woman's education—1907

Rena Rietveld had only a fifth grade education and lived all her life within ten miles of her birthplace, the village of South Holland, Ill. Born into a farm family of Calvinistic Dutch descent, she was sent to relatives to do housework for them at the age of twelve. Later, when her mother became an invalid, she and her two sisters assumed the full burden of doing the housework and farm chores for the large family—there were eleven children in all. At age twenty-eight she married a truck farmer and raised six children of her own, but always managed to stay active in church and community affairs and to teach Sunday school.

The speech recorded in the document below was given in 1907 in a debate organized by the Lansing Country Culture Club, an organization of sixty local men and women. Its members designated themselves "an association for mutual improvement in Pub-

Verduin family document used courtesy of Carl Verduin. I am indebted to Prof. Barbara Fassler, Central Univ. of Iowa, Pella, for bringing this source to my attention.

lic Speaking, Literary Composition, Music, Art, Politics and Literature" and vowed to seek truth and command of temper and to
display "due consideration for the feelings and opinions of others."

Under the leadership of a local brickmaker, the members met
weekly during the winter months and alternately listened to programs by local talent or by invited guest speakers. Over a period of
two years club members debated the following issues of concern to
women, among their other debate topics: "Resolved that Woman is
the Mental Equal of Man"; "Resolved that woman suffrage would
improve the government of the United States"; "Resolved that the
wages of women should not be lower than those of men in the
same occupation"; "Resolved that women should not enter higher
education."

Apparently some of these debates were held in competition with
several other local clubs of a similar nature in the villages of Ross,
Woodbine, and Thornton. The Lansing Country Culture Club
seems to have had a continuing concern with the status of women,
which was reflected in several songs recorded in their minute
book. One of these contains the verse:

> "Now arise and give your thunder,
> Snow those woman haters under,
> Wag your jaw and swell your chest,
> For the ladies fight your best,
> And the judge will do the rest . . ."

However, such Midwestern feminism had its limits. Once, when
volunteers for sergeants-at-arms were called for and two women,
one of them Rena Rietveld, volunteered for the post, the membership voted that only "able bodied men" were suited to fill the
office.

What is remarkable about Rena Rietveld's speech is not only her
saucy homespun feminism, but the fact that arguments presented
by feminist leaders ninety years earlier (see document 40) had
found their way into the consciousness and activities of Midwestern farmers. The time lag between pioneering ideas and their practical implementation was considerable; on the other hand it is interesting to see the way in which Midwestern farm women were
participating in and concerned with the emancipation of women.

The question, as you have heard, to be discussed tonight is: Resolved that women should not enter higher education. Our poor opponents are taking the question as it reads, while my colleague and I will try and convince the audience that women should enter higher education. . . .

Now I did not get up here to show how much I know, but how little I know, and so try and prove that women should have higher education. Through an education girls are enabled to become self-supporting and acquainted with the ways of the world. Through an education girls learn to earn a livelihood and are not so liable to throw themselves away in marriage on some worthless man. A good many men now-a-days think, "Oh, I have but to choose. I can get any girl. The poor things will be too glad to get someone to provide for them and besides they can't do a better thing." . . . And that makes the men think they can get any girl they want, and after marriage use her as a slave.

But when they discover that the girls don't have to marry—by getting an education and going into some profession—they will be more likely to behave themselves and be at some pains to make themselves worthy of the girl's acceptance. . . .

There are circumstances in a family sometimes where it becomes a necessity for the girls to earn a livelihood for themselves not only, but to help support the family also, sometimes through sickness or death. Is it not then much better if these girls are educated and can earn their money in some profession, be it teacher or stenographer, bookkeeper, librarian or any other profession, than to go to the wash tub or serve as a hired girl or work in a shop or factory to ruin her character? . . .

Our opponents may say the education will take away woman's interest in home life. I think our opponents are afraid there won't be any girls left to cook their meals some day. Don't worry, opponents, there will be enough girls left to keep house for you and cook your meals. . . .

Let me tell you that if the educated girl will not have any

interest in the home, the girl that wants an education and it's denied her, will such a girl have any interest in the household duties? *No, never!* . . . A discontented grumbler she'll be, that's all. But give that girl her education and she'll be good for something someday:—and then, opponents, if you want that girl for a wife and she is willing, . . . that woman will step from her education and profession into your house and throw all her interest in her work there. And if she is not willing after her education to go into a home of her own, you will never get her, so don't worry about that, either.

Why, men seem to think that the women have no business on the face of the earth except to work and slave for them. As that grand debater of two weeks ago told us, "Will you work for me?" . . . Women are treated something like this: after a woman is married, that good master of hers takes her, builds four walls around her and *tells* her, "Now little woman you just mind your business in here, and see to it that everything is kept in good order and that the meals are prepared just as *I* want them, and that nothing is prepared that *I* don't like. And if you need any money, come to your Master for it. And never you mind what's going on outside of those walls; that's none of your business. We can do very well without you." And he expects the woman to bow her poor head and say amen to all this. And some are not even satisfied if they take good care of the house, but expect her to keep track of everything in and around the barns and stables too yet, especially if you're unlucky enough to have to deal with farmers. If they lose track of a sack or a bushel basket, a pitch fork, a chicken, or a pig, they march right straight to the house and call the woman or girls and expect them to know just where it is. And poor her if she doesn't. She'll have to leave all her work and hunt for it, and if it isn't found the man will for all the rest of her life think it's the woman's fault. Poor slaves!

Girls, get an education and escape slavery.

Opponents, don't educate the woman or you'll have to

hunt for your missing things yourselves. And that is not so bad yet, but if you can't find them, you won't have a *woman* to blame for it. . . .

My time is up and I know I did not prove much on the subject. . . . This debate was enough to convince anybody that I, at least, should have a higher education, and there are more like me.

BERNICE SANDLER

46. Academic women attack institutional discrimination—1970

With the rise of the new feminist movement, academic women at all levels of the educational establishment began to organize in unprecedented numbers. Women's caucuses sprang up in most of the professional organizations, as did graduate students' groups and university-wide women's coalitions. Their first undertaking was usually a fact-finding survey of the status of women at their own institution or in their academic field. Such surveys quickly proved, what every woman had long suspected, the existence of far-reaching discriminatory practices at every level of academe. The proliferating caucuses and women's groups exchanged and synthesized this information and set up national organizations, such as Women's Equity Action League. They began to attack the system of institutionalized discrimination by exposing it; bringing pressure to bear on individual institutions and professional societies; lobbying for enforcement of existing legislation and for passage of new antidiscrimination laws; finally, by bringing class action suits, described in the document below, which would cut off federal funds from institutions found in violation of federal equal opportunity laws. The universities and colleges, after making

Statement of Dr. Bernice Sandler, Chairman, Action Committee for Federal Contract Compliance in Education of the Women's Equity Action League. U.S., Congress, House, Special Subcommittee on Education of the Committee on Education and Labor, *Hearings*, 91st Cong., 2d sess., June 17, 19, 26, 29, 30, 1970, pp. 298–301, 314.

minor adjustments and offering token remedial action, responded
to the law suits and federal pressure by charging interference with
academic freedom. Without denying the fact of discrimination
against women, academic institutions and their spokesmen asserted that there were not enough "qualified women" to allow
equalization of conditions without lowering standards of academic
excellence.

The issue remained unresolved as the economic retrenchment of
the late 1970s fell with particular severity upon those last-hired
and lowest in rank. Still, opportunities opened for a few of the
best-qualified women. The upsurge in interest and the spread of
courses and programs in Women's Studies, together with the increasing militancy of the young women now entering academic
life, offer hope that future surveys of women's status in the
academic world will not repeat the dismal pattern traced below.

. . . The Women's Equity Action League (WEAL) has initiated since January 31, 1970 formal charges of sex discrimination under Executive Order 11246 as amended, against
more than 100 universities and colleges. This Executive
Order forbids Federal contractors from discriminating
against race, creed, color, national origin, and sex. According to the National Science Foundation report entitled
"Federal Support to Universities and Colleges, Fiscal Year
1968," universities and colleges receive about 3.3 billion
dollars of Federal contracts per year. As Federal contractors,
universities and colleges are subject to the provisions of the
Order.

In its initial complaint, WEAL charged an industry-wide
pattern of sex discrimination and asked for a class action and
compliance review of all universities and colleges holding
Federal contracts. At that time WEAL submitted to the Secretary of Labor, George P. Shultz, more than 80 pages of
documents substantiating its charges of sex discrimination
in the academic community. . . .

The position of women in higher education has been
worsening; women are slowly being pushed out of the university world. For example, in 1870, women were one-third

of the faculty in our nation's institutions of higher learning. A hundred years later, women hold less than one-fourth of the positions. In the prestigious Big Ten universities, they hold 10% or less of the faculty positions. The proportion of women graduate students *is less now* than it was in 1930. The University of Chicago, for example, has a *lower* proportion of women on its faculty *now* than it did *in 1899*.

Women are 22% of the graduate students in the Graduate School of Arts and Sciences at Harvard University. But of the 411 tenured professors at the Graduate School of Arts and Sciences at Harvard University, *not one* is a woman. Let me repeat that. Of the 411 tenured professors at the Graduate School of Arts and Sciences at Harvard University, the number of women is: ZERO. At the University of Connecticut, a state-supported institution, women are 33% of the instructors but only 4.8% of the full professors. On the University of Massachusetts campus at Boston, also a state-supported institution, there are 65 women faculty, but only two of these have tenure. . . .

Even when women are hired they generally remain at the bottom of the academic hierarchy. The higher the rank, the lower the percentage of women, In a typical study of 188 major departments of sociology, Dr. Alice Rossi, a noted sociologist at Goucher College, found that women accounted for—

30% of the doctoral candidates,
27% of the full-time instructors,
14% of the assistant professors,
9% of the associate professors,
4% of the full professors, and
less than 1% of the departmental chairmen. . . .

90% of the women with doctorates are working. Many end up teaching on the faculty of junior colleges and community colleges where they comprise about 40% of the faculty, and where the pay, status, and research opportunities are substantially less than in the major universities. . . .

Undoubtedly the percentage of degrees awarded to women would still be higher if the discriminations based on sex were eliminated. Official and unofficial quota systems for women are widespread. . . .

Women are denied admission to graduate and professional training programs because of the rather odd and illogical reasoning on the part of university decisionmakers: "If a woman is not married, she'll get married. If she is married, she'll probably have children. If she has children, she can't possibly be committed to a profession. If she has older children, she is too old to begin training." Now it is true that she may very well marry. Many of her fellow male students will do likewise. She may very well have children. Men also become parents, but we do not as a society punish them by limiting their professional development and professional opportunities.

Essentially *our universities punish women for being women.* They punish women for not only having children, but even for having the potential to bear children. Such blatant discrimination against women has gone virtually unchecked for years. In every sector of university life, women are losing ground. . . .

At the administrative level, women are most conspicuous by their absence. The number of women college presidents is decreasing, even at women's colleges. Women rarely head departments. Even in the fields where one would expect women to be, such as in education, they simply do not move to the top. At the University of Maryland, for example, in the College of Education, only one department—Special Education—is headed by a woman. Even in women's colleges there has been a decline in the number of high administrative posts held by women. At Smith College, for example (and Smith was a noted pioneer in the education of women), the percentage of women in high administrative posts has declined from nearly 70% in 1962 to less than 50% in 1969.

Many of the best scholarships are limited to men only. It

took a highly active and sophisticated group of New York University Law School students earlier this year to get women to be considered eligible for some highly coveted $10,000 law scholarships. Practically all Federal scholarship and loan aid is for full-time study—a practice that works to virtually eliminate married women with families from receiving such aid, since they may need a part-time schedule. Indeed, many schools forbid or discourage part-time study, particularly at the graduate level, thus punishing women who attempt to combine professional training and home responsibilities simultaneously. . . .

WEAL FACT SHEET ON SOME REASONS WHY IT IS DIFFICULT FOR GIRLS TO GET GOOD COUNSELING

Almost any discussion concerning the role of women in American society sooner or later focuses on the need for better counseling of girls. Recommendations are made, and much is said as to how counseling can be improved. Yet little changes: girls who aspire to be physicians are "counseled" into becoming nurses; still worse, girls who aspire careers are told they will probably get married and therefore shouldn't consider a career; etc.

I recently did a rough tabulation of some 343 departments of counselor education, using data from the *Directory of Counselor Educators, 1967–68* (OE-25036-B). These figures represent virtually *all* of the institutions that train counselors in the United States.

Of the 343 departments:

209 have *no* women at all (61%).
82 have one woman (25%).
52 have two or more women (15%).

In other words, 85% of the departments have only one woman or no women on their faculty. According to U.S. Office of Education figures, women account for 20.9% of the doctorates in Counseling and Guidance.

Moreover, these women who were teaching in counselor education programs had significantly lower ranks than their male counterparts. About one-half (49%) of the women were at the lowest academic rank, that of Assistant Professor. In contrast, only 31% of the male educators were at that rank.

Few, if any, counselor education programs offer courses concerning the counseling of women, although courses concerned with other minority groups are being instituted in several universities. . . .

CHAPTER SIX

Working for a Living

American women have always worked, as have men, and for the same reasons: self-support, support of others, self-expression, and the desire to contribute to the building of society. Unlike men, they have had to justify working for pay and have carried the double burden of work in the marketplace and unpaid domestic work at home. The assignment of work by sex has traditionally expressed not an inherent logic or realistic job specification, but the cultural assumptions and values regarding the place of women in society. There are a few universals in American society in regard to women's work: the jobs women do carry low pay, low status, and inferior working conditions; women follow their traditional domestic occupations into the marketplace; and when jobs or working conditions become upgraded or professionalized women tend to be excluded and must struggle to maintain their former place. Although the woman's movement and reform organizations have historically given more attention to the needs and problems of professional and educated women, most working women don't have careers, but make a living—just barely.

There have been shifts in employment patterns over the past 150 years of industrialization. The percentage of women working for pay has increased; today, one out of every three workers is a woman. While young unmarried women predominated in the female work force until the beginning of the twentieth century, its majority today consists of women over forty years of age.

The position of working women reflects their status in the society. Women's jobs have progressed from unpaid service in the home to paid domestic and service jobs outside of the home; from unpaid home industry to paid industrial factory work; from unpaid labor on the farm to stoop labor in industrial farming and to unskilled labor in food processing.

White women entered the business world in small numbers during the Civil War in clerical and government service and sales work. They retained a hold on these occupations after the war and, with the development of the typewriter and the increasing commercialization of the economy, office work—the service work for business—became a female occupation. Similarly, nursing developed from an unpaid home service to an unskilled, then a professional and largely female occupation. One fact has remained unchanged: regardless of where a woman stands on the occupational status ladder, she is subject to discrimination in earnings, advancement opportunities, and working conditions. Unpaid nursing and child care services became low-paid hospital and welfare work. The myths that women worked for "pin money"; that they worked only temporarily until marriage; that they had no interest and motivation to upgrade their skills, reinforced existing prejudices against women workers and perpetuated their low status.

Figures on women's earnings illustrate the vast inequality of their economic position—the median income (meaning half of the total earned above and half below this figure) of full-time wage earners in 1970 was: $8,014 for white men; $5,603 for black men; $4,700 for white women; and $3,677 for black women. Women earned considerably less than men in every kind of occupation, and they were predominantly employed in low-paying occupations. Figures for 1970 show that 58 percent of the female work force of thirty-one million women were in clerical, sales, or service jobs (factory workers not included). Not surprisingly, considering their position in the work force, roughly two-thirds of all adults living in poverty were women.*

Black women are more affected by race discrimination than by sex discrimination and, except for a very small group of highly skilled black women, lag behind white women in all economic indicators. Fifty percent of all black women work (as against 39 percent of all white women). Race discrimination barriers kept black women out of middle range and skilled jobs such as office work and sales work until the 1960s, and forced even well-educated black women workers into unskilled service jobs. In

---

* U.S., Department of Labor, 1970 figures, Washington, D.C.

1966, 75 percent of all black women workers were employed in service jobs or farm and factory work (as against 38 percent white); 12 percent of all black women workers were saleswomen (34 percent white). A greater percentage of black women work after they have children; they work more years of their lives than do white women; their earnings are lower, their unemployment rate greater.*

The selections in this chapter trace the movement of women's jobs from service work to unskilled factory work and give some examples of the various ways in which women sought to improve their condition.

---

* "Fact Sheet on Non-White Women Workers," U.S., Department of Labor, Women's Bureau, October 1966, Washington, D.C.

DOMESTIC WORK

Sarah Christie Stevens

47. Domestic help on the farm—1894

These entries from the diary of a Minnesota farm woman, herself a
feminist active in the Populist movement of her time (see document 68), illustrate the emergence of domestic work from its ori-
gins in the self-sufficient family farm economy. The "hired girl" (in
this case, "hired couple") employed by the farm family would
usually be a neighbor hired on a part-time, temporary basis, often
not for cash payment but for exchange of goods or services. Hired
help and employer were social equals and, characteristically, did
the same work. In the document below, note that Mrs. Stevens'
daughters pick strawberries and do canning. In an earlier entry not
here reproduced, Mrs. Stevens describes her own work—the usual
domestic work plus care of chickens, tending the vegetable garden
and berry patch, baking, and preserving and pickling the produce
of garden and field. However, despite this shared activity of hired
help and employer, there is a distinct difference in job assignments: Mrs. Vigell is given all the heavy, dirty work; the Stevens
women do the cooking and the less strenuous work. Despite her
own radical political activities, Mrs. Stevens displays a characteristic patronizing attitude toward her hired help, as expressed in
her sneering comments about Mr. Vigell's eating some of her
berries.

June 6th Wednesday.   Mrs. Vigell came up this morning,
washed floor of little room, pantry & dining room, cleaned
out cellar and white-washed walls—she is coming again in
morning to wash safe & stain & scrub tables, clean up back

James C. Christie and Family Papers. Courtesy of the Manuscript Division,
Minnesota Historical Society, St. Paul.

room & help move stove. Also wash screen doors & refrigerator if there is time. When we settled last I forgot to count in the floor. I let her have 27 lbs. = 54 cts. [unclear reference in diary], and I owe her only for this day's work = 75 cts. I therefore owe her tonight 21 cts. She brought me 10 duck eggs also & I gave her a big satchel full of clothes, good, bad & indifferent. . . .

June 7th. Mrs. Vigell here—finished whitewashing, pasted paper on that was coming off ceiling & wall of dining room, helped move stove, scrubbed where it had stood, scrubbed safe in cellar & tables—also cellar stains—back kitchen & pantry table. I owe her 75 cts. for this day.

Vigell here also—fixed fences, mowed some in yard & then hoed in currant and R. [raspberry] bushes. But the old chap discovered the strawberry patch & from thenceforth occupied his time equally between watching for chances for forays into said patch, and the said dashes & excursions. If noticed, he was forthwith eagerly engaged in culling large pig-weeds. His plunder he rendered invisible. Nothing like a long head & short brain. I sent twice today for mail but did not get what I looked for—a letter from Bessie. Terribly warm & threatening rain all day but none came. Picked 4 qts. strawberries this evening—all drying up. . . .

June 11 Monday. We went over (Papa & I) to see Mr. Sanger about Ginseng. . . . I was glad to think as we turned our faces homeward that both girls were at home awaiting us. It was 12:45 when we came back—the girls had been busy, canned 12 pts. of strawberries, washed dishes, dressed two chickens, made biscuits with strawberries for dessert—we had a royal dinner. In the afternoon the girls picked berries & I hulled them & we had the pleasure of sending up some to Mrs. C. Ulrich & to Mrs. Wingen. A most beautiful day—air pure—sun not too warm & a fine breeze. Cloudless.

CATHARINE ESTHER BEECHER (1800–1878)

48. Friendly counsel for domestics

Catharine Beecher in her *Treatise on Domestic Economy* . . . (see also document 22) had offered middle-class urban housewives a "scientific" approach to homemaking and advice on how to perfect their housewifely skills. In a companion volume to this popular manual, she included advice on the handling of servants and the chapter below addressed to domestic servants. It offers a fine illustration of the development of domestic service, with emphasis on the *service*, out of the servant-master relationship. The servant is instructed in knowing and keeping "her place," and biblical authority is invoked for making her accept her inferior status with patience and humility. All the instructions directed at her are such as to enhance her value to her employer. There is an assumption that all her time, not only her long work day, belongs to her employer. In her counsel to the housewives employing servants, Beecher stresses only systematic instruction, conscientious supervision, and firm discipline, but cautions that few "American domestics will long submit" to "a severe and imperious mode of giving orders and finding fault." She also advises tolerance of the religious beliefs of "strangers"—a reference to the many Irish women entering domestic service in the Eastern seaboard cities in the 1840s and '50s. Nowhere in her advice to employers does she mention the human needs of the servant girl, yet her advice to domestic workers places the burden and responsibility for the happiness of the employers' family and children squarely upon the shoulders of the domestic workers.

The document below illustrates the way in which ideology is adapted to and transformed in the interest of class privilege. All women were indoctrinated to service and to placing the interests of others before their own. All women were exhorted and trained to assume responsibility for the smooth functioning of households and for the feeding and maintenance of families. When class differentiation sets in, the "lady" transfers that responsibility to the

Catharine Beecher, *Miss Beecher's Domestic Receipt Book, designed as a supplement to her Treatise on Domestic Economy* (New York: Harper & Bros., 1846), pp. 280–282.

lower-class woman, who is her "domestic help," while her own service function is transformed to that of a "manager," "supervisor" or, ultimately, she is freed for more self-fulfilling work or volunteer service commensurate with her higher status and better education. This actual and attitudinal shift is reinforced by racial and ethnic prejudice, since domestic service, with its long hours, low pay, and stigma of inferiority, was usually sought only by those least able to secure other employment: black women, recent immigrants, or the elderly.

In the nineteenth century, black women coming out of slavery were channelled into domestic service by discrimination barriers in other occupations. The marginal status of black men in the labor force, due to racial prejudice and discrimination, has forced black women to take the only jobs available to them, no matter how bad the conditions. Even at that, black women had to compete with recent immigrant women for jobs. At the time of Catharine Beecher, black women domestics were being replaced by Irish immigrants, leaving them only the heavier jobs such as scrubbing and laundry work. Similarly, the upper ranges of service jobs—governess, cook, and chamber maid—were given to white immigrant women in preference to Blacks.

With industrialization, black women began to enter unskilled factory work, but their greater vulnerability forced them during periods of recession to return to domestic work. Thus the overall employment pattern, by which a disproportionately large percentage of black women held domestic jobs, remained unchanged. In 1966, 5.6 percent of all employed white women were domestic workers; 30.3 percent of all black women workers were so employed.

Domestic work, the quintessential service occupation, is entirely "woman's work." It is, historically in this country, work for women belonging to low-status groups. Typically, when the job becomes upgraded—as in the case of professional cleaning services using machinery—it is a job for men.

My friends, you fill a very important and respectable station. The duties committed to you by God are very apt to be considered of small account, but they are indeed most solemn and important.

On your faithfulness and kindness depends the comfort of

a whole family, and on you often depends the character and happiness of a whole flock of children. If you do your part faithfully in assisting the mother to carry forward her plans, she will be able to train them aright. If you fail to perform your part, she will be perplexed, discouraged, and disabled, and everything will go wrong.

Every person finds troubles and trials in their lot, and so you must find them in yours. But trials are sent by God, not for evil, but for good, so that we, by patiently bearing them, and by striving to improve under them, may grow wiser and better, and thus more happy than we could be without them. . . .

In all your dealings with those who employ you, try to follow *"the golden rule,"* and do by them as you will wish to have others do by you, when you are the mistress of a family, and hire others to help you.

Do you find that many things are uncomfortable and unpleasant in your present lot? Remember that you never can find a place in this world where everything will be just as you want it, and that it is a bad thing for you, as well as for your employers, to keep roving about from one place to another. Stay where you are, and try to make those things that trouble you more tolerable, by enduring them with patience. . . .

Do you think that you are found fault with too much, and that your employer is so hard to please that you wish to change for another? . . . Perhaps she has a great many cares and troubles that you know not of, which try her nerves, and make her feel very irritable, and thus speak hastily when she does not intend it.

Be patient with her failings, if you think you see any, just as you wish to have her bear with your faults, when they trouble her. If you find your patience failing, it may be well in some cases, to say to your employer, that you should do better if she would find fault less and praise you more when you do well. But never say anything of this kind when you are angry yourself or when you see that she is displeased.

Be careful, in all your dealings with children, always *to*

speak the truth, and never let them hear from you any filthy or wicked language. Never promise to do a thing and then break your word, for this teaches them to break promises. . . .

Never take the least thing that does not belong to you, and never tempt children to give you what does not belong to them.

Never tell tales out of the family, nor tell to your employers the bad things you have seen or heard in other families, for this is mean and ungenerous.

Do not spend your money for useless and expensive things, but learn to be economical and prudent, that you may be preparing to be a good housekeeper, wife, and mother, if ever you have a family of your own.

Do not form a habit of roaming about to see company, but be industrious in hours not employed for those who hire you, in mending and making your own clothes.

Take care and keep your person clean, and your hair and clothes in order, and have your chamber always neat and tidy.

Do not be rude and boisterous in manners, but always speak politely to all, especially to those who employ you.

Do not waste any of the provisions, or property of your employers, nor let it spoil by neglect, and never lend or give away anything belonging to the family without leave.

Remember the Sabbath day, to keep it holy.

Read your Bible daily, and try to obey its teachings.

Pray to God to forgive your past sins, and to help you keep all his commands, and live every day so that you will not be afraid to die.

49. Anything but housework—1909

This excerpt from a publication of the Department of Women and Children of the State of Minnesota shows the subtle ways in

Mrs. Perry Starkweather, Department of Women and Children, Part V of the "Twelfth Biennial Report of the Bureau of Labor, Industries, and Commerce of the State of Minnesota, 1909–1910," Minneapolis, 1910.

which women are channeled into sex-role stereotyped occupations. The resistance of Minnesota farm girls to this bureaucratic pressure is representative of a persistently held and widespread attitude toward domestic service on the part of working women.

In 1880 the number of women employed
   in Minnesota was   23,573
In 1890 it had jumped to   62,229
In 1900 it was   90,887

And the most conservative estimate would place it today [1910] at 115,978. . . . This number excludes any enumeration of house servants or waitresses, and of this latter class there are many thousands. . . .

And right here begins the wrong to society that the present system has done and continues to do. In the schools, in the shops, in the streets and all around and about us, women and girls are being weaned from the housewifely arts, from the home, from the industry, the thrift, the sacrifices that build into the home its cornerstone of mutual helpfulness. She is being trained to ignore economics, to buy and throw away and buy again. The limited opportunity for self-development, the long hours of attention to the one minute detail that is hers to do, all these things combine to warp her mind, even as the bending over the machine warps and twists her body. . . . The close student of social conditions must realize the imperative need for so forming the mind of the girl child at an earlier age that they can go into the work of the world along lines that make for home building, home loving, home preserving. . . .

There is no work that women do that is so well paid, where the girl is so well cared for, and where she learns so much that will be of benefit to her in later life as in domestic service. Not only is the wage higher than in many other occupations, but she has in addition room and board, and as a rule is well cared for. But somewhat because of the loneliness of the girl who is so employed, and very largely because she has been trained for so many years to regard housework as drudgery, it seems to be the last form of service that girls are willing to enter.

Society as a whole is to be blamed for this sin against itself.

Of course, there is always the consideration that menial tasks are unpleasant. The girl of today, however, does not have so much of this phase of labor, for much of the heavier burden, as laundry, etc., is now sent out of the home. She does not seek this work because the girl has not been taught as she should be. She feels herself incompetent. The state has three employment bureaus and a division of each one is for women. From early morn until late at night a line of women approach the person in charge of the bureau and they say, "I want some work." "What sort of work?" If the reply was not so sad that it is tragic, it would be funny to hear the almost unvarying reply, "Anything but housework."

50. Our feudal housewives—1938

The article below summarizes the working conditions of domestic workers in major cities. It should be remembered that conditions for domestic workers in suburbs, rural areas, and small towns are usually worse. Thus domestic workers in the South received wages of $1–3 a week during the Depression.

The occupation has been most resistant to unionization. The individual nature of employment in isolated units, the separation of the workers from one another, their low economic and social status and low skill which makes them readily replaceable, are some of the causes. The historic indifference of organized labor toward unskilled women workers certainly contributed to this development, but even when attempts at unionization were made, the results were disappointing.

Evelyn Seeley, "Our Feudal Housewives," *The Nation*, 146, no. 22 (May 28, 1938): 613–614. Used courtesy of *The Nation*.

In 1936, a domestic workers' union was started by seven women in Washington, D.C. It had over a hundred members one year later and had succeeded in raising the prevailing wage from $3 to $10 a week. A Domestic Workers' Association, sponsored by the National Negro Congress, began organizing in New York City in 1937, but was short-lived. The Domestic Workers Union, headed by Dora Jones, a black woman, was founded in 1934 and was affiliated with the Building Service Union, Local 149, in New York City. In 1939 the organization had 350 members, 75 percent of them black women.

Since that period various unions, such as teamsters and laundry workers, have given charters to domestic workers' locals. Unionization has not, generally, resulted in marked improvement of wages and working conditions, except in hotels, institutions, and office cleaning firms. Efforts at ameliorating working conditions through legislation have been equally difficult to accomplish, as the examples below illustrate.

The housewife stands condemned as the worst employer in the country. . . .

The housewives of the United States make their million and a half employees work an average of seventy-two hours a week and pay them lower wages than are paid in any other industry. (Comparatively good wages, $8 to $18 a week, are maintained in some metropolitan areas, but in most sections they average only $3 and $4 a week.) Housewives pay their servants whatever they can squeeze out of their budget after the grocer, the butcher, the laundry, the department store—with means of collection—have been paid; cut them when their own income declines; take from their pay maximum cash value for living quarters and give them minimum value—a room just off the laundry, perhaps, or over the garage; give them no vacations with pay, no sick leave, no insurance against accident, no security of any kind; permit them little freedom to see or make friends; treat them generally in such a way that a social stigma clings to the job of domestic worker.

At the bottom of the worker scale is the "slave market" as

it exists in certain cities. New York has 200 slave markets, according to the Domestic Workers' Union. You can bargain for household help in the Bronx on almost any corner above 167th Street. Colored workers, mostly women, stand there in little groups waiting to be hired. Each carries a bundle containing work clothes and the lunch she will eat hastily on her own time. They work for 35 cents an hour, although 50 cents is the standard rate. Some who are desperate or cold or tired of standing will work for 25 cents. They say that they are sometimes asked to go for 15. Most jobs last three or four hours.

That is the bottom. At the top are the domestic staffs of the big houses, who in many cases have reasonable hours, good pay, security, and some social life among themselves. Between the "cleaning women" and the "staff" come the great majority of domestic workers—those who are the only maid in a home, completely at the mercy of the kindness or carelessness or ruthlessness of the employer. The conditions of their employment are admittedly difficult to change, but certain movements, gathering strength slowly, are under way to help them. Legislation, unionization, training for workers, education of employers, promotion of the working agreement offer hope for the future. . . .

A year ago a bill limiting the hours of domestic work to sixty a week was introduced in the New York legislature. Placing the limit as high as sixty would seem arrogant in any other field, but the home is "different," and to many sputtering housewives, as well as to the domestic-employment agencies, the very idea was revolution. The Women's Trade Union League framed the bill. Such organizations as the Domestic Workers' Union, the National Consumers League, the Women's City Club of New York, and the League of Women Shoppers generally favored it. . . .

It could not be passed. The only thing accomplished for household workers in New York during the past year was the amendment of the workmen's compensation act to apply to employers of two or more household workers. . . .

The Domestic Workers' Union is young and weak. In New York, where there are 100,000 domestic workers, it has not yet 1,000 members. . . . The New York local strives for the sixty-hour six-day week, one full day off, higher wages, better conditions, social security and compensation. The union does not regard sixty hours as a reasonable working week, but it knows it is the best it can ask for now. It suggests working out the sixty-hour six-day week on the basis of two five-hour shifts a day. A ten-hour day seems a great stride ahead, since the average maid works fifteen to sixteen hours a day. . . .

51. Collective bargaining for household technicians—1975

The *New York Times* news story below brings the struggle for upgrading domestic work up to date. The effort to improve the working conditions of domestic workers through legislation has been tried many times and has led to some improvements. It has always depended on the support of middle-class women's organizations, such as the National Consumer League, YWCA, and women's clubs. Such support has always been tempered by the conflict of interest between domestic workers and their female employers. Now, the feminist movement has made this issue a major focus of concern—a "gut issue." Feminists have faced the conflict-of-interest question squarely and have suggested social solutions for housework, maintenance, and child care. This is a novel approach, although some of the pioneering theorists of feminism held similar ideas long ago (see documents 27, 29). It remains to be seen if the organized strength of the feminist movement together with the self-help efforts of domestic workers will bring much-needed amelioration.

Nadine Brozan, "Bargaining Legislation for Domestics May Have Wide Impact," *New York Times* April 28, 1975, p. 24. Reprinted by permission of the *New York Times*, © 1975.

Their average age is 51. Their education ended at the ninth grade. Ninety-eight percent of them are women, an estimated 65 to 80 percent are black. One out of every six is a head of household. And the last time anyone looked, their mean income was $2,243 a year.

They are domestic workers. Their employers call them "my girl." They would rather be known as "household technicians." Recently, they moved one step closer to the negotiating table when the New York State Assembly passed, by a vote of 115 to 20, a bill granting them the right of collective bargaining. . . .

The immediate impact of the bill appears confined to a handful of the 100,000 domestic workers in the state. But it carries implications for every worker.

With the prospect of collective bargaining, activists such as the National Committee on Household Employment and its four affiliates here are already talking of paid vacations, holidays and sick leave, personal days, workmen's compensation, disability insurance, job security and pension plans. For the employers, such proposals mean increased costs. . . .

It is the thorny question of who shall sit across the table from whatever union emerges that perplexes foes and skeptics. Will individual employers be forced to confront a union bargaining team to decide how much they will pay their household help?

The most prevalent solution advocated by legislators and household activists alike is the establishment of union hiring halls, where prospective employers would go to seek workers. Some envision the organization of residents of cooperatives and condominiums into management teams.

For the time being, if his bill is passed, "It will affect essentially the 5,000 or so people who work for contract cleaning firms (those who act as the employer and send their staff to private homes on household assignments)," Assemblyman Seymour Posner conceded. . . .

Predictably, the agencies were opposed to the prospect of unionization. . . .

"Our women wouldn't think of joining a union; they would turn a deaf ear," said a spokesman for Miss Dixie, an employment agency. "They're getting $125 a week and up plus room and board, vacations, bonuses and Social Security. Sometimes it's the employers who are abused while they treat the worker like a doll."

Lester Abrams, field manager for the New York State Department of Labor's household placement offices here said, however, "The employer who gives things like sick leave, paid vacations and holidays is the exception. It is so unusual that we consider it a great plus."

According to Mr. Abrams, the going wage for a day worker in the city is now about $2.25 an hour. The fulltime sleep-out worker gets from $90 to $110 a week; the sleep-in employee gets about $100 a week.

Nationally, Bureau of the Census figures for 1973, the last year for which data is available, showed the median income of the year-round, fulltime worker at $2,243, a drop from the 1972 median of $2,365.

It was not until 1950 that domestic workers gained any legal recognition at all, when an amendment to the Social Security law gave them coverage. . . .

Last May, minimum wage and overtime payment became a national law with an amendment to the Federal Fair Labor Standards Act. . . .

A member of the Women's Political Caucus, Mrs. Carolyn Reed, a leader of the Progressive Household Technicians here, said she considered the women's movement crucial to the uphill battle.

"This is a gut woman's issue. The reason we haven't gotten our rights as a paid person in the labor force is because men think they can get their wives or girlfriends to do the job without pay," she said. . . .

[The bill did not come to a vote in the spring 1975 session of the N.Y. state senate. It awaits further action.]

WOMEN IN INDUSTRIAL EMPLOYMENT

CAROLINE DALL

52. Limited choices—1860

With industrialization women followed their "traditional" occupations into the factory. In Europe, the labor power for early industry had consisted of displaced farmers; in America, men could still make a living at farming and had opportunities for advancing their economic position by migration. Thus, from its beginning, U.S. industry depended on the labor power of women and children.

The textile industry was the chief employer of female labor, but women could be found in over a hundred occupations in 1822. Caroline Dall, in her book from which excerpts appear below, tried to offer a survey of employment opportunities for women. She explains how actuality differed from statistical data: women may have been found in over a hundred different occupations, but most of them were in service jobs or unskilled factory labor. This fact, another universal in the history of American women, has remained constant for over 150 years.

Women might advance from unpaid work in the home to low-paid home industry and from there to unskilled factory work. In hard times, they could return to the home or enter domestic service. These were their limited choices. Only in wartime could they enter different fields or advance according to their abilities and skills. Usually, the gains of war periods were quickly eroded. Last hired, first fired, least paid.

. . . In 1845, there were employed in the Textile manufactures of the United States, 55,828 men and 75,710 women. This proportion, or a still greater preponderance of female labor—that is, from one-third to one-half,—appears in all the factory returns. As an *employed* class, women seem to be more in number than men: as *employers*, they are very few. . . .

Caroline H. Dall, *Women's Right to Labor, or Low Wages and Hard Work* (Boston: Walker, Wise & Co., 1860), pp. 97–103.

In a New-Haven clock factory, seven women are employed among seventy men, on half-wages; and the manufacturer takes great credit to himself for his liberality. At Waltham, also, a watch factory has been lately started, in which many women are employed.* In the census of the city of Boston for 1845, the various employments of women are thus given:—

Artificial-flower makers,	Comb-makers,
Boardinghouse-keepers,	Confectioners,
Bookbinders,	Corset-dealers,
Printers,	Corset-makers,
Blank-book makers,	Card-makers,
Bonnet-dealers,	Professed cooks,
Bonnet-makers,	Cork-cutters,
Workers in straw,	Domestics,
Shoe and boot makers,	Dress-makers,
Band & fancy box makers,	Match-makers,
Brush-makers,	Fringe and tassel makers,
Cap-makers,	Fur-sewers,
Clothiers,	Hair-cloth weavers, and
Collar-makers,	Map-colorers.

I think you cannot fail to see, from this list, how very imperfect the enumeration is: not a single washerwoman not charwoman, for one thing, upon it. Yet here you have the occupations of 4,970 women. Of these, 4,046 are servants,—a number which has, at least, doubled since then;

* I do not dwell upon this watch factory in the text, because, although fifty women are at work with one hundred and fifty men, they are only "tending machines;" so that, although employment is open, a career can hardly be said to be. The watches made at Waltham by machinery are said to be so superior to all others, that they are used by preference on the race-courses to time the horses. Men and women do not compete with each other there; but both are at service, with a steam-engine for their master.

For the first two months, the women earn two dollars and fifty cents *a week;* for the third, three dollars; and, after that, four dollars. The men earn from five shillings to two dollars a *day.* It seems that no special skill is required in the women, while the men in a few departments are still paid according to their ability . . . [—Dall's footnote].

and which leaves only 924 women for all other vocations. . . .

It is probably known to you all how largely the rural post-office duties are performed by women; petty politicians obtaining the appointment, and leaving wives and daughters to do the work. There are several Registers of Deeds; but I know only one,—Olive Rose, of Thomaston, Me. She was elected in 1853, by 469 votes against 205; was officially notified, and required to give bonds. Her emolument depends upon fees, and ranges between three and four hundred dollars per annum. . . .

I am sorry to conclude these attempts at statistics with one reliable estimate, which holds, like a nutshell, the kernel of this question of female labor.

In 1850, there were engaged in shoemaking, in the town of Lynn, 3,729 males and 6,412 females,—nearly twice as many women as men; yet, in the monthly payment of wages, only half as much money was paid to women as to men. The three thousand men received seventy-five thousand dollars a month; and the six thousand women, thirty-seven thousand dollars: that is, the women's wages were, on the average, only one-quarter as much as those of the men. . . .

Salome Lincoln

53. An early "turn-out"—1829

Conditions in the New England textile industry were glowingly described by contemporaries on the basis of their brief visits to the model factory town of Lowell, Mass. Historians have described the transition from the short period of paternalism in the textile mills to industrial conflict brought on by speed-up and the competition of

Almond H. Davis, *The Female Preacher, or Memoir of Salome Lincoln, Afterwards the Wife of Elder Junia S. Mowry* (Providence, R.I.: Elder J. S. Mowry, 1843), pp. 49–52.

immigrant labor. At Lowell, these conditions led to "turn-outs," strike processions, and, between 1834 and 1836, to the formation of a militant union of mill girls, the Female Labor Reform Association.

It is interesting to read the following account of earlier union activity at Taunton, Mass. It describes an episode in the life of Salome Lincoln, one of the earliest female preachers (see document 33). Like most of these early strike actions, the protest of the weavers ended in defeat, and Salome Lincoln's search for other employment may very well have been the result of being blacklisted for her strike leadership. It is difficult to tell from the record to what extent her experiences as a mill girl influenced her future career as a traveling minister, but her leadership qualities must have been obvious to her fellow workers. Here is another instance of the initiative of working women seeking improvement in their condition, and of feminist consciousness emerging from the struggle for economic rights (see also document 54).

In 1822, she [Salome Lincoln] was at work in the weaving room in the factory at Hopewell, Taunton, for the Richmond Company. . . . Salome continued to work in the factory at Hopewell, until the first of May, 1829, when an unforeseen circumstance occurred which deprived her of her work. The circumstance is briefly this:

For some cause, the corporation reduced the wages in the weaving department, where Salome was then at work. The girls indignant at this, bound themselves under an obligation, not to go back into the mill, until the former prices were restored; and this not being granted, they formed themselves into a procession, and marched through the streets, to the green in front of the Court house. . . . They were in uniform,—having on black silk dresses, with red shawls, and green calashes. They then went into a hall near the common, in order to listen to an address. Salome was selected as the orator of the day. She then took the stand, and in her own peculiar style, eloquently addressed them at considerable length, on the subject of their wrongs; after which they quietly returned to their homes.

For one inducement, and another, nearly all who had turned out at this time, returned into the factory again, and resumed their work. But not so with Salome!—She manfully refused to violate her word; but chose rather, to leave business—and break up all the social and religious ties she had formed than to deviate from the paths of rectitude. After this she never worked in the factory again at Taunton, but sought employment elsewhere, and was successful. . . .

54. New York tailoresses organize—1831–1851

The needle trades industry depended on the labor of needy women, who were among the most exploited of all wage earners. Many of the tailoresses and sewing women were single or widowed, barred by lack of skill and training opportunities from more remunerative occupations and forced to work at home at piecework rates, often supplemented by the unpaid labor of their children. It required expertise and fifteen to sixteen hours of daily labor to earn a dollar and a half per week in Philadelphia and New York City, according to contemporary testimony, with the average income of a seamstress at $1.25 a week. This was not enough income for survival, and many seamstresses had to accept supplementary charity.

Under these circumstances, it is not surprising that the several efforts of sewing women to organize were easily defeated. The documents below describe one of the earliest attempts to organize women workers.* The United Tailoresses Society of New York was formed in February 1831 in response to a cut in piecework rates. They held several meetings and adopted a "bill" of wages which they considered adequate for maintenance, and tried to enlist public support for these minimum wages. They also hoped to put pressure on their employers by publicizing their needs. A committee, headed by a man, was appointed to receive contributions from

---

* I am indebted to my former student, Dolores Janiewski, for calling these sources to my attention and for their interpretation.

the public. The speech by Lavinia Waight, who was elected secretary of the society and is thus one of the earliest women trade union leaders known, is remarkable for its feminist tone. In fact, such forthright feminist statements by working-class women may make it necessary to revise current historical interpretations of the rise of feminist ideology as being a middle-class phenomenon. In the case of the tailoresses it was middle-class influence, that of their "benevolent" supporters, which apparently caused them to forsake their strongly feminist, militant stance after the defeat of their brief strike in June 1831. The women went back to work at the lower rates and the organization dissolved.

The next effort at organizing the sewing women of New York City occurred in 1836, and another one in 1845 with the formation of the militant Ladies Industrial Association, which lasted only a few months. Following this, reformers set up another organization which appealed to the public's generosity and chivalry, did not stress strike action, but rather aimed to set up a "cooperative" which would employ sewing women at better wages and for which the support of the public was sought. The association was led by a committee of middle-class men and women who collected money, set up the Shirt Sewers' Cooperative Union, and for a few years employed forty women, paying them about one and a half dollars a week above prevailing wages. Even this small effort at improving conditions failed and the organization of sewing women lapsed for several decades.

It is worth noting how the phenomenon of working women attempting to organize was treated in the press as an occasion for sly innuendo, sexual jokes, and "witty" writing.

Remarks of the Secretary, Lavinia Waight

I shall offer no other prelude to the following remarks, than the simple expression of a desire on my own part, to augment the excitement that I have perceived to exist among my female friends who were present at the last meeting, which had for its laudable object a subversion of the most flagrant abuses that disgrace the policies of men. That females are imposed upon, and oppressed in almost every stage of action to which the circumstances of their existence

New York Daily Sentinel, Thursday, February 17, 1831.

render them liable, is a fact, that, . . . requires only the reiteration of cases, great in number, wretched in their character, and calculated to draw forth the sympathies of the benevolent. . . . Are not females in the first place excluded from equal liberality in the circumstances of their education, incapacitated for the duties of legislation and other matters of like importance, in which, you will all allow, they are equally interested? Their parents, as *they* are taught to do, offer as an apology for this partiality, the inutility of their children's acquiring knowledge which can never become practically important to them. I would ask why it should not? Why should not women engage in the duties of trade and legislation? to whom shall I put the question? to those helpless and oppressed beings who are, and have been, blindfolded by a cunning and designing policy, from a fair view of their own interests? Here are only a small portion, whom some uncommonly fortunate circumstance, perhaps existing in the very extremity of their oppression, has convinced of their delusion: I here allude to the present assembly. Shall I then question the lords and tyrants of the world, and the monopolizers of all interest? It is unnecessary. Look to the baneful effects that a degraded and major portion of mankind exhibit to your view? Shall I ask *Nature* if the physical inequalities which she has made, furnish a cause for these evils? or shall I argue from her decrees, a total reversion of the present degraded order of things.

These remarks may be thought by some of too extensive a nature and irrelevant to the immediate purposes of this meeting. I have thought them important links in the chain of oppressions against the truly dominated *weaker sex.* . . .

Another Organizing Attempt:
The Newspaper Reaction—1836

The Seamstresses—We are happy to hear that there is a determination universally expressed throughout this indus-

New York Sun, 1st year, no. 788, March 15, 1836.

trious, lovely and very numerous class of our population, to combine and demand of their employers a more adequate remuneration for the productions of their hands—However unfavorable the late decree of Chief Justice Savage may be interpreted with regard to the right of combination in the male operatives of this community we cannot believe that any lawyers in the land would be so thoroughly savage as to deny this right to the fair stitchers of society. . . . Certain it is that the legislators of modern days, at least, have favored few laws for the gentle sex but what are protective rather than restrictive. The feminine gender therefore, has privileges in the Syntax of life which the masculine has not; there is no rule to compel it to agree either with the nominative or genitive case, however desirable such a concord may be; and its relation to any copulative or disjunctive function is entirely voluntary. Thus a woman may separate from her husband and there is no law to compel her to return to him, or to set a single stitch for his maintenance but a man cannot degrade himself to single wretchedness without incurring a magisterial visitation and a certain demand upon his exchequier (or ex-check-her) as Aunt Tabitha spells it and thus, although, the Chief Justice of this state may have decided that men have no right to combine, to demand an increase of wages, he would no more think of deciding against the rights of women to obtain this object than of deciding that men and women have not a right to combine in matrimony for the increase of the population of this extensive country.

Conscious of this right, we are assured by several fair correspondents, that the seamstresses of this city are going, one and all, to stick their needles in their cushions, take . . . the yoke of oppression from their necks, shake the shreds from their laps, and stand upon their footstools for higher prices. Nothing can be more commendable and nothing more successful, but we trust that they will render their strike more striking by exhibiting their striking beauties to the eyes of our sex, in a pretty procession round the Park. It would be the most striking spectacle ever witnessed in this city for so many dears in one park were never seen in the lordly domain of Europe, and will it not accomplish something more than a mere matter of money—say matrimony? O yes it would! The fusty bachelors of this city have never seen a thousandth part of the beauteous faces and forms that are bent over the vests which enwrap their torpid hearts and the pantaloons which enclose their inamative legs. . . . When they see this unexceptional array of beauty on whom they have been dependent for every article of their raiment larger than a fig leaf, will not the ungrateful rascals begin to thirst of Hymen as the only appropriate portion of these high-minded women? Will the recreant dastards then think it unreasonable that wives should wear the breeches when they reflect upon the many pairs they have made for them whilst in their maiden state, and all unpaid themselves?

The suffering of the seven classes of seamstresses in this city is intolerable. . . . Only think how these lovely girls are confined before they get married; and how little they get for all this labor from the grinding avarice of their employers, and then ask if they are not justified in throwing up their needle work for higher prices? One fair correspondent . . . in a well written, sensible letter, makes us acquainted with these serious grievances of the sweet stitching species of our race. . . .

"I hope and trust that the male will act with a whole heart . . . and if they are not disposed to lend their aid in this way, I fear many of us will fall on them with a heavier claim, both directly or indirectly, for it is utterly impossible for us to obtain an honest living at the present price of provisions, fuels, and house rent." . . .

Bless their dear little souls and bodies, we shall feel as happy in being on their side and taking their part as we always feel in being by their side and taking their delicate little hands. . . .

If the stockmakers do not give you better wages for making stocks, we will torment their faces with our bristling quills until they wish they were in the pillory, and others who oppress you we will press until they wish they were under their own heated irons for giving you under prices and so we will enter upon that Christian duty tomorrow, but do, oh, do, give us a procession in the Park!

Another Try: Ladies' Industrial Association—1845

NEW YORK SUN, MARCH 3, 1845

"Mass Meeting of Young Women"—We are requested to call the attention of the young women of the city engaged in industrious pursuits to the call for a mass meeting in the Park this afternoon at 4 o'clock.

We are also requested to appeal to the gallantry of the men of this city, young and old, and respectfully ask them not to be present at this meeting as those for whose benefit it is called prefer to deliberate by themselves.

NEW YORK HERALD, MARCH 8, 1845

Seldom or never did the Superior Court of City Hall contain such an array of beauty under suffering, together with common sense and good order, as it did yesterday, on the occasion of the meeting of the Female Industrial classes in their endeavor to remedy the wrongs and oppression under which they labor, and from some time past, have labored. At the hour appointed for the adjourned meeting, four o'clock, about 700 females, generally of the most interesting age and appearance, were assembled, and after a trifling delay, a young lady stepped forward and in rather a low, diffident tone, moved that Miss Grey (Gray) take the chair, which, having been put forward and carried in the usual business like way—Miss Grey (a young woman, neatly dressed, of

New York Sun, 12th year, no. 3570, March 3, 1845.

Reprinted article from the *New York Herald* in the *Working Man's Advocate*, March 8, 1845.

New York Herald VI, no. 77 (March 19, 1845).

some 22 or 24 years of age, fair complection, interesting, thoughtful and intellectual cast of countenance), came forward from the back part of the room. She . . . stated that finding the class she belonged to were unable to support themselves honestly and respectably by their industry . . . had therefore come to the determination of endeavoring to obtain something better, by appealing to the public at large, and showing the amount of the sufferings under which they at present labored. She then . . . mentioned several employers by name who only paid them from 10 to 18 cents per day; others who were proficient in the business after 12 or 14 hours of hard labor, could only get about 25 cents per day; one employer offered them twenty cents per day, and said that if they did not take it, he would obtain girls from Connecticut that would work for less even than what he offered. The only employer who had done them justice was Mr. Beck of 14th Street, who only allowed his girls to be out about two hours when he complied with their reasonable demands. He was a man who was worthy of the thanks of every girl present and they wished him health, wealth and happiness. How was it possible that on such an income they could support themselves decently and honorably, let alone support widowed mothers, and some two, three or four helpless brothers and sisters, which many of them had. Pieces of work for which they last year got 7 shillings, this year they could get only three shillings. . . .

Another female of equally interesting appearance [Mrs. Horn] then came forward and said that it was necessary . . . their own position should be fully known. If the supply of labor in the market was greater than the demand, it followed in a matter of course that they could not control the prices and therefore, it would be well for those present to look around to see into what other channels they could [put] their industry with advantage. There were many branches of business in which men were employed that they could as well fill. Let them memorialize the merchants in the dry goods department for instance and show them this also.

That there were hundreds of females in this city, who were able to keep the books as well as any man in it. There were various other branches of business in which men were employed for which females alone were suitable and intended. Let those men go into the fields and seek their livelihood as men ought to do and leave the females to their legitimate employment. . . .

A number of delegates of the following trades entered their names to act as a Committee to regulate future proceedings—tailoresses, plain and coarse sewing, shirt makers, book-folders and stitchers, cap makers, straw workers, dress makers, crimpers, fringe and lace makers, etc., etc. . . . [They planned a fund-raising meeting at the Opera House, and]

Resolved that an address be prepared by a committee to present our wrongs to the public in their true and proper light and advising such measures as may be best calculated to remedy them. . . .

New York Herald, MARCH 19, 1845

The "Female Industrial Association"—We have given frequent notice of the association bearing this title, recently attempted in this city and said a great many favorable things in behalf of the enterprise but we very much doubt whether it will terminate in much good to female labor of any description. . . . We remember very well how the generous attempt in this city a few years ago . . . terminated. Vast sums of money were collected, powerful appeals made to public sympathy, and a great amount of parade and noise perpetuated, but no permanent benefit accrued to the sufferers. A few stray women who became the managers of the Concern, appropriated the good that was done to their own private emolument, advantage and credit, and this is, we believe, in most cases the result of such movements. In this country every individual of every class of society must trust to individual effort, individual prudence, individual skill and enterprise. All combinations end in nothing.

Shirt Sewers' Cooperative Union

The public are aware that a portion of the Shirt Sewers of New York made an effort early last summer to better their condition and raise themselves from the low and abject condition of toiling from fifteen to eighteen hours per day for a bare pittance to sustain life by associating together for the purpose of dividing the larger share of profits now accruing to the employers among the employed, thereby bringing the producer and consumer together for purposes of mutual aid and profit. . . . We have had kind friends to help us, and to such we are grateful, but they have been few, and we begin to despond. Our work is falling off, we are unable, from our very limited means to give employ to but few of our suffering and needy sisters, when there are thousands ready and anxious to unite with us, if our facilities would allow us to give them employ. Society is not extending to us the helping hand that we were fain led to expect. We are too poor to make our case known to you by paid advertisement and we now make this last appeal to you, believing that it will not pass unheeded. Upon our failure or success depends the future comfort or misery of thousands in our city, who are even now "sewing at once with a double stitch, a shroud as well as a shirt."

The condition of the Shirt Sewers is lamentable and calls for your kindest and warmest sympathies. It is estimated that their numbers at present exceed six thousand. Many of these are young and friendless orphans, early left to struggle with poverty and solely dependent upon the precarious pittance of wages doled out by employers. Others are widows, depending upon the needle for support of helpless children, and with the pittance of some $2 or $2.50 per week, trying to feed and clothe, and pay rent of a family. We need not tell you this cannot be done. They bear in silence, sufferings and trials that would chill the sternest heart, to recount. The defenceless girl often wrestles with poverty, hunger, temp-

Broadside, c. 1851. Courtesy of the New York Historical Society.

tation until dire neçessity forces sad and fearful alternatives
upon her. Is this Christian? Is it Human?

> Oh men with sisters dear,
> Oh men with mothers and wives,
> It is not linen you're wearing out,
> It's human creatures' lives.

But we will not murmur; we are ready to make personal
sacrifices to sustain and build up our association. To this end
we appeal to a generous public.

We need your assistance now. We need a store in which to
dispose of stock when made, and the patronage of those who
have employment to give. We need to be placed on a permanent basis, where disabilities, necessities and wants will
not circumscribe our usefulness, and dampen our energies.
Kind friends! Will you aid and assist us? The present office
of our Association is at 9 Henry Street, where orders will be
thankfully received and our wants made known to such as
will interest themselves in the cause of our suffering sisters.
Who will hear? Who will regard our humble and earnest
appeal? Signed on behalf of the Shirt Sewers' Cooperative
Union by the following members of the Board of Managers:
Mrs. Moody, Dunn, J. H. Keyser, Loveland, Manageress.

RHETA CHILDE DORR

55. Protective legislation—1908

The long struggle to win labor protective legislation for women
workers arose out of the grim realities of the working conditions in
an industrializing society, where neither strong labor unions nor

Rheta Childe Dorr, *Women's Demand for Humane Treatment of Women
Workers in Shop and Factory* (New York: The Consumers League of the
City of New York, 1909). Reprinted from *Hampton's Magazine* (December
1909).

sympathetic public opinion existed to check the exploitation of unskilled workers. Trade unions had failed repeatedly to organize these workers and were, in any event, indifferent to the conditions under which women worked. The courts, led by the Supreme Court, had upheld the fictitious equality between the bargaining power of the corporation and of the lone worker, considering both of them equally "free" to negotiate the conditions under which labor would toil. As long as the courts refused to accept any restraints on hours and wages, considering these restraints on the "freedom to contract," the only hope for winning an improvement in the condition of unskilled workers was an appeal to morality and social interest. It was this appeal—the need to protect the health of working women in the interest of the entire community and the race—which finally won what economic arguments had failed to win: a legal limit on the length of the working day, in the 1908 *Muller* v. *Oregon* decision discussed in the article below. Although this court-imposed restraint on the rights of employers applied to working women only, male workers would have to be granted the same protections sooner or later.

Labor protective legislation, then as now, was needed for *all* workers, but in the U.S. setting, was won first for women. The struggle for winning these rights was further remarkable for the close alliance between working-class and middle-class women in the interest of the former. The National Consumers League and the National Women's Trade Union League were the leading forces welding this alliance into a workable tool for social change.

In the headquarters of the National [Consumers'] League in New York City, a group of trained experts work constantly, collecting and recording a vast body of facts concerning the human side of industry. It is ammunition which tells. One single blast of it, fired in the direction of a laundry in Portland, Oregon, two years ago, performed the wonderful feat of blowing a large hole through the Fourteenth Amendment to the Constitution of the United States.

There was a law in Oregon which decreed that the working day of women in factories and laundries should be ten hours long. The law was constantly violated, especially in the steam laundries of Portland. One night a factory inspector walked into the laundry of one Curt Muller, and found working there, long after closing time, one Mrs. Gotcher. The inspector promptly sent Mrs. Gotcher home and arrested Mr. Muller.

The next day in court Mr. Muller was fined ten dollars. Instead of paying the fine he appealed, backed up in his action by the other laundrymen of Portland, on the ground that the ten-hour law for women was unconstitutional. The Fourteenth Amendment of the Constitution guarantees to every adult member of the community the right freely to contract. . . .

The case was appealed, and appealed again, by the laundrymen, and finally reached the Supreme Court of the United States. Then the Consumers' League took a hand.

The brief for the State of Oregon . . . was prepared by Louis S. Brandeis, of Boston, assisted by Josephine Goldmark, one of the most effective workers in the League's New York Headquarters. This brief is probably one of the most remarkable legal documents in existence. It consists of one hundred and twelve printed pages, of which a few paragraphs were written by the attorney for the State. All the rest was contributed, under Miss Goldmark's direction, from the Consumers' League's wonderful collection of reasons why women workers should be protected. . . . The Consumers' League convinced the Supreme Court of the United States, and the Oregon ten-hour law was upheld. . . .

Waitresses' Union, Local No. 484, of Chicago, led by a remarkable young working woman, Elizabeth Maloney . . . drafted, and introduced into the Illinois Legislature, a bill providing an eight-hour working day for every woman in the State. . . .

The "Girls' Bill," as it immediately became known, was the most hotly contested measure passed by the Illinois Legislature during the session. Over 500 manufacturers appeared at the public hearing on the bill . . . presenting the business aspect of the question; the girls showed the human side. . . .

"I am a waitress," said Miss Maloney, "and I work ten hours a day. In that time a waitress who is tolerably busy *walks* ten miles, and the dishes she carries back and forth aggregate in weight 1,500 to 2,000 pounds. Don't you think eight hours a day is enough for a girl to walk?"

Only one thing stood in the way of the passage of the bill after that day. The doubt of its constitutionality proved an obstacle too grave for the friends of the workers to overcome. It was decided to substitute a ten-hour bill, an exact duplicate of the "Oregon Standard" established by the Supreme Court of the United States. The principle of limitation upon the hours of women's work once established in Illinois, the workers could proceed with their fight for an eight-hour day.

The manufacturers lost their fight, and the ten-hour bill became a law of the State of Illinois. The Manufacturers' Association, through the W. C. Richie Paper Box Manufactory, of Chicago, immediately brought suit to test the constitutionality of the law. Two Richie employees, Anna Kusserow and Dora Windeguth, made appeal to the Illinois courts. Their appeal declared that they could not make enough paper boxes in ten hours to earn their bread, and that their constitutional rights freely to contract, as well as their human rights, had been taken away from them by the ten-hour law. . . .

One point the courts cannot escape: the revelation of the state of women's wages in Illinois. If women of mature years—one of the petitioners has been a box-maker for over thirty years—are unable, in a day of ten hours, to earn enough to keep body and soul together, is it not proved that women workers are in no position freely to contract? For who, of her own free will, would contract to work ten hours a day for less than the price of existence? There is a terrible confession, on the part of the employers, involved in this protest against the ten-hour day.

It seems to the women who have studied these things that proper sanitary conditions, lunch room, comfortable seats, provision for rest, vacations with pay, and the like, are no more than the wage-earners's due. They are a part of the laborer's hire, and should be guaranteed by law, exactly as wages are guaranteed. An employer deserves gratitude for overtime pay no more than for fire escapes. . . .

57. How to live on 46 cents a day—1929

For more than a hundred years working women have sought to improve their conditions by organizing. This account of the daily life of a South Carolina cotton mill worker and her family reveals how little has changed in the condition of unskilled women workers.

Gladys Caldwell* met us at the door of her four-room cottage in the mill village. It was one of a row of dingy cottages out in Poinsett, across the meadows at the edge of Greenville, just beyond "nigger town." . . .

Here is Gladys Caldwell's story:

I have a husband and five children. I'm a weaver. . . . I get paid by the day. . . .

I get up at four to start breakfast for the children. When you got five young 'uns it takes a while to dress 'em. The oldest is nine and she helps a lot. The others are seven, five, four, and three. . . .

After I've got the children dressed and fed I take 'em to the mill nursery, that is three of 'em. Two go to school, but after school they go to the nursery until I get home from the mill. The mill don't charge anythin' to keep the children there. I couldn't afford it anyway. We have breakfast about

Paul Blanshard, "How to Live on Forty-six Cents a Day," *The Nation* 128 no. 3332 (May 15, 1929): 580–581. Used courtesy of *The Nation*.

* Gladys Caldwell is not the real name of the mill woman Mr. Blanshard interviewed. Otherwise her story is set down as she related it, the story of how a family of seven finds it possible to live on $22.80 a week or $.46 each per day.—EDITOR, THE NATION.

five, and I spend the rest of the time from five to seven gettin' the children ready and cleanin' up the house. That's about the only time I get to clean up. Ruby washes the dishes. Ruby is nine.

My husband and I go to the mill at seven. He's a stripper in the cardin' room and gets $12.85 a week, but that's partly because they don't let him work Saturday mornin'. They put this stretch-out system on him shore enough. You know he's runnin' four jobs ever since they put this stretch-out system on him and he ain't gettin' any more than he used to get for one. Where'd they put the other three men?—why they laid 'em off and they give him the same $12.85 he got before.

I work in the weavin' room and I get $1.80 a day. That's $9.95 a week for five and a half days. I work from seven to six with an hour for dinner. I run up and down the alleys all day. No, they ain't no chance to sit down, except once in a long time when my work's caught up, but that's almost never.

At noon I run home and get dinner for the seven of us. The children come home from school and the nursery. . . . We have beans and baked sweets and bread and butter, and sometimes fat-back and sometimes pie, if I get time to bake it. Of course I make my own bread.

It takes about $16 a week to feed us. . . .

After dinner I wash the dishes and run back to the mill. We don't have any sink but there's a faucet with runnin' water on the back porch and a regular toilet there, too. . . .

When the whistle blows at six I come home and get supper. Then I put the children to bed. There's a double bed here and a double bed in that other room and a double bed out in the back room. That's for seven of us. The baby's pretty young. I 'spose all of the children'll go into the mills when they get a bit older. We'll need the money all right. Yes, my father and mother were mill workers, too, and they're still livin' and workin'. He gets $18 a week and my mother gets about $3 a week for workin' mornin's. . . . I went through the third grade in school and then I went to work in the mill. I was nine years old when I started work at

Number 4 in Pelzer. My husband didn't go to school neither but he managed to pick up readin' and he reads books. Yes, we take a paper.

When supper is over I have a chance to make the children's clothes. Yes, I make 'em all, and all my own clothes, too. I never buy a dress at a store. I haven't no sewin' machine but I borrow the use of one. On Saturday night I wash the children in a big wash-tub and heat the water on the oil stove. Then I do the week's ironin'. I send the washin' to the laundry. I just couldn't do that, too. It costs nearly $2 a week. Our rent in this house is only $1.30 a week for the four rooms and we get water and electric lights free.

I always make a coat last seven or eight years. My husband gets a suit every two years but he ain't had one for the last six years. He got an overcoat about four years ago. Things have been pretty hard. . . .

Maybe my children ought to get away from the mill village, but if they went anywhere they would go back to the farm and there ain't no use doin' that. The farmers haven't got it as good as we have. . . .

Sunday's about the only day I get to rest any. Seems as if I just have to have a little rest then.

Let's see, my babies cost $25 except the first one and that cost $30. 'Taint every doctor will do it for that. I never had any trouble. I worked up to two months before, mostly, an' I went back when the children was about four months old. The nursery'll take 'em when they're three weeks old. I had to hire a colored girl when the babies come. That cost $7 a week.

Birth control? What's that? . . . Oh! Sure, we'd be glad to have that if it didn't cost no money. . . .

Once I mashed my thumb in the mill. I was out for two months with it and I didn't get anythin'. I went to pull a loom and the handle on the lever slipped because the gear was too tight and it mashed my thumb. The company don't pay anythin' for a thing like that.

Usually I get to bed between ten and eleven at night.

ORGANIZING WOMEN WORKERS

Leonora M. Barry

57. Report of the general investigator, Knights of Labor—1886–1887

Ever since they had entered the factories, women had attempted to organize in their own behalf. Previous documents have shown that these efforts met with failure. In the second half of the nineteenth century, as labor unions began to grow in strength and confidence, male unionists had to deal with women workers, whom they regarded as mostly unwanted competitors, potential strikebreakers, and only rarely as potential valuable allies. The principle of organizing women workers alongside men was proclaimed successively by the National Labor Union, the Knights of Labor, and the American Federation of Labor. Of these, only the Knights of Labor, founded in 1869, actually attempted to unionize women on a national scale. The Knights of Labor accepted women for membership both in mixed "assemblies" and in sex-segregated locals. In 1886, when the union reached its peak strength, it had chartered 113 women's assemblies.

A "Committee on Women's Work" of the union had succeeded in securing the appointment of Mrs. Leonora M. Barry as a "general investigator" or national organizer. A hosiery worker by trade, she had started work in a mill at sixty-five cents a week. In the document below she describes her first year's activities, which revealed some of the problems of organizing working women. Women workers were generally young, many of them children, and hoped to leave their work as soon as possible through marriage. That such ideas proved to be illusions did not alter their impact. Their extreme exploitation, the long hours of work, and the exhaustion and fatigue which resulted from these conditions were obvious obstacles to any sustained organizational activity. For married women, the double burden of factory work and household responsibilities made trade union activity extremely difficult. Nevertheless, as her

Pamphlet, Sophia Smith Collection (Women's History Archive), Smith College, Northampton, Mass.

report shows, women could be organized and, with some support and understanding of their special needs, could become good trade unionists. However, the Knights of Labor, beset by many problems, could not sustain this effort and its female membership shared in the general decline of that organization. The American Federation of Labor, which took its place, gave lip service to the principle of organizing women workers. Several AFL unions, such as the Cigarmakers and Typographers, admitted women to membership, but except for the short-lived appointment of a female organizer in 1892, little progress was made until the early twentieth century.

General Master Workman and
Members of the General Assembly:

One year ago the Knights of Labor, in convention assembled at Richmond, Va., elected me to a position of honor and trust—the servant and representative of thousands of toiling women. . . .

Having no legal authority I have been unable to make as thorough an investigation in many places as I would like, . . . consequently the facts stated in my report are not all from actual observation but from authority which I have every reason to believe truthful and reliable.

Upon the strength of my observation and experience I would ask of officers and members of this Order that more consideration be given, and more thorough educational measures be adopted on behalf of the working-women of our land, the majority of whom are entirely ignorant of the economic and industrial question which is to them of such vital importance; and they must ever remain so while the selfishness of their brothers in toil is carried to such an extent as I find it to be among those who have sworn to demand equal pay for equal work. Thus far in the history of our Order that part of our platform has been but a mockery of the principles intended. . . .

Men! ye whose earnings count from nine to fifteen dollars

a week and upward, cease, in the name of God and humanity, cease your demands and grievances and give us your assistance for a time to bring some relief to the poor unfortunate, whose week's work of eighty-four hours brings her but $2.50 or $3 per week. . . .

[She toured mill towns in western New York and Pennsylvania, investigating conditions, organizing, and holding meetings of women workers.]

December 10 went to Newark to investigate the matter concerning the sewing-women of that city, which was referred to our committee at the General Assembly at Richmond. Found, after a careful study of the matter, that the case reported by the boys' shirt-waist makers was not only true, but that in general the working-women of Newark were very poorly paid, and the system of fines in many industries were severe and unjust. Instance: a corset factory where a fine is imposed for eating, laughing, singing or talking of 10 cents each. If not inside the gate in the morning when the whistle stops blowing, an employee is locked out until half past seven; then she can go to work, but is docked two hours for waste power; and many other rules equally slavish and unjust. Other industries closely follow these rules, while the sewing-women receive wages which are only one remove from actual starvation. In answer to all my inquiries of employer and employed why this state of affairs exists, the reply was, monopoly and competition. . . .

Went to Auburn, N.Y., Feb. 20. I found the working-women of this city in a deplorable state, there being none of them organized. There were long hours, poor wages, and the usual results consequent upon such a condition. Not among male employers alone in this city, but women in whose heart we would expect to find a little pity and compassion for the suffering of her own sex. To the contrary, on this occasion, however, I found one who, for cruelty and injustice toward employees, has not an equal on the pages of labor's history—one who owns and conducts an establishment in which is manufactured women's and children's wear. Upon accepting a position in her factory an employee is compelled to purchase a sewing machine from the proprietress, who is agent for the S.M. Co. This must be paid for in weekly payments of 50 cents, provided the operative makes $3. Should she make $4 the weekly payment is 75 cents. At any time before the machine is paid for, through a reduction of the already meagre wages, or the enforcement of some petty tyrannical rule—sickness, anger, or any cause, the operative leaves her employ, she forfeits the machine and all the money paid upon it, and to the next applicant the machine is resold. She must also purchase the thread for doing the work, as she is an agent for a thread company. It takes four spools of thread at 50 cents a spool to do $5 worth of work, and when $2 is paid for thread, and 50 cents for the machine, the unfortunate victim has $2.50 wherewith to board, clothe and care for herself generally; and it is only experts who can make even this. . . .

I succeeded in organizing two Local Assemblies in this city, one of wood-workers, and one women's Local Assembly, numbering at organization 107 members, which has grown rapidly and is now one of the most flourishing Local Assemblies in the State. Here it was that Sister Annie Conboy was discharged from the silk mill for having taken me through the mill, although she had received permission from her foreman to take a friend through, yet, when the proprietor found out I was a Knight of Labor she was discharged without a moment's warning.

March 14 was sent to Paterson to look into the condition of the women and children employed in the Linen-thread Works of that city. There are some fourteen or fifteen hundred persons employed in this industry, who were at that time out of employment for this reason: Children who work at what is called doffing were receiving $2.70 per week, and asked for an increase of 5 cents per day. They

were refused, and they struck, whereupon all the other employees were locked out. This was what some of the toady-
ing press called "Paterson's peculiar strike," or "unexplain-
able phenomena." The abuse, injustice and suffering which
the women of this industry endure from the tyranny, cruelty
and slave-driving propensities of the employers is something terrible to be allowed existence in free America. In
one branch of this industry women are compelled to stand
on a stone floor in water the year round, most of the time
barefoot, with a spray of water from a revolving cylinder
flying constantly against the breast; and the coldest night in
winter as well as the warmest in summer those poor creatures must go to their homes with water dripping from their
underclothing along their path, because there could not be
space or a few moments allowed them wherein to change
their clothing. A constant supply of recruits is always on
hand to take the places of any who dare rebel against the
ironclad authority of those in charge. . . .

[There follows a description of visits to Massachusetts, New
Hampshire, Washington, D.C., Maryland, and Philadelphia.]

I left Philadelphia on July 15 to make investigation of the
condition of New York City's sewing-women, in compliance
with the request presented at the session of the General
Assembly at Richmond. . . . I can truthfully say that more
injustice, scheming, trickery, and frauds of all kinds are practiced upon the helpless, poverty-bound sewing-women of
New York City by the greedy, heartless employer, than on
any other class of wage-workers on the American continent.
The price paid for all kinds of women's and children's wear,
also that of men and boys, manufactured on the slop-shop
system, is simply a means of slow starvation, being insufficient to procure the amount of food necessary to appease the
pangs of hunger, much less pay the exorbitant rent for their
miserable tenement to the pitiless landlord, or cover the
wasted form with comfortable clothing. And ofttimes, when

work is finished and returned to the sweater, or middleman, whose object is to shave in every direction for the least flaw in one garment, the price for making the dozen is deducted, even though hungry stomachs are at the wretched home waiting the loaf that those few pennies would purchase, and the seamstress dare not resent or she would be discharged from his employment. A proof that New York City is the centre of underpaid labor may be understood from the assertion of a reliable gentleman, who stated that material could be shipped from Philadelphia to New York, then cut and made up into garments and returned to Philadelphia from 30 to 40 percent cheaper than they could get it made in Philadelphia. . . .

Another cause of the misery of these poor creatures is the large amount of work that is taken on the outskirts of the city by women who are not dependent on their earnings for a livelihood. Whole cases of goods are sent to parties who make ladies' lawn and muslin suits, consisting of three pieces and trimmed with lace, for $1 and $2 per dozen; this is also true of all other garments. This compels the poor dependent seamstress to accept work at these prices or get none at all. The state law, while prohibiting children under a certain age from working in factories, etc., seems powerless to reach the numbers of children from four to six and eight years of age who ply the needle as industriously the twelve and fourteen hours of the day as does the unfortunate mother whom they assist to earn their coarse and scanty meal. This fact of infant labor is also noticeable in the tobacco industry. . . .

I reached Pittsburgh, June 11, by invitation of L.A. 7228. Here would be a good place for some to come who are constantly talking of *women's sphere*. Women are employed in the manufacturing of barbed wire, under-ground cable, cork works, pickle factories, bakeries, sewing of all kinds and all the other branches of business at which women are employed, elsewhere. I visited a large establishment, a part of which is to be fitted for the manufacturing of nails, at which women are to be employed. There are also many laundries here in which women are compelled to work, . . . ten hours per day. . . . Also, in a tailoring establishment here I found that whatever wages are made by the employee, she must pay her employer 50 cents per week for the steam-power which runs the machines. There is but little organization here among the women, consequently their condition is similar to that of all others who are unprotected—small pay for hard labor and long hours. While the cause of their lack of interest in organized labor is largely due to their own ignorance of the importance of this step, yet much blame can be attached to the neglect and indifference of their brother toilers within the jurisdiction of D.A. 3, who seem to lose sight of one important fact, that organization can never do the work it was intended to do until every competitor in the labor market can be taught its principles. Having assisted to renovate and revive Ladies' L.A. 7228, I have every reason to believe that it will continue to grow and flourish and achieve great success in the future. . . .

[She continued her trip through Ohio, Indiana, and Michigan.]

In submitting my report to the members of the Order and the public at large, I ask only one favor, namely, a careful perusal and just criticism. . . . I can only hope that my labor will yet bear good fruit, and that in the near future fair consideration and justice will be meted out to the oppressed women of our nation. . . .

> Fraternally yours,
> *Leonora M. Barry, General Investigator,*
> *Knights of Labor*

[Leonora M. Barry continued in her post until 1890. By that time the Knights of Labor had been greatly weakened and interest in organizing women had vanished. She was not replaced. Her greatest achievement was passage of a factory inspection bill in Illinois, which helped to curb child labor.]

Rose Schneiderman (1882–?)

58. A cap maker's story—c. 1905

Rose Schneiderman, a Jewish immigrant who came to the United States as a child, was one of the rank and file garment workers who rose to union leadership in the course of the organizing drives of 1905–1913. She describes her beginnings as a trade unionist in the selection below. She was soon to be an organizer of the International Ladies Garment Workers Union, becoming the organization's vice-president in 1907. At the same time she rose to leadership in the National Women's Trade Union League, becoming its president in 1918. A staunch trade unionist, feminist, and suffrage leader, she was appointed secretary of the New York State Department of Labor in 1937. (See also document 7.)

. . . After I had been working as a cap maker for three years it began to dawn on me that we girls needed an organization. The men had organized already, and had gained some advantages, but the bosses had lost nothing, as they took it out on us. . . .

Finally Miss Brout and I and another girl went to the National Board of United Cloth Hat and Cap Makers when it was in session, and asked them to organize the girls. [Instead, the women organized their own shop.]

Then came a big strike. . . . About 100 girls went out.

The result was a victory, which netted us—I mean the girls—$2 increase in our wages on the average.

All the time our union was progressing very nicely. There were lectures to make us understand what trades unionism is and our real position in the labor movement. I read upon the subject and grew more and more interested, and after a time I became a member of the National Board, and had duties and responsibilities that kept me busy after my day's work was done.

Rose Schneiderman, "A Cap Maker's Story," *The Independent* LVIII, no. 2943 (April 27, 1905): 935–938.

But all was not lovely by any means. . . . Soon notices
. . . were hung in the various shops:

> After the 26th of December, 1904, this shop will be run on
> the open shop system, the bosses having the right to engage
> and discharge employees as they see fit, whether the latter are
> union or nonunion.

Of course, we knew that this meant an attack on the
union. The bosses intended gradually to get rid of us, employing in our place child labor and raw immigrant girls
who would work for next to nothing. . . .

Our people were very restive, saying that they could not
sit under that notice, and that if the National Board did not
call them out soon they would go out of themselves.

At last word was sent out, and at 2:30 o'clock all the workers stopped, and, laying down their scissors and other tools,
marched out, some of them singing the "Marseillaise."

We were out for thirteen weeks, and the girls established
their reputation. They were on picket duty from seven
o'clock in the morning till six o'clock in the evening, and
gained over many of the nonunion workers by appeals to
them to quit working against us. . . .

During this strike period we girls each received $3 a
week; single men $3 a week, and married men $5 a week.
This was paid us by the National Board.

We were greatly helped by the other unions, because the
open shop issue was a tremendous one, and this was the
second fight which the bosses had conducted for it.

Their first was with the tailors, whom they beat. If they
now could beat us the outlook for unionism would be bad.

Some were aided and we stuck out, and won a glorious
victory all along the line. That was only last week. The
shops are open now for all union hands and for them
only. . . .

Our trade is well organized, we have won two victories
and are not going backward.

But there is much to be done in other directions. The shop

girls certainly need organization, and I think that they ought to be easy to organize, as their duties are simple and regular and they have a regular scale of wages.

Many saleswomen on Grand and Division streets, and, in fact, all over the East Side, work from 8 a.m. till 9 p.m. week days, and one-half a day on Sundays for $5 and $6 a week; so they certainly need organization.

The waitresses also could easily be organized, and perhaps the domestic servants. I don't know about stenographers. I have not come in contact with them.

Women have proved in the late strike that they can be faithful to an organization and to each other. The men give us the credit of winning the strike. . . .

The girls and women by their meetings and discussions come to understand and sympathize with each other, and more and more easily they act together. . . .

So we must stand together to resist, for we will get what we can take—just that and no more.

IDA M. VAN ETTEN—1890; NATIONAL
WOMEN'S TRADE UNION LEAGUE—1929

59. How to organize women workers

The selections from a report given to the 1890 national convention of the American Federation of Labor by Ida Van Etten, discuss in detail the special problems of trade union women workers. The impact on women of long hours and the "double burden" under which they labored was insufficiently understood by male trade unionists. This lack of understanding of the special needs of women workers was one reason why it proved to be more effective to organize them in separate locals under female leadership. The selections below explain why, and stress the unity of interest between women workers in shops and those in other occupations.

The second pamphlet represents a more sophisticated approach to the same problem. Published in 1929, it incorporates the experience of several decades of women's trade union activity led by feminist-oriented women in the National Women's Trade Union League.

The NWTUL, founded during the 1903 AFL convention, provided a much-needed impetus toward organizing women workers. It established a unique working cooperation between women from the ranks of labor and the middle- and upper-class women in the woman's movement. Combining trade union activity with political action, the organization supported strikes of women workers, set up educational and leadership training classes, and worked and lobbied for passage of protective legislation. In turn, it generated support among trade unionists for passage of the woman suffrage amendment. Not the least of the organization's achievements was to help secure the establishment of the Women's Bureau of the Department of Labor, and to bring a number of trade union women, such as Mary Anderson of the shoe workers, Agnes Nestor of the glove workers, Rose Schneiderman and Leonora O'Reilly of the garment workers, to national prominence.

Ida M. Van Etten—1890

. . . [The] influx of women and children into large numbers of trades has been fraught with the most disastrous consequences to themselves; it has reduced them as workers to the most miserable conditions. . . . I think I can claim, without fear of honest criticism, that fully one-half of the working-women of New York work from sixteen to eighteen hours a day. Of course, a less number of hours constitute a day's work in a factory, but in the great majority of women's trades, night work, done at home, is the rule. . . .

The saleswomen in New York, especially those on the East Side and in the stores frequented by the working population, are another class of working-women among whom long hours prevail to an injurious extent. . . .

During the holiday season nearly all the stores remain open from 8 A.M. to 9 and 10 P.M., while those on the East

Ida M. Van Etten, "The Condition of Women Workers under the Present Industrial System," Address to the National Convention of the AFL, Detroit, Mich., December 8, 1890 (American Federation of Labor, 1891).

Side are open *every* Saturday until late at night and often on Sundays. When we take into consideration that saleswomen are obliged to stand from 8 o'clock until after 11 at night, with only a few moments, and in the busy season no time at all, for lunch, we can realize something of the physical and nervous strain it must be upon the young girls who constitute the greater part of the saleswomen. It is simply an inhuman day's work. The effect of such a day's work was graphically told me by a saleswoman, who said: "It is usually 11 o'clock before the last customer leaves the store on Saturday night, and then it takes an hour or more to arrange our stock. As most of us live a long distance from the store, it is nearly always 1 or 2 o'clock before we reach home. Then, tired out with the week's hard work, ending with such a superhuman workday on Saturday, we usually lie in bed on Sundays until noon, or later. Thus we have no day of recreation, only week after week of hard, uninterrupted toil." . . .

In New York State the factory laws only prescribe sixty hours per week for minors and women under twenty-one years of age. Thus the law, for even this class of workers, is easily evaded by false statements as to age, etc. Last winter the Working Women's Society of the City of New York introduced a bill in the Legislature providing for women factory inspectors, including mercantile establishments in the operations of the factory law, and limiting the hours of labor for *all* women to sixty per week. It gained the women factory inspectors, but the clauses relating to mercantile establishments and hours of labor were defeated. . . .

From my own experience in organizing women I would give the following brief suggestions as to some of the methods to be employed:

Let them have their own separate organizations, even in the mixed trades, with their own meetings carried on entirely by themselves, with their own presiding officers, treasurers, secretaries, etc.

Do not expect them to become mere addenda to men's organizations, or they will be failures. Neither men nor women will long feel an interest in an organization that is not under their direct management.

The very qualities that most need encouragement and development in the characters of working-women will be brought into play by the carrying on of their own organizations, viz., the formation of exact business methods and habits, a sense of the order and courtesy required in meetings, the habit of expressing themselves readily and easily in public, and a knowledge of their own condition as workers.

Another, and to me a powerful argument in favor of separate organizations for women lies in the fact *that they are women,* and that therefore many subjects which are of vital importance to them as workers are of only secondary interest to men. . . . Then, too, women being so much newer in organization than men, need a vast amount of elementary education in its principles, methods and aims that is naturally not given in the older trade unions of men. . . .

Just here I cannot refrain from speaking a word for the public school teachers. The most zealous, efficient and devoted co-workers I have in the work of organizing women are public school teachers. . . .

A widespread effort is now being made by women teachers in all our large cities to equalize the salaries of men and women teachers.

In every city the labor organizations can be of most effective assistance by sending committees to the Board of Education, endorsing the movement and working for it in various ways that will suggest themselves in each locality. This is a simple act of justice, and would bring into sympathy the working people and the educators of their children.

And now, in conclusion, is not the strongest condemnation of the present industrial system furnished by the condition of its working women and children? . . .

National Women's Trade Union League—1929

How Can Women Be Interested?

Success in interesting women depends upon the attitude of women toward vocations. If they have enthusiasm for economic independence and are ambitious to succeed in their work, they will more readily see the importance of a union.

For many of them it will no longer be possible to choose between marriage and a job. They must have both, and it must be part of the work of a union with women members to encourage the women to stand on their feet and to find out how they can combine marriage and a job to the best advantage of their families and themselves. The union might well study the ways of relieving women of unnecessary burdens in the home, developing co-operative methods of getting housework done and especially letting the women see that they must secure a high enough wage to enable them to pay for service in the households (be it doing the weekly cleaning or preparing the evening meal). . . .

The direst appeal of the union to the individual needs reinforcement by more discussion of trade unionism in the home, particularly in the families of trade unionists. Women's auxiliaries and the closely allied device of the union label can be of great assistance in developing the homes of trade unionists as centers of education of children in the principles of the labor movement. As one delegate at Waukegan said: "My father, a miner, carried a card for years, and he never said to me when I went into industry that I ought to belong to a trade union. I think the responsibility lies largely on the trade union man, that our women are not in the organization today."

"How to Organize: A Problem, Resume of Findings, One Day Institute on Trade Union Organization" (1929), NWTUL Papers, Schlesinger Library, Radcliffe College, Cambridge, Mass.

SEPARATE LOCALS FOR WOMEN

> Is it easier to interest women if they are organized separately?
>
> Is it more effective to have men and women workers in the same local unions?

An organizer in the millinery trade put the answer in this way: "In our particular line we have to organize the women separately because, although there is no reason in it, matters have come to the stage that you cannot get women to come to the men's organization. A great many men have entered the industry. They are saying that women are not organizable. The women, on the other hand, say: "We can't have anything to do with the men, because in a strike they will scab on us. It is our industry. They took it from us." That is the fault of education. In time we will overcome it, but right now we are faced with the problem of organizing the women separately. . . . Another delegate gave other reasons for separate organization: "Whenever men and women are in one organization, the women don't get any representation. Our international union has been organized since 1898 and we had quite a fight to elect a woman on the international executive board. But finally we did it. There is no law against it, but the men are absolutely against it. I think it is better for men to organize by themselves and the women by themselves, but to belong to the same international union."

Another delegate, representing the postoffice clerks, contributed the idea that "in the trades where men and women are somewhat of the same age, they seem to work together best. When you find the men older, the women don't have a chance. In the postoffice union they are about the same age, and the men and women have a great deal in common. The experience there is that the young man is interested in the union and the young woman is satisfied to leave it to him. It is generally when the woman is older that you can get her interested to come to the meetings. The men always seem to be glad when a woman shows interest. We have many women officers in the locals, and the men were delighted when they were able to get a woman who would fill a position on the executive board, and when after years of serving most brilliantly she had to leave the service because of poor health we have not been able to find another woman to take her place. From my own observation I cannot agree that a woman does not have a chance to express her personality in a union where men and women are organized together."

An officer of the League, speaking of experience in several industries, said: "In the garment trades they formed a woman's local because when they were organized with the men in an election of delegates to the national convention not one woman was chosen. The men believe they can handle these things better. One reason is that it is hard to get men and women to the meetings at the same time. The women would rather have a meeting at five o'clock than to come in the evening when they have work to do at home. Sometimes the meeting is held in a place where women do not like to go. Sometimes the women are timid about taking an active part when men are attending the meeting. I don't know whether it is because we are so honest in admitting inexperience, but you often hear a woman say: 'I don't feel equal to taking the office.' A man will never say that. He will say: 'I haven't got the time.' If we wish to develop leadership, our women must be in an organization by themselves, because then they are thrown on their own resources and they must function to manage their own organization. We have found that it is not that the men are trying to keep the women down, but that the women don't push themselves. Take the elevated railway employes. They think it is great because they put one woman on the board. The International Ladies' Garment Workers, with 80 per cent women, have only one woman on their national executive board. It was by a resolution of the Women's Trade Union League that a delegate went to the National Convention of Hotel and Restaurant Workers, authorized to present a resolution for women to serve on the joint boards, and she got it. We must remember that this great labor organization, the American Federation of Labor, has not one woman on its executive council."

[This condition has not changed from 1929 to date.]

UNITED AUTO WORKERS

60. A union protects its women members—1955

There are some unions which have successfully organized women and have consistently protected their rights. The United Auto Workers Union and its Women's Department has, since its inception in 1937, an admirable record of service to its female members.

The UAW has over 200,000 women members; thousands of them serve as shop stewards; over 800 of them hold union leadership posts at all levels (including the top levels). All UAW contracts provide for equal pay, and equal job and training opportunity; maternity clauses in UAW contracts have become models for maternity protection in other industries and businesses. The UAW has long been a pioneer in legislative work in behalf of women workers.

The following excerpts from a UAW convention debate illustrate the level of understanding of male and female union members in regard to issues affecting working women and show how the acceptance of such an advanced program is reached by debate and persuasion. Under debate at the 1955 convention was a resolution affirming the union's dedication to the principle of nondiscrimination based on sex and marital status.

DELEGATE LOVELAND, LOCAL 174: I rise to speak in favor of this resolution. . . . We all know that employers discriminate against women more than any other group. In

Proceedings, 15th Annual Constitutional Convention, Union of Auto, Aerospace and Agricultural Implement Workers of America (UAW-CIO), Cleveland Public Auditorium, March 27, 1955–April 1, 1955, pp. 52–57, 61–62.

my own particular plant, to my knowledge they haven't hired a woman in the factory since 1944, even though they did hire quite a few employees in 1950. . . .

While I have the floor I would like to express my opinion on married women working. I don't think that any of the delegates in this room have the right to challenge the necessity of two incomes, and I don't think it is too much of our business. I also say that I believe married women work only because they have to, the majority of them. Therefore, I urge the adoption of this resolution.

DELEGATE BERRY, LOCAL 835:   I urge the adoption of this resolution for the reason that there are too many women that work merely because they are the breadwinners for the family. In the case of Negro women if they don't work in the plant they are then forced to go out and do day work for $6 a day and carfare. In some instances that I personally know about some of them are taking care of crippled husbands and a lot of children that nobody else will help support. I urge the adoption of this resolution.

DELEGATE SOMERLOTT, LOCAL 1055:   Brothers and sisters, I would like to urge the adoption of this resolution. . . .

I work in a plant where there is only a small percentage of women, and they grow less every day because they are being forced out by the Company making the jobs heavier and using the argument that they cannot let women do them because it is against the state labor law.

And I would like to add this, backing up the sister on married women working. Maybe there are some married women who do not have to work, but let me point out to you the jobs that they create by working—the extra refrigerators and automobiles and homes that are paid for that help create your jobs, and I mean you brother delegates, where there are large families where the father and mother both work are paid for by the married women working. . . .

DELEGATE CARRIGAN, LOCAL 887:   In my Local there are approximately 2,000 women members, and in a group that size we find practically all the problems you will find in any given set of workers who have discrimination at the hiring gate and then promotion and termination. We have our Company using state laws to keep us in lower classifications and thereby cut the ground from under our brothers who are on the same jobs. Many of us have ten or more years of seniority in our jobs and are still in the lowest classifications. . . .

The resolution states that an average income is 44 per cent less for women than for men. This 44 per cent represents purchasing power which should be in the workers' pockets instead of in management's till. . . .

DELEGATE DRENNON, LOCAL 662:   Brother Chairman, I am in support of this resolution. In our Local we have a real problem with this. There are over 14,000 people working in our plants. Over 4,000 of them are women. In many cases they do identical work with the men and draw 16 cents less an hour. We feel that is wrong and we intend to do something about it. . . .

PRESIDENT [WALTER] REUTHER: The Chair has been admonished because he has not been asking whether you are for or against. Are there any delegates who wish to speak in opposition to this resolution? . . .

DELEGATE HILL, LOCAL 961:   Mr. Chairman, fellow delegates and sister delegates: I rise to oppose the particular resolution on the floor at this time for the simple reason that I think that our International Union is trying to create a condition whereby it will require two paychecks in every home in order that we might live like decent human beings. . . .

How about the poor fellow who has a big family and his wife has to stay at home and take care of those kids in order that there won't be juvenile delinquency, and there is only one paycheck coming into that home? That fellow simply cannot keep pace with the two paychecks. . . .

I am not opposed to single women and widows working

in the shop, but I am opposed to married women working in the shop, and I think that the Committee should withdraw this resolution. . . .

DELEGATE EMMA MURPHY, LOCAL 3: . . . Year after year we come to convention, and the same resolution is passed every time. We are just giving lip service to the women in industry. We go back for two years and the same thing happens over and over again.

Certainly I am in favor of the resolution, but let's do something about it and not just say we are going to and forget about it.

I am sort of burned up at some of the previous speakers, and I would like to get one of them in a debate where I could just talk back and forth to him. Two pay checks in a family are fine. I happen to be married. My husband happens to be one of those unfortunate people with 22 years seniority in Hudson Local Union No. 154. Today he has no job. What would happen if I wasn't able to work? My family would be going hungry. And a new car—I would be driving a jalopy or else I would be walking.

The same thing happened in Murray Local. Those people don't have any jobs any more. The ones whose wives are not working there are just out of luck.

So let's not talk about two paychecks in a family. The only thing I can figure out is that the man who made that statement is only jealous because his wife either won't work or doesn't have a job to go to.

PRESIDENT REUTHER: All right, everybody has their rights.

The Chair will ask for one in this section to speak in opposition. . . .

DELEGATE RUTT, LOCAL 195: A good deal of discussion has been going on about married women working. I don't know why the men married the wives if they can't keep them.

Several years ago when I was married I was working at the Timken-Detroit Axle plant, which I believe is President Reuther's local. At that time my wife was working in an office in Detroit, although we both lived in Windsor. When we decided to get married she said, "I think I will keep my job after I am married." I said "Fine, I will quit mine." She has only worked one day since we have been married, which is 32 years on the 31st of this month.

The trouble today is that married people, as I see it, want everything. They want a car, a home, a TV. You can't do that on one weekly pay, I will admit. They are not prepared to do as we did 30 or 40 years ago. We bought things as we needed them. True, we didn't have everything we needed then. We haven't got everything we need today. But as long as there are single women looking for jobs the married woman's place is in the home. If the husband isn't working, as the previous speaker said, I can understand that. . . .

We have had some trouble in the Detroit locals, but as long as the husband is working it is his place to provide for his wife and family.

DELEGATE SZUR, LOCAL 174: I have been warned by my delegation first to watch my language, so with a tremendous effort I will try very hard.

In the first place, I would like to say give us good-looking men with enough money and we don't have to work.

But to get down and be real serious about it, who is to say a woman should work or should not? Where is our democracy in this country if a woman cannot be a free individual and make up her own mind? I think that when you start telling women you can or cannot work you are infringing upon their civil rights, which I as a woman resent.

I am not ashamed of some of the various speakers. They are union people, but I am disgusted with them. One of the brothers spoke about women working. I would like to ask that brother what he would do if he had the finances and wanted to start a business, and some other guy said, "You can't do it because you haven't got five kids; you have got to have five or you can't start a business." Must a woman have children that she can't work? Must she not be married and have to work, or just what is it? If they told him he couldn't have a business, he would blow his fuse more than he did.

We women helped organize this Union. We pay our dues; we attend our meetings, and many of us stand up to management better than some of our weak-spined brothers. . . .

We walk the picket line in the ice and snow—and I did at General Motors as long as we had the strike and I haven't forgotten it, and believe me I am willing to do it again. . . .

I am not married—happily. And I want to stay that way, believe it or not. But I say that a woman who works and leaves her children at home, a normal, good mother, sees that they have adequate care. It is not the quantity of the time they spend with the children; it is the quality of the training they give them while they are with them.

I say that a working mother is not a bad mother, any more than a mother who does not work and spends her time at bridge clubs and leaves her kids with somebody else.

DELEGATE TABACHNICK, LOCAL 424: . . . I believe this convention owes a deep vote of thanks to those brothers who have spoken against the resolution. I think it is better that if and when we pass the resolution we pass it . . . after a thorough discussion of a problem that I know there is a difference of opinion on in our Union. . . .

DELEGATE COLIN, LOCAL 1200: . . . There is one provision in this resolution that I cannot go along with. Surely no one can question the need for women in industry now. No one questions that. But I cannot agree with the sentiment that I see on the floor saying that a woman has a right to compete with a man for a job. I say this, that the economic standing of our country today, the conditions we have today, force women to go into industry. . . . The brothers in favor of this motion should consider this fact, that this came as a result of the last war, and it came as a result of the rising cost of living.

But I say this, when it comes to the basic principle of who should provide for the family, that the father has that responsibility. . . . We are not endorsing the principle that a woman has a right to compete with a man for a job. I think it is basic. I think that the sacrament of matrimony bears out the fact that the man has the responsibility of providing for his family.

I think that there are those women, a minority of women, that need a job, widows and women who are not married, and things of that kind. We can agree with that. . . .

DELEGATE CHANTRES, LOCAL 600: . . . If you will look closely at the resolution all that is asked in this resolution is job security for women workers. . . . Job security for women workers does not mean whether they should work or not. They already have the right to work. They already have been working in the plants for years and years, and all they want now is job security as the men have today, like seniority. . . .

By the way, I want to inject this before anyone believes that my wife is working. My wife is not working; she is taking care of three kids. Incidentally, I am one of those people that is opposed to women working. But this resolution does not mean whether we are opposed or in favor of women working. It says whether we are in favor of job security for women workers. . . .

PRESIDENT REUTHER: . . . I would like to say . . . that I believe what we have done here is that a lot of people have substituted emotion for what the resolution calls for. . . . I come from a family that, thank God, had a mother who stayed home and took care of her children. But there are good mothers and there are bad mothers, and there are good fathers and bad fathers.

What we are talking about is if a woman is working whether we are going to protect her rights. That is a decision that people of a free country make. But where people are working who are women, are we going to protect their standards, are we going to permit management to exploit them and use them to undermine our standards? That is what we are dealing with here. So we ought to understand that.

Now, on the resolution which says that we will protect women workers against discrimination by appropriate contract provisions, all those in favor of that motion signify by saying aye; those opposed [nay].

The resolution is carried overwhelmingly.

CHAPTER SEVEN
Women and Politics

Disfranchised groups in a democracy can hope to influence those holding political power only by persuasion, by educational activity, or by exerting pressure in a variety of forms—personal, economic, and through mass action. All hopes of enfranchisement similarly rest on the ability of such groups to change public opinion sufficiently to make their cause appealing to politicians.

Women have shared this experience with other disfranchised groups, with the major differences that women were at all times at least half of the population; were distributed evenly through all strata of the population; and were the group longest disfranchised in U.S. history. The seventy-two year-long struggle for woman suffrage is well recorded and has received some critical analysis by historians, to the exclusion of other aspects of women's history. But that focused campaign for the passage of the federal suffrage amendment, with its associated state-by-state campaigns, was only the tip of the iceberg. The broad range of political activities of women, carried on at the grassroots and designed to exert pressure for social change, which in turn made legal changes possible, was of greater scope and more far-reaching effect than the legislative campaign; it has remained almost entirely unrecognized by historians.

The documents in this chapter will highlight both aspects of women's political activity and illustrate their interdependence. Since the suffrage movement itself has received more attention and documents pertaining to it are readily accessible, the other aspect of women's political activity has been stressed here.

Their peculiar relationship to political power caused women to use a variety of political techniques, transform old tools into weapons, and innovate methods of pressure and persuasion. Petitions and memorials to legislatures had been used traditionally by voters and nonvoters alike to try to influence their legislators. Mass petitioning first occurred in the 1820s as part of the work of missionary societies, and was then taken on by the American Anti-Slavery Society as a chief means of educating congressmen and the public. Antislavery women transformed this tool into an instrument for mass organizing (see documents 62). In order to circulate petitions, they had to learn how to organize on a community level, to set up a network of gatherers, letterwriters, agents, and lecturers. This activity in turn created local grassroots organizations, which led to the formation of permanent antislavery societies.

In 1838 Angelina Grimké brought an antislavery petition with 20,000 signatures before a committee of the Massachusetts legislature, and formally spoke to the politicians. The importance of her presentation did not so much lie in the fact that she was the first woman ever to address an American legislature, as in the fact that she represented an organized network of female antislavery societies. Here was indeed a new force on the political scene; it was only a matter of time before it would be transformed into a powerful pressure group.

Fundraising and the distribution of literature followed from petitioning; all three of these activities were carried out mostly by women. Later, other organizations of subordinated and out-of-power groups, such as working people trying to organize into unions, adopted these techniques to good effect. From petitioning to the canvassing of candidates it was only a small step, one which antislavery women in New England and Ohio took in the 1840 and 1842 elections.

Memorials to various legislative bodies were also used effectively (see documents 62 and 64). A memorial might be the expression of an individual opinion or it might represent the consensus of a group organized for just such a purpose. With the convening of the first woman's rights convention at Seneca Falls, N.Y., in 1848, this ancient method of petitioning one's lawmakers was raised to a new level of meaning. The resolutions, memorials, and appeals which issued from local, state, and national woman's rights conventions for more than seven decades, became instruments for changing public attitudes and educating legislators. Equally important was the function this activity performed for the participants in such conventions—an ideology was created by a collective process, in which a first-time participant in the convention contributed as much to the shaping of policy as did veteran leaders. The various state conventions and their resolutions differed significantly from national resolutions, reflecting the level of local consciousness on various issues. Woman's rights conventions served to teach organizational skills, reinforce self-confidence, and provide a female support group. They taught women how to speak in public, to engender mass campaigns, to stand up to the abuse and ridicule of hecklers, disparaging family members, and the press. Woman's rights conventions helped women to develop strategy and tactics, to test them in various places, to compare their effectiveness, and to try out innovations.

An example of this process can be seen in document 65 in the development of a legal-constitutional challenge to the exclusion of women from suffrage. The argument that women, as citizens, were already entitled to the ballot, was first developed in a state woman's rights convention. The interpretation was accepted by the national movement and led to a variety of tactics for confronting the courts with a challenge: tax protests, attempts at registering female voters, and demonstrations at the polls. The test case, which finally reached the Supreme Court, led to a change in tactics, but the process had been educational. Seeing a group of respectable women appearing at the polls, only to be turned away, brought home to many citizens the fact that woman suffrage was not something advocated by a few deviant women, but was an issue of concern to their neighbors, sisters, and mothers. The heated family debates that preceded and followed such a local protest converted many a male voter. Each local action, regardless of its outcome, added publicity, spread discussion of the issues, and, indirectly, prepared the public for changes in opinion.

When an individual woman staged a tax protest, presented a petition, or visited the representative of her district at the state legislature, groups of women joined her. This helped to give her courage and support; more importantly it turned individual action into public protest. In this way women proceeded from scattered protests to organized lobbying. In the latter decades of the century they would actively participate in electoral campaigns in order to exert influence on the men elected to office. The Women's Christian Temperance Union, under the leadership of Frances Willard, would turn the election day activities of women at polling places into dignified public demonstrations. Through such work, women learned to speak the language of politics, mobilize support where it counted, and keep up persistent, year-round pressure on reluctant legislators. They also learned to think of themselves in new ways and to absorb the lesson of trade unionism: in unity there is strength.

Legal challenges could take the form of running for office. As documents 65, 67, and 68 show, the campaigns women ran for school board offices, superintendents, and for the presidency of the United States all had the effect of bringing their cause to widespread attention. Two women actually ran for the presidency: Victoria Woodhull (1872) and Belva Lockwood (1884). In both cases, the practical effect was insignificant, but the spectacle of a woman running for the highest office in the land before women even had the right to vote, much as it contributed to public hilarity, had the effect of making women appear in a new role. The unsuccessful national campaign prepared the public for the effective local campaign, which would result in putting a female into the office of superintendent of schools. This, in turn, would prepare the ground for the concept that women, conceivably, might hold other political offices with dignity and competence. The activities of radical and socialist women had a similar effect beyond their direct programmatic and political impact. Radical women in politics represented a new model of womanhood in their person, educating men to accepting women in new roles and influencing women to trust in themselves and in other women for improvement in their condition (document 69).

Another innovative political technique developed by women was the public opinion survey. Challenged by opponents of woman suffrage with the accusation that they did not represent the majority of women, suffragists began to develop the technique of "enrollment," that is they assembled lists of "enrolled" supporters of woman suffrage, male and female, arranging such lists by sex, county, community, and election district. These lists became the basis for mobilization around particular issues and for pressure on legislators, by showing them the actual state of public opinion in their districts. The technique, which was perfected in the 1880s in

Ohio, was used on a nationwide basis in the "winning campaign" between 1912 and 1919. It has served as a model for mobilizing grassroots opinion ever since.

Working women in the New England textile industry were the first to utilize the legislative fact-finding inquiry for purposes of generating political pressure. When in 1844 the Massachusetts legislature set up a special committee to investigate working conditions in the textile mills, women workers, under the leadership of Sarah G. Bagley, organized the Lowell Female Labor Reform Association and collected two thousand signatures on a petition calling for a ten-hour day. Sarah Bagley testified before the committee and continued to organize the mill girls, although the legislature rejected their plea. The Female Labor Reform Association is credited with bringing about the defeat of a hostile Lowell representative in the elections following this hearing.

A formidable woman, acting without the support of any organization, developed the fact-finding survey into an innovative technique for influencing politics. A frail, thirty-nine-year-old spinster in ill-health, Dorothea Dix accidentally discovered the deplorable conditions under which insane persons were held in common jails in Boston. Outraged, she set out to visit every jail and almshouse in New England and to record the results of her eighteen-month investigation in a survey, which she presented to the legislature of Massachusetts in 1843. Her *Memorial* in behalf of the insane and helpless was a remarkable document, the first of its kind, and led to passage of the two reform bills she had requested. Dorothea Dix went on to reform the penal system and the care of the mentally ill by the techniques of exposé survey, publicity, and lobbying, in every state of the union and in several countries of Europe. In 1848 she presented Congress with another "Memorial" on behalf of the mentally ill, a well-thought-out program of care and treatment to be financed with a federal land grant. Her one-woman, six-year lobbying campaign which resulted in passage of a bill in 1854 (vetoed by President Pierce) set a unique model for political effectiveness for the disfranchised.

It would take a book the size of this one to document fully the scope, breadth, and achievement of the seventy-two-year campaign for woman suffrage. There is no intention to do justice to the subject of the political activities of women since the passage of the Nineteenth Amendment by inclusion of document 70, the debate

around the Equal Rights Amendment in the 1940s. This item
merely serves to indicate the pros and cons of an ongoing political
issue of primary concern to women. It is obvious that the enactment of the ERA, like that of the Nineteenth Amendment, will be
the result of not only the direct political support engendered by
women, but of changes in public opinion and in the status of
women in society. Anything promoting such changes and improving this status can properly be regarded a women's political
activity.

61. Women vote in New Jersey—
1790–1807

In colonial times the franchise was, in practice, restricted to land-holders. Since free men and unmarried women were entitled to become freeholders upon arrival in the colonies and indentured servants could obtain freehold rights at the end of their service, this assured relatively wide access to the ballot. By category and in practice slaves, women, Indians, and imbeciles were excluded from voting.

The first time a woman asserted her right to vote, it was on the basis that she was a property holder. Mistress Margaret Brent, to-gether with her sister Mary and a large group of servants, arrived in Maryland as a proprietor. She increased her properties by shrewd management and, like any man, exercised on her own estate the right of "court-baron"—court sessions in which she dispensed jus-tice. She also frequently filed suits to collect debts, acting as her own and other people's attorney. She was so well respected that Governor Calvert named her the executor of his will. In 1647 she asked the state assembly to seat her and grant her two votes, one as a freeholder, the other as Calvert's attorney. She was denied any vote in the assembly and promptly protested that therefore all proceedings of the assembly were illegal.

The subject of woman's right to the franchise was not raised again until, in the period of the American Revolution, the demand for wider access to the franchise began to be expressed in popular petitions. In 1776 the Provincial Congress prepared an ordinance containing an extension of the franchise to "every person worth fifty pounds." This provision was incorporated in the state constitu-tion of New Jersey. The exercise of the franchise by New Jersey women under this definition occurred as a result of the turbulent political struggles of the next ten years. Women voters undoubt-edly were manipulated by male voters. Their voting was made possible by an ambiguity in the law and the indifference of the community. When widespread voting frauds alerted the commu-nity, the first step taken to "purge" the ballot was to make certain

Proceedings of the New Jersey Historical Society VIII, 1856–1859 (Newark, N.J., 1859), first series, pp. 101–105.

of the exclusion of women by explicitly limiting the right of franchise to "free white male citizens, twenty-one years of age and worth fifty pounds . . ." in the act passed November 16, 1807. In interpreting this isolated incident of female voting in the colonies it is well to remember, as the historian of this incident states: "It is true that exclusion was owing partly to the fraud and illegal practices of some women voters, but these women were not worse than the men among whom they voted."*

In the document below, it is interesting to note the more contemporary prejudices against female voting expressed in the interpretation of the gentleman making his presentation before the New Jersey Historical Society.

A Brief Statement
Read before the [New Jersey Historical] Society, January 21, 1858, by William A. Whitehead

By the Proprietary laws, the right of suffrage in New Jersey was expressly confined to the free *men* of the province, and, in equally explicit terms, a law passed in 1709, prescribing the qualifications of electors, confined the privilege to male freeholders, having one hundred acres of land in their own right, or worth fifty pounds, current money of the province, in real and personal estate, and during the whole of the colonial period these qualifications remained unaltered.

By the Constitution adopted July 2, 1776, the elective franchise was conferred upon *all inhabitants* of this colony, *of full age,* who are worth fifty pounds, proclamation money, clear estate in the same, and have resided within the county in which they claim a vote for twelve months immediately preceding the election; and the same, or similar language, was used in the different acts regulating elections until 1790; but I have not discovered any instance of the exercise of the right by females, under an interpretation which the full import of the words, "all inhabitants," was sub-

* Edward R. Turner, "Women's Suffrage in New Jersey: 1790–1807," *Smith College Studies in History* I, no. 4 (June 1916): 187.

sequently thought to sanction, during the whole of this period.

In 1790, however, a revision of the election law then in force was proposed, and upon the committee of the Legislature to whom the subject was referred was Mr. Joseph Cooper, of West Jersey, a prominent member of the Society of Friends. As the regulations of that society authorized females to vote in matters relating thereto, Mr. Cooper claimed for them the like privilege in matters connected with the State, and to support his views quoted the provisions of the constitution as sanctioning such a course. It was therefore to satisfy him that the committee consented to report a bill in which the expression "he or she," applied to the voter, was introduced into the section specifying the necessary qualifications; thus giving a legislative endorsement of the alleged meaning of the constitution. Still, no cases of females voting by virtue of this more definite provision are on record, and we are warranted in believing that the women of New Jersey then, as now, were not apt to overstep the bounds of decorum, or intrude where their characteristic modesty and self respect might be wounded.

This law and its supplements were repealed in 1797, and it is some proof that the peculiar provision under review had not been availed of to any extent, if at all, (as its evil consequences would otherwise have become apparent) that we find similar phraseology introduced into the new act. The right of suffrage was conferred upon "all *free* inhabitants of this State of full age, &c.," thus adopting the language of the constitution with the addition of the word "free," and "no person shall be entitled to vote in any other township or precinct than that in which *he* or *she* doth actually reside, &c.," and in two other places is the possible difference in the sex of the voters recognized.

The first occasion on which females voted, of which any precise information has been obtained, was at an election hall this year, (1797) at Elizabethtown, Essex County, for members of the Legislature. The candidates between whom the greatest rivalry existed, were John Condit and William Crane, the heads of what were known a year or two later as the "Federal Republican" and "Federal Aristocratic" parties, the former the candidate, of Newark and the northern portions of the county, and the latter the candidate of Elizabethtown and the adjoining country, for the Council. Under the impression that the candidates would poll nearly the same number of votes, the Elizabethtown leaders thought that by a bold *coup d'etat* they might secure the success of Mr. Crane. At a late hour of the day, and, as I have been informed, just before the close of the poll, a number of females were brought up, and under the provisions of the existing laws, allowed to vote; but the manœuvre was unsuccessful, the majority for Mr. Condit, in the county, being 93, notwithstanding. . . .

[The incident aroused a good deal of hostile and "humorous" comment in the local press, of which the following poem, circulated as a song, gives a good example. Note that this poem was not cited in the original article by William Whitehead, but was taken from page 171 of the Turner article and inserted here by the editor.]

. . . What tho' we read, in days of yore,
    the woman's occupation, .
Was to direct the wheel and loom,
    not to direct the nation:
This narrow-minded policy
    by us hath met detection;
While woman's bound, man can't be free,
    nor have a *fair Election*.

Oh! what parade those widows made!
    some marching cheek by jole, sir;
In stage, or chair, some beat the air,
    and press'd on to the *Pole*, sir:
While men of rank, who played this prank,
    beat up the widow's *quarters*;
Their hands they laid on every maid,
    and scarce spar'd wives, or daughters!

This precious clause of section laws
  we shortly will amend, sir;
And woman's rights, with all our might,
  we'll labour to defend, sir:
To Congress, lo! widows shall go,
  like metamorphosed witches!
Cloath'd with the dignity of state,
  and eke, in coat and breeches!

Then freedom hail! thy powers prevail
  o'er prejudice and error;
No longer men shall tyrannize,
  and rule the world in terror:
Now one and all, proclaim the fall
  of Tyrants!—Open wide your throats,
And welcome in the *peaceful* scene,
  of government in petticoats!!!

[Whitehead's report continues:]

So discreditable was this occurrence thought that, although another closely contested election took place the following year, we do not find any other than male votes deposited then in Essex County, or either there or elsewhere, until the Presidential election of 1800, between Mr. Adams and Mr. Jefferson, at which females voted very generally throughout the State; and such continued to be the practice until the passage of the act positively excluding them from the polls. At first the law had been so construed so as to admit single women only, but as the practice extended, the construction of the privilege became broader and was made to include females 18 years old, married or single, and even women of color. At a contested election in Hunterdon County, in 1802, the votes of two or three such, actually electing a member of the Legislature. It is remarkable that these proceedings did not sooner bring about a repeal of the laws which were thought to sanction them. . . .

[In 1806 the issue of the location of a Court House and jail made the State Legislature election highly controversial. The Board of Elections qualified "women of full age, whether single or married, possessing the required property qualification" to vote. However, not only did all females vote, but many several times. The legislature set aside the election as fraudulent and passed a new election law which "confined the right of suffrage to *free white male citizens* twenty-one years of age, worth fifty pounds proclamation money. . . ."]

The law remained unchanged until the adoption of a new constitution a few years since, which instrument is equally restrictive as to persons who shall vote, and removes the property qualification altogether.

Very recently a refusal to respond to a demand for taxes legally imposed, was received from a distinguished advocate of "Woman's Rights" in one of the northern counties. . . .*

Similar arguments were advanced by a sister of Richard Henry Lee, in 1778, . . . yet the distinguished Virginian did not hesitate to show the unreasonableness of the demand . . . remarking that . . . "perhaps 'twas thought rather out of character for women to press into those tumultuous assemblages of men where the business of choosing

* The following letter contains the sentiments referred to in the text—

Orange, N.J., Dec. 18, 1858

Mr. Mandeville, Tax Collector: Sir—Enclosed I return my tax bill, without paying it. My reason for doing so, is, that women suffer taxation, and yet have no representation, which is not only unjust to one half the adult population, but is contrary to our theory of government. For years some women have been paying their taxes under protest, but still taxes are imposed, and representation is not granted. The only course now left us is to refuse to pay the tax. We know well what the immediate result of this refusal must be.

But we believe that when the attention of men is called to the wide difference between their theory of government and its practice, in this particular, that they cannot fail to see the mistake they now make, by imposing taxes on women, while they refuse them the right of suffrage, and that the sense of justice which is in all good men, will lead them to correct it. Then we shall cheerfully pay our taxes—not till then.

Respectfully,

LUCY STONE.

representatives is conducted!" And as it is very evident that when in times past the right was, not only claimed, but exercised in New Jersey, it never accorded with public sentiment; so it may be safely predicted that, as was the case in 1807 "the safety, quiet, good order and dignity of the State," will ever call for its explicit disavowal in times to come.

62. Petitioning

Petitioning as a form of political activity antedates the formation of the republic. Slaves, women, and various reform societies had petitioned since colonial days. By 1830 petitions reached the House of Representatives in large numbers on such varied issues as the tariff, currency reform, abolition of Sunday mail, the ten-hour day, and support of the cause of the Cherokee Indians.

As early as 1836, in her *Appeal to the Christian Women of the Southern States,* Angelina Grimké had pointed out that petitions were a particularly apt means of political expression for women, since they were excluded from other means. She urged Southern women to take up petitioning and cautioned them not to be disappointed if progress were slow: "If you could obtain but six signatures to such a petition in only one state, I would say, send up that petition, and be not in the least discouraged."*

The 1837 Anti-Slavery Convention of American Women made this work the focus of their activities, using petitioning in a systematic way as a basis for local organizing.

Antislavery petitions began to flood the Congress, especially following passage of the "gag," a rule establishing the practice of tabling without further action all petitions on the subject of slavery. The "gag rules" passed by succeeding Congresses at the insistence of Southern congressmen broadened the abolition campaign into a campaign in defense of free speech. The political effect was far-reaching and decisive in widening the base of the antislavery movement.

---

* Angelina Grimké, *Appeal to the Christian Women of the Southern States* (New York: n.p., 1836), p. 26.

The "Address to Females in the State of Ohio" explains the purpose and organizational tactics of petitioning. The "fathers and rulers" petition, which was the most widely circulated of all the antislavery petitions, is noteworthy because it was particularly written for women in 1836 and continued to be used thereafter. It is devoid of feminist rhetoric and uses instead the submissive appeal of the helpless for the protection of their "fathers and rulers." The tone of this petition compares interestingly with the strongly feminist resolutions passed by the same convention (see document 64). In 1838, Ohio abolitionists claimed to have gathered one hundred thousand signatures to antislavery petitions; tens of thousands of these were collected by women. James Birney, a leading abolitionist, estimated in 1838 that the total number of petitions to the third session of the 25th Congress had been one-half million. In 1840, when the House no longer accepted antislavery petitions and kept no record of their number, John Quincy Adams noted that during that session "a greater number of petitions than at any former session" had been sent.

The speech of Ohio Representative Benjamin Tappan upon refusing to present the women's petitions is typical of the majority response to this activity. It also repeats the major arguments against the involvement of women in political activities. It expressed the attitude of the majority of men and women. The small, dedicated band of abolitionist and feminist women was unimpressed and continued to organize.

In 1863 the Women's Loyal National League was formed for the express purpose of collecting one million signatures to a petition asking for passage of the Thirteenth Amendment, ending slavery. A letter, over the signature of Susan B. Anthony, was sent to hundreds of potential petition gatherers, enlisting their aid in circulating the petitions. The goal of one million signatures was not reached, but Charles Sumner presented a roll of petitions with three hundred thousand signatures in 1863, all of them gathered by women.

Another letter from Susan B. Anthony, in correspondence with a friend who was attempting to write a history of the early suffrage campaign, recapitulates the highlights of organized feminist activity. At the time of her writing, the major work of organizing the campaigns in behalf of woman suffrage lay ahead. Anthony did not include in her summary the political activities of the reform organization which, at the time of her writing, had organized the biggest mass movement of American women in the nineteenth century—the Women's Christian Temperance Union. This organization was able to mobilize one million members in every state of the union, plus an equal number of teenage members in separate youth groups. No one has yet attempted a summary of the numbers of petitions and memorials circulated and rallies held by the WCTU in behalf of its main cause, temperance, and its many subsidiary causes, among which woman suffrage featured prominently. A historical analysis of this organization from the point of view of its political impact, and as an instrument for community organizing, waits to be done. Until it is done, no realistic appraisal of women's political activity in the nineteenth century is possible.

Address to Females in the State of Ohio
PUTNAM, JUNE 13TH, 1836

Beloved Sisters—We beg leave to call your attention to the importance of petitioning Congress, at its next session, for the abolition of slavery in the District of Columbia. It has been recommended, that a single form of petition for females, should be circulated throughout the state, instead of using different forms in every town and county. . . . You will oblige us by giving to these petitions as rapid and as extensive a circulation as possible, and returning them with their signatures, to the Secretary of the Female A.S.S. for Muskingham County, as early as the 1st of October. We wish the signatures may be written in a fair legible hand, with their appropriate titles of Mrs. or Miss, that it may appear what proportion of them are adults. . . .

The capital of our nation is the citadel of slavery. . . . *Women* are in captivity and degradation, subject to the most cruel and humiliating bondage; and this, too, without the power to plead their own cause, or appeal to the virtuous and humane for protection from insult and outrage. This is enough to call forth our sympathies, and nerve our souls, if need be for persecution and conflict. . . . Let us labor, then,

The Emancipator, July 21, 1836, p. 46.

with untiring vigor, in behalf of the poor captives in our
land. . . .

To petition for the removal of an evil, is but one mode for
expressing our detestation of it. By this measure we shall at
least clear our skirts of the blood of souls. . . .

We have also a deep personal interest in this matter, and it
has so much connection with the fire-side and the nursery,
that we hope our enemies even will do us the justice to
acknowledge, that it forms a very laudable apology for
female action. . . .

Dear Sisters, we have fallen upon troublous times, and
the weal of future generations demands of us the most vigorous effort. . . . If our husbands, and fathers, and brethren, are ready to prostrate themselves before the swift running car of this mighty Juggernaut which slavery hath set
up—we hope the women of our country, untrammelled by
party politics, and unbiased by the love of gain, will exert a
countervailing influence, and endeavor to open afresh the
fountains of human sympathy and lofty patriotism, which
seem to be well nigh closed by long delay and criminal
familiarity with existing abuses. . . .

May it please the Lord to give to our oppressed brethren
and sisters forebearance under injuries, and a patient waiting for deliverance from bondage. . . .

> *Mrs. Maria A. Sturges,* Corresponding Secretary
> *Of the Female A.S.S. for Muskingham Co.*

Petition of Ladies Resident in the State of Ohio [1836]

To the Hon. the Senate and House
of Representatives of the United
States in Congress Assembled.

Fathers and rulers of our country:—

Constrained not only by our sympathy with the suffering,
but also by a true regard for the honor and welfare of our

beloved country, we beg leave to lay before you this our
humble memorial in behalf of that oppressed and deeply
injured class of native Americans who reside within the
limits of your exclusive jurisdiction. We should poorly estimate the virtues which ought ever to distinguish your honorable body, could we anticipate any other than a favorable
hearing when our appeal is to men, to philanthropists, to
patriots, to the legislators and guardians of a christian
people. We should be less than women, if the nameless
wrongs of which the slaves, of our sex, are made the defenceless victims, did not fill us with horror, and constrain
us, in earnestness and agony of spirit, to pray for their deliverance. By day and by night, their woes and injuries rise
up before us, throwing shades of mournful contrast over all
the joys of domestic life, and filling our hearts with sadness
at the recollection of those whose hearts are desolate.

Nor do we forget, in the contemplation of their other sufferings, the intellectual and moral degradation to which
they are doomed: how the soul, formed for companionship
with angels, is despoiled and brutified, and consigned to
ignorance, pollution and ruin.

Surely then, as the representatives of a people professedly christian, you will bear with us, when we say with
Jefferson, "we tremble for our country, when we remember
that God is just, and that his justice cannot sleep for ever;"
and when—in obedience to a divine command, "we remember them that are in bonds as bound with them." Im-
pelled by these sentiments, we solemnly purpose, the grace
of God assisting, to importune High Heaven with prayer,
and our National Legislature with appeals, until this christian people abjure, forever, a traffic in the souls of men, and
the groans of the oppressed no longer ascend to God from
the dust where they now welter.

We do not ask your honorable body to transcend your
constitutional powers, by legislating on the subject of slavery within the boundaries of the slave-holding states—but
we do conjure you to abolish slavery in the District of Columbia, where you exercise "exclusive jurisdiction." In the

name of humanity, justice, equal rights, and impartial law, our country's weal, her honor, and her cherished hopes, we earnestly implore for this our humble petition, your favorable regard. If, both in christian and heathen lands, kings have revoked their edicts at the intercession of woman, and tyrants have relented when she appeared a suppliant for mercy, surely we may hope that the legislators of a free, enlightened and christian people, will not regard our prayer as "abominable, malicious and unrighteous," when the only boon we crave is the deliverance of the fettered and the downtrodden from the bondage under which they groan.

And, as in duty bound, your petitioners will ever pray.

Remarks of Mr. Tappan of Ohio on abolition petitions, delivered in the Senate, Feb. 4, 1840

Mr. President, I hold in my hand a number of petitions, purporting to be signed by inhabitants of Harrison Co., in the state of Ohio, praying Congress to abolish the slave trade in the District of Columbia. These petitions are signed by both males and females, in the proportion of about 2/3 of the former, 1/3 of the latter.

[Rep. Tappan proceeded to attack the petitioners and claimed they had no right to interfere in the domestic affairs of other states.]

As to the female signers of these petitions, I have a word to say. Nature seems to have given the male sex exclusive powers of government, by giving to that sex the vital strength and energy which the exercise of those powers call into constant and active exertion. To the female a more delicate physical organization is given: and she need not repine that she has not the iron nerve of her protector, man: He has the storms of life to encounter; she the calm and sunshine of

Printed pamphlet, Benjamin Tappan Papers, Manuscript Division Library of Congress, Washington, D.C.

domestic peace and quiet to enjoy. Hers is the domestic altar; there she ministers and commands, in all the plentitude of undisputed sway, the fountain of love and pleasantness to all around her; let her not seek madly to descend from this eminence to mix with the strife and ambition of the cares of government; the field of politics is not her appropriate arena; the powers of government are not within her cognizance, as they could not be within her knowledge unless she neglected higher and holier duties to acquire it. . . .

For myself, I cannot recognize the right of my fair countrywomen to interfere with public affairs. Whether slavery shall be abolished in the District of Columbia or not belongs not to them to say, much less does it belong to the women of Ohio to agitate questions of public policy which their own state government has often declared it wrong in her citizens to meddle with. For these reasons, I decline presenting these petitions to the Senate.

Women's Loyal National League

NEW YORK. JUNE 20TH 1863.

Dear Madam,

Informed of the interest taken by you in the great struggle in which our nation is engaged, with its causes and issues, the Women's L.N.L. instructs us to ask your aid in procuring signatures to the enclosed petitions. We hope to obtain not less than one million of names, before the meeting of Congress. But to succeed is so vast an undertaking, earnest zeal and untiring perseverance are needed, on the part of all interested.

Under the arrangements already made, it is estimated that the expense of preparing, circulating, and presenting these petitions will amount to a sum not exceeding one cent for

Susan B. Anthony letters, Clara Berwick Colby manuscripts, Courtesy of the Huntington Library, San Marino, Calif.

each name. Therefore, we beg you, in returning the blanks with the signatures attached, to let them be accompanied with this penny contribution, or a larger one if may be, from the signers and other friends in your neighborhood. Every effort in this cause will be richly rewarded, if, as we confidently hope, the objects of the petition be thereby attained.

If the clergyman of your church, any pastors in your vicinity, or the teachers in your schools, be willing to aid in this object, will you hand to them copies of these petitions for presentation to their congregations or schools.

Will you also circulate and cause to be read, as far as is in your power, the accompanying Tract, setting forth the necessity of the proposed work of the League.

We earnestly solicit you to initiate and organize Auxiliary Leagues in your town or neighborhood, to be in constant correspondence with the Central League in New York, as this will materially facilitate the collection and forwarding of names and monies for the furtherance of the grand object in view. Enclosed are copies of our Pledge, to be signed by those desirous of membership with us. The badge of the L.N.L. will be forwarded at its original cost to any members desirous of possessing it, also to local Auxiliary Leagues.

The Central League will bestow their badge and membership as a gift upon any boy or girl under 18—who, being by their age prevented from signing the petitions, shall collect and forward 50 or more names and as many cents.

They will also bestow a handsomely bound copy of each of the two celebrated and recently published works of Augustin Cochin on Slavery, and Emancipation, as follows,—On the person who shall collect and send the largest number of signatures from any City of the Union, having a population of over twenty-five thousand: also—On the person who shall collect the largest number of signatures outside of said Cities, from any State in the Union. . . .

Yours in behalf of the Women's L.N.L. League
Susan B. Anthony Secy./S. E. Draper—Con. Secy.

SUSAN B. ANTHONY TO CLARA B. COLBY/*JANUARY 10, 1900.*

I think when you speak of Ben Butler's report and the committees which follow you should state that *hundreds* of *thousands* of petitions were sent to Congress during that year and the next two or three. Miss [Frances] Willard took in a petition of 80,000 names, asking for suffrage, and our own special petitions during '71–72 had 280,000 more. I just wish somebody could take the time to go into the vaults of the two Houses, and figure up the entire number of petitions that have been sent to Congress since '65. Our very first petition to Congress was in '65, praying that the word "male" should not go into the Fifteenth Amendment, and from that time on there have been more or less petitions sent in every year—for thirty-five years you see! I presume the suffrage petitions are all piled up in a compartment by themselves in a vault in each House. . . .

I think you should make a graphic picture of the Women's Loyal League petition of 300,000 signatures, presented by Charles Sumner, in 1863. It did not ask for anything for women but it was their work. Our second appeal to Congress was in December, 1865, and January, 1866, when we sent in our petitions remonstrating against the word "male" in the 14th Amendment; then in 1867 and 1868 urging that the word "sex" should be added to the 15th Amendment; then in the last of 1868 and 1869 we sent petitions for the 16th Amendment, Pomeroy in the Senate and Julian in the House championed our demands.

In the winter of '66 and '67 came the action on the D.C. suffrage bill, nine votes in the Senate and I forget how many in the House in favor of leaving the word "male" out of it.

In 1869 we had a hearing before the Joint Committee of the D.C. and again in 1870, when Mrs. Stanton made an argument in favor of our right to vote under the 14th Amendment, based on the resolution of Francis Miner, which he presented and were [!] adopted in the St. Louis Convention, in October, 1869; then in December, 1870 Victoria Woodhull stole the march on us, got her resolution claiming the right to vote under the 14th Amendment, introduced in the House and Judge Bingham pledged to give her a hearing on the very morning of the day that our National Convention opened in Lincoln Hall in Jany. 1871! . . .

LYDIA DRAKE (WESTERVELT)

63. Why women should not meddle with politics—1840

Nothing is known about the circumstances which prompted the preparation of this outline for an essay or a speech by an Oberlin College student, and little is known about her. Lydia Drake had entered Oberlin College in 1837, and she completed the college course in 1845. Oberlin in 1833 was the first college to admit female students, but these students were taught in a separate Ladies Department. In 1837 four female freshmen enrolled in the regular college course, making the institution truly coeducational. Lucy Stone, who was one of the pioneer group at Oberlin, frequently protested the discriminatory treatment of women students. In particular her determination to become a public lecturer and that of her friend and classmate Antoinette Brown to train for the ministry, were met by disapproval and dismay on the part of the faculty.

In 1840, the problems raised by coeducation and those engendered by the activities of antislavery women, who no longer seemed satisfied with taking a subservient, merely auxiliary role in their organizations, put the "woman question" at the center of controversy at Oberlin and in reform circles in general. Should women participate equally in the leadership of abolition societies? Should they work only in separate female societies? Was it proper for them to lecture in public? to become ministers? to enter medical school? Woman suffrage had not yet become a public issue; it was fully eight years before it would first be raised as a feminist demand. Even then, the woman suffrage resolution almost failed of

Lydia Drake (Westervelt), manuscript copy, Western Reserve Historical Society, Cleveland, Ohio.

acceptance by the 1848 Seneca Falls Convention, because it was considered too daring.

How then can one explain the preparation of Lydia Drake's speech on woman suffrage? Chances are it was intended to answer the main objection to any demand for advancing the status of women: "If they can go to college, they'll be asking to vote next." The specter of women voting was the clinching argument of all those who objected to granting women access to higher education and professional training, and to equal participation in reform organizations and in community leadership.

Lydia Drake, in her slyly humorous rebuttal, thought to hold up all these patriarchal arguments to ridicule. She succeeded admirably. The existence of this kind of speech draft, written by a young woman in Ohio as early as 1840, indicates that the demand for woman suffrage raised at Seneca Falls was perhaps not as outrageously radical a demand as historical scholarship has made it appear.

1. Her mind is inferior to that of man, and we know that it requires the strongest of minds to become a good politician. . . .

2. It is beneath her dignity. . . .

3. She has no right to vote and there is no use in her being prepared to do intelligently what she is not permitted to do at all.

4. She has not sufficient stability of character. She would always follow the opinions of her father, brother or husband . . . and this might do more hurt than good.

5. We should soon see ladies mounted on the public stage addressing her listening audience on the subject of politics and that would not look very well.

6. She is too capricious and full of new-fangled notions.

7. Women would soon enough occupy the Presidential chair and the legislative halls of our country, and we do not know what the consequences of that might be.

8. There is no need of it. There are men enough who have nothing else to do who can transact all necessary business.

9.   If permitted to study politics she would understand the art of governing and she might usurp the authority of men and it would be rather revolting to our feelings to see her holding it over the lords of creation.

10.   It would increase her responsibility, and it is well known that she has more now than she sustains with credit.

11.   She would be entirely out of her sphere. . . .

12.   She has not sufficient strength of body and mind.

13.   Too fond of novelty.

14.   Woman is too ambitious and cruel to be invested with power. . . .

15.   Has not time to attend to politics. She has enough of it to do.

16.   [illegible]

17.   She is talkative. . . .

18.   She is too fastidious. This needs no comment.

19.   It is contrary to the direction of St. Paul, who said "I suffer not woman for to usurp authority over the man. . . ."

20.   It would exceedingly blunt her moral susceptibilities, her sense of propriety.

21.   If woman should have the control of affairs, we should soon see woman placed in every department of office in the country, thus throwing many of our most distinguished men out of office, and of course out of employment, for they would not do anything else to support themselves, and would soon become pests to security.

22.   Too whimsical.

23.   She would soon be able to converse intelligently on the subject of politics, and on this subject equal men. . . .

24.   There are more engaged in politics now than know what they are about.

25.   She would understand the principles of government and would be constantly practicing them in her own little empire home. . . .

26.   She's too fond of fashion to attend to the interests of her country.

27.   If we should see ladies attending conventions,

traveling about the country in great carts drawn by many yoke of oxen, waving their pocket handkerchiefs to assembled multitides, it would greatly shock our sensibilities.

28. It is contrary to the Bible. I know that some move forward the cases of Deborah and others to prove woman's capability, but others think that they were perfect Amazons and very different from the refined ladies.

29. Woman influences mind only when too young to have anything to do with politics. . . .

30. Ladies would attend to nightly caucus of their political party and that would be improper.

31. She was never designed for it. Her eyes were never made to be spoiled in *plodding* over political trash.

32. It would lead to the neglect of family duties.

33. She is too energetic. She would carry. . . .

34. Veria et muta tabilis femina est. I know that some would say, semper, but that would not make much difference.

35. It is not fashionable and some appear to think that we might as well be out of the world as out of fashion.

36. It would give offense to some, and it is woman's province to please not to offend.

37. She could never equal men in intellectual and political power, therefore it would be useless for her to attempt it.

38. It is contrary to public opinion, when we might as well attempt to stop the mountain torrent in its course as to stem the tide of public opinion.

39. She would lose her sense of dependence on man, and of course forfeit his protection.

40. She has not wit enough for a politician, "for wit, like wine, intoxicates the brain,—too strong for feeble woman to sustain."

I presume it would be quite as easy to give 40 times 40 reasons why gentlemen should not engage in politics with such fiery zeal that they sometimes do, as it is to give 40 why ladies should not engage in them as well.

64. The Salem, Ohio, woman's rights convention—1850

Two years after the first woman's rights convention at Seneca Falls, N.Y., the assembling of a convention for the purpose of amending the Ohio state constitution prompted Ohio women to organize a convention of their own in that state. "We saw that the fullness of time had come to make a public protest," Emily Robinson, one of the signers of the convention call, later explained.* The April 1850 woman's rights convention in Salem, Ohio, was distinguished by being the first and only such convention which deliberately excluded men from participation and leadership. As the first historian of this event recorded: "*Never did men so suffer.* They implored just to say a word; but no; the President was inflexible—no man should be heard. If one meekly arose to make a suggestion he was at once ruled out of order. For the first time in the world's history, men learned how it felt to sit in silence when questions in which they were interested were under discussion.†

Emily Robinson, reminiscing about the event some thirty years later, gave these reasons for the exclusion of men: "The movers [in planning the meeting] had been long and thoroughly indoctrinated in coeval-coequal-coextensive rights, but they were not yet quite ready to stand afresh face to face with that mighty force prejudice to convince them that the fullness of time had come to precipitate the matter—to get them in line of battle was the work of the movers of the convention. When once in line, there was no hesitancy, no doubting, no tremulousness. . . ."

Interestingly, the exclusion of men which had been regarded as a weakness by the organizers, affected the content of the convention. The memorial to the constitutional convention was accompanied by a call to action, addressed to the women of Ohio. The twenty-two resolutions passed by the convention offer an interesting comparison to those passed at Seneca Falls. Their stronger

Anti-Slavery Bugle 5 (April 27, 1850).

* Emily Robinson to Susan B. Anthony, Jan. 9, 1882, Marius Robinson Papers, Western Reserve Historical Society, Cleveland, Ohio.
† Elizabeth C. Stanton, Susan B. Anthony, and Matilda J. Gage, *History of Woman Suffrage*, 6 vols. (New York: Fowler & Wells, 1881–1922) I:110.

feminist rhetoric, the increased stress on sex role indoctrination as a cause for the oppression of women, and the emphasis on winning economic rights probably reflect the greater self-confidence and freer discussion engendered by this convention. The strong comparison of the status of women to that of slaves may have been due to the fact that many of the women, including the president of the convention, Betsey Cowles, and some of its organizers, such as Emily Robinson, Elizabeth Jones, and Josephine Griffing, had long been active abolitionists.

The more militant tone of this document may also be an indication of the ideological progress of the feminist movement in the two years since the Seneca Falls convention. The Salem convention represented a great advance in the political consciousness of women: two years earlier the suffrage resolution had been the only convention resolution to engender serious conflict. Now, political action on the part of women was an integral part of their organization, and the suffrage plank had moved to a central place in their resolutions.

Memorial to the Constitutional Convention

ADOPTED BY THE WOMAN'S RIGHTS CONVENTION,
SALEM, OHIO, APRIL 19TH AND 20TH, 1850.*

Presented by Mariana W. Johnson:

We believe the whole theory of the common law in relation to woman is unjust and degrading, tending to reduce her to a level with the slave, depriving her of political existence, and forming a positive exception to the great doctrine of equality as set forth in the Declaration of Independence. In the language of Prof. Walker, in his "Introduction to American Law": "Women have no part or lot in the foundation or administration of the government. They can not vote or hold office. They are required to contribute their share, by way of taxes, to the support of the Government, but are allowed no voice in its direction. They are amenable to the

---

* The only woman's rights convention from which men were excluded.—ED.

laws, but are allowed no share in making them. This language, when applied to males, would be the exact definition of political slavery." Is it just or wise that woman, in the largest and professedly the freest and most enlightened republic on the globe, in the middle of the nineteenth century, should be thus degraded?

We would especially direct the attention of the Convention to the legal condition of married women. Not being represented in those bodies from which emanate the laws, to which they are obliged to submit, they are protected neither in person nor property. "The merging of woman's name in that of her husband is emblematical of the fate of all her legal rights." At the marriage-altar, the law divests her of all distinct individuality. . . . Legally, she . . . becomes emphatically a new creature, and is ever after denied the dignity of a rational and accountable being. The husband is allowed to take possession of her estates. . . . He can collect and dispose of the profits of her labor without her consent, as he thinks fit, and she can own nothing, have nothing, which is not regarded by the law as belonging to her husband. Over her person he has a more limited power. Still, if he render life intolerable, so that she is forced to leave him, he has the power to retain her children, and "seize her and bring her back, for he has a right to her society which he may enforce, either against herself or any other person who detains her" (Walker, page 226). Woman by being thus subject to the control, and dependent on the will of man, loses her self-dependence; and no human being can be deprived of this without a sense of degradation. The law should sustain and protect all who come under its sway, and not create a state of dependence and depression in any human being. The laws should not make woman a mere pensioner on the bounty of her husband, thus enslaving her will and degrading her to a condition of absolute dependence.

. . . We earnestly request that in the New Constitution you are about to form for the State of Ohio, women shall be secured, not only the right of suffrage, but all the political and legal rights that are guaranteed to men.

Resolutions, Ohio Women's Convention April 19 and 20, 1850

Whereas, all men are created equal and endowed with certain God-given rights, and all just government is derived from the consent of the governed; and whereas, the doctrine that "man shall pursue his own substantial happiness" is acknowledged by the highest authority to be the great precept of Nature; and whereas, this doctrine is not local, but universal, being dictated by God himself; therefore. . . .

2. Resolved, That the prohibition of Woman from participating in the enactment of the laws by which she is governed is a direct violation of this precept of Nature, as she is thereby prevented from occupying that position which duty points out, and from pursuing her own substantial happiness by acting up to her conscientious convictions; and that all statutes and constitutional provisions which sanction this prohibition are null and void.

3. Resolved, That all rights are *human* rights, and pertain to human beings, without distinction of sex; therefore justice demands that all laws shall be made, not for man, or for woman, but for mankind, and that the same legal protection be afforded to the one sex as to the other.

4. Resolved, That the servile submission and quiet indifference of the Women of this country in relation to the unequal and oppressive laws by which they are governed, are the fruit either of ignorance or degradation, both resulting legitimately from the action of those laws.

5. Resolved, That the evils arising from the present social, civil and religious condition of women proclaim to them in language not to be misunderstood, that not only their *own* welfare, but the highest good of the race demands of them, as an imperative duty, that they should secure to themselves the elective franchise.

6. Resolved, That in those laws which confer on man the

power to control the property and person of woman, and to remove from her at will the children of her affection, we recognize only the modified code of the slave plantation; and that thus we are brought more nearly in sympathy with the suffering slave, who is despoiled of all his rights.

7.   Resolved, That we, as human beings, are entitled to claim and exercise all the rights that belong by nature to any members of the human family.

8.   Resolved, That all distinctions between men and women in regard to social, literary, pecuniary, religious or political customs and institutions, based on a distinction of sex, are contrary to the laws of Nature, are unjust, and destructive to the purity, elevation and progress in knowledge and goodness of the great human family, and ought to be at once and forever abolished.

9.   Resolved, That the practice of holding women amenable to a different standard of propriety and morality from that to which men are held amenable, is unjust and unnatural, and highly detrimental to domestic and social virtue and happiness. . . .

11.   Resolved, That the political history of Woman demonstrates that tyranny, the most degrading, cruel and arbitrary, can be exercised and produced the same in effect under a mild and republican form of government as by an hereditary despotism.

12.   Resolved, That while we deprecate thus earnestly the political oppression of Woman, we see in her social condition, the regard in which she is held as a moral and intellectual being, the fundamental cause of that oppression.

13.   Resolved, That amongst the principal causes of such social condition we regard the public sentiment which withholds from her all, or almost all, lucrative employments, and enlarged spheres of labor.

14.   Resolved, That in the difficulties thus cast in the way of her self-support, and in her consequent *dependence* upon man, we see the greatest influence at work in imparting to her that tone of character which makes her to be regarded as the "weaker vessel." . . .

16. Resolved, That we regard those women who content themselves with an idle, aimless life, as involved in the guilt as well as the suffering of their own oppression; and that we hold those who go forth into the world, in the face of the frowns and the sneers of the public, to fill larger spheres of labor, as the truest preachers of the cause of Woman's Rights.

Whereas, one class of society dooms woman to a life of drudgery, another to one of dependence and frivolity; and whereas, the education she generally receives is calculated to cultivate vanity and dependence, therefore. . . .

18. Resolved, That the education of woman should be in accordance with responsibility in life, that she may acquire the self-reliance and true dignity so essential to the proper fulfillment of the important duties devolving on her.

19. Resolved, That as woman is not permitted to hold office, nor have any voice in the government, she should not be compelled to pay taxes out of her scanty wages to support men who get eight dollars a-day for *taking* the right to *themselves* to enact laws *for* her.

20. Resolved, That we, the Women of Ohio, will hereafter meet annually in Convention to consult upon and adopt measures for the removal of various disabilities—political, social, religious, legal and pecuniary—to which women as a class are subjected, and from which results so much misery, degradation and crime. . . .

VIRGINIA MINOR (1824–1894)
VICTORIA CLAFLIN WOODHULL (1838–1927)

65. Women are enfranchised by the Constitution

The argument that women, since they were citizens, were already enfranchised by the Constitution, was first offered to a woman's suffrage convention held in St. Louis in October 1869, by Mrs.

Virginia L. Minor, president of the Woman Suffrage Association of Missouri, at the suggestion of her lawyer husband, Francis Minor.

The Minors urged the National Woman Suffrage Association to adopt this argument, which in fact became the official position of the organization. Their interpretation of the Constitution found expression in speeches, resolutions, and hearings before Congress, as well as in the tactic of groups of women trying to vote in the hope of establishing a test case. The first such action in defiance of local electoral laws took place in Vineland, N.J., and ended simply with the registrar's refusal to enroll the female voters.

Mrs. Virginia Minor next attempted to register to vote in St. Louis in 1872 and was refused, whereupon she and her husband sued the registrar of voters for denying her her constitutional rights. In the same year Susan B. Anthony led a group of Rochester, N.Y., women to the polls and was arrested for her action, found guilty, and fined one dollar. Susan B. Anthony, in a principled protest, refused to pay the fine, but she was prevented by a technicality from appealing the case to a higher court. Meanwhile the Minor case, which had been decided against the plaintiffs, had reached the Supreme Court. Ruling in 1875 in *Minor* v. *Hapersett** the court upheld the lower court judgment in a unanimous decision. While affirming that women were citizens, it held that suffrage was not coextensive with citizenship. It was up to the states to decide which of its citizens could vote and under what conditions. The ruling stated, "certainly, if the courts can consider any question settled, this is one. . . . Our province is to decide what the law is, not to declare what it should be. . . . If the law is wrong, it ought to be changed; but the power for that is not with us."

Spurred on by this judicial setback and inspired by its language, advocates of woman suffrage embarked on the long uphill struggle to "change the law." One group of the now-divided movement— the National Woman Suffrage Association led by Susan B. Anthony and Elizabeth Cady Stanton—worked for passage of a federal amendment to the Constitution, while the other group—the American Woman Suffrage Association, led by Lucy Stone and her husband Henry Blackwell—concentrated on enfranchising women state by state. Eventually, after the merger of the two factions in 1890 in the National Woman Suffrage Association (NAWSA), both

---

* *Minor* v. *Hapersett* (U.S. Reports) 21 Wallace 162.

approaches would be coordinated in a strategy which was, at long last, successful in 1920 in securing passage of the Nineteenth Amendment.

Before the adverse Supreme Court ruling in 1875, another attempt had been made to prove that women were, by the Constitution and especially by the Fourteenth and Fifteenth Amendments, entitled to vote. The highly controversial petitioner Victoria Claflin Woodhull, a protégé of Cornelius Vanderbilt, acted as an individual and without consultation with the leaders of the woman's movement when she asked to present a memorial to the Congress. On January 11, 1871, she was granted a hearing before the house Judiciary Committee to present her petition, which she followed by an "address" to the committee three weeks later. Despite her creditable presentation, the committee tabled the memorial on the grounds that the right to vote could only be granted by state government. Victoria Woodhull, undaunted by this setback, attempted first to use the woman's movement to further her political ambitions. She was quickly rebuffed by the more conservative suffrage leaders in the AWSA, who were scandalized by her life style and her advocacy of free love and legalized prostitution. Woodhull then attempted to organize a "People's Party" to promote her candidacy for president of the United States. Anthony and Stanton, who had supported her up to then, feared this would discredit the woman's movement and disavowed her. Woodhull set up an "Equal Rights Party" which nominated her for president in May 1872, with Frederick Douglass as her running mate. The black leader did not accept and campaigned for Ulysses S. Grant instead. Woodhull's campaign ground to a halt and her support among suffragists vanished, as she attempted to defend herself against charges of concubinage by leveling charges against respectable leaders of society, specifically by accusing the highly popular preacher of Brooklyn's Plymouth Church, Henry Ward Beecher, of immoral conduct and adultery. The ensuing "Beecher-Tilton scandal" caused a great deal of embarrassment to suffragists and led to the prosecution and temporary jailing of Woodhull and her sister on charges of libel. The sisters were acquitted of these charges after seven months of litigation, but Woodhull's political career, always controversial and somewhat ephemeral, was ended.

The selection below, which consists of excerpts from her address to the Judiciary Committee and from her platform as a presidential candidate, are of interest for the constitutional questions raised and for the boldness and originality of her approach. Woodhull, like Frances Wright, was a woman ahead of her time, who dared link her feminism publicly with unorthodox and radical ideas about politics and sexual mores. The approach toward the emancipation of American women advocated by Wright and Woodhull, that of asserting women's constitutional rights while attempting to change societal views about sexuality and family structure, failed and was lost for several decades. It would arise again in the twentieth century when later generations, discouraged by the limited changes brought about in the position of women through the winning of suffrage, would once again search for a way to change the patriarchal ideas and values which permeated American society.

Virginia Minor

I believe that the Constitution of the United States gives me every right and privilege to which every other citizen is entitled; for while the Constitution gives the States the right to regulate suffrage, it nowhere gives them power to prevent it. The power to regulate is one thing, the power to prevent is an entirely different thing. Thus the State can say where, when, and what citizens may exercise the right of suffrage. If she can say that a woman, who is a citizen of the United States, shall not vote, then she can equally say that a Chinaman, who is not a citizen, shall vote and represent her in Congress. The foreign naturalized citizen claims his right to vote from and under the paramount authority of the Federal Government, and the State has no right to prevent him from voting, and thus place him in a lower degree or grade of citizenship than that of free citizens. This being the case, is it presumable that a foreign citizen is intended to be placed higher than one born on our soil? Under our Constitution

Virginia L. Minor, President of the Woman Suffrage Association of Missouri, opening address to the convention, St. Louis, October 1869. In Elizabeth C. Stanton, Susan B. Anthony, and Matilda J. Gage, *History of Woman Suffrage*, 6 vols. (New York: Fowler & Wells, 1881–1922) II: 408–410.

and laws, woman is a naturalized citizen with her husband. . . .

[A]ll rights and privileges depend merely on the acknowledgment of our right as citizens, and wherever this question has arisen the Government has universally conceded that we are citizens; and as such, I claim that if we are entitled to two or three privileges, we are entitled to all. This question of woman's right to the ballot has never yet been raised in any quarter. It has yet to be tested whether a free, moral, intelligent woman, highly cultivated, every dollar of whose income and property are taxed equally with that of all men, shall be placed by our laws on a level with the savage. I am often jeeringly asked, "If the Constitution gives you this right, why don't you take it?" My reply is both a statement and a question. The State of Massachusetts allows negroes[!] to vote. The Constitution of the United States says the citizens of each State shall be allowed all the privileges of the citizens in the several States. Now, I ask you, can a woman or negro[!] vote in Missouri? You have placed us on the same level. Yet, by such question you hold us responsible for the unstatesmanlike piece of patchwork which you call the Constitution of Missouri! Women of the State, let us no longer submit to occupy so degraded a position! Disguise it as you may, the disfranchised class is ever a degraded class. Let us lend all our energies to have the stigma removed from us. Failing before the Legislatures, we must then turn to the Supreme Court of our land and ask it to decide what are our rights as citizens, or, at least, not doing that, give us the privilege of the Indian, and exempt us from the burden of taxation to support so unjust a Government.

Victoria Claflin Woodhull

. . . I now do proclaim, to the women of the United States of America, that they are enfranchised. That they

Victoria Claflin Woodhull, *A Lecture on Constitutional Equality* (New York: Journeymen Printers Cooperative Association, 1871).

are, by the Constitution of the Union, by the recognition of its Congress, by the action of a State, by the exercise of its functions, henceforth entitled in all the States of the Union, and in all its territories, *to free and equal suffrage with men.*

This has been established by Wyoming.* In the elections therein held women voted. . . .

From this exercise of female suffrage in Wyoming comes the legal, the undeniable fact, that each State has now imposed upon it the necessity, *not of granting* the right of suffrage to woman, for it exists, but of denying it if it is to be restrained—but how! Not by a legislative act, that is not sufficient, but by a convention, with its act to be approved by a vote of the *people* of whom the women would be voters also! Until a denial is accomplished in this manner woman HAS now, and will retain, *the right of suffrage in every State and Territory of this Union.* . . .

That the framers of the Constitution had Woman's Rights clearly in their minds is borne out by its whole structure. Nowhere is the word *man* used in contradistinction to *woman.* They avoided both terms and used the word "persons" for the same reason as they avoided the word "slavery," namely, to prevent an untimely contest over rights which might prematurely be discussed to the injury of the infant republic. . . .

The issue upon the question of female suffrage being thus definitely settled, and its rights inalienably secured to woman, a brighter future dawns upon the country. Woman can now unite in purifying the elements of political strife— in restoring the government to pristine integrity, strength and vigor. To do this, many reforms become of absolute necessity. Prominent in these are:

A complete reform in the Congressional and Legislative work, by which all political discussion shall be banished from legislative halls, and debate be limited to the actual business of the people.

A complete reform in Executive and Departmental con-

* Woodhull ignored the fact that Wyoming was at the time not a state, but a territory.—ED.

duct, by which the President and the Secretaries of the United States, and the Governors and State officers, shall be forced to recognize that they are the servants of the people, appointed to attend to the business of the people, and not for the purpose of perpetuating their official positions, or of securing the plunder of public trusts for the enrichment of their political adherents and supporters.

A reform in the tenure of office, by which the Presidency shall be limited to one term, with a retiring life pension, and a permanent seat in the Federal Senate, where his Presidential experience may become serviceable to the nation, and on the dignity and life emolument of Presidential Senator he shall be placed above all other political positions, and be excluded from all professional pursuits. . . .

[Items omitted here include a plank for federal control over railroads and transportation, and several planks elaborating protectionist policies for U.S. industries.]

A reform between the relations of the employer and employed, by which shall be secured the practice of the great natural law, of one-third of time to labor, one-third to recreation and one-third to rest, that by this intellectual improvement and physical development may go on to that perfection which the Almighty Creator designed. . . .

A reform in the system of crime punishment, by which the death penalty shall no longer be inflicted—by which the hardened criminal shall have no human chance of being let loose to harass society until the term of the sentence, whatever that may be, shall have expired, and by which, during that term, the entire prison employment shall be for—and the product thereof be faithfully paid over to—the support of the ciminal's family, instead of being absorbed by the legal thieves to whom, in most cases, the administration of prison discipline has been intrusted, and by whom atrocities are perpetrated in the secrecy of the prison inclosure, which, were they revealed, would shock the moral sense of all mankind.

In the broadest sense, I claim to be the friend of equal

rights, a faithful worker in the cause of human advancement; and more especially the friend, supporter, co-laborer with those who strive to encourage the poor and the friendless. . . .

If I obtain . . . the position of President of the United States, I promise that woman's strength and woman's will, with God's support, if he vouchsafe it, shall open to them, and to this country, a new career of greatness in the race of nations. . . . In accordance with the above, we shall assume the new position that the rights of women under the Constitution are complete, and here-after we shall contend, not for a Sixteenth Amendment to the Constitution, but that the Constitution already recognizes women as citizens, and that they are justly entitled to all the privileges and immunities of citizens.

It will therefore be our duty to call on women everywhere to come boldly forward and exercise the right they are thus guaranteed. It is not to be expected that men who assume that they alone, as citizens of the United States, are entitled to all the immunities and privileges guaranteed by the Constitution, will consent that women may exercise the right of suffrage until they are compelled. . . . We will never cease the struggle until they are recognized, and we see women established in their true position of equality with the *rest of the citizens* of the United States.

FRANCES ELLEN WATKINS HARPER (1825–1911)

66. A black woman appeals to white women for justice for her race

In a period when throughout the nation the hard-won rights of Blacks were being eroded by restrictive legislation, Frances Ellen

Rachel F. Avery, ed., *Transactions of the National Council of Women of the United States, assembled in Washington, D.C. on Feb. 22–25, 1891* (Philadelphia: J. B. Lippincott, 1891), pp. 86–91.

Watkins Harper—poet, lecturer and organizer of black women—in this speech made before a national assembly of women's clubs leaders, seized the opportunity to appeal for political rights for her race. Southern states had gradually eroded Negro suffrage and by 1901 the last elected black representative left the House. For twenty-seven years there would be no Black represented in the federal government. To Frances Ellen Watkins Harper, as to most other black women, the political and economic needs of her race were more urgent than the needs of black women. She confidently expected white women to be more sympathetic and supportive of these demands than were white men, a confidence which was not often justified.

I deem it a privilege to present the negro,* not as a mere dependent asking for Northern sympathy or Southern compassion, but as a member of the body politic who has a claim upon the nation for justice, simple justice, which is the right of every race, upon the government for protection, which is the rightful claim of every citizen, and upon our common Christianity for the best influences which can be exerted for peace on earth and good-will to man.

Our first claim upon the nation and government is the claim for protection to human life. That claim should lie at the basis of our civilization, not simply in theory but in fact. Outside of America, I know of no other civilized country, Catholic, Protestant, or even Mahometan, where men are still lynched, murdered, and even burned for real or supposed crimes. . . . A government which has power to tax a man in peace, and draft him in war, should have power to defend his life in the hour of peril. A government which can protect and defend its citizens from wrong and outrage and does not is vicious. A government which would do it and cannot is weak; and where human life is insecure through either weakness or viciousness in the administration of law, there must be a lack of justice, and where this is wanting nothing can make up the deficiency.

The strongest nation on earth cannot afford to deal unjustly towards its weakest and feeblest members. . . . I

* F. W. Harper's lower case spelling "negro" is retained.—ED.

claim for the negro protection in every right with which the government has invested him. Whether it was wise or unwise, the government has exchanged the fetters on his wrist for the ballot in his right hand, and men cannot vitiate his vote by fraud, or intimidate the voter by violence, without being untrue to the genius and spirit of our government, and bringing demoralization into their own political life and ranks. Am I here met with the objection that the negro is poor and ignorant, and the greatest amount of land, capital, and intelligence is possessed by the white race, and that in a number of States negro suffrage means negro supremacy? . . .

It is said the negro is ignorant. But why is he ignorant? It comes with ill grace from a man who has put out my eyes to make a parade of my blindness,—to reproach me for my poverty when he has wronged me of my money. If the negro is ignorant, he has lived under the shadow of an institution which, at least in part of the country, made it a crime to teach him to read the name of the ever-blessed Christ. If he is poor, what has become of the money he has been earning for the last two hundred and fifty years? Years ago it was said cotton fights and cotton conquers for American slavery. The negro helped build up that great cotton power in the South, and in the North his sigh was in the whir of its machinery, and his blood and tears upon the warp and woof of its manufactures.

But there are some rights more precious than the rights of property or the claims of superior intelligence: they are the rights of life and liberty, and to these the poorest and humblest man has just as much right as the richest and most influential man in the country. Ignorance and poverty are conditions which men outgrow. Since the sealed volume was opened by the crimson hand of war, in spite of entailed ignorance, poverty, opposition, and a heritage of scorn, schools have sprung like wells in the desert dust. It has been estimated that about two millions have learned to read. Colored men and women have gone into journalism. Some of the first magazines in the country have received contributions from them. Learned professions have given them diplomas. Universities have granted them professorships. Colored women have combined to shelter orphaned children. Tens of thousands have been contributed by colored persons for the care of the aged and infirm. . . . Millions of dollars have flowed into the pockets of the race, and freed people have not only been able to provide for themselves, but reach out their hands to impoverished owners. . . .

Instead of taking the ballot from his hands, teach him how to use it, and to add his quota to the progress, strength, and durability of the nation. . . .

Underlying this racial question, if I understand it aright, is one controlling idea, not simply that the negro is ignorant; *that* he is outgrowing; not that he is incapable of valor in war or adaptation in peace. On fields all drenched with blood he made his record in war, abstained from lawless violence when left on the plantation, and received his freedom in peace with moderation. But he holds in this Republic the position of an alien race among a people impatient of a rival. And in the eyes of some it seems that no valor redeems him, no social advancement nor individual development wipes off the ban which clings to him. It is the pride of Caste which opposed the spirit of Christ, and the great work to which American Christianity is called is a work of Christly reconciliation. . . .

MRS. CAROLINE MCCULLOUGH EVERHARD

67. Voting for school boards in Ohio—1894

The story of the campaign for passage of the Ohio law enabling women to vote for school board elections is told here by one of its

"Report by Mrs. Caroline McCullough Everhard, President, Ohio Woman Suffrage Association," Harriet Taylor Upton Papers. Courtesy of the Western Reserve Historical Society, Cleveland, Ohio.

chief organizers, Mrs. Caroline McCullough Everhard, president of the Ohio Woman Suffrage Association. The Ohio campaign was representative of the legislative struggle in most states in the post-Civil War decades. Fourteen states had already granted woman suffrage on school bond issues; Montana allowed the vote on local budget propositions and Kansas had extended municipal suffrage to women. Only two territories, Wyoming (1869) and Utah (1870), had enfranchised women for state and federal elections. These territories would later be among the first states to enact woman suffrage—Wyoming in 1889, Colorado in 1893, Idaho and Utah in 1896.

The documents below illustrate the massive activity necessary for pressuring male politicians to share some of their offices and power with disfranchised women. Every obstructionist tactic possible was used to keep the bill from passing and, once passed, to challenge its legality. The list of legislative gains made by Ohio women illustrates the way in which moderate reforms in property and legal rights changed public opinion sufficiently, so that more dramatic changes became politically acceptable.

For women, the skills, fighting spirit, and organizational clout developed in the countless minor skirmishes provided the necessary know-how and stamina for the long struggle for suffrage.

The attainment of school suffrage for women in Ohio, like other reform measures, was attended by many discouragements in consequence of repeated defeats. First in 1892 a bill was introduced into the House of Representatives by Mr. Doty of Cleveland providing that women could vote for members of school boards and be eligible to serve on such boards. The bill was lost by seven votes, it was reconsidered in the adjourned session of 1893 and lost again by six votes. A similar bill was introduced in January 1894 by Representative [Gustavus A.] Wood of Washington county and was [defeated (47–43). A similar bill was again introduced and passed in the Senate on the 10th of April (20–6), and was passed in the House (55–25, 11 abstaining.)] The measure became a law April 24th and victory followed defeat.

In December 1894 Mrs. Ida M. Earnhart of Columbus . . . was one of the first women to register for voting at

the school elections to be held the following April. Whereupon . . . [the state of Ohio petitioned] to strike the name
of Mrs. Earnhart from the registration list because it was
claimed the law was unconstitutional. . . . The court
[ruled that] the act . . . granting women the right to vote
in school elections [was] constitutional. The decision of this
court was appealed to the Supreme Court of the state where
the decision of the lower court was sustained. This completed the victory which the Ohio Woman Suffrage Association worked so hard to win. . . . [More than 30,000 women
voted at the first election. In the winter of 1898 a bill to
repeal the school suffrage law was introduced.] Forthwith
letters were sent to all the suffrage clubs. . . . Petition
heads protesting against the repeal of the woman suffrage
law were circulated and more than 40,000 names were sent
to the legislature on these papers in a very short time. On
February 10th, 1898, representatives of the committee on
legislation of the state Suffrage Association appeared before
the committee on elections in the House of Representatives,
and spoke against the repeal bill. Through courtesy to Mr.
Hazlett, who was a member of the committee on elections,
the bill was reported back, without recommendation however, and was overwhelmingly defeated when brought to
vote in the House, leaving to the women of Ohio their fragmentary suffrage, which has unquestionably been the
means of educating them on broader lines. In the spring of
1900 they voted in greater numbers than any previous election, and are serving acceptably on the school boards of a
fair number of cities and towns.

Legislative Activities of Ohio Women, 1888–1894

In 1888 the Legislature was asked to submit to the voters
an amendment giving Full Suffrage to women. This measure was lost, and a Municipal Suffrage Bill met a like fate.

Elizabeth C. Stanton, Susan B. Anthony, and Matilda J. Gage, *History of
Woman Suffrage,* 6 vols. (New York: Fowler & Wells, 1881–1922) IV:880–
882.

In 1889 a bill for Full Suffrage was defeated in the Senate by 19 ayes, 9 noes, a three-fifths majority being required.

In 1890 a similar bill was introduced in the House and discussed at length. It received 54 ayes, 47 noes, but not a constitutional majority.

In 1891 the Legislature was petitioned without result, and in 1892 and 1893 School Suffrage Bills were defeated by small majorities.

It was enacted in 1893 that mayors in cities of 10,000 inhabitants and upwards shall furnish proper quarters for women and female children under arrest, and that these shall be out of sight of the rooms and cells where male prisoners are confined. The law further provides for the appointment of police matrons.

In 1894 a Municipal Suffrage Bill was introduced but was not reported from committee. This year, however, School Suffrage was granted to women. . . .

In 1894 the Legislature was asked to enact a law making women eligible as trustees of homes and asylums for women and children. The request was refused on the ground that the law would be declared unconstitutional because such trustees must be electors.

In 1896 Free Traveling Libraries were established.

In 1898 the Legislature provided that a woman could be a notary public. Two months later the law was declared unconstitutional, as notaries must be electors.

In 1884 a law was enacted giving a married woman the right to sue and be sued and to proceed in various other matters as if unmarried. Her personal property and real estate were liable to judgment, but she was entitled to the benefits of all exemptions to heads of families.

In 1887 married women obtained absolute control of their own property. This act gave a wife the right to enter into any engagements or transactions with her husband, or any other person, to hold and dispose of real and personal property and to make contracts. . . .

Either husband or wife on the death of the other is now entitled to one-third of the real estate for life. . . .

In 1893 it was made legal for a married woman to act as guardian; and in 1894 as executor or administrator.

By the code of 1892 the father is the legal guardian of the children and may appoint a guardian by will, even of one unborn. If he has abandoned the mother, she has custody.

The husband must support his wife and minor children by his property or labor, but if he is unable to do so, the wife must assist as far as she is able. . . .

The [school election] law of 1894 permits women, on the same terms as men, to vote for members of the boards of education (trustees), but not for State Commissioner (superintendent) nor on any question of bonds or appropriations. . . .

SARAH CHRISTIE STEVENS (1844–1920)

68. A Minnesota farm woman in politics

The following selections from the diaries and letters of Mrs. Sarah Christie Stevens afford an unusual insight into the political life of a Minnesota farm woman with a large family (see also document 47). Mrs. Stevens ran for superintendent of schools of Mankato County in 1890, attempting first to secure the Democratic party nomination and, when that failed, securing the nominations of the Alliance (Populist) and the Prohibition parties. She won, and served in office, running for reelection in 1894.

At the time of her candidacy, Minnesota women had voted for school officers for fifteen years and had also been eligible for "any office pertaining solely to the management of schools." This 1875 law was interpreted as entitling women to run for school boards, but not for the office of school superintendent. It took passage of another bill in 1885 to give women the right to run for that post. Since then, more than seventy women had been elected superintendents in Minnesota's seventy-six counties. The minor parties,

James C. Christie and Family Papers. Courtesy of the Manuscript Division, Minnesota Historical Society, St. Paul.

Prohibition and Populist, favored women's municipal suffrage and their representatives at various times offered bills advancing women's rights.

The correspondence of Mrs. Stevens offers many interesting insights into the early political activities of women. The detailed description of her 1890 campaign shows that she sought and gained the support of many influential men in her community; that she bargained political influence for votes, like any good politician; that she had considerable support from rural women, but not as much from women in the city. This may reflect the greater strength of major party machinery in the urban centers. Mrs. Stevens enjoyed the support of veterans of the Union Army, who campaigned for her and stressed her Civil War services as a volunteer nurse. Personal attacks made upon her and her family by her Republican opponent, F. L. Patterson, not only incensed her male family members, but apparently backfired, arousing male voters to a chivalrous defense of her. Obviously, Mrs. Stevens campaigned hard—notice her diary for the 1894 campaign with its enumeration of personal visits to many people in her community—and accepted support from outstanding Populist speakers, like Eva McDonald. The latter apparently hoped for a patronage post in return for her services. Finally, it is obvious from Mrs. Stevens' correspondence and diaries that she was a family-loving, outgoing person, whose commonsense approach to community problems must have recommended her to the voters.

Sarah Christie Stevens was born in Ireland and brought as a child to Wisconsin by her immigrant parents. She attended Wisconsin Female College, opened a dressmaking shop, and at various times taught at Carleton College, Northfield, Minn., and Wheaton College, Wheaton, Ill. She married William L. Stevens, a widower with four children, at age thirty-four, and had two daughters. Her husband, a farmer, was active in local politics.

J. L. WASHBURN TO MRS. S. J. C. STEVENS
DULUTH, MINN., SEPT. 9, 1890

Dear Madam:—

Your [letter] of the 2d [Sept. was received] and since its writing and receipt the conventions have been held and the story is over. You ask to whom did I write. I wrote to Mr.

Wise, Mr. Diamond and some half dozen others whose names perhaps I might as well not mention, some of whom I think will work for you in the election, although another candidate was nominated. I think it is a great misfortune that you were not nominated by the Democrats. If you had been I have very little doubt of your election. So far as I can read the delegates, which I had prior to the slip which you enclose me, as I take the papers from Mankato, they were largely in the interest of one or two candidates. I knew it would largely depend upon what sort of a trade they made where their vote would go.

J. L. Washburn [Atty.]

MRS. S. J. C. STEVENS TO HER BROTHER, FRANK
GOOD THUNDER, MINN., SEPT. 29, 1890

. . . About the Collectorship, if you want a position with Kellie after you have helped me out, or *in*, I will do my best to help you secure this place you mention or some other. . . .

We are all as usual. My election *is not at all sure*, it is quite doubtful. It will be a "nip & tuck"—I need all the help I can get. . . .

BESSIE STEVENS TO HER BROTHER, FRANK
MINNESOTA, OCT. 14, 1890

. . . Mamma is away from home today and has been gone away since Friday. I suppose that you know that Mamma is trying to get the suprintendency. Mr. Whitelaw wrote a poem about Mr. Patterson and published it in all the papers that were for Mamma. I will send you a copy of the poem. . . .

The sun is shining today. I do not think Mamma will be home today or tomorrow. She was going to Mankato and then to Madison lake and then I don't know where she is going maybe she will come home. . . .

Little Paul has been having truble with his eyelid the

Doctors had to take a peace out of Aunt Carmonies eyelid and graft it into Paul's eyelid.

I wish you would come home and see us again we would have such fun. I hope you will answer soon your loving sister Bessie.

ALEX J. CHRISTIE TO HIS BROTHER
WASHINGTON, OCT. 26, 1890

. . . send me the name of the ablest lawyer you know in Blue Earth County. I intend bringing suit for libel against the Mankato *Journal* for its infamous publication over my signature. They meant mischief toward me and I suspect toward Sarah as well. Of course people won't vote for any candidate who has a low blackguard for a brother, and the soldiers in particular won't stand an insult of that kind. If she is defeated it will be largely due to the *Journal*. . . .

POEM IN SUPPORT OF MRS. STEVENS' CAMPAIGN,
ADDRESSED TO THE VETERANS OF THE CIVIL WAR
[PROBABLY WRITTEN BY J. L. WASHBURN]

A word I wish to speak with you,
    Comrades of the Grand Old Blue,
Concerning a sister of the G. A. R.,
    And the part she bore all through the war.

Miss S. J. Christie was then her name,
    Now Mrs. Stevens, yet still the same
Loyal friend to the boys in blue,
    As when with Sherman they marched clear through

The state of Georgia—and suspense,
    The state of hunger—at times intense,
The state of pain and suffering, too,
    Both by disease and the piercing through

With bayonet, or sword, or ball,
    By which so many had to fall;
And then, as some of us do know,
    To the Hospital we had to go.

And there it was, my comrades dear,
  That we were made to so revere
The women north of Dixon's line,
  Who, with the spirit of one divine,

Sent us stores of things to eat,
  A blessed gift, a royal treat: then,
The Christian commission, a blessing
  Of heroic women for heroic men.

Miss Sarah Christie—Mrs. Stevens now,
  With valor stamped upon her brow,
Offered to go as an army nurse,
  And share with us the dreadful curse

Of a civil war, and a bloody one,
  As e'er was fought beneath the sun;
But being too young, as she was told,
  To go as nurse to join the fold.

She went back home and organized
  An aid society; then so prized,
By loyal people, brave and true,
  Also the boys that wore the blue.

Hard she worked for the boys in blue,
  An what, my Comrades, shall we do?
To help her to an office good?
  She has helped our brotherhood.

Let us work for her tomorrow morn,
  In the sunshine or in a storm,
Work all day till the sun goes down;
  Work for her all through the town.

  —A soldier vet,
    Who can't forget
  Such kindness to him shown,
    And which tomorrow—
  Clear or wet,
    In voting he will own.

The Journal, Oct. 25, 1890

Rev. F. L. Patterson, the republican candidate for county superintendent, is reported having said at Mapleton Monday night that all the papers that are supporting Mrs. Stevens, the alliance candidate for superintendent are "puppies and doggies," and intimated that they had all been bought up. To say the least the above is very inelegant language for a minister of the gospel who ought to be in language and deportment, as a humble follower of the meek and the lowly an example. The JOURNAL takes no stock in ministers on politics, and sincerely hopes that the voters of Blue Earth county will do nothing to impair the usefullness of Rev. Patterson. Let him stay home.

To the Editor of The Journal, *Oct. 25, 1890:*

The principal hall at Garden City was packed to overflow Monday evening to hear Mrs. Stevens, the candidate for county superintendent of schools, Miss Eva McDonald the "girl orator" of Minneapolis. The meeting opened by an able, scholarly address from Mrs. Stevens. In a concise logical manner she discussed the position of women in regard to voting, to office holding, urging that, as the legislature had conferred on her the privilege of voting for school directors to superintendent, woman failed in her duty to the state and to society did she fail to accept these responsibilities. Many historical instances were quoted where women had gone out of the usual circumscribed realm and successfully administered affairs without losing their womanly graces. Mrs. Stevens did not desire to pose as a politician or an office seeker, but wished to put the question at issue in an impartial manner and leave the citizens of Blue Earth county to decide which candidate should receive their votes. Mrs. Stevens was frequently interrupted by applause as she made a witty or epigrammatic remark. Her manner was so ladylike, yet unassuming that it produced a very favorable impression and many flattering comments were made at the close.

Miss Eva McDonald then delivered an address, lasting an hour and a quarter, in which she discussed industrial conditions, the effects of the tariff, the railroads, the policy of the two parties, alliance movement and the question of woman's fitness for holding office. The audience listened attentively and seemed well pleased. It is evident that Mrs. Stevens will get the solid vote of Garden City.

ALEXANDER ("SANDY") CHRISTIE TO HIS SISTER,
SARAH J. C. STEVENS/*Nov. 3, 1890*

If defeated do not be cast down. The campaign has brought out a warmth of support from your friends of whom you may well feel proud. The utterances of those on the other side have been respectful or anonymous. Very few disrespectful things have been said, these few most probably by low saloon keepers. To have such people for you would be intolerable. In fact, we expect their enmity. . . . Yes, the campaign has been well worth it even if you don't get the office. . . . And if you are elected you must do your very best for the schools of Blue Earth County, and I will help you all I can.

[The election took place on November 6, 1890, and resulted in a victory for Mrs. Stevens. In the morning, an enthusiastic supporter dashed off a cheering note:]

GEORGE R. BEALES TO MRS. S. J. C. STEVENS/*Nov. 6, 1890*

Mankato, Thursday, 10:30 [probably a.m.] *Victory.* You are way ahead. . . . the Alliance Representatives all elected. *Victory* on our *Banner.*

[The official election result reported on November 11 was as follows:]

W. Schellbach (Dem.)	1955
F. L. Patterson (Rep.)	2301
Mrs. Stevens (Alliance)	2602

ALEXANDER CHRISTIE TO HIS SISTER, SARAH J. C. STEVENS
WASHINGTON, NOVEMBER 6, 1890

My dear Sister:

Your telegram received this forenoon. But I feel like waiting for the figures 48 hours later, when every vote is in and
counted and the ballots burned, before throwing up my
[hat] . . . as soon as you are *sure,* let me know and I will
send you some books. The term begins I presume with the
calendar year. I see that Mr. Stevens got mad and went for
Patterson. Well, that was right. I would like to know who
wrote the [illegible] in the Free Press signed "Humanity."
He intended to be insulting and I would like to get in range
of him. The editor of that paper is not a gentleman to admit
the piece as it reads and I intend to tell him so. I suppose
Hunt is the editor. He will probably be here again. I met
him once at Linds. When I meet him again he will explain
things or take a whipping. . . .

NEWSPAPER OPINION: *FREE PRESS,* NOV, 7, 1890

As conceded in last evening's paper, the Alliance-
Democratic county ticket made a clean sweep with a single
exception. It was well known from the outset that if the
Alliance members adhered strictly to the ticket the result
could not be otherwise than it is, but it was expected that
the lines would give way and most of the old party members
return to their first love. This hope proved a delusion. The
Alliance-Democrats and Republicans alike, stood firm and
unyielding and by so doing they have scored nothing less
than a triumphant victory. . . .

Mrs. Stevens, for County Superintendent of Schools, surprised even her friends, and it is more than likely that she
was surprised herself at the outcome. She was on only two
tickets, the Alliance and Prohibition, and the gallant fight
made for her resulted in a victory that she can feel justly
proud of. Mr. Patterson unquestionably hurt his own cause

through his injudicious remarks, and he has no one to blame for his defeat but himself. . . .

REVIEW, NOV. 11, 1890

The official canvass of this county, which we print elsewhere, shows the election of Mrs. S. J. C. Stevens, for county superintendent, by a plurality of 301 over Mr. Patterson, the next highest, in a total vote of 6,858. She owes her election to the country vote, receiving only 495 votes in the city, to 902 for Mr. Schellbach and 760 for Mr. Patterson. In the city the female vote was largely against Mrs. Stevens, and in a majority of instances it was because she was a woman, the general belief being that women should not hold office. Ladies worked in getting out voters, and some worked with the energy of male politicians. In one instance a male voter being importuned to vote against Mrs. Stevens, and resisting the argument of words, was set upon and scratched and bitten, and the loss of a finger nail will signalize the occasion to him for many days. In the country districts, however, Mrs. Stevens received a large vote from the members of her own sex, and the alliance vote was very strongly in her favor. She is elected, will enter upon the discharge of her duties the first of January, and we hope the expectations so confidently entertained by her friends may be realized.

MRS. FLORENCE STUART PARKER TO MRS. SARAH J. C. STEVENS
GARDEN CITY, MINN., NOV. 8, 1890

I've only a minute to write and the baby is in mischief, but I want to let you know how glad we are that you are elected; not only Ned and I but a great many others in the community. You had 194 votes here, 68 of them women. Quite a number worked for you more or less, but perhaps Addie Murphy put in the most time and labor. She fought many a sharp battle for you. She was very much in earnest about it, believing it to be a righteous cause. Others deserve honorable mention too, and I would like to have you come over and talk things over. I don't see that it will ever be possible for me to go to see you. I've had no help for weeks except two days washing.

The little girls are very well I'm thankful to be able to say. . . .

L. G. CULVER TO MRS. SARAH J. C. STEVENS
MANKATO, NOV. 9, 1890

> I thought perhaps you'd like to know,
> That Comrad Bean, of Mankato:
> Worked well for you on Election day,
> Had some good things of you to say
> To a crowd of men upon the street,
> And his arguments they could not meet.
> A man of logic and real good sense,
> He spoke so well in your defense
> As to win for you a few good votes
> From those who had to change their coats. . . .
>
> Few business men would dare to do,
> As did this Comrad that day for you.
> They were non-committed sometimes with me,
> For fear of losing trade you see.
> But Comrad Bean, like a soldier true,
> Stood for a woman he never knew,
> Except by name, and a record good
> All through the war toward his brotherhood. . . .

With respect & esteem, L. G. Culver

EVA McDONALD TO MRS. SARAH J. C. STEVENS
MINNEAPOLIS, MINN. NOV. 15, 1890

Allow me to congratulate you with all my heart upon your election. You deserved it and I am sure you will fulfill the duties of the office in a manner satisfactory to every-body. . . . I feel a little personal pride in having contrib-uted to the result. I see my legislative candidates in every district I spoke have been elected. I would like a clerkship in the House this winter, but don't know whether my alliance friends will see it in that light or not. . . .

EXCERPTS FROM SARAH CHRISTIE STEVENS DIARY, 1894

Monday, June 18. . . . F. Leaving asked me today, in front of Mr. Allen's Store, if I intended to run for superintendent of schools. He said he had heard such a rumor. I replied in the affirmative—but asked him not to publish such a statement. He then asked me to let him know when I wished it announced & he would give me "a good send off."

He advised that I have it announced soon and then go out and make a thorough canvass of the county—said that he knew I could have a big Republican vote—said that there was dissatisfaction with Scherer everywhere!! . . .

Thursday, June 21. . . . I talked to Mr. Graham about the superintendency. He will help me in every way he can. Thinks my chances are good to secure it. Advised me to announce myself soon—would have a tendency he thinks to discourage others. Advised an Independent Candidacy *before the people* & then go *out & work.*

Just as Geddes advised and as I think myself, must send to the Labor Com. of U.S. or to the Com. of Ed. for Report on Industrial Education. Give a talk on it. Look up old papers of mine for talks to the people. School Laws etc. Must make out points for announcement and also point for letter to the people of Blue Earth County & get it into every paper.

Friday, June 22. . . . I cooked all day—the children in school. After coming home Bessie helped her Papa clean bee sections for a while—drove up the cows—made frosting for cake & helped with the supper. Mary watered the chickens & helped Frank sow or plant cucumber seed. . . .

Sat. June 23. . . . Exceeding hot day & storm of rain & lightning about supper time—lasted but about 45 minutes. Rained again in the evening. Two loads of people from the circus sought shelter in the barn. Mr. Furman, one of the people, came to the house. Told me how the people of Sterling disliked Scherer [candidate opposing her]—except as he said J. A. Harbison & Mr. Ellis & wife. I cannot believe that Mr. Ellis himself is really & truly a friend, either politically or otherwise, of Scherer. We will see! I finally told Mr. Furman that I was to try for the office again, and he replied heartily that he was *"glad of it."* Said Scherer would never get the Sterling delegation again & promised to do what he could for me. Said A. Benedict was with him & shared in the same sentiments with himself, & also said they heard frequent favorable mention of myself. I must go to Mankato tomorrow and see Geddes & Mr. Wise & perhaps others & then out into the County. . . .

Monday, June 25. . . . Saw Geddes—says that Charlie Schellbach thinks of running. Geddes is to make out list of names of men I ought to see in each township—says Dave Cross is opposed to Scherer but says (D.C.) that Mrs. Stevens would not run well at Amboy. . . .

Wednesday, June 27. . . . Saw Millie and Bessie Jamison and Miss Kennedy—she told me Freeman had been at their house & said he was a candidate. Her father and all of them, she said, would work for me however. Had a nice visit at Reynolds—told him about delegates to Peoples Party Convention July 7. We appointed 7 p.m. next Sat. . . . at school house for Caucus. . . .

Thursday, June 28. . . . Bessie and I went to Mankato— stopped & told John Layman about Caucus. He is to see others—told me to see Charlie Yaeger on my way down, which I did—was not very enthusiastic but said he would do what he could. . . .

Saturday, July 7. . . . Peoples' Party [Populist] Con. at Good Thunder. Mary & I went and stayed in sitting room of Graham house. Saw Carrier, Pratt, Reynolds & Glynn. O'Conner is not to run—but Fleming certainly is working hard for it. Saw Mr. Jewett who told me Scherer told him that Stillwell was to run. Mr. J. volunteered to help me.

Sunday, July 8. Bessie, Mary & I went to Church. Saw Rev. Flockhart & heard him. Stayed for S. School. He volunteered to help me.

Wednesday, July 11. . . . Spoke to Geo. R. Clark of my candidacy & he promised to help me. Saw Geddes—he said Ben Williams told him that none of the Welsh liked Scherer & spoke favorably of me. . . . Saw Dunning—he was enthusiastic in his offer of help: *"No use for Scherer!"*

LENA MORROW LEWIS (1862–1950)

69. A woman in Socialist politics—1907

The radical labor and Socialist movements offered to women, as to men, a philosophy and world view which explained their present-day problems and gave them a vision of a better future. Within these movements women could work for needed reforms and more fundamental social change on a basis of equality with men. Here many women, for the first time in their lives, experienced the increase in self-confidence which comes from group solidarity and joint action. In the document below, Socialist organizer and journalist Lena Morrow Lewis briefly traces her political development and career and defines her political position. Her lifelong dedication to her cause and her energetic activism are characteristic of this small band of radicals, who thought of themselves as Socialists first, women second.

. . . For a number of years I worked in the temperance cause, and while that movement partakes of all the characteristics of a reform movement as related to the social system, yet within its own field or limitations it is revolu-

Lena Morrow Lewis, "Experiences as a Socialist Propagandist," (Chicago) *Daily Socialist*, July 3, 1907.

Lena Morrow Lewis to Morris Novik, Lena Morrow Lewis letter files, 1929–1939, Tamiment Library, New York City. I am indebted to Prof. Mari Jo Buhle, Brown University, for bringing both of these items to my attention.

tionary, in that it seeks not to reform, but to abolish the institution against which it directs its force. But when one perceives that the saloon is not the cause that menaces the safety and welfare of society, that it is not the cause of poverty and crime, one must, if honest with one's self, and if possessed of a truly revolutionary spirit, transfer activities to other fields.

For a number of years I also believed that political bondage was the cause of many of the ills endured by those of my own sex; until I discovered that the man without a job was about as badly off as the woman without a ballot. In fact, a little worse, for we can live without voting but we cannot live without eating.

The real antagonism is not that which exists or is supposed to exist between the sexes; but between the capitalist class and the proletariat. Women are victims of class distinctions more than of sex distinctions and when I perceived this fact, I changed my course of action and whatever revolutionary spirit there is in me finds expression today in the Socialistic movement.

Something more than three years ago I looked over the field to see what were the prospects to do propaganda work in this State. There were comparatively few locals in the central and northern part of the state. . . . So I decided to go into unorganized towns, and speak on the street, and sell literature.

The novelty of one of my sex speaking on the street on social and economic problems is of some advantage in gathering a crowd, but this of itself will in time wear away, and either man or woman must have something worth while to offer if they would hold a crowd on the street.

My first street work was done in Stockton, and I had no sooner returned to San Francisco before the Oakland Comrades arranged a hall meeting for me which was afterwards followed by several street meetings.

Meantime some of the Comrades in Humbolt Co. were writing to friends in Oakland to send a speaker up that way, and . . . the Oakland Comrades of the Karl Marx Club sent me up into the "wood country" to talk socialism.

That six nights' work done on the streets of Eureka did not please the capitalistic press of that city is evidenced by the following extract from the Eureka Standard of June 13, 1902.

> The appearance of a woman mounted on a cracker box at the corner of Second and F Streets, mouthing Socialist vaporing brings forcibly to mind the detested Emma Goldman and the cowardly act of her weak-minded disciple Czolgosz.

Such misrepresentation and uncomplimentary notice did not deter me in the least, and from Eureka I proceeded to visit the lumber camps, some of which were accessible only by riding the engine of the work train. Several hundreds of workingmen were addressed and the literature sold in those camps has undoubtedly opened the eyes of many a wage-slave.

As I look over the list of Locals today I see many that were unorganized when I visited them, some of which are Dinuba, Elk Grove, Fort Bragg, Klamathon, Lenmoore, Modesto, Campbell, Los Gatos, Shasta Co., Selma, Stockton, Tipton, Watsonville, Crockett, Mokolumne Hill, Mendecino, Bakersfield. . . .

In addition to this . . . my trips have extended from the Oregon State line to the Mexican border. . . .

Since my marriage two years ago this coming summer, most of my work . . . has been about San Francisco and Oakland. For weeks, night after night, I have addressed meetings on Grant Ave. . . .

During the summer of 1903, the Chief of Police of San Francisco took it into his head to stop the Socialist speaking on the streets. Comrade Holmes was the first to be arrested. His case was tried and dismissed. Upon the strength of this we proceeded to hold a meeting at the same corner where he had been arrested. Hardly had I spoken ten minutes when a couple of policemen came up and ordered me to move on. I refused to do so and was at once placed under arrest. This of course broke up the meeting and I was taken to the police station. My husband walked along with us and upon arriving at the police station, was obliged to witness the humiliating scene of the police searching my body for whatever valuables might be on me, and handling me in a coarse, brutal manner. A more impulsive man would have resented it, but he was discreet enough to know that he was no match for three or four big, burley six-foot policemen. But when his time came, he hurled such singing invectives against the police for their trampling on the rights of the people and their unwarranted actions in the whole proceeding as to arouse the public until it contributed most generously toward the expense of our injunction case against the police of the city, restraining them from arresting the Socialist street speakers. . . .

As the spring days pass by, I find myself rapidly recovering from my long and dangerous illness of the winter, and I expect in a very short time to be out in the State doing active service.

LENA MORROW LEWIS TO MORRIS NOVIK,
AMERICAN LABOR PARTY/*AUGUST 3, 1936*

My dear Comrade Novik—

In compliance with your request for details concerning my activities and experiences in the Labor and Socialist movements, I am submitting the following—

My membership in the Socialist party began in April 1902 and ended March 1st 1936, when it became a party of dictators and lost its democratic soul. I have now cast my political lot with the Peoples Party affiliated with the American Labor Party.

During my years of membership in the Socialist Party, I have covered every state in the union except Mississippi in organization and educational work. . . .

From 1912 to Nov. 1917 excepting for the winter months

of 1912–3 I spent in Alaska. During that time I organized the Alaska Territorial Socialist Party. Had charge of the Delegate to Congress campaign in 1912 and in 1916 was the candidate myself. In many of the mining camps I received the largest vote of any of the candidates. The winter of 1916 and '17 I served as vice-president of the Alaska Labor Union in Anchorage. . . . It fell to my lot to serve as Acting President a good deal of the time. A membership of more than 3200 with some score or more nationalities required skill in handling the meetings and often interpreters were needed to explain what was said to the various language groups.

In 1920 had charge of the Debs campaign in the Northwest and looked after the work of placing the tickets on the ballot in Washington and Oregon. In 1932 managed the Socialist campaign in Salt Lake City and also campaigned that year in Wyoming, Colorado, Utah and Idaho.

Served as State Secretary of California Socialist Party from 1925 to 1930 and from 1925–31 inclusive was managing editor of the Labor World, official organ of the Socialist Party of California. In 1926 ran for Lieut. Governor in California and polled 10,506 votes more than Upton Sinclair who was the head of the ticket. As candidate for the U.S. Senate, I ran ahead of Norman Thomas—Presidential candidate—nearly 8,000 votes. I made a vigorous campaign for the whole ticket but apparently profited most thereby.

Had a very active part in the campaign of 1924 and spoke for the LaFollette and Wheeler ticket in Michigan, Ill., Indiana, Iowa, Nebraska, Idaho and California.

During periods covering time from 1922 to spring of 1924 was in New York City and served for a while as organizer for the Umbrella Workers Union. Also assisted in the work of the Paper Box workers Union and helped in their strike. . . .

Was the first woman elected to membership on the National Executive Committee of the Socialist Party and served from 1907 to 1912. Was elected by the party membership to serve as a delegate to the International Labor and

Socialist Congress in Copenhagen, Denmark in 1910 and addressed a number of meetings in various parts of England enroute the Congress and return.

Was active in the Leage of Women Voters when in San Francisco. Have been an interested student of the labor and Socialist movements for more than 30 years.

I believe that Labor should have a directing voice in the economic, political and social life of the nation. I believe that political and industrial changes should be brought about by democratic methods and policies. . . .

I shall be very happy to serve the cause of the American Labor Party and trust that out of this election may come a clear-cut labor party, whose triumph in the political life of this nation will soon become a reality. . . .

Yours fraternally, *Lena Morrow Lewis*

70. Rights, not roses: the debate around the Equal Rights Amendment— c. 1942, 1970

Section 1. Equality of rights under the law shall not be denied or abridged by the United States or by any state on account of sex.

Section 2. The Congress shall have the power to enforce, by appropriate legislation, the provisions of this article.

Section 3. This amendment shall take effect two years after the date of ratification.

The Equal Rights Amendment (ERA) was first introduced in Congress in 1923 due to the efforts of the National Woman's Party. This small and socially conservative group consistently supported and worked for passage of ERA by lobbying and political pressure, but made little headway until the upsurge of the women's movement in the 1970s. In the decades prior to World War II, ERA was opposed by most of the large women's organizations, by trade unions and by the Women's Bureau, primarily because it was seen as a threat to labor protective legislation. The Supreme Court had outlawed labor protective legislation in principle as an infringement of the Fourteenth Amendment, and had allowed such legislation for women only on the grounds that their biological function as mothers and prospective mothers demanded protection. Thus, opponents argued convincingly that ERA, in conferring legal rights which would mainly benefit middle- and upper-class women, would deprive most working women and the poor of hard-won economic gains. The position of ERA opponents of this period is summarized by Blanch Freedman of the Women's Trade Union League.

After earlier Supreme Court rulings were superseded by acceptance of New Deal legislation, such as the Fair Labor Standards Act, and unionization afforded better protection to larger numbers of women workers, the possibility of extending labor protective legislation to both men and women seemed more realistic. Support for ERA slowly began to build, and was reflected by its inclusion in the platforms of both major parties. In 1950 and 1953 the Senate passed ERA, but it lingered in the House Judiciary Committee, which refused to hold hearings on the bill. It was only in May of 1970, in response to increasing pressure from NOW and other militant feminist organizations, that a subcommittee of the House Judiciary Committee, chaired by Congressman Birch Bayh, held hearings on the bill.

Passage of ERA would have both symbolic value and practical impact. By now supporters of ERA represent the vast majority of all U.S. women, women's organizations and trade unions, including the Executive Council of the AFL-CIO. They agree that ERA's greatest importance lies in making women legally persons under the Constitution, and in extending equal treatment under the law to 53 percent of the population. Symbolically, its passage would represent a serious commitment to equal rights for women on the part of the nation.

Opponents are to be found both among those who approve of its stated goals and those who do not: the first consider passage of a constitutional amendment an unnecessary and ineffective means to a worthy goal; the latter regard the social changes implicit in wiping out legal inequality as undesirable.

Two documents reprinted here reflect only one aspect of the

conflict, that centering on protective labor legislation. They highlight the conflicting views of trade union women in regard to the impact of ERA on working women.

It should be noted that the UAW women's department, which has been one of the most active organizations in behalf of trade union women since its inception in 1935, formerly was among the opponents of ERA. The organization changed its position due to the shop experiences of women members, who found so-called protective laws used as tools for discrimination against them, and due to successive changes in law and court rulings. Among these are passage of the Equal Pay Act of 1963 and of Title VII of the Civil Rights Act of 1964, which make equal pay for equal work and equal opportunity in the labor market the law of the land; guidelines and enforcement of these principles on the part of the Equal Employment Opportunity Commission (EEOC); interpretation of state courts which invalidated labor protective laws in several states under Title VII; and the passage in these and other states of laws protecting both men and women from employment hazards. The most recent position of UAW women found expression in the full acceptance of their platform, which represents the most advanced program for equality of working women in any labor organization, by the 1970 UAW convention.

The Equal Rights Amendment, which was passed by both houses of Congress in 1972, has been ratified by thirty-four states. Thirty-eight states are needed for final ratification and passage, which is expected in the bicentennial year, 1976.

New York Women's Trade Union League

STATEMENT BY BLANCH FREEDMAN,
EXECUTIVE SECRETARY—C. 1942

We oppose the so-called "Equal Rights" Amendment which is dangerous and vicious because:

> The Proposed Amendment Deprives the State of Its Inherent Right to Protect Itself by Taking Cognizance of the Special Role of Women as Mothers or Potential Mothers.

Blanch Freedman, "Statement of the Women's Trade Union League in Opposition to the Equal Rights Amendment (Proposed by the National Woman's Party)," NWTUL Papers, Schlesinger Library, Radcliffe College, Cambridge, Mass.

On the statute books of most of the states of the Union, laws exist which prescribe conditions under which women shall work. They regulate the hours of employment and fix maximums; they sometimes establish minimum-wage rates; they often require the establishment of certain facilities for the maintenance of health. The purpose behind this legislation is readily understandable. Experience as well as scientific knowledge has demonstrated that unless the conditions under which women work are controlled there is grave danger that their health and well-being will be impaired to a degree that will affect their offspring injuriously. . . .

We are now engaged in a great war. The manpower of the Nation has been *conscripted for active combat service.* Only a madman would urge that, except under conditions of absolute desperation, the *women of the Nation* should be simultaneously and similarly conscripted for *active combat service.* . . . The proposed amendment brushes aside the tremendous social significance to the State in this difference of sexes and would require no discrimination between them in the carrying on of the war. The good sense and the instinct of all right-minded people rebel at such suggestion. . . .

The havoc of industry and its wear and tear upon the life and health of many of its workers is not so apparent, but in the long run its toll may be equally as great and the concern of the State in its future citizens requires that it protect through legislation the health of the women who are the mothers of the race to the maximum extent possible. THIS IS NOT DISCRIMINATION AGAINST WOMEN AND THIS IS NOT SPECIAL LEGISLATION IN THEIR BEHALF! . . . We protect the young with child labor laws; shall we not then protect them while still unborn to the fullest extent that medical science has taught us, including the protection of the health of the mothers to be? . . .

> The Proposed Amendment Asserts as Public Policy a Rigid Equality of Sexes; a Fact which Is Not True in Nature or Society and Would, Therefore, Result in Contradiction Between Life and Law.

. . . Implicit in the proposed amendment is the idea that as between men and women there is an absolute equality. This is contrary to fact. It needs no learned, scientific citation to establish that there are many physical differences between men and women and that in the mores of our time the social functions of men and women also differ. This is not the same kind of physical difference that exists between one man and another or the different roles that men play in society. Those differences are accidental; they can be altered or modified during a lifetime. Healthy men can become disabled; a poor boy may become president. The sex differences we refer to are the fundamental differences inherent in the nature of men and women and the different roles they play as such in our present society. Thus, the bulk of our adult female population are housewives and not wage workers, while on the other hand the bulk of our adult men are wage workers. This and other differences, in some degree, are reflected in differing rights and obligations of men and women under our laws. For example: since under the prevailing mode of existence in our society, mothers of small children are not generally self-supporting while fathers are, the laws of most States make provision to widows for the support of infant children, while no similar provisions are made for widowers. The proposed amendment requiring "equal rights" for men and women would ignore completely this social experience and would demand equal treatment for these differing social situations.

Therefore, because the amendment actually disregards the decisive differences between men and women in nature and society, and completely discounts our experience, its effect would be to produce not equality, but grievous inequality.

CONCLUSION

There would be less serious objection to the amendment—however impractical it would be—if it were not for the fact that its adoption threatens all social labor legislation affecting women. In justification of this threatened assault, the defenders of the proposed amendment insist that some of these laws are detrimental and not beneficial to the women involved. Their argument that the adoption of the amendment is a panacea for all such "ills" at one fell swoop is utterly specious. The fact is that 36 legislatures must be convinced to adopt this amendment. Needless to say, if legislation in a State is undesirable, its legislators can be persuaded more easily to remedy it specifically by amendment or repeal rather than by adopting the blanket provisions of this amendment. . . . But the proposed amendment would prohibit the enactment of *any* legislation for the safeguarding of women alone. An amendment to the U.S. Constitution, such as the proposed "Equal Rights" amendment, would be a stone wall against which the waves of experience would pound in futility.

1970 U.S. Senate Hearings on ERA, Committee on the Judiciary

STATEMENT BY EVELYN DUBROW, LEGISLATIVE
REPRESENTATIVE, ON BEHALF OF THE INTERNATIONAL
LADIES' GARMENT WORKERS' UNION (AFL–CIO):

On behalf of the ILGWU and its more than 420,000 members in the United States—80 percent of whom are women—I welcome this opportunity to make known our views in opposition to the Equal Rights Amendment to the Constitution.

The Constitution of the United States already fully guarantees equal rights to all persons regardless of sex, age, race, religion or national origin. Laws to accomplish this end have also been adopted by the Congress on numerous occasions and have been upheld by our courts. Thus, no Constitutional amendment is required to achieve equality of the sexes.

U.S., Congress, Senate, Committee on the Judiciary, *Equal Rights, 1970*, 91st Cong., 2d sess., May 5–7, 1970, pp. 642–643; pp. 611–613.

Of course, the existence of a right under the Constitution does not automatically guarantee that discrimination will not exist. More than 100 years after the adoption of the 15th Amendment guaranteeing suffrage regardless of race, there is still inequality to be eliminated at the polls. And more than 100 years after adoption of the 14th Amendment, the federal courts had to rule unconstitutional a state law barring women from jury service. . . .

Although women faced discrimination in many areas of society . . . the most serious deprivation of their rights occurs in their role as employees. From the time women began to enter the labor force in substantial numbers, their substantially weaker bargaining power made them the target of many discriminatory practices. . . . They had no alternative—accept or starve.

Under pressure from an aroused and irate citizenry, state and federal governments enacted legislation to alleviate the discrimination to which working women were subject. Laws set minimum wages and maximum hours; they provided rest periods, sanitary facilities, ventilation, seating and limited work before and after childbirth. All of these laws have been upheld as proper actions of the states and the federal government. . . .

Under the proposed Amendment, a number of essential legislative safeguards of women's rights as industrial citizens would be wiped out. This should not be permitted to happen.

The proposed "Equal Rights" Amendment is unnecessary. . . .

STATEMENT BY OLGA M. MADAR, VICE PRESIDENT,
UNITED AUTOMOBILE, AEROSPACE AND AGRICULTURE
IMPLEMENT WORKERS OF AMERICA (UAW):

These hearings take place on the eve of Mother's Day, a ritual observance which celebrates not so much mothers and motherhood as the American genius for wedding sentimentality and profitable commercialism. . . . But Mother's

Day 1970 may usher in a new era, for it comes at a time when a very strong tide is running in behalf of the proposition that American women, while they may like candy and roses, really need basic rights still denied them. Rights not roses is the watchword for an increasing number of American women. . . .

The UAW supports the Equal Rights Amendment for Women for a number of reasons. We seek its enactment because it will reinforce Title VII of the Civil Rights Act and make it more difficult for employers to circumvent the Equal Employment Opportunity Commission.

The amendment will also reinforce the "equal pay for equal work" principle, which is so often disregarded by employers, especially in small plants.

The Equal Rights Amendment is also needed because the 14th Amendment has proven to be vague and inadequate in assuring women of equal protection of the laws. In case after case over the years, the Supreme Court has failed to find ground in the 14th Amendment to find unconstitutional laws which classify persons on the basis of sex. Despite the 14th Amendment and in the absence of the Equal Rights Amendment for Women, most states still have laws regarding property rights, inheritance rights and marriage, which make women if not indentured servants then certainly second-class citizens vis-a-vis their husbands.

In a number of states, unequal treatment adds absurdity to injustice in criminal statutes which provide for harsher sentences for women than for men upon conviction of identical crimes. . . .

Opponents of the Equal Rights Amendment have played upon fears that certain social legislation would be endangered if the Amendment were enacted. Such fears, however, are groundless. Maternity laws, for example, would not be affected because such laws do not apply to women as a class (not all women are mothers). Nor would special legislation for mothers with dependent children be invalidated by enactment of the Amendment.

It should also be stressed that with enactment of the Equal Rights Amendment, benefits such as a minimum wage or guarantees of seating facilities and lunch periods which cover women workers would automatically be extended to men. The position of the UAW regarding laws limiting and restricting the employment of female workers is as outlined . . . by President Reuther in Administration Letter No. 10* . . .

Walter P. Reuther, President

TO ALL LOCAL UNIONS: POLICY REGARDING
CHALLENGE TO STATE PROTECTIVE LAWS

Many states have statutes which prohibit or limit . . . the employment of females in certain occupations, in jobs requiring the lifting or carrying of weights exceeding certain prescribed limits, during certain hours of the night or for more than a specified number of hours per day or per week. The Equal Employment Opportunity Commission (EEOC), the federal agency charged with enforcing Title VII, has now unequivocally ruled, with Court approval, that Title VII supersedes such state laws because they do not take into account the capacities, preferences, and abilities of individual females, and tend to discriminate against them rather than to protect them. This has been the position of the International Union since the enactment of Title VII. . . .

Many employers have utilized the so-called "state protective laws" to deny women as a class, opportunities to work overtime, for recall, to bid on certain jobs, work in certain departments and on certain shifts, notwithstanding the fact that an individual woman might have had the seniority, skill and ability which should have been recognized in any of these situations. Employers have followed this course despite the absence of any contract language requiring women to be treated any differently from men. WHEREVER SUCH A

* Letter from p. 595 of the hearing record inserted here by the editor.

PRACTICE STILL EXISTS, THE LOCAL UNION SHOULD CHALLENGE IT
BOTH IN THE GRIEVANCE MACHINERY AND WITH THE EEOC.

There is a larger and fundamental point . . . regarding
the Equal Rights Amendment which argues eloquently and
imperatively for its enactment. The point is that . . . over
180 years since the ratification of the Constitution of the
United States, American women are still second-class
citizens. . . .

The Equal Rights Amendment is not a panacea, but it will
bring us closer to the goal of equal justice under law. We in
the UAW know no valid reason why this Amendment, which
proposes equal treatment for men and women, should not
be incorporated into the U.S. Constitution. . . .

SENATOR BAYH [SUBCOMMITTEE CHAIRMAN]. . . . Is it your
judgment that the vast number of working women who are
the recipients of the so-called benefits of these protective
laws really do not feel they need them and that these working women would support the proposed amendment as a
step forward?

MRS. MADAR. Yes. Well, let me put it this way, though,
Senator. I think the kind of protective legislation that we
have now that supposedly protects women has not protected them . . . and discriminates against them. I do think
that we do need to have protective legislation for people at
the work place, and this is one of the issues . . . we are
dealing with right now as we . . . bring the whole question
of in-plant environmental pollution to the collective bargaining table. . . .

I think you have to deal with specific legislation that has
application for the general population in order to get the
kind of protection that workers need. . . .

III

A New Definition of Womanhood

CHAPTER EIGHT

Creating the New Woman

The first step women took toward their own definition of womanhood was to defy traditional sex roles. There is only one case documented of a woman serving as a soldier in the American Revolution, that of Deborah Sampson. There were several women who served in the armed forces during the Civil War, disguised as men. There were others, like Dr. Mary Walker, who served in the army as women but wore men's clothing, possibly for its greater practicability. The women who served disguised as men can certainly be considered to have expressed dissatisfaction with and rebellion against the roles society assigned to them because of their sex. Whether their motivation was excessive patriotism, personal dissatisfaction, or a desire for adventure, is irrelevant. One can assume that it did not essentially differ from that of the male volunteers to service except in its defiance of traditional sex roles. In each of these cases the women must have shown unusual nerve, guile, and willpower, for their disguises were only uncovered with hospitalization and several of them suffered minor injuries and wounds without discovery.

Another step toward a new definition of womanhood was the creation of new female roles: the emergence of the educated, independent professional woman. She came into being through the efforts and struggles of many nineteenth-century women—the early teachers, the school founders, the pioneers in professional schools, the lonely few who had to win entry into male-dominated professions in each state, each city, each town. Due to the force of tradition and the strength of patriarchal ideas and values, discrimination barriers had to be broken down over and over again, profession by profession. The following three documents highlight the emergence of the female physician. Experiences in the medical field closely duplicate those in the other professions: first the work of lonely, embattled pioneers; then the building of sex-segregated institutions to counter the resistance of patriarchal professions; and finally, as more and more professional women received better training, their painfully slow acceptance by male colleagues and by the professional establishment.

The process of creating this new kind of woman was unthinkable without the support of ideas and organizations which advocated justice and rights for women. The emergence of feminist consciousness is documented throughout this volume. It rested on the existence and continuity of woman's rights conventions, the suffrage and woman's club movements, and feminist organizations. In this chapter, two nineteenth-century feminists discuss aspects of creating the newly defined woman. One of the foremost leaders of American feminism, Elizabeth Cady Stanton, proposes a new approach to training girls so as to create self-reliant women. Belva Lockwood, herself an accomplished professional woman, outlines some of the principles which guided her career.

To millions of less-privileged women, a new consciousness would come through trade union organization, strikes, struggles, and radical political activity. Working-class women rose to leadership in the trade union or radical movements through their organizing work. Some of them confined themselves deliberately to women's work within their organizations, while others were integrated in the general struggle, often emerging to leadership just because they were rare types. Just such a leader was Elizabeth Gurley Flynn, who saw herself representing the female arm of the working-class movement, united with male radicals for the common goal of transforming society, but stressing the separate needs and interests of working-class women. To such women, their feminism was subordinated to their radical Socialism, but they created a feminist socialist ideology and became heroines to thousands of workers, who regarded them as a new breed of women.

The new consciousness brought new issues to the fore. Several of these issues had been of great concern to women at an earlier time, but such concern had found different expression. What the twentieth century would know as "a woman's right to her own body" was in the nineteenth century discussed as "the sacredness of marriage and motherhood." Liberalized divorce laws, protection of the rights of illegitimate children and their mothers, contraception and planned parenthood were all issues around which women organized, for which they educated and lobbied, and which ultimately expressed their determination to take charge of their own lives. Historians have recently pointed out that the nineteenth century "social purity" and temperance movements had feminist content. Women's concern with curbing prostitution could be viewed as an attack on male prerogatives under the double standard of sexual behavior. Temperance as an issue helped to mobilize millions of women in defense of their homes and children, and to teach them that they needed political power if they wanted to effect any significant change in their communities. Even antifeminist women, in order to gain their objectives, had to enter politics and to take part in the creation of the woman citizen.

The nineteenth-century American woman sought to advance women to equal citizenship, but she discovered in the process that this was not enough. Since the regulation of female sexuality has always been one of the root causes of the oppression of women, female autonomy must include, beyond equal economic and political rights, female control of female sexuality.

Finally, the new definition of womanhood encompasses the concept of sisterhood, of the communality of interest of women as a group. The sharing of the experience of subordination, the common aspects of their past experience, a new sense of their strength as they organize around specific goals—all of these give women a new perception of themselves.

The strengthening effect on the individual working woman of organizing for her own interests, has often been described in history and literature. For working women, unionization has frequently been the first step in gaining self-confidence, learning new skills, and discovering an untapped reservoir of strength and leadership within themselves. As documented earlier, the initial trade union experience for women often also led to problems with trade union men, who tended to subordinate the issues important to women to "broader" trade union issues. On the other hand, women, even in sex-segregated "auxiliaries," have been able to make important advances for themselves, for their union, for men. An example of such step-by-step progression in consciousness and initiative is given in document 81.

An organizational innovation of the modern feminist movement which arose in the 1960s is the consciousness raising (CR) group, described in document 82. Such groups proliferated throughout the country, creating a new kind of grassroots organization for the otherwise amorphous women's liberation movement. The highly personal network of friendships and joint activity generated a dynamic movement spirit. Interestingly, modern feminism has revitalized the mode of cooperation by which American women traditionally lightened their burdens.

The final document—an action agenda of political priorities for American women as expressed through eighty national organizations—represents a blueprint for the making of a future new womanhood. Even if only part of this agenda were to be realized, the effect would be a major transformation of American society.

DEFINING HER OWN SPHERE

Deborah Sampson (1760–1827)

71. A female soldier in the American Revolution

Deborah Sampson of Massachusetts, bound out to service as a child, acquired a little education, and after her term of indenture ended in 1779, she taught school for a short while. In 1782 she enlisted in the Continental Army, Fourth Massachusetts Regiment, under the name Robert Shurtleff. She was able to perform her military duties adequately, participating in several engagements. Even though she was once wounded in action, her sex was not discovered until she was hospitalized with a fever in Philadelphia. She was discharged at West Point in 1783.

After returning to Massachusetts, she resumed life as a female. In 1785 she married Benjamin Gannett, a farmer. She gave birth to three children. In 1797 she told the story of her war service to Herman Mann, who wrote a romanticized biography and furnished her with a lecture which she gave on a tour of New York and New England towns. She was awarded a war pension by the State of Massachusetts in 1792 and in 1805 she was awarded a partial pension of $4.00 a month by the United States. After her death her husband, claiming heavy expense for medical care for her service-incurred injuries, was awarded a full pension of $80.00 a year through an Act of Congress, "Act for the relief of the heirs of Deborah Gannett, a soldier of the Revolution, deceased."

Below is a 1797 pension petition by her, which was rejected.

TUESDAY, NOVEMBER 28, 1797

A petition of Deborah Gannett of the town of Sharon in the state of Massachusetts, was presented to the house and read, stating that the petitioner, though a *female,* enlisted as a continental soldier, for the term of three years, in the Massachusetts line, of the late American Army, by the name of Robert Shurtleff; that she faithfully performed the duties of

Manuscript copy of petition by Deborah Gannett. Courtesy of the Huntington Library, San Marino, Calif.

a soldier during the time above specified, and received a wound while in the actual service of the United States, in consequence of which she is subjected to pain and infirmities; and praying that she may receive the pay and emoluments granted to other wounded and disabled soldiers.

Ordered, that the said petition; together with the petition of Andrew Pepin, presented the nineteenth of November, one thousand seven hundred and ninety-two, and the report of the Secretary of War thereon, of the second of March, one thousand seven hundred and ninety three, be referred to the Committee of Claims.

[Journals of the House of Representatives, Vol. III, page 90]

FRIDAY, MARCH 9, 1798

Mr. Dwight Foster, from the committee of claims, to whom were referred the petitions of James Brown, of Deborah Gannett, of John Smuck, one of the heirs of Francis Koonz, deceased, and of John Henry Zimmerman, made a report, which was read and considered: Whereupon,

Resolved, that the prayer of the petitions of the said James Brown, Deborah Gannett, John Smuck and John Henry Zimmerman, cannot be granted.

[Journals of the House of Representatives, Vol. III, page 220]

HARRIOT K. HUNT (1805–1875)

72. The female physician: an unlicensed practitioner

These excerpts from Harriot Hunt's autobiography illustrate the work and struggles of a woman who was kept out of professional

Harriot K. Hunt, M.D., *Glances and Glimpses; or Fifty Years Social, Including Twenty Years Professional Life* (Boston: John P. Jewett and Co., 1856), pp. 265–272.

training and accreditation by discrimination barriers. Harriot Hunt had been prompted to become a physician by the harrowing medical treatment given to her sister. She was privately trained in her native Boston by a British practitioner. Convinced of the inefficacy of much then-current medical work, she went into medical practice in 1835, mostly among women and children. Her system was a blend of good nursing, attention to diet, homeopathy, and psychological consultation. She attempted to channel the energies of her patients into benevolent activities and inform them of sound rules of hygiene, physical exercise, and mental health. After successfully practicing in this manner for twelve years, she applied in 1847 to Harvard Medical School for permission to attend their lectures, but was refused. Three years later, she made another attempt, recorded below. The refusal of Harvard in no way curbed her flourishing practice, which she continued until shortly before her death.

Convinced that ignorance of their physiology was harmful to the health of women, she organized a Ladies Physiological Society in 1843, to which she gave monthly talks. She was an active feminist and annually dramatized her demand for woman suffrage by paying her taxes under protest. A woman who chose to remain single and referred to herself as married to her profession, Harriot Hunt lived her life in self-conscious defiance of convention and became a model for the nineteenth-century career woman.

Boston, Nov. 12, 1850

Gentlemen of the Medical Faculty of Harvard College:—

In addressing you again on a subject of so much moment, permit me to bring to it the same earnest, trusting spirit that prompted me when I asked leave to attend your medical lectures in December, 1847, and was refused on the ground of inexpediency. Nay, a deeper, more interior motive operates upon me now, than even then; for public sentiment has been bending more and more in this direction, and the idea that delicacy, propriety, and necessity require for woman one of her own sex, properly educated, to consult with in many cases, has gained a stronger foothold. . . .

The want and need of female physicians must be seen, I should think, by every philanthropic and delicate mind. . . . There is a gap in society, a true legitimate want in our midst, to satisfy which, a separate female medical college is even now struggling for life. . . . A feeling of disorder is active in community, and the question is even now put, Do you employ a male or female physician?

In my previous letter I stated plainly my desire for medical knowledge, to aid me in an extensive practice among the highly intelligent. That desire deepens with years and with the responsibility of being a precedent in so high a vocation. Your refusal in the city of my birth, education, and life, seemed unjust to me, and I now hope for something better, and would respectfully ask you to investigate this subject further, and . . . open your institution (as in other States) to prepare woman for one of the noblest callings in life, or through refusal again, cause further agitation on this great subject. . . .

These remarks are respectfully offered, gentlemen, by one, who, in this city for fourteen years, undiplomaed and unacknowledged by the Medical Faculty, has been permitted to establish and continue herself in a new, true, elevating path for woman. And now . . . she asks for you, clearness of vision, strength of purpose, and high justice, in your deliberations on these great questions:—

Shall woman be permitted all the Medical advantages she desires? Shall mind, or sex, be recognized in admission to medical lectures?

An answer will be awaited with deep interest.

Respectfully yours, Harriot K. Hunt

BOSTON, DEC. 5, 1850

Dear Madam:—

It was voted by the Medical Faculty of Harvard University, on the 23d of November, "That Miss Hunt be admitted to the lectures on the usual terms, provided that her admission be not deemed inconsistent with the statutes."

On communicating this vote to the President and Fellows, the answer was returned that no objection was perceived arising from the statutes of the Medical School to admitting female students to the lectures, but that no opinion was expressed by that answer as to the claims of such students to a medical degree.

You can therefore obtain tickets. . . .

> *Yours, respectfully,*
> *O[liver] W[endell] Holmes, Dean of the Faculty*

[Harriot Hunt was ill at the time she received the letter of reply above, and had to postpone her attendance at Harvard Medical School lectures. Meanwhile, students had heard of her admission and reacted angrily. Their actions were described in a letter by one of them to the Boston *Evening Transcript*.]

The Female Medical Pupil—Mr. Editor:—

. . . Allow me to . . . claim space for an insertion of the following series of resolutions passed at a meeting of the medical class with but *one* dissenting vote, and afterwards respectfully presented to the Faculty of the Medical College.

Whereas, it has been ascertained that permission has been granted to a female to attend the Medical Lectures of the present winter, therefore

Resolved, That we deem it proper both to testify our disapprobation of said measure, and to take such action thereon as may be necessary to preserve the dignity of the school, and our own self-respect.

Resolved, That no woman of true delicacy would be willing in the presence of men to listen to the discussion of the subjects that necessarily come under the consideration of the student of medicine.

Resolved, That we object to having the company of any female forced upon us, who is disposed to unsex herself, and to sacrifice her modesty, by appearing with men in the medical lecture room.

Resolved, That we are not opposed to allowing woman

her rights, but do protest against her appearing in places where her presence is calculated to destroy our respect for the modesty and delicacy of her sex.

Resolved, That the medical professors be, and hereby are, respectfully entreated to do away forthwith an innovation expressly at variance with the spirit of the introductory lecture, with our own feelings, and detrimental to the prosperity, if not to the very existence of the school.

Resolved, That a copy of these resolutions be presented to the Medical Faculty.

SCALPEL.

[Harriot Hunt continues her narrative of the incident:]

My letter was then requested and appeared in the same paper. I am aware that at the time of my application, the college was involved in some difficulty. . . . It seems that at the commencement of the lectures two colored persons were found to be of the number of students. This occasioned a good deal of feeling in the school. In a few weeks another black made his appearance, and anon a report was circulated that a woman had taken tickets for the lectures. The pent up indignation now burst forth, and two series of resolutions were passed, remonstrating against this amalgamation of sexes and races.

The class at Harvard in 1851, have purchased for themselves a notoriety they will not covet in years to come. The publication of their resolutions has done good service to the cause of woman; they have elicited discussion, sharpened wit, called forth satire, and furnished subject for thought. . . .

It is in place for me here to record my thanks to the Female Medical College of Philadelphia, for the honorary degree which they conferred upon me in January, 1853. Courtesy and respect had led many of my patients for many years to address me as Dr., but the recognition of that College was very pleasant after eighteen years practice. . . .

ELIZABETH BLACKWELL, M.D. (1821–1910)

73. The female physician: pioneer work

The creation of a "new woman"—the qualified professional woman—was an agonizingly slow process, in which certain pioneers invested their lives. Gaining access to professional training was only the first step in that process. The case of Elizabeth Blackwell, generally known as "the first woman doctor" in the United States, illustrates the way in which well-trained women found themselves barred from their professions and had to proceed to the building of sex-segregated institutions, if they wished to practice their skills. Elizabeth Blackwell deserves to be better known than she is for her work in founding the institutions in which the first generation of fully qualified female physicians could be trained, supported, and employed.

After a long struggle to win admission to a medical school and to overcome the prejudices of her fellow students and staff of Geneva College (N.Y.), where she finally was admitted, Elizabeth Blackwell received the M.D. in 1849. She had to overcome more sex discrimination barriers before she could receive additional advanced training in France and England. But her fine training was insufficient to overcome the wall of sex prejudice which met her on her return to New York City in 1851. In the document below she describes her struggle for establishing a private practice. She was denied access to hospitals, prevented from renting quarters for her home or office, insulted, and vilified. Her opening a one-room dispensary was a step forced on her by necessity.

Elizabeth Blackwell describes the successive stages in her institution-building: from one-room dispensary to the New York Infirmary for Women and Children, the Woman's Central Association of Relief which helped to pave the way for the professionalization of nursing, and, finally, her establishment of the Woman's Medical College of New York. This institution upgraded medical training for women and functioned independently until 1899,

Elizabeth Blackwell, *Pioneer Work in Opening the Medical Profession to Women* (New York: E. P. Dutton Co., 1895).

when Cornell University Medical School in New York began to admit women students.

. . . I employed the leisure hours of a young physician in preparing some lectures on the physical education of girls, which were delivered in a basement Sunday school room in the spring of 1852.

These lectures, owing to the social and professional connections which resulted from them, gave me my first start in practical medical life. They were attended by a small but very intelligent audience of ladies, and amongst them were some members of the Society of Friends, whose warm and permanent interest was soon enlisted. Indeed, my practice during those early years became very much a Quaker practice; and the institutions which sprang up later owed their foundation to the active support of this valuable section of community. . . .

First Annual Report of the New York Dispensary for Poor Women and Children, 1855*

The design of this institution is to give to poor women an opportunity of consulting physicians of their own sex. The existing charities in our city regard the employment of women as physicians as an experiment, the success of which has not yet been sufficiently proved to admit of cordial cooperation. It was therefore necessary to form a separate institution which should furnish to poor women the medical aid which they could not obtain elsewhere. . . .

The Eleventh Ward was chosen as the location for the dispensary, it being destitute of medical charity, while possessing a densely crowded poor population. The necessary rooms were found in Seventh Street, near Tompkins Square, and were ready for the reception of patients in the month of March. The dispensary has been regularly opened through the year, on Monday, Wednesday, and Friday after-

---

* I insert this document here, out of sequence.—ED.

noons, at 3 o'clock. Over 200 poor women have received medical aid. All these women have gratefully acknowledged the help afforded them, and several of the most destitute have tendered their few pence as an offering to the institution. . . .

My first medical consultation was a curious experience. In a severe case of pneumonia in an elderly lady I called in consultation a kind-hearted physician of high standing who had been present in Cincinnati at the time of my father's fatal illness. This gentleman, after seeing the patient, went with me into the parlour. There he began to walk about the room in some agitation, exclaiming, "A most extraordinary case! Such a one never happened to me before; I really do not know what to do!" I listened in surprise and much perplexity, as it was a clear case of pneumonia and of no unusual degree of danger, until at last I discovered that his perplexity related to *me*, not to the patient, and to the propriety of consulting with a lady physician! I was both amused and relieved. I at once assured my old acquaintance that it need not be considered in the light of an ordinary consultation, if he were uneasy about it, but as a friendly talk. So, finally, he gave me his best advice; my patient rapidly got well, and happily I never afterwards had any difficulty in obtaining a necessary consultation from members of the profession. . . .

Establishment of a hospital.—In 1856 my working powers were more than doubled by the arrival of my sister, Dr. Emily Blackwell, who became henceforth my partner and able co-worker. Dr. Maria E. Zackrzewska also joined us as soon as she had graduated at Cleveland, and became for some years before her removal to Boston our active and valued assistant in the New York work. . . .

Many cases of extreme destitution have come to the dispensary. These have been chiefly emigrants, mostly Germans, without friends or money, and ignorant of the language. Several families have been visited where some member was sick, and found utterly destitute, suffering from hunger, and though honest and industrious, disappointed in every effort to obtain work. To such families a little help with money, generally in the form of a loan till work could be procured, has proved invaluable, and a small poor fund placed by some friends in the hands of the attending physician, for this special object, has saved several worthy families from despair and impending starvation. . . .

Poor women and children may be sent from any part of the city to receive the medical aid of the dispensary, it being free to all.

This institution was commenced by the subscriptions of a few friends; its expenses have been kept within its means, but the power of doing good has necessarily been limited by the smallness of its funds. It is found desirable to enlarge its operations, and place it on a permanent basis. For this purpose, the trustees wish to raise the sum of 5,000 dollars, and contributions are earnestly solicited. . . .

The amount raised will be invested as a permanent fund for the institution. It is the hope of the founders of this charity to make it eventually a hospital for women and a school for the education of nurses. . . .

Thus reinforced, an advanced step was made in 1857 by the renting of a house, No. 64 Bleecker Street, which we fitted up for a hospital where both patients and young assistant physicians could be received. This institution, under the name of "The New York Infirmary for Women and Children," was formally opened in the May of this year by a public meeting, in which the Rev. Henry Ward Beecher, Dr. Elder of Philadelphia, and the Rev. Dr. Tyng, jun., warmly supported the movement. In this institution Dr. Zackrzewska accepted the post of resident physician, Dr. Emily becoming chiefly responsible for the surgical practice.

This first attempt to establish a hospital conducted en-

tirely by women excited much opposition. . . . Our difficulties are thus noted in the Annual Report for 1864:—
"But to this step (the establishment of a hospital) a host of
objections were raised by those whom the early friends of
the institution attempted to interest in their effort. They
were told that no one would let a house for the purpose, that
female doctors would be looked upon with so much suspicion that the police would interfere; that if deaths occurred
their death certificates would not be recognised; that they
would be resorted to by classes and persons whom it would
be an insult to be called upon to deal with; that without men
as resident physicians they would not be able to control the
patients; that if any accident occurred, not only the medical
profession but the public would blame the trustees for supporting such an undertaking; and, finally, that they would
never be able to collect money enough for so unpopular an
effort."

Through a cloud of discouragement and distrust the little
institution steadily worked its way, its few friends holding
to it the more firmly for the difficulties it experienced. The
practice of the infirmary, both medical and surgical, was
conducted entirely by women; but a board of consulting
physicians, men of high standing in the profession, gave it
the sanctity of their names. . . .

The pecuniary support of this institution, in addition to
the medical responsibility involved in its conduct, was no
small burden. . . .

At one time Fanny Kemble was giving a series of Shake-
spearian readings in New York, and often rendered generous
help to benevolent institutions by the use of her great talent.
We hoped that she might aid our struggling infirmary by
giving a public reading in its behalf. So on one occasion I
called with our fellow-worker Dr. Zackrzewska at the hotel
where she was staying to prefer our request. She received
us courteously, listened with kindness to an explanation of
the object of our visit and of the needs of the infirmary; but

when she heard that the physicians of the institution were *women* she sprang up to her full height, turned her flashing eyes upon us, and with the deepest tragic tones of her magnificent voice exclaimed: "Trust a *woman*—as a DOCTOR!— NEVER!" . . .

The necessity, however, of a separate hospital for the general training of women students had by this time been recognised. Experience both at the New York Hospital and at the large Bellevue Hospital, where classes of imperfectly trained women had failed to maintain their ground, proved that a special woman's centre was needed, not only as affording them practical instruction, but for the purpose of testing the capacity and tact of the students themselves, before admitting them to walk the general hospitals where male students were admitted. The New York Infirmary for Women therefore gradually enlisted the active help of enlightened men and women. . . .

In the full tide of our medical activity in New York, with a growing private practice and increasing hospital claims, the great catastrophe of civil war overwhelmed the country and dominated every other interest.

The first shot at Fort Sumter aroused the whole North, and the assassination of Lincoln enlisted the indignant energy of every Northern woman in the tremendous struggle. As the deadly contest proceeded, and every town and village sent forth its volunteers to the fearful slaughter of civil war, the concentration of thought and action on the war dwarfed every other effort. . . .

On the outbreak of the war, an informal meeting of the lady managers was called at the infirmary to see what could be done towards supplying the want of trained nurses so widely felt after the first battles. A notice of this meeting to be held at the infirmary having accidentally found its way into the "New York Times," the parlours of the infirmary were crowded with ladies, to the surprise of the little group of managers.

The Rev. Dr. Bellows and Dr. Elisha Harris being present, a formal meeting was organised. Whilst the great and urgent need of a supply of nurses was fully recognised, it was also felt that the movement would be too vast to be carried on by so small an institution. A letter was therefore drafted on this occasion, calling for a public meeting at the Cooper Institute, and a committee of the ladies present was appointed to obtain signatures to this call.

The meeting at the Cooper Institute was crowded to overflowing. The National Sanitary Aid Association was then formed, in order to organise the energetic efforts to help that were being made all over the country.

The Ladies' Sanitary Aid Association, of which we were active members, was also formed. This branch worked daily at the Cooper Institute during the whole of the war. It received and forwarded contributions of comforts for the soldiers, zealously sent from the country; but its special work was the forwarding of nurses to the seat of war. All that could be done in the extreme urgency of the need was to sift out the most promising women from the multitudes that applied to be sent on as nurses, put them for a month in training at the great Bellevue Hospital of New York, which consented to receive relays of volunteers, provide them with a small outfit, and send them on for distribution to Miss Dix, who was appointed superintendent of nurses at Washington. . . .

It was not until [the] great national rebellion was ended that the next step in the growth of the infirmary could be taken.

The infirmary service of young assistant physicians, which had been hitherto supplied by students whose theoretical training had been obtained elsewhere, no longer met the New York needs.

In 1865 the trustees of the infirmary, finding that the institution was established in public favour, applied to the Legislature for a charter conferring college powers upon it.

ANN PRESTON, M.D. (1813–1872)

74. The female physician: an attack and a reply

The struggles of Elizabeth Blackwell for access to professional training were duplicated by Ann Preston of Philadelphia who, denied admission to all Philadelphia medical colleges, entered the first class of the newly founded Female (later Woman's) Medical College of Pennsylvania at the age of thirty-seven. Unlike the lonely Blackwell, she obtained her training and practical experience with other women in a sex-segregated institution. Dr. Preston would spend her life in building up the Woman's Medical College; she was appointed professor in physiology and hygiene in 1853 and later became the first woman dean.

Establishing a woman's college was only the beginning in a continuous struggle for professional equality. In 1858 the Philadelphia Medical Society formally ostracized this institution, making women inadmissable to membership in any of the state's medical societies and closing teaching opportunities to them. Although Ann Preston later won the right for her students to attend the general clinics at Philadelphia Hospital, resistance of male professionals surfaced again in the statement printed here. Dr. Preston's reply is interesting not only for its well-reasoned argument, but for its strongly feminist tone: "We have decided ourselves that the study and practice of medicine are proper, womanly, etc." she states, asserting feminine autonomy with confidence and authority. "We suppose that our sense of what is right and fitting for ourselves [is] as reliable [as that] . . . of the men who condemn our course."

Preamble and Resolution Passed By The Philadelphia County Medical Society

Looking to the usefulness and dignity of the profession, which are inseparably connected with the welfare of the

"Preamble and Resolution of the Philadelphia County Medical Society upon the Status of Women Physicians with *A Reply by a Woman*" (Philadelphia: Stuchey, 1867), pamphlet.

community, we are not without very grave objections to women taking on themselves the heavy duties and responsibilities of the practice of medicine. . . .

. . . The physiological peculiarities of woman even in single life, and the disorders consequent on them, cannot fail frequently to interfere with the regular discharge of her duties as physician in constant attendance on the sick. How much greater must be the interruption to her duties if she enters the marriage state, and becomes a mother and nurse. The delicate organization and predominance of the nervous system render her peculiarly susceptible to suffer, if not to sink, under the fatigue and mental shocks which she must encounter in her professional round. Man, with his robust frame and trained self-command, is often barely equal to the task. The home influence of woman is one of the greatest benefits growing out of christian civilization. More especially is this manifest when we look at her as the head of the household, a helpmate to her husband, and the confidante, guide, instructor, and loving friend of her children, whose future happiness and respectability so much depend on her tuition and example. What would be the state of the household, what the present condition and future prospects of the children, deprived to a considerable extent of their natural guardian, who would be engaged all day and not secure against calls in the night, in the service of the sick? Nor when at home, can the mother, worried and fretted and anxious about her patients, give healthy milk to her infant, or be in a fit frame of mind to interchange endearments with her beloved little ones, to receive their confidences and offer advice.

Once embarked in the practice of medicine, a female physician will not long confine herself to attendance on persons of her own sex. Curiosity, caprice, the novelty of the thing, would induce some men to ask the professional advice of a woman doctor. It is sufficient to allude merely to the embarrassments which would be encountered on both sides, in her visiting and prescribing for persons of the opposite sex. If her services be restricted to the female portion of the family, then must there be a male physician to attend on the males, and thus there will be constantly two physicians in the regular service of the family, with all the chances of counterprescriptions and advice and breach of ethics, misunderstandings and heartburnings, by each one passing the lines of the other. If a female physician be once received in full standing, and professional intercourse by consultation or at other times with a physician of our sex be allowed, the greatest latitude will be taken and given in the statement of the case of disease, whatever it may be, its symptoms and causes, and questions of treatment therapeutical and psychical. Will woman gain by ceasing to blush while discussing every topic as it comes up with philosophic coolness, and man be improved in the delicate reserve with which he is accustomed to address woman in the sick room? The bounds of modesty once passed in this professional intercourse, will the additional freedom of speech and manner thus acquired impart grace or dignity to a woman in her new character?

Could women be induced to see the true line of duty in relation to medical study, it would be to learn preventive medicine and acquire a suitable knowledge of physiology and hygiene, so as to be able to preserve their own health and that of their children, and to inculcate on the latter the close connection between the physical and mental well being of our nature. The field is large, and its cultivation would richly repay the laborers in it.

In no other country than our own is a body of women authorized to engage in the general practice of medicine. The specialty of midwifery practice in France is hedged in by regulations which call for the assistance of medical men in any case of difficulty or doubt.

Moved by these considerations, be it therefore

RESOLVED, *That, in conformity with what they believe to be due to the profession, the community in general and the female portion of it in particular, the members of this Soci-*

ety cannot offer any encouragement to women becoming practitioners of medicine, nor, on these grounds, can they consent to meet in consultation such practitioners.

Reply by Ann Preston, M.D.

Editor, Medical and Surgical Reporter:

I have read with surprise the preamble and resolution adopted by the Philadelphia County Medical Society, and published in the MEDICAL AND SURGICAL REPORTER of the 6th ult., in reference to the status of women-physicians; and as a subscriber to the REPORTER, and one personally interested in the bearing of that decision, I trust I may be permitted, through the same channel, to examine the arguments which support the resolution. . . .

The "very grave objections to women taking on themselves the heavy duties and responsibilities of the profession" appear to be based, in the *first* place, upon the assumption that they do not possess the "ability to bear up under the bodily and mental strain to which they would be unceasingly subjected in this new vocation;" in the *second,* upon the presumed incompatibility of professional practice with the best home influence of the woman and the duties of the mother; in the *third* place, upon the collision and practical difficulties that might arise if different members of the same family should employ two physicians—a man and a woman; and *lastly,* the objections are made upon the ground of the equivocal effect of medical consultations upon the modesty and delicacy of feeling of those who may thus meet; and also upon the fact, that "in no other country but our own is a body of women authorized to engage in the general practice of medicine."

In regard to the *first* difficulty, few words need be expended. Pausing merely to allude to the fact, that in barbarous communities woman is pre-eminently the laborious drudge, and that in civilized society she is the *nurse,* keeping her unceasing vigils not only by the cradle of infancy, but by every bed of sickness and suffering, with a power of sustained endurance that man does not claim to possess; that her life is as long, and her power of surmounting its painful vicissitudes not inferior to his, we come to the open, undeniable fact, that women *do* practice medicine, that they *are* able to "bear up under the bodily and mental strain" that this practice imposes, and that "natural obstacles" have not obstructed their way.

There are in this city women who have been engaged in the practice of medicine a dozen years, who to-day have more vigor and power of endurance than they possessed in the beginning of their career; and the fact of "their delicate organization and predominance of the nervous system," combined with their "trained self-command," is the very reason that in some cases their counsel has been preferred to that of the more robust man.

The *second* objection, bearing upon the home influence of woman, has certainly another side.

Probably more than half the women of this city and country are under the stern necessity of supporting themselves by their own exertions. Some mothers leave their young children day by day and go out to labor, in order to be able to bring them bread at night; others sew away their strength for the pittance which barely keeps famine from their doors, and, exhausted with their labors, they are indeed not in "a fit frame of mind to interchange endearments with their beloved little ones;" nor can they, even with the price of life itself, surround them with the home influence and comforts needful to their healthful and harmonious development.

If the woman who has studied medicine should be surrounded by a family of young children, we should surely regard it as a misfortune if the same overpowering necessity should compel her to follow an active practice during the period that these heavy maternal claims were pressing upon her; although even then, her duties would be less exhausting, and her time less continuously occupied than are hers who supports her family by sewing or washing. . . .

The *third* objection, in regard to collisions and "heartburnings," could scarcely apply to high-toned physicians who know what belongs to the proprieties of their position. The danger would seem to be equally imminent if the medical advisers were both of the same sex, and yet we all know it is quite common in this city for more than one practitioner to attend the different members of the same family—one being preferred for his supposed skill in one class of cases, another for his superior reputation in another class; and we have yet to learn that injurious results follow this proximity of practitioners.

The natural tendency would seem to be, to foster care and research; and if mutual observation of the results of treatment should occasionally suggest improved methods and break up old, sluggish routine in either party, the profession and the community will surely be gainers by this mutual stimulus.

The objection upon the ground of the invasion of delicacy in examining questions of disease and treatment is indeed an astonishing one, to come from a body of scientific and right-minded physicians. Who are the patients treated by these men? Often women—the sensitive and refined. The whole nature of the malady must be investigated and the means of recovery enforced. If, as frequently happens, to save the shrinking sensitiveness of the young woman, some tender experienced mother or elder friend informs the physician of the symptoms and conveys to the patient his conclusions, she, for the time, performs the part of the attending physician in reference to the consulting one; yet who will dare assert that her womanly modesty is compromised, or that "the delicate reserve with which" a man "is accustomed to address woman in the sick-room" is injuriously affected by this necessary and humane intervention?

. . . But leaving these special points, there are broad, general grounds upon which, as physicians and as women, we stand, and appeal from the resolution of the Philadelphia County Society to the better judgment of true-hearted professional men.

When once it is admitted that women have souls, and that they are accountable to God for the uses of the powers which He has given them, then the exercise of their own judgment and conscience in reference to these uses, becomes a thing which they cannot, rightfully, yield to any human tribunal.

As responsible beings, who must abide by the consequences of our course for time and for eternity, we have decided for ourselves that the study and practice of medicine are proper, womanly, and adapted to our mental, moral, and physical constitution.

We will scarcely be charged with presumption in supposing that our instincts may be as pure, our intuitions as clear, our sense of what is right and fitting for ourselves as reliable, as are those of the men who condemn our course. . . .

That we have not had the facilities for acquiring medical information is a charge that, it seem to us, should hardly come from those who have systematically closed hospitals and colleges against our applications for admission, and who have endeavored to prevent the members of their fraternity from assisting us in our struggle for knowledge.

That we have stemmed this tide of opposition, and found opportunities for obtaining medical instruction—some in other cities and across the ocean, some by persevering and long-continued efforts in various ways at home; that we have found noble men in the profession to assist us, and that we have been able to found hospitals and open various channels for practical education—*is due to the inherent vitality of our cause,* and its strong hold upon the sympathies and convictions of the community.

That we have not yet all the facilities for instruction that are needed, we are fully aware.

That "there are female graduates who are a disgrace to the medical profession," we also know too well: for the sake of humanity we would that we could truly add, that the graduates who disgrace the profession are found *only* among women!

From the nature of the relation of physicians to society, not more than one man in hundreds follows medicine as a profession, and the proportion of women, under the most favoring circumstances, will probably not be greater; but the systematic training, and the knowledge of physiological functions and hygienic conditions involved in a thorough medical education for the few, will, we believe, be reflected in many homes, and be one of the means of radically changing that mistaken plan of education, and those destructive social customs and habits, which are now undermining the health, and darkening the lives of so many of the women of this country. . . .

But on behalf of a little band of true-hearted young women who are just entering the profession, and from whose pathway we fain would see annoyances and impediments removed, we must protest, in the sacred name of our common humanity, against the injustice which places difficulties in our way,—not because we are ignorant, or pretentious, or incompetent, or unmindful of the code of medical or Christian ethics, but because we are women.

Philadelphia, April 22, 1867.   ANN PRESTON, M.D.

ELIZABETH CADY STANTON

75. The best protector any woman can have is courage

Freedom of mind and body, courage, self-reliance—these were the virtues Elizabeth Cady Stanton sought all her life to win for the new generation of girls. In this astonishingly modern approach to

Elizabeth C. Stanton, Susan B. Anthony, and Matilda J. Gage, *History of Woman Suffrage*, 6 vols. (New York: Fowler & Wells, 1881–1922), I:816.

counteracting sex-role indoctrination, Elizabeth Cady Stanton summarizes her views on creating the new feminist consciousness. (See also document 89).

ELIZABETH CADY STANTON TO THE WOMAN'S
CONVENTION, HELD AT AKRON, OHIO, MAY 25, 1851.

Dear Friends:—. . . The great work before us is the education of those just coming on the stage of action. Begin with the girls of *to-day,* and in twenty years we can revolutionize this nation. The childhood of woman must be free and untrammeled. The girl must be allowed to romp and play, climb, skate, and swim; her clothing must be more like that of the boy—strong, loose-fitting garments, thick boots, etc., that she may be out at all times, and enter freely into all kinds of sports. Teach her to go alone, by night and day, if need be, on the lonely highway, or through the busy streets of the crowded metropolis. The manner in which all courage and self-reliance is educated *out* of the girl, her path portrayed with dangers and difficulties that never exist, is melancholy indeed. Better, far, suffer occasional insults or die outright, than live the life of a *coward,* or never move without a protector. The best protector any woman can have, one that will serve her at all times and in all places, is *courage;* this she must get by her own experience, and experience comes by exposure. Let the girl be thoroughly developed in body and soul, not modeled, like a piece of clay, after some artificial specimen of humanity, with a body like some plate in Godey's book of fashion, and a mind after the type of Father Gregory's pattern daughters, loaded down with the traditions, proprieties, and sentimentalities of generations of silly mothers and grandmothers, but left free to be, to grow, to feel, to think, to act. Development is one thing, that system of cramping, restraining, torturing, perverting, and mystifying, called education, is quite another. We have had women enough befooled under the one system, pray let us try the other. The girl must early be impressed with the idea that she is to be "a hand, not a mouth"; a worker, and not a drone, in the great hive of human activity. Like the boy, she must be taught to look forward to a life of self-dependence, and early prepare herself for some trade or profession. Woman has relied heretofore too entirely for her support on the *needle*—that one-eyed demon of destruction that slays its thousands annually; that evil genius of our sex, which, in spite of all our devotion, will never make us healthy, wealthy, or wise.

Teach the girl it is no part of her life to cater to the prejudices of those around her. Make her independent of public sentiment, by showing her how worthless and rotten a thing it is. It is a settled axiom with me, after much examination and reflection, that public sentiment is false on every subject. Yet what a tyrant it is over us all, woman especially, whose very life is to please, whose highest ambition is to be approved. But once outrage this tyrant, place yourself beyond his jurisdiction, taste the joy of free thought and action, and how powerless is his rule over you! his sceptre lies broken at your feet; his very babblings of condemnation are sweet music in your ears; his darkening frown is sunshine to your heart, for they tell of your triumph and his discomfort. Think you, women *thus* educated would long remain the weak, dependent beings we now find them? By no means. Depend upon it, they would soon settle for themselves this whole question of Woman's Rights. As educated capitalists and skilled laborers, they would not be long in finding their true level in political and social life.

BELVA LOCKWOOD (1830–1917)

76. A new self-consciousness

In her brief letter cited below, Belva Lockwood modestly downgrades the several ways in which she contributed to the crea-

Belva A. Lockwood to J. A. Cruikshank, Miriam Y. Holden Library, New York City. Courtesy of Miriam Y. Holden.

tion of a new woman. She was among the first class of women admitted to study at National University Law School in Washington, D.C., and one of two female students to complete the law course. Still, she was not granted her degree until she protested in the following words to Ulysses S. Grant, then President of the United States and thereby president of the National University Law School:

"You are, or you are not the President of The National University Law School. If you are its President I wish to say to you that I have been passed through the curriculum of study of that school, and am entitled to, and demand my Diploma. If you are not its President then I ask you to take your name from its papers, and not hold out to the world to be what you are not."*

The letter had its effect and she received her diploma at the age of forty-three. This was followed by her admission to the bar of the District, but in 1876 her petition for admission to the Supreme Court was denied on the ground of custom. Mrs. Lockwood thereupon lobbied energetically for passage of a bill which would enable women lawyers to pursue cases to the highest court in the land. The bill was passed, and in 1879 she became the first woman to practice before the Supreme Court and opened the way to full acceptance of other women as professional lawyers.

Her suffrage activities in Washington, D.C., culminated in her campaign for President of the United States as candidate of the National Equal Rights Party in 1884 and 1888. The last decades of her long life were devoted to public lectures, law practice, and her activities in the international world peace movement.

WASHINGTON, D.C., NOV. 21, 1897

Your favor containing the question, as to whether I consider myself a "new woman" is before me. As a rule I do not consider myself at all. I am, and always have been a progressive woman, and while never directly attacking the conventionalities of society, have always done, or attempted to do those things which I have considered conducive to my

---

* Madeline Stern, "The First Woman Admitted to Practice Before the United States Supreme Court—Belva Ann Lockwood, 1879," *We the Women: Career First of Nineteenth Century America* (New York: Schulte Publishing Co., 1963), p. 211.

health, convenience or emolument, as for instänce: Attended college and graduated when the general sentiment
of the people was against it, and this after I had been a
married woman.

Entered a law school and graduated, at a time when there
was much opposition to such a course.

Applied for, and was admitted ultimately to the United
States Supreme Court. Such a course had been previously
unknown in our history. I was the first woman to ride a
wheel in the District of Columbia, which I persisted in
doing notwithstanding newspaper comments.

I accepted a nomination to the Presidency by the Equal
Rights Party, and my letter of acceptance was published
throughout the length and breadth of 2 worlds.

I do not believe in sex distinction in literature, law, politics, or trade; or that modesty and virtue are more becoming
to women than to men; but wish we had more of it
everywhere.

I was new about 60 years ago, but did not then appreciate
my privileges.

Yours truly, Belva A. Lockwood.

ELIZABETH GURLEY FLYNN (1890–1964)

77. The woman revolutionary

The woman revolutionary came out of a long radical tradition in
the American working-class movement. Mother Jones of the min-
ers, Emma Goldman, Kate Richards O'Hare, and Ella Reeve Bloor
were some of the leading figures of American radicalism. None
captured the imagination as strongly as did young "Gurley," the

Mary Heaton Vorse, "Elizabeth Gurley Flynn," printed in *The Nation* 122,
no. 3163 (February 17, 1926): 175–176. Original manuscript in Mary
Heaton Vorse Papers, Wayne State University Labor Archives, Detroit,
Mich.

"Rebel Girl." Here one of the young radical women of the middle class, the writer and trade union organizer Mary Heaton Vorse, describes young Elizabeth Gurley Flynn. Later Flynn would become a leader of the Communist Party, U.S.A. As such, she was convicted under the Smith Act in 1952 and served a five-year jail sentence at the age of sixty-five. On her release, she became chairman of the Communist Party, U.S.A., a post she held from 1959 until her death in 1964.

1906–16, Organizer, lecturer for I.W.W.;

1918–24, Organizer, Workers Defense Union;

Arrested in New York, 1906, free-speech case, dismissed; active in Spokane, Washington, free-speech fight, 1909; arrested, Missoula, Montana, 1909, in free-speech fight of I.W.W., Spokane, Washington, free-speech fight of I.W.W., hundreds arrested; in Philadelphia arrested three times, 1911, at strike meetings of Baldwin Locomotive Works; active in Lawrence textile strike, 1912; hotel-workers strike, 1912, New York; Paterson textile strike, 1913; defense work for Ettor-Giovannitti case, 1912; Mesaba Range strike, Minnesota, 1916; Evertt I.W.W. case, Spokane, Washington, 1916; Joe Hill defense, 1914. Arrested Duluth, Minnesota, 1917, charged with vagrancy under law passed to stop I.W.W. and pacifist speakers, case dismissed. Indicted in Chicago I.W.W. case, 1917. Arrested in Philadelphia, 1920, at Sacco-Vanzetti meeting, no police permit. Active in Sacco-Vanzetti defense, 1921–24.

She began this amazing record by getting arrested on a street corner when she was fifteen. Her father was arrested with her. He never has been arrested since. It was only the beginning for her.

The judge inquired, "Do you expect to convert people to socialism by talking on Broadway?"

She looked up at him and replied gravely, "Indeed I do."

The judge sighed deeply in pity. "Dismissed," he said.

Joe O'Brien gives me a picture of her at that time. He was

sent to cover the case of these people who had been arrested for talking socialism on Broadway. He expected to find a strong-minded harpy. Instead he found a beautiful child of fifteen, the most beautiful girl he had ever seen. A young Joan of Arc is what she looked like to him with her dark hair hanging down her back and her blue Irish eyes ringed with black lashes. That was how she entered the Labor movement. Since then she has never stopped.

Presently she joined the I.W.W., which was then in its golden age. Full of idealism, it swept the Northwest. They had free-speech fights everywhere. The authorities arrested them and more came. They crammed the jails to bursting.

"In one town," said Elizabeth, "there were so many in jail that they let them out during the day. We outside had to feed them. Every night they went back to jail. At last the wobblies decided that when the jail opened they would not come out. People came from far and near to see the wobblies who wouldn't leave jail."

This part of her life, organizing and fighting the fights of the migratory workers of the West, is the part of her life that she likes most. . . . Her marriage did not affect her activities. The arrival of her son did. His birth closed this chapter of her life.

My first sight of her was in Lawrence in the big strike of 1912. I arrived just after the chief of police had refused to allow the strikers to send their children to the workers' homes in other towns. There had been a riot at the railway station. Children had been jostled and trampled. Women fainted. The town was under martial law. Ettor and Giovannitti were in jail for murder as accessory before the fact.

I walked with Bill Haywood into a quick-lunch restaurant. "There's Gurley," he said. She was sitting at a lunch counter on a mushroom stool, and it was as if she were the spirit of this strike that had so much hope and so much beauty. She was only about twenty-one, but she had gravity and maturity. She asked me to come and see her at her house. She had gone on strike, bringing with her her mother and her baby.

There was ceaseless work for her that winter. Speaking, sitting with the strike committee, going to visit the prisoners in jail, and endlessly raising money. Speaking, speaking, speaking, taking trains only to run back to the town that was ramparted by prison-like mills before which soldiers with fixed bayonets paced all day long. Almost every night when we didn't dine in the Syrian restaurant we dined in some striker's home, very largely among the Italians. It seemed to me I had never met so many fine people before. I did not know people could act the way those strikers could in Lawrence. Every strike meeting was memorable—the morning meetings in a building quite a way from the center of things, owned by someone sympathetic to the strikers, the only place they were permitted to assemble. The soup kitchen was out here and here groceries were also distributed and the striking women came from far and near. They would wait around for a word with Gurley or with Big Bill. In the midst of this excitement Elizabeth moved calm and tranquil. For off the platform she is a very quiet person. It was as though she reserved her tremendous energy for speaking.

The Paterson textile strike followed Lawrence. In Lawrence there was martial law and militia. It was stern, cruel, and rigorous. The Paterson authorities were all of that and besides they were petty, niggling, and hectoring. Arrests were many. Jail sentences were stiff and given for small cause. Elizabeth was also arrested, but set free again. The Paterson strike of all the strikes stands out in her memory. She got to know the people, and their courage and spirit were things that none of us who were there could ever forget. . . .

The strike on the Mesaba Range was the end of Elizabeth Gurley Flynn's activities as organizer in the I.W.W. Just after the Espionage Act had been passed it happened that we went to the theater together. "If I were in the I.W.W. now," she said, "whether I opened my mouth or didn't I would surely be arrested. It's rather nice to draw a long breath." Next day she was arrested just the same. She was one of the 166 people associated with the I.W.W. indicted for conspiracy.

Defense work was no new thing to her, and from 1918 until recently her major activities have been getting political prisoners out of jail. And since 1921 she has concentrated on the Sacco-Vanzetti case. There has been constant work, there have been arrests, there has been her preoccupation with comrades in jail for their opinions. She comes out of her first twenty years in the labor movement undimmed and undiscouraged.

THE RIGHT TO HER OWN BODY

78. Unwanted motherhood

"No woman can call herself free who does not own and control her own body. No woman can call herself free until she can choose conscientiously whether she will or will not be a mother."

> *Margaret Sanger,* Woman and the New Race *(New York: Truth Publishing Co., 1920), p. 94.*

For thousands of years women have been subject to their biology, being unable to avoid the automatic link of sexuality and reproduction. Even when birth control knowledge was well-advanced scientifically and technology was available to limit reproduction, such information and technology were withheld from women by man-made laws and social customs. Women were culturally conditioned to regard unwanted pregnancies as their fate and to submit to "the will of God" or to the marital rights of their husbands. How women responded to these traditional attitudes is shown in the first two selections below.

Margaret Sanger was the pioneer in placing contraception in the center of feminist concerns (see document 17). The organized woman's rights movement of her day ignored and bypassed her. Women of all classes continued to resort to illegal and highly dangerous abortions. It was only after the advent of the new feminism that young feminists in the National Organization of Women insisted on making abortion law repeal a key plank in their 1967 platform. The cry of Margaret Sanger, "A woman has a right to control her own body," became the basis for the new feminist position, that abortion and contraception were not properly the subject of laws. Abortion law repeal, not reform, was the only way in which to institutionalize a woman's right to make autonomous decisions regarding her own body.

The first two selections that follow are a hundred years apart in time, but their likeness in tone and content is striking. One consists of a letter by an anonymous "lady" to Henry C. Wright, the abolitionist utopian reformer, which he included in his book, *The Unwanted Child.* The passage was reprinted, as typical and representative of conditions in their day, by Dr. Cowan and Mr. Latson, authors of a sexual advice book, originally printed in 1869 and reissued in 1903. It speaks to the prevalence of abortion practiced by middle- and lower-class married women throughout the nineteenth century, a fact which is reflected in the steady decline of the birth rate during that century. It speaks also to the sacrifice of physical health and the unhappiness and mental anguish of women through unwilling sexual intercourse—little more than legal rape—in marriage.

The second selection includes a case history from the files of the National Florence Crittenton Mission by a woman seeking advice and help for an unwanted pregnancy. Initially founded in 1883 to "rescue prostitutes" and carry on an evangelical mission, the organization became, under the leadership of Dr. Kate Waller Barrett, primarily a shelter and home for unwed mothers, providing maternity care and vocational guidance. The limitations of the social welfare approach it represented can be seen in the denial of birth control and abortion referral information to applicants—and in the fact that the over sixty-five homes throughout the United States were race segregated, and only two of them accepted black women.

The third selection summarizes the major arguments advanced in favor of abortion law repeal by reformers in the late 1960s and '70s. The "action resolution" passed by NOW in its 1967 convention has helped to advance the new feminist interpretation that abortion is a civil right of women.

[c. 1845]

Before we married, I informed him (the husband) of my dread of having children. I told him I was not yet prepared to meet the sufferings and responsibilities of maternity. He entered into an arrangement to prevent it for a specified time. This agreement was disregarded. After the legal form was over and he felt that he could now indulge his passion without loss of reputation, and under legal and religious sanctions, he insisted on the surrender of my person to his will. He violated his promise at the beginning of our united life. That fatal bridal night! . . . I can never forget it. It sealed the doom of our union, as it does of thousands.

He was in feeble health; so was I; and both of us mentally depressed. But the sickly germ was implanted, and conception took place. We were poor. . . . In September, 1838, we came to ____, and settled in a new country. In the March following my child . . . was born. After three months' struggle, I became reconciled to my, at first, unwelcome child. . . .

In one year I found I was again to be a mother. I was in a state of frightful despair. My first-born was sickly and troublesome, needing constant care and nursing. My husband chopped wood for our support. . . . I felt that death would be preferable to maternity under such circumstances. A desire and determination to get rid of my child entered into my heart. I consulted a lady friend, and by her persuasion and assistance killed it. Within less than a year, maternity was again imposed upon me, with no better prospect of doing justice to my child. It was a most painful conviction to me; I felt that I could not have another child at the time. . . .

Henry C. Wright, *The Unwelcome Child* (Boston: B. Marsh, 1858) as cited in John Cowan, M.D. and W. R. C. Latson, *What All Married People Should Know* (Chicago; G. W. Ogilvie & Co., 1903), pp. 214–218.

I consulted a physician, and told him of my unhappy state of mind. . . . He told me how to destroy it. After experimenting on myself three months, I was successful. I killed my child about five months after conception.

[A fourth unwanted pregnancy followed, and the baby was carried to term.]

Soon after the birth of my [second] child, my husband insisted on his accustomed injustice. Without any wish of my own, maternity was again forced upon me. I dared not attempt to get rid of the child, abortion seemed so cruel, so inhuman, unnatural and repulsive. I resolved again, for my child's sake, to do the best I could for it. Though I could not joyfully welcome, I resolved quietly to endure its existence.

After the birth of this child, I felt that I could have no more to share our poverty, and to suffer the wrongs and trials of an unwelcome existence. I felt that I had rather die at once, and thus end my life and my power to be a mother together. My husband cast the entire care of the family on me. . . .

In this state, known as it was to my husband, he thrust maternity upon me twice. I employed a doctor to kill my child, and in the destruction of it, in what should have been the vigor of my life ended my power to be a mother. . . . I suffered, as woman alone can suffer, not only in body, but in bitter remorse and anguish of soul. . . .

Such had been my false religious and social education, that, in submitting my person to his passion, I did it with the honest conviction that, in marriage my body became the property of my husband. He said so; all women to whom I applied for counsel said it was my duty to submit; that husbands expected it, had a right to it, and must have this indulgence whenever they were excited, or suffer; and that in this way alone could wives retain the love of their husbands. I had no alternative but silent, suffering submission to his passion, and then procure abortion or leave him, and thus resign my children to the tender mercies of one with whom I could not live myself. Abortion was most repulsive to every feeling of my nature. It seemed degrading, and at times rendered me an object of loathing to myself.

When my first-born was three months old, I had a desperate struggle for my personal liberty. My husband insisted on his right to subject my person to his passion, before my babe was two months old. I saw his conduct then in all its degrading and loathsome injustice. I pleaded, with tears and anguish, for my own and my child's sake, to be spared; and had it not been for my helpless child I should then have ended the struggle by bolting my legal bonds. For its sake I submitted to that outrage, and to my own conscious degradation. For its sake, I concluded to take my chance in the world with other wives and mothers, who, as they assured me, and as I then knew, were all around me subjected to like outrages and driven to the degrading practice of abortion.

But, even then, I saw and argued the justice of my personal rights in regard to maternity. . . . I insisted on my right to say when and under what circumstances I would accept of him the office of maternity, and become the mother of his child. I insisted that it was for me to say when and how often I should subject myself to the liability of becoming a mother. But he became angry with me; claimed ownership over me; insisted that I, as a wife, was to submit to my husband *"in all things;"* threatened to leave me and my children, and declared I was not fit to be a wife. Fearing some fatal consequences to my child or to myself—being alone, destitute, and far from helpful friends, in the far West, and fearing that my little one would be left to want—I stifled all expression of my honest convictions, and ever after kept my aversion and painful struggles in my own bosom. . . .

Every feeling of my soul did then, does now, and ever must, protest against the cruel and loathsome injustice of husbands toward their wives, manifested in imposing on them a maternity uncalled for by their own nature and most repulsive to it, and whose sufferings and responsibilities they are unprepared and unwilling to meet.

An Unwed Mother

FOUR CORNERS, GA. (ROUTE 2) / JUNE 23, 1938

Reading your letters in the Romantic Story, I am asking you to please help me. Its like this:

Last December I went to visit my Uncle . . . and I met a boy and fell in love with him and he said he loved me and showed it in many ways. Well, in January I was in a wreck with my Uncle and stayed in the hospital three weeks with a broken knee. I came home in April and found I was going to have a baby. I had to go back for trial and told him he promised to marry me. In fact he wanted to marry me before but his foster mother objected (he is an orphan). Well, I came home again. He promised to write but two weeks passed and I did not hear from him so I wrote begging him to do something. He never answered and so I forgot my pride and wrote again.

That has been two months ago and still I haven't heard a word from him. I sent the letters to a boy I knew I could trust as I couldn't send them to him on account of his foster mother. Now I don't know what to do. It would kill my Daddy and brother to know what I've done, but I love him and it couldn't be so terribly wrong loving him as I did.

My Daddy worries over everything and has the heart trouble and I'd rather die than for him to know. I've even thought of ending it all but then the whole world would know. And I haven't any money to go away and my Daddy is a poor man and he paid all my hospital bills and I can't ask him for money, if he had it. I have thought of just disappearing and never be heard from again but the thought of what it

National Florence Crittenton Mission Papers, Social Welfare History Archives, Univ. of Minnesota, Minneapolis. Courtesy of the American Social Health Association. Names omitted and place names changed, by editor.

would cause makes me want to die and I love my brother so much. He's the only brother I have. My Mother has been dead since I was small. I have one sister but I can't bear to have them know.

My life has been lonely. My sister married young to get away from my step-mother. I am desperate; have no one to help me; no money. . . .

I have thought of just going as far as my lame knee would carry me, where I'm not known and just do oh I don't know what. Please understand if you can. I've heard of homes where girls like I am can go. I thought maybe you could tell me some place where I could work for my board until then and after maybe the Good Lord will help me. I want to keep my baby, if possible. . . .

Please, don't think I'm bad. I loved him and no man ever made me have the feeling I did. I'm 21 and he is just 18. Is that why he has forgotten me? He said he loved me and I believed him.

I am miserable because I am beginning to show some and I'm afraid to go any place. I just want to die but I know I'm not fit to now, so please, if you can help me, won't you write and tell me which way to turn? . . .

Just a heart-broken girl, L. N.

[In her reply, Reba B. Smith urged L. N. to muster her courage to tell her family. She suggested the girl should try to confide in her married sister, and secure the help of the pastor of her church to see the young man and plead with him. She informed her that "maternity homes will not accept the responsibility of taking girls for confinement unless some member of the family knows." She offered to use her influence to secure L. N.'s admittance to the state's Florence Crittenton home.]

Four Corners, Ga. / July, 1, 1938

My dear Mrs. Smith:

I received yours and Dr. P.'s letters today, and I can't tell you how much I appreciate the kindness of both of you. I didn't think such kind, understanding people were living any more, and I'll admit it made me cry like my heart would break. It was almost like having my mother back again. Mrs. Smith, I cannot tell my people. I know you meant well and its kind of you to advise me to do so and I appreciate it. Most girls could and I wish so much that I could and have them understand. I'm sure my brother and sister would, but there is nothing they can do—they haven't anything. My brother is here on the farm and my sister has three children to care for, so it would only break their hearts to know and they couldn't do anything.

I wish I could picture to you what kind of a person my daddy is; he is good in his way and a good provider, but, though I hate to say it, he is a hard man and has never understood such things. Although he has been married twice, he thinks people that make mistakes like that are bad and people, good people, shouldn't have anything to do with them. If my mother was living, I wouldn't mind telling him. I know she would understand and he would be different, but to tell him now, Mrs. Smith, I hate to think of what would happen. I've heard him say that he would kill any man that mistreated one of us, and that's just what he'd do. He has a terrible temper, and to see him another way, Mrs. Smith, he worries over everything and he has had a lot of bad luck, and it, I'm afraid, would kill him to know. . . . Mrs. Smith, would you write [this boy] for me, and tell him just what this means and what he could prevent if he would. I know you could make him see things as they are. . . . If he doesn't want a family, Mrs. Smith, it's like you said I'd know he's young, but if he would marry me and keep my family from knowing and give my baby a name, I'd go as soon as I could and he'd never be sorry, that is, if he didn't want me. . . . His name is T. M. [Name and address deleted]. Mrs. Smith, I hope I'm not asking too much, but when anyone gets to the place I am they do the only things they can. . . .

I can't understand why he hasn't written. . . . Mrs. Smith, if he won't marry me, would you take me in one of

your Homes and let me work for my board, please? I can
sew and do cooking and cleaning. . . . I'll try to be brave
and maybe there will be a way for me, and may the Good
Lord bless you and Dr. P. for your kindness toward me, and
I hope I can be worthy of it. . . .

L.N.

[A case worker connected with the state "Children's Home Society" went to visit young T. M. and his foster mother. She described them as poor, T. being "an unprepossessing looking boy
who does not seem to be particularly intelligent . . . he seemed
frightened and belligerent." He admitted that he drank too much,
that he had had sexual relations with her, but he blamed the girl for
being the "aggressor." He refused to marry her or have anything
further to do with her, giving as his reason that he did not love her.
The caseworker considered this "a hopeless situation as far as any
help from T.M. is concerned," especially since the young man was
employed irregularly, earning only $8.00 a week when he was
working.

The concerted effort of Reba Smith, Dr. P., who had initially
brought the girl's plight to the agency's attention, and of the Children's Home Society, resulted in L. N. being assigned a place in
the Florence Crittenton home. She arrived there at the end of August and expressed her gratitude to all concerned. She felt
homesick, especially for her younger brother, and was still terrified
at the thought that her Dad would find out where she was.

Others applying for help were not as fortunate as L. N. The following appeal was made to a different agency than the preceding
one.]

JULY 22, 1952

Please help me, I wrote to Family Service Ass. of American and they told me to write to you. I'm desperate, we can't
be like other people and have one baby at a time, we have
twins. Twin boys that are six, twin girls 3 and a boy & girl 9
months old and thier [!] more than I can take care of with

American Social Health Association Papers, General Correspondence, Social Welfare History Archives Center, Minneapolis, Minn. Courtesy of
ASHA.

the constant fear of having more. My family Dr. won't help me, all he would suggest is counting the days of each month. But this won't help me as I have never been regular, sometimes my (menstrual) period is a week ahead of time and sometimes 3 or 4 days later.

I read about getting help in magazines etc. But have not gotten any so far. Please help me.

Mrs. [name deleted]

[The agency offered expressions of support, informational literature and referral to local social service agencies. Neither abortion nor birth control information was offered.]

The Facts About Abortion—[c. 1970]

All states—even those that have "reformed" their abortion laws—still severely curtail woman's right to abortion. In most states, the present criminal laws make it illegal for a doctor to perform an abortion for any reason other than to save the woman's life.

But in spite of these laws, about 1 woman in 4 will have had an abortion by the end of her childbearing years.

1,000,000 or more abortions are performed in the U.S. every year—1 for every 4 births, and at least 100 illegal abortions for every one performed legally. Since most women are forced to go underground for abortions, usually to people who are not qualified doctors, 500 to 1000 women die each year.

When it is performed under clinical conditions, an abortion is safer than a tonsillectomy—and many times safer than childbirth.

But *illegal* abortion is the leading cause of the deaths associated with pregnancy in this country. Significantly, New York City's death rate from illegal abortion is about 5 times as high for Puerto Ricans as for whites, and 8 times as

Pamphlet, National Association for Repeal of Abortion Laws.

high for black women as for white women. This difference is obviously due to the fact that poor people cannot afford the $500 to $1000 often required to pay for an abortion from a qualified doctor. Poor women are discriminated against even in the interpretation of the present rigid laws: many times more legal abortions are performed in private than in public hospitals.

Since millions of women are in fact determined to get abortions even at the risk of their lives, it is not a question of whether abortions will be performed, but whether they will be performed under the right conditions.

THE SOLUTION

All laws and practices that compel any woman to bear a child against her will must be abolished. Abortion law "reform" measures must therefore be opposed: they merely institutionalize the existing injustices.

> Only REPEAL of abortion laws will make a woman's decision about this simple operation a private matter between her and her doctor.

> Only REPEAL will make abortion a legal medical procedure governed solely by medical-practice codes.

> Only REPEAL can prevent the needless deaths that result from the illegal trade in abortion.

79. Protection from rape and sexual exploitation

The ideology of sexism, which "explains" and justifies the subordination of women, depends for its existence on the separating of women, one from the other. Women are defined—by male standards—into normal or deviant, good or bad, feminine or unfeminine, with women of one group being made to feel superior to women of another. The isolation of women, each considering her own position a merely personal matter and a result of free choice, keeps the ideology unchallenged. The fact that women have for centuries internalized this division, which has been reinforced by race and class prejudices, and have transmitted it to their children, in no way contradicts its essential purpose. On the contrary, the ideology *must* be internalized by its victims in order to bolster the system of oppression.

In earlier periods attitudes toward divorce, illegitimacy, and sexual freedom were the great dividers, separating "good" women from "bad." Today, sexual permissiveness and shifting marital standards have made much formerly deviant behavior more acceptable. Now, women are divided and separated from each other by their attitudes toward the still controversial subjects of rape, prostitution, and homosexuality. Like birth control and abortion, these issues touch upon the personal right of women to make decisions regarding their bodies and on the powers of society and of its institutions to regulate women's bodies and sexuality. In that sense, these are the core issues affecting women.

The fear of rape and the myths surrounding the rapist are highly effective means of social control. The principal myths concerning rape are (1) rapists are insane, psychotic, or characterized by criminal personalities; (2) certain types of men such as strangers, black men, and lower class and uneducated men commit most rapes and do so in "unsafe" areas such as dark streets and disreputable neighborhoods; (3) the female victim of rape has (a) wished for her fate, (b) enjoyed it, (c) contributed to it by her behavior; (4) the fact that the vast majority of rapes go unreported indicates female complicity; and (5) of rapes committed across race lines more are by black men on white women than by white men on black women. All the myths regarding rape serve to throw the responsibility for rape on the victim and to keep women divided as a group, defenseless, and in need of male protection.

The selections below address themselves to most of these myths and refute them. In fact, most rapes are committed by men known to the victim, near the victim's home or workplace or in it, by premeditation and by men distinguishable from other men only by their tendency toward violence. Black women are more likely to be victims of rape than white, and their rapists are more likely to be

white men than black. The majority of rapes go unreported because of the humiliation and abuse to which rape victims, not their
attackers, are subject.*

Rape is a weapon of terror and violence, aimed at keeping
women subordinate to men and divided from each other. But it is
more: it is also a symbol and manifestation of power aimed at the
men of a subordinate group. The practice of symbolizing the con-
quest of another tribe or people, by making captives of their men
and sexually abusing—that is raping or prostituting—their women
as a means of humiliating the males of the conquered group, antedates history. This practice only incidentally serves the sexual
pleasure of the rapist and more importantly serves to impress upon
the conquered and subordinate of both sexes that they are the
helpless victims of power and mastery. During classical antiquity
slave women were routinely turned into prostitutes and con-
cubines. Those conquered were different from the conqueror, belonging to different tribes, races, and religions. Thus, not only did
the sexual exploitation of conquered women become casual and
acceptable, but it reinforced stereotypes of race. Their women—all
women of such "lower" races—could henceforth be sexually
abused with impunity.

With the rise of class society the practice of sexually exploiting
the women of the subordinate class became sanctioned by custom
and institutionalized by law. *Le droit du seigneur,* which granted
the lord of the manor sexual rights to the bride of any of his serfs
prior to the serf's marriage, represented a legal vestige of a widespread custom. Examples of this are the practices prevalent in
French society after the Revolution; use by men of the Russian
nobility of women of the serf class; and reflections of such practices
in the plays of Ibsen and Strindberg in even such democratic countries as those of Scandinavia at the end of the nineteenth century.

In the American setting, these traditions surfaced in the complex
sexual relationships between the races. The sexual exploitation of
slave women by white men during and after slavery affirms the
colonial nature of the oppression of black people in the United
States. Black men, like all conquered foes, were symbolically cas-
trated and effectively humiliated by being prevented from defend-

---

* Susan Griffin, "Rape: The All-American Crime," *Ramparts* 10 (September 1971): 26–35.

ing their wives and daughters from the sexual abuses of white men. The sexual exploitation of black women by white men is an essential feature of race-caste oppression in the United States and continued unabated until very recently, when the militancy of the black movement helped to reduce it. It was upheld by laws forbidding intermarriage, enforced by terror against black men and women and, though frowned upon by the white community, was tolerated in both its clandestine and open manifestations. It is reflected in the monotonous one-sidedness of rape conviction statistics, especially in the Southern states, which reveal the essential double standard: the rape of black women by white men goes unpunished; the rape of white women by black men is severely punished.

The dual function of rape as a means of sexual and caste oppression is no place more evident than in the death penalty statistics which reveal that rape, the very crime for which most white men escape punishment or are lightly punished, is the cause of more death penalty sentences if the rapist or alleged rapist is black. In the post-Civil War period and as late as the 1940s the accusation of rape against black men was the chief cause of lynchings. Historical records of the antilynching movement point out the use of lynching as a weapon of terror to uphold this sexual double standard.

The new feminist movement has made protection from rape a central issue. The first selection describes the kind of rape case which never shows up in crime statistics. The second and third define the position of present-day feminists toward the rape issue and illustrate some ways in which women are organizing to protect each other from rape. Recently, feminists have succeeded in altering some of the laws and practices in rape cases to afford better protection to the victim.

Prostitution, documented and analyzed from the woman's point of view, is a vast and unexplored subject, which could well furnish material for a separate volume of documents. The selection printed here merely indicates the modern feminist approach to the subject, in a speech protesting a legislative hearing on prostitution. It connects the question of prostitution with that of the general sexual exploitation of women and insists that the woman's view of this subject must be seriously considered. It also strongly manifests the determination of the new feminists not to allow the division of women into "good" or "bad" to continue.

A *Common Case of Rape*

JULY 29, 1952.

Dear Sir,

Never use to read your [column] in the paper, but now I've made a habit of reading it every day. And yesterday or the day before I read where you could get a booklet for 5¢ [birth control information booklet]. And so I sat right down and wrote to you, because we have some neighbor boys, that when ever they see my Mom and Dad drive out then the 4 boys come over they are all around 18 years old. And they get me in the bedroom up stairs and lock the door. I try to get away but I am only 15 and I can't get away from 4 boys. And then two of them hold me down and take all my clothes off and the other two do the dirty work. I just cry and cry and I'm scared to tell my parents because they would probably kick me off of the place but if it happens much more I am going to tell them. But this is the question I would like to ask. These boys are about 18 yrs. old would you please tell me if they are old enough to cause trouble? I sure would appreciate it if you would just please answer this question because I would not like to get in trouble. And also I'm sending 5¢ for that booklet.

Please do not put in the paper.

I would like to have your answer soon if possible.

Sincerely yours, J. S. [name deleted]

Rape: An Act of Terror

. . . Terror is an integral part of the oppression of women. Its purpose is to ensure, as a final measure, the acceptance

General Correspondence, American Social Health Association Papers, Social Welfare History Archives, Univ. of Minnesota, Minneapolis. Courtesy of ASHA.

Barbara Mehrhof and Pamela Kearon, "Rape: An Act of Terror," *Notes From the Third Year: Women's Liberation*, n.p., 1971, pp. 79–81. Courtesy of the authors.

by women of the inevitability of male domination. . . . The most important aspect of terrorism is its indiscriminateness with respect to members of the terrorized class. There are no actions or forms of behavior sufficient to avoid its danger. There is no sign that designates a rapist since each male is potentially one. While simple fear is utilitarian, providing the impetus to act for one's safety, the effect of terror is to make all action impossible.

. . . Rape is a punishment without crime or guilt—at least not subjective guilt. It is punishment rather for the *objective* crime of femaleness. That is why it is indiscriminate. It is primarily a lesson for the whole class of women—a strange lesson, in that it does not teach a form of behavior which will save women from it. *Rape teaches instead the objective, innate, and unchanging subordination of women relative to men.*

Rape supports the male class by projecting its power and aggressiveness on the world. For the individual male, the possibility of rape remains a prerogative of his in-group; its perpetration rekindles his faith in maleness and his own personal worth.

Rape is only a slightly forbidden fruit. . . . In New York State, for instance, the law stipulates that the woman must prove she was raped by force, that "penetration" occurred, and that someone witnessed the rapist in the area of the attack. Although the past convictions of the defendant are not admissable evidence in a rape trial, the "reputation" of the rape victim is. The police will refuse to accept charges in many cases, especially if the victim is alone when she comes in to file them. In New York City only certain hospitals will accept rape cases and they are not bound to release their findings to the courts. Finally, the courts consistently refuse to indict men for rape.

It is clear that women do not come under the law on anything like an equal footing with men—or rather, that women as women do not enjoy the protection of law at all. Women as victims of rape, unlike the general victim of assault, are not assumed to be independent, indistinguishable, and equal citizens. They are viewed by the law as subordinate, dependent, and an always potential hindrance to male action and male prerogative. Rape laws are designed to protect males against the charge of rape. The word of a peer has a special force; the word of a dependent is always suspicious, presumed to be motivated by envy, revenge, or rebellion.

Rape . . . is not an arbitrary act of violence by one individual on another; it is a political act of *oppression* (never rebellion) exercised by members of a powerful class on members of the powerless class. Rape is supported by a consensus in the male class. It is preached by male-controlled and all-pervasive media with only a minimum of disguise and restraint. It is communicated to the male population as an act of freedom and strength and a male right never to be denied. . . .

Many women believe that rape is an act of sick men or is provoked by the female. Thus women as a class do not yet have a consensus on a counter-reality which defines the true meaning of rape for us. . . .

The first step toward breaking the debilitating hold on us of the Sexist Ideology is the creation of a counter-reality, a mutually guaranteed support of female experience undistorted by male interpretation. . . . We *must* understand rape as essentially an act of terror against women—whether committed by white men or minority group males. This is the only means of freeing our imagination so that we can act together—or alone if it comes to it—against this most perfect of political crimes.

LETTER TO THE EDITOR OF *WOMEN: A JOURNAL OF LIBERATION*, BY THE RAPE CRISIS CENTER COLLECTIVE, WASHINGTON, D.C.

. . . Rape is an institutionalized act of power, aggression and terror performed by men against women. We want to

Women: A Journal of Liberation III, no. 2 (1972): 68–69.

stress the importance of destroying the myth of rape as a sexual act. . . .

The issue of rape is increasingly becoming a major focus of the women's movement. . . .

Increasing numbers of women are developing self-defense skills. The psychological readiness to react to aggression is formed by the continuous development and strengthening of our bodies through basic self-defense tactics, judo, and karate. The possession of weapons does not give us the mind-set to use them; if taken from us, we are left not only undefended, but also in an even more vulnerable position by virtue of the fact that the weapon may be used against us. . . . To attempt running and screaming is never futile. Until women learn self-defense, have access to weapons and are prepared to use them, running and screaming are our only defenses. . . .

Women have been kept powerless through isolation, thus having to develop individual solutions to their oppression. *You do not have to do it yourself!* Collectively, we are creating solutions to rape. The Rape Crisis Center is one such collective action. We are a volunteer group of women who staff a 24 hour crisis phone for women who have been raped or attacked. As a result of our own experience we recognize the necessity of women supporting women. We provide this support for those women who call us. We will accompany a woman to the police station or to court if she wants. However, realizing the emotional strain of reporting this crime, we do not take a position that it is necessary to report it. The decision must be made by the individual women. We support and provide the same services regardless of her decision. These services are legal, medical, and psychiatric information and referrals, explanations of police and court procedures and emergency housing. Both to educate women about rape, the needs and reactions of the rape victim and the politics of rape and to give women an opportunity to discuss their experiences with other victims, we coordinate seminars and direct conferences. . . .

A *"Victimless" Crime*

The following is an abbreviated version of a paper presented at a feminist filibuster of a New York state legislature hearing on "Prostitution as a Victimless Crime." The speaker is an active member of New York Radical Feminists.

Gentlemen, you state that the purpose of your hearing today is to listen to testimony on the subject of prostitution, what you refer to as "a victimless crime." Prostitution is a crime, gentlemen, but it is not victimless. There is a victim, and that is the woman. . . .

One fact about prostitution I'm sure has not escaped your notice: the buyers, the ones who hold the cash in their hand, the ones who create the market by their demand, they are all men, gentlemen, the same sex as yourselves.

In the 1940s, the Kinsey Report—which was probably the last really documented report on sexuality—stated that two-thirds of all American men have some experience with a prostitute. In 1964, R.E.L. Masters estimated that the figure was closer to 80 percent. Now, having counted the men in this room, I don't think we need to play a shell game to figure out which one of you might have a clean slate.

Now the stock your sex is buying with their dollar bills is human flesh, for the most part, but not always, the same sex as myself. . . .

Now the myth has it that the female prostitute is the seller of her own flesh, that she is a free participant in her act, that she has made a conscious choice to sell her body. That is a male myth, gentlemen, one that your sex has rather successfully popularized for your own self-interest. It has not only absolved you of your responsibility in this terrible crime of buying another human being's body, it has conveniently shifted your guilt onto our shoulders. The law in this city is applied to punish the woman and let the man go scot-free.

Susan Brownmiller, "Speaking Out on Prostitution," *Notes from the Third Year: Women's Liberation* (New York, 1971), pp. 37–39. Courtesy of the author.

Now there is something else that the male sex has always tried to do to cover up its crime: it has tried to separate the woman engaged in prostitution from the rest of the women in the culture. It calls her "the other," it marks her the bad woman, it sends her to jail, and it tells the rest of us that we are very good and virtuous and we have nothing in common with her.

Well, gentlemen, I have good news for you. We have seen through *that* little myth: the feminist movement identifies itself with the female victims of the male-created institution known as prostitution. . . .

Now, I am white, and middle-class and ambitious, and I have no trouble identifying with either the call girl or the street hustler, and I can explain why in one sentence: I've been working to support myself in the city for fifteen years, and I've had more offers to sell my body for money than I have had to be an executive. . . .

I don't think that anyone has ever asked you to sell your body, or presumed that your body was for sale. I wonder if a cab driver has ever turned around to you and remarked, "I see you're a little short of change. Perhaps we could work together. I could steer some customers your way." I wonder if a man has ever walked up to you in a hotel lobby, and muttered, "What's your price? Ten? Twenty? I'll pay it. I'll pay it." That happened to me in the Hotel Astor. . . .

Now these were all experiences that happened to me at a time of my life when perhaps I looked more vulnerable than I am today, and when I was certainly more desperate. And I want to say without theatricality that I was lucky. I had options that most other women don't have. I managed to use my ambition in a positive manner. I managed to become a writer, what Caroline Bird called "a loophole woman." There was, of course, one other option I could have exercised. I could've gotten married.

So now, perhaps you can understand why I identify with the prostitute, and why, when I see a front page headline in

the *New York Times*, "Mayor Stepping Up Drive on Prostitutes and Smut," I know that in a very real sense it is me and
my entire sex that the mayor and the *New York Times* are
talking about. And when this mayor appoints a task force of
six men and no women to study the problems of pimps,
pornography, and prostitution, giving equal moral weight to
each category, I know that his failure to appoint even one
woman to this task force is not an oversight, it's just that the
boys decided they've got to get together and do a little superficial something to preserve their fun. . . .

Gentlemen, if you intend to extend the definition of
government-inspected meat to the sale of human flesh, you
will do it over our dead bodies. The women's movement
will not tolerate the legalization of sexual slavery in this
state. Yes, there is a prostitution problem. . . .

There is a serious problem in our society, when women
with ambition must sell their bodies because there is no
other way that they can earn fifteen thousand a year. There
is a serious problem in our society when men think that
access to the female body is, if not a divine right, at least a
monetary right.

There has been but one in-depth study on the gratification
men get from paying for sex, and that study was conducted
in the 1920s. And perhaps that is the area in which you
gentlemen could begin your research. Perhaps it is the only
valid study a man could make in this day and age on the
subject of prostitution. . . .

Prostitution will not end in this country until men see
women as equals. And men will never see women as equals
until there's an end to prostitution. So it seems that we will
have to work for the full equality of women and the end to
prostitution side by side. One cannot occur without the
other. In the meantime, it seems to me, it's foolish to prose-
cute a woman for a crime in which she is the victim. But it is
equally reprehensible to let a man go free for the criminal
act of purchasing another's body. . . .

80. Freedom of sexual preference

The right to her own body must include the freedom to express sexual preference without societal strictures. The right to choose lesbian relationships without being discriminated against for "deviance" falls within the broader context of an expansion of personal civil rights, represented by the gay liberation movement. Lesbians, who had long felt oppressed both for their sex and their sexual preference, and had been active in the new feminist movement without revealing their sexual orientation for fear of hurting that movement, "came out of the closet" in 1969–1970. In so doing they brought up to date the old issue of the "normal" and the "deviant" woman and forced contemporary feminists to reexamine their ideas and values. Lesbians, forming their own groups within the feminist movement, challenged the traditionalist approach of reform feminists and posed the same disturbing questions posed in regard to other controversial issues connected with female sexuality. Their position quickly moved from self-defense to a militant assertion of leadership.

The first document below represents an influential statement of the radical lesbian position. It raises lesbianism from a personal civil rights and civil liberties question to a political question. Then Anne Koedt engages in serious debate of some of the issues raised and offers an alternative radical feminist position. The discussion, within the feminist movement and without it, is far from over and the documents here can merely serve to introduce some of the issues. In the general context of this chapter, they represent a further extension of the search for female autonomy, for self-definition, and for the insistence on sisterhood—the unity of all kinds of women.

The Woman-Identified Woman

What is a lesbian? A lesbian is the rage of all women condensed to the point of explosion. She is the woman who, often beginning at an extremely early age, acts in accor-

New York Radicalesbians, "The Woman-Identified Woman" (1970). Used by permission of the publisher.

dance with her inner compulsion to be a more complete and freer human being than her society—perhaps then, but certainly later—cares to allow her. . . . She is forced to evolve her own life pattern, often living much of her life alone, learning usually much earlier than her "straight" (heterosexual) sisters about the essential aloneness of life (which the myth of marriage obscures) and about the reality of illusions. . . . Those of us who work that through find ourselves on the other side of a tortuous journey through a night that may have been decades long. The perspective gained from that journey, the liberation of self, the inner peace, the real love of self and of all women, is something to be shared with all women—because we are all women.

It should first be understood that lesbianism, like male homosexuality, is a category of behavior possible only in a sexist society characterized by rigid sex roles and dominated by male supremacy. Those sex roles dehumanize women by defining us as a supportive/serving caste *in relation to* the master caste of men, and emotionally cripple men by demanding that they be alienated from their own bodies and emotions in order to perform their economic/ political/military functions effectively. Homosexuality is a by-product of a particular way of setting up roles (or approved patterns of behavior) on the basis of sex; as such it is an inauthentic (not consonant with "reality") category. In a society in which men do not oppress women, and sexual expression is allowed to follow feelings, the categories of homosexuality and heterosexuality would disappear.

But lesbianism is also different from male homosexuality, and serves a different function in the society. . . . Lesbian is a label invented by the Man to throw at any woman who dares to be his equal, who dares to challenge his prerogatives (including that of all women as part of the exchange medium among men), who dares to assert the primacy of her own needs. To have the label applied to people active in women's liberation is just the most recent instance of a long history; older women will recall that not so long ago, any woman who was successful, independent, not orienting her whole life about a man, would hear this word. . . .

"Lesbian" is one of the sexual categories by which men have divided up humanity. While all women are dehumanized as sex objects, as the objects of men they are given certain compensations: identification with his power, his ego, his status, his protection (from other males), feeling like a "real woman," finding social acceptance by adhering to her role, etc. Should a woman confront herself by confronting another woman, there are fewer rationalizations, fewer buffers by which to avoid the stark horror of her dehumanized condition. Herein we find the overriding fear of many women toward being used as a sexual object by a woman, which not only will bring her no male-connected compensations, but also will reveal the void which is woman's real situation. . . .

Women in the movement have in most cases gone to great lengths to avoid discussion and confrontation with the issue of lesbianism. It puts people up-tight. They are hostile, evasive, or try to incorporate it into some "broader issue." . . . But it is no side issue. It is absolutely essential to the success and fulfillment of the women's liberation movement that this issue be dealt with. As long as the label "dyke" can be used to frighten women into a less militant stand, keep her separate from her sisters, keep her from giving primacy to anything other than men and family—then to that extent she is controlled by the male culture. Until women see in each other the possibility of a primal commitment which includes sexual love, they will be denying themselves the love and value they readily accord to men, thus affirming their second-class status. As long as male acceptability is primary—both to individual women and to the movement as a whole—the term lesbian will be used effectively against women. . . . On one level, which is both personal and political, women may withdraw emotional and sexual energies from men, and work out various alternatives for those energies in their own lives. On a different political/

psychological level, it must be understood that what is crucial is that women begin disengaging from male-defined response patterns. In the privacy of our own psyches, we must cut those cords to the core. For irrespective of where our love and sexual energies flow, if we are male-identified in our heads, we cannot realize our autonomy as human beings.

But why is it that women have related to and through men? By virtue of having been brought up in a male society, we have internalized the male culture's definition of ourselves. That definition consigns us to sexual and family functions, and excludes us from defining and shaping the terms of our lives. . . . We are authentic, legitimate, real to the extent that we are the property of some man whose name we bear. To be a woman who belongs to no man is to be invisible, pathetic, inauthentic, unreal. . . . As long as we are dependent on the male culture for this definition, for this approval, we cannot be free.

The consequence of internalizing this role is an enormous reservoir of self-hate. This is not to say the self-hate is recognized or accepted as such; indeed most women would deny it. . . . Women resist relating on all levels to other women who will reflect their own oppression, their own secondary status, their own self-hate. For to confront another woman is finally to confront one's self—the self we have gone to such lengths to avoid. And in that mirror we know we cannot really respect and love that which we have been made to be.

As the source of self-hate and the lack of real self are rooted in our male-given identity, we must create a new sense of self. . . . Only women can give to each other a new sense of self. That identity we have to develop with reference to ourselves, and not in relation to men. This consciousness is the revolutionary force from which all else will follow. . . . As long as women's liberation tries to free women without facing the basic heterosexual structure that binds us in one-to-one relationships with our oppressors, tremendous energies will continue to flow into trying to straighten up each particular relationship with a man, into finding how to get better sex, how to turn his head around—into trying to make the "new man" out of him, in the delusion that this will allow us to be the "new woman." . . .

It is the primacy of women relating to women, of women creating a new consciousness of and with each other, which is at the heart of women's liberation, and the basis for the cultural revolution. Together we must find, reinforce, and validate our authentic selves. . . .

Lesbianism and Feminism

. . . With the increased interaction between the gay and women's liberation movements, a heightened consciousness about lesbianism has evolved among feminists—and along with it a corresponding disagreement and confusion as to what exactly it means to be a lesbian. . . . For the purposes of this discussion the meaning of the word lesbianism is restricted to its simplest definition of "women having sexual relations with women," so that the various "life style" arguments which are sometimes added to the basic definition can be looked at separately.

I think that the first thing to do is to define radical feminism: To me it means the advocacy of the total elimination of sex roles. A radical feminist, then, is one who believes in this and works politically toward that end.* Basic to the position of radical feminism is the concept that biology is not destiny, and that male and female roles are learned—indeed that they are male political constructs that serve to ensure power and superior status for men. Thus the

Excerpts from "Lesbianism and Feminism," © 1971 by Anne Koedt. In *Radical Feminism*, ed. Anne Koedt, Ellen Levine, and Anita Rapone (New York: Quadrangle, 1973), pp. 246–258. This article first appeared in *Notes from the Third Year: Women's Liberation* (New York, 1971, pp. 84–89). Reprinted by permission of the author.

* She does not by this definition live a life untouched by sex roles; there are no "liberated" women in that sense.

biological male is the oppressor not by virtue of his male biology, but by virtue of his *rationalizing* his *supremacy* on the basis of that biological difference. The argument that "man is the enemy" is then true only insofar as the man adopts the male supremacy role.

What then is the relationship between lesbianism and radical feminism? Taking even the most minimal definitions of lesbianism and feminism, you can find one major point of agreement; biology does not determine sex roles. Thus since roles are learned there is nothing inherently "masculine" or "feminine" in behavior.

Beyond these basic assumptions, however, there are important differences. . . . The following are some of the points of disagreement:

The agreement that there is nothing innately sick about persons having sex with someone of their own sex does not mean that therefore all gay behavior is healthy in feminist terms. A lesbian acting like a man or a gay man acting like a woman is not necessarily sicker than heterosexuals acting out the same roles; but it is not healthy. *All role playing is sick*, be it "simulated" or "authentic" according to society's terms. . . .

One position advanced by some lesbians is the idea that lesbians are the vanguard of the women's movement because (1) they broke with sex roles before there even was a feminist movement, and (2) they have no need for men at all. . . .

Several points seem to be ignored with this kind of argument. For one, there is a confusion of personal with a political solution. Sex roles and male supremacy will not go away simply by women becoming lesbians. It will take a great deal of sophisticated political muscle and collective energy for women to eliminate sexism. So at best a lesbian relationship can give a woman more happiness and freedom in her private life (assuming both women are not playing roles). But a radical feminist is not just one who tries to live the good non-sexist life at home; she is one who is working

politically in society to destroy the institutions of
sexism. . . .

Any woman who defies her role—be it refusing to be a
mother, wanting to be a biochemist, or simply refusing to
cater to a man's ego—is defying the sex role system. It is an
act of rebellion. In the case of lesbianism, the act of rebellion often has earned the woman severe social ostracism.
However, it becomes radical only if it is then placed in the
context of wanting to destroy the system as a whole, that is,
destroying the sex role system as opposed to just rejecting
men. . . .

The organized gay movement seeks to protect the freedom of any homosexual, no matter what her or his individual style of homosexuality may be. This means protection of
the transvestite, the queen, the "butch" lesbian, the couple
that wants a marriage license, or the homosexual who may
prefer no particular role. They are all united on one thing:
the right to have sex with someone of one's own sex (i.e.,
"freedom of sexual preference"). . . .

In uniting to change oppressive laws, electing officials
who will work toward these ends, and changing social attitudes which are discriminatory against homosexuals, the
gay movement is addressing itself to its civil rights. It is my
feeling that the gay liberation issue is in fact a civil rights
issue (as opposed to a radical issue) because it is united
around the secondary issue of "freedom of sexual preference." Whereas in fact the real root of anti-homosexuality is
sexism. . . . That is, the *radical* gay person would have to
be a feminist.

It is not with the actual gay counterculture that I want to
quarrel; I think it is a very understandable reaction to an
intolerable exclusion of homosexuals from society. To be
denied the ordinary benefits and interaction of other people, to be stripped of your identity by a society that recognizes you as valid only if your role and your biology are
"properly" matched—to be thus denied must of course
result in a new resolution of identity. Since gays have been

rejected on the basis of their homosexuality, it is not surprising that homosexuality has become the core of the new identity.

The disagreement with feminism comes rather in an attempt to make a revolutionary political position out of this adjustment. The often heard complaint from feminists that "we are being defined once again by whom we sleep with" is correct, I think. . . . A woman has historically been defined, on the basis of biology, as incomplete without a man. Feminists have rejected this notion, and must equally reject any new definition which offers a woman her identity by virtue of the fact that she may love or sleep with other women.

It is for this reason, also, that I disagree with the Radicalesbian concept of the "woman-identified-woman." For we ought not to be "identified" on the basis of whom we have relationships with. . . .

The original genius of the phrase "the personal is political" was that it opened up the area of women's private lives to political analysis. Before that, the isolation of women from each other had been accomplished by labeling a woman's experience "personal." Women had thus been kept from seeing their common condition as women and their condom oppression by men.

However, opening up women's experience to political analysis has also resulted in a misuse of the phrase. While it is true that there are political implications in everything a woman *qua* woman experiences, it is not therefore true that a woman's life is the political property of the women's movement. . . .

Even the most radical feminist is not the liberated woman. We are all crawling out of femininity into a new sense of personhood. Only a woman herself may decide what her next step is going to be. I do not think women have a political obligation to the movement to change; they should do so only if they see it in their own self-interest. If the women's movement believes that feminism *is* in women's self-interest, then the task at hand is to make it understood through shared insights, analysis, and experience. That is, feminism is an offering, not a directive, and one therefore enters a woman's private life at her invitation only. . . .

Homosexuality, with its obvious scorn for the "rules" of biology, challenges a cornerstone of sexist ideology and consequently makes most men nervous. There is at this time less fear of female homosexuality than of male homosexuality, possibly because men still feel secure that isolated lesbian examples will not tempt women away from their prescribed feminine roles. . . .

With male homosexuality, however, men (and thus male society) are more personally threatened. . . . [F]or a man to leave the "superior" group is to go down—that is, become "inferior" or "feminine." Frequently male homosexuals may touch on the unspoken fears in many men that they are not powerful and "manly" enough to fulfill their supremacy destiny, and the gay male thus becomes a symbol of total male "failure." . . .

To understand men's fear of homosexuality, then, is above all to understand men's fear of losing their place of power in society with women. And to hold that power, men must preserve both the "absoluteness" of their ideology and the group unity of their members.

It must be kept in mind that while homosexuality does contain an implicit threat to sexist ideology, it is, at best, only a small part of the whole fight to bring down the sex role system. . . .

Thus it is only in the most radical interpretations that lesbianism becomes an organic part of the larger feminist fight. In this context it joins the multitude of other rebellions women have been making against their prescribed role—be it in work, in law, or in personal relationships. As with all such rebellions, they are only personal accommodations to living in a sexist society unless they are understood politically and fought for collectively. The larger political truth is still that we are women living in a male society where men have the power and we don't; that our "female role" is a creation that is nothing more than a male political expediency for maintaining that power; and that until the women's movement alters these ancient political facts we cannot speak of being free collectively or individually.

IN UNION THERE IS STRENGTH

AUDIE LEE WALTERS

81. "We didn't none of us eat there"—1971

The meaning of sisterhood differs from place to place, from group to group. What does not differ is the exhilarating process of change, that slow day-by-day process of gaining new perspective, a new sense of strength and goals. Sometimes, it can be summed up in a moment—perhaps a simple gesture, a statement never made before. In this story, told by a middle-aged white Southern woman, there occurs such a rare moment when the new insight finds concrete expression in action. White and black working-class women learn, during a long and bitter strike, that unity means supporting their men, supporting each other. Finally, cutting across the ancient barriers of prejudice, they express their common sisterhood.

My husband is 53 years old. He's been hauling wood since way before we were married. And we've been married 37 year. Fred makes about fifteen hundred dollar a year. We got four boys and two girls. When we was raising our kids, my husband hauled wood a lot of times barefooted.

What shoes we did have, they had holes in the feet. But he had to work, even when he didn't have no shoes, to keep all the bills paid. I never did go out with him to cut wood.

Audie Lee Walters, *Southern Patriot* 29, no. 10 (December 1971): 5.

He never would let me. I always had a baby to tend to. I don't know how we've kept our young'uns in school, but we have, some way or another. . . .

Some days Fred didn't bring in but one load, then other days he'd get two, three loads. Sometimes, they didn't haul at all. Them's the days we didn't eat. You know, a wood hauler, they live from today until tomorrow. So if you haul a load of wood today, you eat today. But if you don't haul a load of wood tomorrow, you don't eat.

So, when Fred quit hauling wood, went out on strike, I didn't know what to think. We got to talking about it and now I realize what the strike's all about. I know they can't haul wood and take a beat of ten or fifteen dollar a load. The day they went out on strike, one man hauled a load in there and he got a dollar and a half bring-home pay. A dollar and a half. That ain't hardly enough.

So I kept talking to Fred about the strike and I realized what he was trying to do. And I found out that there was some other way, that we could hope there was some other way to get better wages for hauling wood.

Fred told me he was going to walk the picket line, get something done so Masonite wouldn't take everything that belonged to him. He just couldn't haul wood and let them take his money, what belonged to him. And he convinced me it was the right thing for him to do.

It don't take a man to walk the picket line. Annie Belle Pulliam, she says she'd walk the picket line every day if they'd let her. There's a lot of women that's not afraid of it. Some of the other places that are out in Mississippi have women walking the picket lines. But they're afraid for us to walk it here at Masonite in Laurel.

Me and my daughter, Elaine and Annie Belle and three colored women, we went up to Canton last week to talk to Brother Ralph and some Presbyterian church people about raising something for Christmas for the families that's out on strike.

Well, we started out, it's about a hundred and fifty mile drive, and we got along a ways and we was getting hungry. So we stopped at this little cafe in Bay Springs. The colored women, they told us white women to go on in there and eat and just bring them something out to the car to eat.

We said, no, if they didn't serve all of us we wasn't going to eat there. Well, they wouldn't serve the colored women, so we went on. We didn't none of us eat there.

So we drove on up the road until we come to the next town. That was Raleigh. The colored women said for us white women to go in there and ask if they serve colored foks in there. So me and Annie Belle and Elaine, we went in. The lady in the cafe, she put glasses of water down in front of us. And we asked did they serve colored women in there. The lady said, no, they didn't. She said if they were colored and served on the Grand Jury she'd serve them. She told us if the colored women wanted any service they'd have to go around to the back of the cafe to get their food.

So Annie Belle, she just shoved her water glass at the lady and said we wouldn't eat in no damn place that refused to serve colored folks. Then I asked the lady could I use her bathroom. I says, "I would like to use your bathroom." She told me to go up the street to the courthouse if I wanted to use a bathroom.

Well, we left out of there, went on up the road, still looking for a place to eat. Finally, when we got to Canton, we found a cafe that said they served both white and colored. And we all ate there together. On the way back home, we stopped at a shopping center in Raleigh and there was a place there that had a bathroom.

Annie Belle, she got the key to the bathroom and when she had finished using it, she give the key to one of the colored women. A lady come running out and said, "You can't use it. You're colored." Well, the colored lady just looked at her and said, "Lady, I'm human." And she took the key and went on in and used the bathroom.

82. Consciousness raising—1970

The document below describes the growth and progress of one of
the thousands of consciousness-raising groups generated in the
new feminist movement. In weekly "rap sessions" small groups of
women discuss their common experiences and problems. Great
care is taken to create a supportive atmosphere and to allow each
woman to participate equally, without the creation of "leaders."
Shyness and the inability to speak soon vanish, as women develop
feelings of trust and love for women. The discovery that what they
had considered personal problems are in fact social phenomena
has a liberating effect and frees the energies of group members for
social action. Women become stronger, take pride in themselves,
and see in the group a community, a substitute family.

Liberation is a constant process and since a woman's liberation involves an end to her loneliness and isolation from
other women, it would be both agonizing and impossible
without their support. Because we have kept our thoughts
inside for most of our lives, and because we must begin to
challenge those parts of our lives we have always considered the most personal, the most private, we have sought
this support through the "small group." Unique to the
women's movement, the small group is our greatest
strength. It is the means through which women reach out to
each other, search together, grow together. Our best method
of raising consciousness, our most effective organizing tool,
it is, at the same time, our most human structure.

Every Sunday night I meet with ten other women. Two
high school students, two high school teachers, a social
worker, three college students, three drop-outs. . . . Mari-
lyn and Janice are sisters; Kay and I, quite accidentally, are
old family acquaintances; Ronny and Paula are close school
friends; Bette knew none of the others until our first
meeting.

Ronnie Lichtman, "Getting Together: The Small Group in Women's Liberation," *Up From Under* 1, no. 1 (May/June 1970): 23–24.

Our first discussions were fumbling; in our enthusiasm we would jump from topic to topic as new ideas flew from one to another, fragmenting the political from the personal. Until we realized that we had to begin with our most potent political force—our lives. And the best way to do that, we discovered, was for each of us to speak about her life—her childhood, her family, her friendships, ambitions, lovers, husbands, career: a method in itself revolutionary, a way of breaking down one of the strongest bulwarks of our society—the belief that an individual's perceptions of himself cannot be understood by anyone else, that individual problems must therefore be dealt with in isolation and loneliness.

For the past few months each meeting has been devoted to one of us—to listening to her "story," dealing with her life. . . .

For many of us this openness demanded a tremendous, sometimes overwhelming, emotional effort, one which necessitated the laying aside of life-long inhibitions. In our society, it is always a risk to relinquish the security of anonymity, one of the few securities allowed us. We each had to overcome the additional fear of losing the support and friendship of the group. How did any of us know to what extent we could trust each other? How could we know that we wouldn't meet with hostility, disapproval, ridicule? These fears, though real, proved to be unfounded. In fact, our group has drawn much closer since these intense personal analyses began. . . .

Listening to other women, learning about their feelings, their weaknesses and strengths, their fears, their experiences, has helped me to accept myself as a woman. I'm not the only one whose sexual initiation was difficult and painful; I'm not the only one who won't open her mouth in a large group unless I know the indisputable truth and even then, only if I've rehearsed it a dozen times; I'm not the only one struggling to overcome dependency on men, to experience healthy relationships with both sexes.

But perhaps most important to me—to my self-image—was the realization that the dynamic woman is not a rarity, an aberration of the natural order. Every woman in our group is an exciting person. . . . For me, to enjoy women *en masse* was an almost totally new experience. . . .

As a group we must also start to piece together the commonalities of our experiences to come to a greater understanding of the conditions in society which have kept many women separate from each other, unfulfilled. . . . We must begin to define the kinds of changes we as women must make, not only individually in our personal lives, but together, united against crippling institutions that shape and mold us.

The concept of women's liberation understood through participation in the movement has already made profound differences in many lives. . . .

I'm growing stronger, more confident, though sometimes I have to fight to make it show. And that's when I know I can turn to my sisters. And I know they'll understand.

83. U.S. National Women's Agenda—1975

This agenda, a list of priorities for 1976, was developed by eighty national and regional women's organizations, representing over thirty million American women. One hundred women's organizations, ranging from Girl Scouts to radical women's liberation groups, were queried by questionnaires as to their legislative and programmatic priorities for 1976. Eighty of them replied, and the items on which they agreed were incorporated into the agenda. It represents an expression of consensus not reached since the woman suffrage movement mobilized a broad spectrum of feminist

Excerpts from a leaflet circulated by Women's Action Alliance, New York City, in behalf of the sponsoring organizations, 1975.

organizational strength around the single issue of passage of the Nineteenth Amendment.

What is remarkable in the agenda below is not so much that consensus was reached on passage of ERA as a top priority, but that so many diverse organizations reflect a feminist awareness in a broad program for societal change.

I. *Fair Representation and Participation in the Political Process*

Encouragement for women to run for elective office, and provision of the necessary resources for women candidates; appointment of increased numbers of women to political positions.

Provision of opportunities for women and girls to develop and exercise leadership skills; systematic preparation and examination of all legislation, taking into account its effects on women; commitment to and enforcement of equal access and affirmative action rules within political parties. . . .

II. *Equal Education and Training*

Enforcement of laws which guarantee equal access to and treatment in all educational, vocational and athletic programs and facilities; equalization of financial aids, research opportunities and educational funds for girls and women.

Development of continuing education programs to meet the needs of varying life patterns, and to assess and give education credits for appropriate life experiences.

Increased numbers of women on faculties, administrations and policy making bodies, at all levels of educational systems.

Incorporation of women's issues into all areas of educational curricula.

III. *Meaningful Work and Adequate Compensation*

Enforcement of legislation prohibiting discrimination at all levels of employment.

Extension of the basic workers' benefits to household workers, migrant and agricultural workers, and homemakers.

Economic and legal recognition of homemakers' work.

Recognition of pregnancy related disabilities as normal, temporary employment disabilities.

Attainment of equal pay for comparable work, that is, work frequently performed by women which is equivalent to work performed by men, but for which women receive less pay.

Review of widely used industrial designs and machinery which inhibit women's work production.

IV. *Equal Access to Economic Power*

A minimum standard of income for low income and disadvantaged persons.

Elimination of discrimination in income tax laws and the social security system, and introduction of coverage under S.S. for unpaid homemakers; elimination of discrimination against women in credit, insurance, and benefit and pension plans.

V. *Quality Child Care for All Children*

Creation of a comprehensive system of child care which includes parent involvement; child care as a tax deductible business expense.

VI. *Quality Health Care and Services*

Support for and expansion of medical and mental health services available without regard to ability to pay.

Implementation of the legal right of women to control their own reproductive systems.

Expansion of private and public health insurance to provide for women's special needs.

Increased attention to and support for research into new drugs and medical procedures which have special significance for women.

VII. *Adequate Housing*

VIII. *Just and Humane Treatment in the Criminal Justice System*

Repeal of laws which treat women and men differently within the criminal justice system; equalization of services for women and men offenders.

Achievement of expanded representation and participation of women in positions of authority in the criminal justice system.

Improved treatment of rape victims by personnel within the criminal justice system; re-examination of laws pertaining to victimless crimes.

IX. *Fair Treatment By and Equal Access to Media and the Arts*

X. *Physical Safety*

Recognition of and respect for the autonomy and dignity of the female person; recognition of rape as a violent and serious crime.

Reform of laws which make it unduly difficult to convict rapists and which place victims of rape in the role of the accused in the legal system; creation and expansion of support programs for rape victims.

XI. *Respect for the Individual*

Protection of the right to privacy of relationships between consenting adults.

Extension of all civil rights legislation to prohibit discrimination based on affectional or sexual preference.

End to prejudice and discrimination against women who wish to determine their own names.

Elimination of discrimination against women based on marital status.

Recognition that women are individuals with full rights to make the choices affecting their lives.

CHAPTER NINE

The Search for Autonomy

In the previous chapters women's experiences of family life, community, and work have been documented as has been their long struggle for equal rights and equal access to all the economic and legal benefits of citizenship. In this final chapter another process is delineated—the step-by-step progression by which women emancipate themselves intellectually: First, self-consciousness—an awareness of their separate needs as women; then an awareness of a female collectivity—the reaching out toward other women, first for mutual support and then in order to improve their condition. Out of the recognition of communality there emerges feminist consciousness—a set of ideas by which women autonomously define themselves in a male-dominated world and seek to substitute their vision and values for those of the patriarchy. In its early stages, illustrated by Anne Hutchinson and Mary Dyer, this simply is manifested in the insistence by women that they define their own role in society. The refusal to abide by patriarchal assumptions of woman's place is the first step toward autonomy. Historically, it was repeated over and over again, by succeeding generations of women until enough of them had done so to generate a shift in societal values.

The tentative formulation of feminist theory did not occur in one place and at one time—it did not, certainly, "begin" at the first woman's rights convention in 1848—rather, it evolved in many places simultaneously and perhaps successively, through the tentative thoughts, prayers, and diary musings of many kinds of women. The range and the breadth of this wavelike movement cannot adequately be traced as yet, since we still know far too little of the female past. Space permits only an indication and symbolic representation of the process in the documents below, from the touching prayer of Marian Louise Moore, frontier woman, to the fragments of an advanced feminist theory, formulated by the aging Sarah Grimké, an inadequately trained woman of superior intellectual ability. The speech by the former slave Sojourner Truth belongs here not so much because of its content, but because of its tone. This old black woman, a charismatic leader possessed of a sense of prophetic mission, had finally and completely transcended societal restraints—she spoke to anyone, regardless of their race, station, and rank, to freedmen, white upper-class intellectuals, presidents, and generals, with the self-assured confidence of one who has received revelation. Sojourner Truth's feminism was an integral part of her being, and so she projected it outward with the utmost sincerity, simplicity, and assuredness: "I am about the only colored woman that goes about to speak for the rights of the colored women." She personifies the liberated woman, who defines herself, her place, and her role.

Elizabeth Cady Stanton's inspired challenge reduces feminism to its most fundamental principle: women are responsible individuals and, under divine and human law, should be treated as such. It is here that the new history must begin. A world in which women are only grudgingly admitted and in which they are subordinated to patriarchal judgments is no longer tolerable. A history which loses sight of women, admits them only grudgingly, and subordinates them to value judgments based on patriarchal assumptions, is no longer adequate. The "solitude of self" and the collective female experience impose the necessity for, and the direction of, societal changes. The last two selections in this book, two contemporary poems by women, point to the future.

ANNE HUTCHINSON (1591–c.1643)

84. The trial of a heretic

Anne Hutchinson, a member of a highly respected merchant family, came to Massachusetts Bay in 1634, together with her husband William and their children. They had fifteen children, the youngest of whom was born in Massachusetts. Highly respected among the colonists for her knowledge of midwifery and herbal healing, Anne Hutchinson, who in religious doctrine was a follower of John Cotton, began gathering women in her home to comment on John Cotton's sermons. Going further than her spiritual mentor, she soon expounded a permissive doctrine of salvation by a gift of grace, a mysterious indwelling of the spirit of the Lord which relieved sinners of their transgressions. This heretical doctrine, which downgraded the role of the learned ministry and denied the absolute authority of the elect, became a highly controversial issue, when Anne Hutchinson criticized all but two of the Massachusetts clergy for failing to have the right spirit.

Tried first by the General Court in November 1637, then by the clergy in March 1638, Anne Hutchinson was formally banished from the colony by the former and excommunicated by the latter. When she and her family fled to the more tolerant climate of Roger Williams' colony in Rhode Island, thirty-five other families followed. The family later migrated once more to the shores of Long Island Sound, where in 1643 Anne Hutchinson and most of her family were killed by Indians.

Her trial had political and economic dimensions arising from the tensions between the Puritan ministry and the merchant class with which the Hutchinsons identified. The following document was written by John Winthrop, the governor of the colony, who took the prosecutor's part in her civil trial. His version of her trial and his comments concerning the "monstrous" births reproduced below, show that the fact that this particular heretic was a *woman*, who dared to assert the right of women to instruct others and "proph-

John Winthrop, *The Short Story of the Rise, Reign, and ruine of the Antinomians . . . of New England . . .* (London, 1644), reprinted in C. F. Adams, *Antinomianism in New England* (Boston: The Prince Society, 1894).

esy," lent special emphasis to the case. It can be said that part of Anne Hutchinson's heresy was her challenge to the doctrine of female submissiveness in word and deed.

The First Trial of Anne Hutchinson

. . . One Mistris Hutchison,* the wife of Mr. William Hutchison of Boston (a very honest and peaceable man of good estate) and the daughter of Mr. Marbury, sometimes a Preacher in Lincolnshire, after of London, [was] a woman of a haughty and fierce carriage, of a nimble wit and active spirit, and a very voluble tongue, more bold then a man, though in understanding and judgement, inferiour to many women. This woman had learned her skil in England, and had discovered some of her opinions in the Ship, as shee came over, which has caused some jealousie of her, which gave occasion of some delay of her admission, when shee first desired fellowship with the Church of Boston, but shee cunningly dissembled and coloured her opinions, as shee soon got over that block, and was admitted into the Church, then shee began to go to work, and being a woman very helpfull in the times of child-birth, and other occasions of bodily infirmities, and well furnished with means for those purposes, shee easily insinuated her selfe into the affections of many. . . . But when shee had thus prepared the way by such wholesome truths, then shee begins to set forth her own stuffe, and taught that no sanctification was any evidence of a good estate, except their justification were first cleared up to them by the immediate witnesse of the Spirit, and that to see any work of grace, (either faith or repentance, &c.) before this immediate witnesse, was a Covenant of works: whereupon many good soules, that had been of long approved godlinesse, were brought to renounce all the work of grace in them, and to wait for this immediate revelation. . . . Indeed it was a wonder upon what a sudden the whole Church of Boston (some few excepted) were become

* The misspelling "Hutchison" has been retained from the original document.

her new converts, and infected with her opinions, and many also out of the Church, and of other Churches also, yea, many prophane persons became of her opinion, for it was a very easie, and acceptable way to heaven, to see nothing, to have nothing, but waite for Christ to do all; so that after shee had thus prevailed, and had drawn some of eminent place and parts to her party (whereof some profited so well, as in a few moneths they outwent their teacher) then shee kept open house for all commers, and set up two Lecture dayes in the week, when they usually met at her house, threescore or fourescore persons, the pretence was to repeate Sermons, but when that was done, shee would comment upon the Doctrines, and interpret all passages at her pleasure. . . .

[Anne Hutchinson was tried in Boston court. At the time of her first trial she was pregnant.]

COURT: What say you to your weekly publick meetings? can you shew a warrant for them?

HUTCH.: I will shew you how I took it up, there were such meetings in use before I came, and because I went to none of them, this was the speciall reason of my taking up this course, wee began it but with five or six, and though it grew to more in future time, yet being tolerated at the first, I knew not why it might not continue.

COURT: There were private meetings indeed, and are still in many places, of some few neighbours, but not so publick and frequent as yours, and are of use for increase of love, and mutuall edification, but yours are of another nature, if they had been such as yours they had been evill, and therefore no good warrant to justifie yours; but answer by what authority, or rule, you uphold them.

HUTCH.: By Tit. 2. where the elder women are to teach the younger.

COURT: So wee allow you to do, as the Apostle there meanes, privately, and upon occasion, but that gives no warrant of such set meetings for that purpose; and besides, you take upon you to teach many that are elder than your selfe, neither do you teach them that which the Apostle commands, *viz.* to keep at home.

HUTCH.: Will you please to give mee a rule against it, and I will yeeld?

COURT: You must have a rule for it, or else you cannot do it in faith, yet you have a plaine rule against it; I permit not a woman to teach.

HUTCH.: That is meant of teaching men.

COURT: If a man in distresse of conscience or other temptation, &c. should come and ask your counsell in private, might you not teach him?

HUTCH.: Yes.

COURT: Then it is cleare, that it is not meant of teaching men, but of teaching in publick.

HUTCH.: It is said, I will poure my Spirit upon your Daughters, and they shall prophesie, &c. If God give mee a gift of Prophecy, I may use it. . . .

COURT: Yes, you are the woman of most note, and of best abilities, and if some other take upon them the like, it is by your teaching and example, but you shew not in all this, by what authority you take upon you to bee such a publick instructer: (after shee had stood a short time, the Court gave her leave to sit downe, for her countenance discovered some bodily infirmity.)

HUTCH.: Here is my authority, Aquila and Priscilla, tooke upon them to instruct Apollo, more perfectly, yet he was a man of good parts, but they being better instructed might teach him.

COURT: See how your argument stands, Priscilla with her husband, tooke Apollo home and instruct him privately, therefore Mistris Hutchison without her husband may teach sixty or eighty.

HUTCH.: I call them not, but if they come to me, I may instruct them.

COURT: Yet you shew us not a rule.

HUTCH.: I have given you two places of Scripture.

COURT: But neither of them will sute your practise.

HUTCH.: Must I shew my name written therein?

COURT: You must shew that which must be equivalent, seeing your Ministry is publicke, you would have them receive your instruction, as coming from such an Ordinance.

HUTCH.: They must not take it as it comes from me, but as it comes from the Lord Jesus Christ, and if I tooke upon me a publick Ministery, I should breake a rule, but not in exercising a gift of Prophecy, and I would see a rule to turne away them that come to me.

COURT: It is your exercise which drawes them, and by occasion thereof, many families are neglected, and much time lost, and a great damage comes to the Common-Wealth thereby, which wee that are betrusted with, as the Fathers of the Common-wealth, are not to suffer. . . .

[As a result of this first trial Anne Hutchinson was banished, but since the season was too advanced for her departure from the colony she was confined at the Rev. Joseph Welde's home in Roxbury, Massachusetts until March.

Anne Hutchinson was very weak physically at the time of her second trial in January 1638. She first admitted to some errors, but refused to recant completely. She was thereupon excommunicated by the following decree:]

Forasmuch as you, Mrs Huchison, have highly transgressed & offended, & forasmuch as yow have soe many ways *troubled the Church with yor Erors* & have drawen away many a poor soule, & have *upheld yor Revelations:* & forasmuch as *you have made a Lye,* &c. Therfor in the name of our Lord Je: Ch: & in the name of the Church I doe not only pronownce yow worthy to be cast owt, but *I doe cast yow out* & in the name of Ch. *I doe deliver you up to Sathan,* that yow may learne no more to blaspheme, to seduce & to lye, & I doe account yow from this time forth to be a Hethen & a Publican & soe to be held of all the Bretheren & Sisters, of this Congregation, & of others: therfor *I command yow* in the name of Ch: Je: & of this Church *as a Leper to wthdraw*

yor selfe owt of the Congregation; that as formerly yow
have dispised & contemned the Holy Ordinances of God, &
turned yor Backe one them, soe yow may now have no part
in them nor benefit by them.

[Anne Hutchinson and her children left for Rhode Island, where
her husband and sons had set up a home for them.

Shortly after her arrival in Rhode Island she miscarried as a
result of a post-menopausal pregnancy. The "monstrous birth"
was used by the Boston Puritans as an argument against her, and
was described by John Winthrop in the following manner:]

Then God himselfe was pleased to step in with his casting
voice, and bring in his owne vote and suffrage from heaven,
by testifying his displeasure against their opinions and practises, as clearely as if he had pointed with his finger, in
causing the two fomenting women in the time of the height
of the Opinions to produce out of their wombs, as before
they had out of their braines, such monstrous births as no
Chronicle (I thinke) hardly ever recorded the like. Mistris
Dier brought forth her birth of a woman child, a fish, a beast,
and a fowle, all woven together in one, and without an
head. . . .

Mistris Hutchison being big with child, and growing towards the time of her labour, as other women doe, she
brought forth not one, (as Mistris Dier did) but (which was
more strange to amazement) 30, monstrous births or there-
abouts, at once; some of them bigger, some lesser, some of
one shape, some of another; few of any perfect shape, none
at all of them (as farre as I could ever learne) of humane
shape.

These things are so strange, that I am almost loath to be
the reporter of them, lest I should seeme to feigne a new
story, and not to relate an old one, but I have learned otherwise (blessed be his name) then to delude the world with
untruths. . . .

And see how the wisdome of God fitted this judgement to
her sinne every way, for looke as she had vented mishapen

opinions, so she must bring forth deformed monsters; and as about 30. Opinions in number, so many monsters; and as those were publike, and not in a corner mentioned, so this is now come to be knowne and famous over all these Churches, and a great part of the world.

MARY DYER (DYAR) (?–1660)

85. Preparation to the death of a Quaker witness

The case of Mary Dyer is usually seen simply as an episode in the struggle for religious toleration. But on closer observation, the historical record reveals a feminist aspect to the case—Mary Dyer's refusal to take advantage of the "protection" and leniency society was willing to grant her as a woman, even if it meant giving up her life. She was born Mary Barrett and raised in England, where she was married to William Dyer in 1633. Of the couples' many children, five survived infancy. The family emigrated to Massachusetts and was admitted to the Boston church in 1635. Mary Dyer was an adherent of Anne Hutchinson. For this sinfulness she too, according to John Winthrop, was delivered of a stillborn "monster."

When Anne Hutchinson was excommunicated, Mary Dyer the only person to accompany her out of the church, for which she, in turn, was excommunicated. The family settled in Newport, R.I. Mary Dyer became a follower of George Fox, founder of the Society of Friends during a five-year stay in England. On her return she was imprisoned in Boston in 1657, under a law against "the cursed sect of heretics." Her husband secured her release by promising to keep her incommunicado until she left the colony. But Mary Dyer returned to Boston two years later to visit two male Quakers imprisoned there under a more recent law banishing Quakers under pain of death. Again arrested, she and the two men

George Bishop, *New England Judged by the Spirit of the Lord* (1611), reprinted in Horatio Rogers, M.D., *The Quaker Martyr that was hanged on Boston Common, June 1, 1660* (Providence: Preston and Rounds, 1896), pp. 84–93.

were banished under threat of execution should they return. Within a month the three were back in Boston, determined to defy the "bloody laws." The three Quakers were condemned to death and on October 27, 1659, were led to the gallows through the streets of Boston, with drums beating to prevent them from speaking to the crowd. Mary Dyer was forced to watch the execution of the two men, then, with the hangman's noose around her neck, she received a prearranged reprieve, due to the intervention of both the Governer, John Winthrop, and her own son, William. The document below gives her statement to the Court upon receiving the death sentence and her statement refusing reprieve. Still, she was deported to Rhode Island; but feeling herself under the command of God, she was back in Boston in May 1660. Once again she was "to offer up her life there." She was tried and sentenced to death, but this time the sentence was carried out swiftly, despite a moving plea from her husband who was not a Quaker and who declared himself unable to understand her "madness." On June 1, 1660, Mary Dyer was hung in Boston, "as a flag for others to take example by," as one witness phrased it. In death, she bore her witness. Only one other Quaker was executed in Massachusetts after her, and then the persecution of Quakers was ended by intervention of the Crown.

Mary Dyer was given several chances to subordinate herself to her husband and to heed the pleas of her son, which would, according to law and custom, have permitted the court to exercise leniency because she was a wife and mother. Her refusal to do so and her insistence that she came at the command of the Lord "and go at his command" are strong assertions of her autonomy as a human being. God spoke directly to Mary Dyer; it was her firm conviction that as a human being she was accountable only to God and to herself, and so she chose death.

LETTER TO THE MASSACHUSETTS GENERAL
COURT AFTER SHE HAD RECEIVED
SENTENCE OF DEATH. [1659]

To the General Court now in Boston.

Whereas I am by many charged with the Guiltiness of my own Blood; if you mean, in my coming to Boston, I am therein clear, and justified by the Lord, in whose Will I

came, who will require my Blood of you, be sure, who have
made a Law to take away the Lives of the Innocent Servants
of God, if they come among you, who are called by you,
Cursed Quakers; altho' I say, and am a living Witness for
them and the Lord, that he hath Blessed them, and sent
them unto you: Therefore be not found Fighters against
God, but let my Counsel and Request be accepted with you,
To Repeal all such Laws, that the Truth and Servants of the
Lord may have free Passage among you, and you be kept
from shedding Innocent Blood, which I know there are
many among you would not do, if they knew it so to be: Nor
can the Enemy that stirreth you up thus to destroy this Holy
Seed, in any measure countervail the great Damage that you
will by thus doing procure: Therefore, seeing the Lord hath
not hid it from me, it lyeth upon me, in Love to your Souls,
thus to persuade you: I have no self-ends, the Lord
knoweth, for if my Life were freely granted by you, it would
not avail me, nor could I expect it of you, so long as I should
daily hear or see the Sufferings of these People, my dear
Brethren and Seed, with whom my Life is bound up, as I
have done these two Years; and now it is like to encrease,
even unto Death, for no evil Doing, but coming among you:
Was ever the like Laws heard of, among a People that profess Christ come in the Flesh? And have such no other
Weapons, but such Laws, to fights against Spiritual Wicked-
ness withall, as you call it? Wo is me for you! Of whom take
you counsel? Search with the Light of Christ in ye, and it
will shew you of whom. . . . You will not Repent, that you
were kept from shedding Blood, tho' it were from a woman:
It's not mine own Life I seek (for I chuse rather to suffer
with the People of God, than to enjoy the Pleasures of
Egypt) but the Life of the Seed, which I know the Lord hath
Blessed. . . . Therefore let my Request have as much Acceptance with you (if you be Christians) as Esther had with
Ahasuerus (whose Relation is short of that that's between
Christians) and my Request is the same that hers was; and
he said not, that he had made a Law and it would be dishon-

ourable for him to Revoke it; but when he understood that these People were so prized by her, and so nearly concerned her (as in Truth these are to me) as you may see what he did for her: Therefore I leave these Lines with you, Appealing to the faithful and true Witness of God, which is one in all Consciences, before whom we must all appear; with whom I shall eternally Rest, in everlasting Joy and Peace, whether you will hear or forbear; With him is my Reward, with Whom to live is my Joy, and to dye is my Gain, tho' I had not had your forty eight Hours warning, for the Preparation to the Death of Mary Dyar.

And know this also, That if through the Enmity you shall declare your selves worse than Ahasuerus, and confirm your Law, tho' it were but by taking away the Life of one of us, That the Lord will overthrow both your Law and you, by his righteous Judgments and Plagues poured justly upon you, who now whilst you are warned thereof, and tenderly sought unto, may avoid the one, by removing the other; If you neither hear nor obey the Lord nor his Servants, yet will he send more of his Servants among you, so that your end shall be frustrated, that think to restrain them, you call *Cursed Quakers,* from coming among you, by any Thing you can do to them. . . . In Love and in the Spirit of Meekness I again beseech you, for I have no Enmity to the Persons of any; but you shall know, That God will not be mocked, but what you sow, that shall you reap from him, that will render to everyone according to the Deeds done in the Body, whether Good or Evil; Even so be it, saith

MARY DYAR.

LETTER TO THE MASSACHUSETTS GENERAL
COURT, WRITTEN THE DAY AFTER MARY DYAR
WAS REPRIEVED ON THE GALLOWS TREE.
THE 28TH OF THE 8TH MONTH, 1659.

Once more to the General Court, Assembled in Boston, speaks Mary Dyar, even as before: My Life is not accepted, neither availeth me, in Comparison of the Lives and Liberty of the Truth and Servants of the living God, for which in the Bowles of Love and Meekness I sought you; yet nevertheless, with wicked Hands have you put two of them to Death, which makes me to feel, that the Mercies of the Wicked is Cruelty; I rather chuse to Dye than to Live, as from you, as Guilty of their innocent Blood: Therefore, seeing my Request is hindred, I leave you to the Righteous Judge, and Searcher of all Hearts, who, with the pure measure of Light he hath given to every Man to profit withal, will in his due time let you see whose Servants you are. . . .

When I heard your last Order read, it was a disturbance unto me, that was so freely Offering up my Life to him that gave it me, and sent me hither so to do, which Obedience being his own Work, he gloriously accompanied with his Presence, and Peace, and Love in me, in which I rested from my labour, till by your Order, and the People, I was so far disturbed, that I could not retain any more the words thereof, than that I should return to Prison, and there remain Forty and Eight Hours; to which I submitted, finding nothing from the Lord to the contrary, that I may know what his Pleasure and Counsel is concerning me, on whom I wait therefore, for he is my Life, and the length of my Days; and as I said before, I came at his Command, and go at his Command.

MARY DYAR.

MARIAN LOUISE MOORE

86. A frontier woman discovers her own kind of feminism—1839

At a time when societal taboos made it very difficult for them to express unconventional opinions, women tended to express their

Journal of Marian Louise Moore. Courtesy of the Western Reserve Historical Society, Cleveland, Ohio.

truest feelings in religious terms, either in prayer or in inspired interpretations of biblical texts. The following excerpts from the diary of Marian Louise Moore—unfortunately fragmentary and frustratingly short due to the poor condition of the manuscript— give a startling glimpse into the inner world of an ordinary woman (see also document 35). Having lived most of her life on the frontier and in rural isolation, Marian Louise Moore had rejected a marriage proposal from a suitable suitor and chosen to live the customary life of the spinster, caring for her mother and relatives. At the time of the first diary entry she was thirty-six years old. Unacquainted with any literature but the religious writings of Hannah Moore, the sentimental tales of Lydia Sigourney, and the inspirational poetry of Mrs. Hemans, the young woman reasoned her way to a feminism of her own definition. Three years later, having suffered much family trouble she raised a challenge to the Lord, couched somewhat in the form of a prayer, but strikingly assertive in tone. She asks for no more nor less than the emancipation of woman. "If there is not another woman in America pleading to that effect, *I* am pleading," she states with amazing self-confidence, and promises to praise the Lord if he will only grant her "the heaven of my . . . desires." One wonders in how many farmhouses and log cabins, anonymous women groped in the quiet of the night for a similar vision of opening vistas for women.

Diary, Jan. 5, 1839.   And now another year rolled off, never to return. How beautifully does Our Lord address Himself to a female. The kingdom of heaven is like to a leaven which a woman took and [illeg.] until the whole was leavened. Is it not profitable that many a Hannah Moore, Hemans, and Mrs. Sigourney may grace our literary world. Ah, methinks, were I to address myself to mothers, my language should be thou art inexorable to a woman, yes, were I possessed of the tongue of a seraph I would still proclaim thou art responsible . . . oh mothers. . . . [She cites various biblical passages about women prophesizing, and recounts Queen Elizabeth and other eminent women.] I have now penetrated the philosophers' stone, have I discovered wherein the female can be useful by pen, diligence, and deeds of benevolence, like an angel here to guide, aid and accompany man to a nobler paradise. . . .

Feb. 20, 1842. Yesterday was . . . one of the most sorrowful days that ever I opened my eyes upon. . . . Today I am prepared to say my trust is in God. . . . For the last four years of my life I have experienced many conflicts: I have seen my brother taken from one toil to another unjustly by wicked men until he was almost wasted by grief, whilst his family & almost orphan children were thrown upon my parents' kind care. . . . Today I have been trying to suspend this sorrow, and now my Savior I ask that woman may be found worthy before God to stand upon a platform of equal rights as the first major stroke in these United States of America. Thou hast blessed woman and exalted her in England, canst thou not in America? My faith staggers not; Lord, increase my faith. I wish her to be exalted, not to do evil but to do good. Let her influence be greater in the path of virtue. . . . I pray to God to this effect. If there is not another woman in America pleading to that effect, *I* am pleading. O thou, who first taught my little hands to work, my fingers to fight, thou who inspired me with intellect when first my little feet wendeth their way to school. . . . I have been looking over my diary and find that sorrow and troubles have compressed me about, and oh my savior, if I may but experience the heaven of my late-mentioned desires, my soul shall praise thee.

Sarah Moore Grimké

87. She is the arbiter of her own destiny

In chapter two, the essay "Marriage" by this early feminist theorist was reproduced in print for the first time. The three fragments of essays—"Marriage," "Sisters of Charity," and "Education of Women"—and some scattered diary notes are all that is left of a larger work, a synthesis of feminist theory, on which the mature Sarah Grimké worked in the period 1852–1857. Below, the essay "Education of Women" is reproduced in its entirety, along with selected passages from "Sisters of Charity."

The author surveys the ground covered in her earlier major work, *Letters on the Equality of the Sexes* (1838), with special emphasis on the adverse effects on women of the denial of education. The earlier book preceded the first woman's rights convention by ten years, and inspired many of its conveners. The later essay was written after an organized woman's movement had become a reality. "Marvel not that so few have joined our band," exclaims the sixty-year-old rebel, which invokes at once the image of the small band of patriots who began the American Revolution.

Sarah Grimké soon leaves familiar legal arguments and deals with the psychological effect of the inequality between the sexes. As she has been all her life, Sarah Grimké is intellectually ahead of her time. In 1852, she demands that women be represented on school boards; she predicts that social change will be welcomed most by lower-class women, and she analyzes insightfully the way in which sex role stereotyping hampers female ambition and aspirations.

In the brief excerpt from "Sisters of Charity" which concludes this selection, she asks for greater access of women to industrial employment. She decries the fact that woman was deprived of rights and opportunities by law and custom and that she was made ignorant of her own power. "Woman has struggled through life with bandaged eyes, accepting the dogma of her weakness." But now she seeks "to give to her whole being the opportunity to expand to its essential nobility." Sarah Grimké's ringing call for woman's "self-reliance" repeats the theme of woman's autonomy, which she, first of all U.S. feminists, stressed in her earlier writings.

Education of Women

The reason why women effect so little & are so shallow is because their aims are low, marriage is the prize for which they strive, if foiled in that they rarely rise above the disappointment. . . .

Many a woman shudders . . . at the terrible eclipse of those intellectual powers which in early life seemed prophetic of usefulness and happiness, hence the army of

Sarah M. Grimké, "Education of Women," Miscellaneous Essays, Weld-Grimké Papers. Courtesy of the William L. Clements Library, Univ. of Michigan, Ann Arbor.

martyrs among our married & unmarried women who, not having cultivated a taste for science, art or literature form a corps of nervous patients who make fortunes for agreeable physicians. . . .

Freedom and equality of rights and privileges, furnish a salutary discipline for the mind and open a vast field for intellectual effort. . . . Education furnishes the means for extensive information and widens the bounds of human experience, which embraces the past and the present. It is doubtless a feeling of injury on the part of woman which has induced a few of us to claim the Rights so unjustly withheld. It is because we feel we have powers which are crushed, responsibilities which we are not permitted to exercise, duties which we are not prepared to fulfill. Rights vested in us as moral and intellectual beings which are utterly ignored and trampled upon. . . . It is because we feel this so keenly we now demand an equal education with man to qualify us to be co-workers with him in the great arena of human life. We come before him not in fear and trembling; we come filled with the sense of the moral sublimity of our present position . . . as equals to demand in the name of Him who created us, our appropriate purpose in the scale of humanity. Marvel not that so few have joined our band. The mightiest river drops a little streamlet from the mountainside. The most stupendous mountain is gathered grain by grain. But two or three were gathered together at the first meeting of our revolutionary fathers. But fifty-six signed the Declaration of Independence. Nevertheless, the grand and glorious words had been uttered, "liberty or death," "taxation and representation," and they reigned [rang] through the land with magic power. . . . Will it not be so with the words woman utters? The Rights, Quality [Equality], Education, Self-Support and Representation. . . .

Can we marvel that woman does not immediately realize the dignity of her own nature when we remember that she has been so long used as the means to an end and that end, the comfort and pleasure of man, regarded as his *property*, a being created for *his* benefit, and living like a parasite on *his* vitality. When we remember how little her intellect has been taken into account in estimating her value in society, and that she received as truth the dogma of her inferiority? . . .

The conflict of interests and opinions between the sexes cannot fail to create antagonistic feelings and this will necessarily be felt in all their relations to each other. This conflict arises from withholding rights on one side and the injury sustained from this injustice on the other. Perhaps there is nothing that will tend as rapidly and so powerfully to the equalization as similar education advantages. . . . The fellow feeling which universal education produces among people, is clearly discernable in America, and its influence in strengthening that sympathy is incalculable when learning in all its higher branches shall become the common property of both sexes; when the girl, as well as the boy, may anticipate with earnest delight a complete course of study which will enable her to look forward to a life full of continuous culture and of independence and of the fulfillment of high and honorable trust. The contemplation of such a future will raise her ideas of herself beyond the ephemeral sphere of fashion by the toilsome drudgery of that incessant manual labor which is calculated in most cases to stultify intellect and which may be performed for small compensation by those who have hands but are nearly destitute of brains. It would be as wise to set an accomplished lawyer to saw wood as a business as to condemn an educated and sensible woman to spend all her time boiling potatoes and patching old garments. Yet this is the lot of many a one who incessantly stitches and boils and bakes, compelled to thrust back out of sight the aspirations which fill her soul. Think not because I thus speak, that I would draw woman from the duties of domestic life—far from it. Let her fulfill in the circle of the home all the obligations that rest upon her but let her not waste her powers on inferior objects, when higher and holier responsibilities demand her attention. . . .

The common school system of education which was adopted in New England when the colony consisted of only a few thousand is now established nearly all over the United States and there can be no doubt that it has contributed more than any single institution to the advancement of the people in arts and manufactures, in commerce, in morality and religion and literature. . . . Among the most extraordinary and flagrant violations of the spirit of Republicanism is the exclusion of women from school committees although the schools are composed of daughters as well as sons. It would be extremely difficult to repress the feeling of indignation at this ignoring of the feelings and rights of women if I did not clearly see that it originated from circumstances over which neither sex could exercise any control. In the early settlement of every country the men greatly outnumber the women, schoolhouses are often at a distance from most of the dwellings of the pupils' parents, the access to them is difficult and women with families and few conveniences to aid in domestic labor are too busy and too much worn from fatigue to attend anything but the immediate duties of home. This is now no longer the case. Women can afford the time quite as well as men, and their judgment, their sympathy, their maternal care is needed in all such committees. That they have abundant leisure to attend to this important duty is manifest from the fact that they devote so much time to benevolent associations, none of which has so strong a claim upon them as the sacred duty of examining and ascertaining the qualifications and characters of those to whom is entrusted the care of their children. "But," said a gentleman, "you cannot find women fit to put on such committees." I shall not stop to disprove this assertion but simply state, that I have known committee *men* who certainly were more unfit for their business than any *women* who would be likely to be placed in that position because unusual care would be taken in the selection of women, as is always the case in the introduction of any innovation. We have, moreover, an admirable provision in human nature which prevents change from being brought about too

rapidly. The love of old usages emphasizes a sort of guard-
ianship over society somewhat resembling the tutelage of a
parent toward a child. . . . And as many parents find it
difficult to recognize the manhood and womanhood of their
children albeit they are sometimes far ahead of them in
clear-sightedness as to what will be most conducive to their
own benefit, so conservatism is very slow to acknowledge
any proposed amendment in the structure of society will be
really beneficial.

. . . We cannot easily foresee what will be the result of
placing men and women on an equality in education. One
thing, however, is certain. It will be an unspeakable advantage to society. The community must increase in wisdom
and strength in proportion to the diffusion of learning since
there is nothing so admirably calculated to strengthen individual character than the unlimited extension of knowledge.
In a popular government this is of paramount importance. . . . If then the diffusion of the elements of education produces such blessed effects, is it not clear that to give
to such women as desire it and can devote themselves to
literary and scientific pursuits all the advantages enjoyed by
men of the same class will lessen essentially the number of
thoughtless, idle, vain and frivolous women and thus secure
the society the services of those who now hang as dead
weight? The number of these is indeed already lessened, for
women have shared to some extent in a general diffusion of
knowledge through the common school system. The multiplication of newspapers and periodicals, the rapid increase
of which is one of the most remarkable features in the history of our country, has also greatly enlarged their means of
information. . . .

It is not from women who are reclining in the lap of opu-
lent splendor and eating the bread of idleness that we can
expect aid; they have all they are capable of enjoying, nor
ask a better lot. Reformists have almost universally arisen
among what are termed the inferior classes of society. They

are not so steeped in the enjoyment of material delights to be unable to appreciate moral and intellectual pleasures. They are not unfitted by luxury and selfish indulgence from casting their eyes over the condition of society and pondering the best means of advancing the happiness and prosperity of the race. . . . Those who feel the daily calamity of unjust laws, the degradation of being in an inferior and abnormal position, whose souls are on fire because of oppression and imprisonment, these are the men and women who awaken public attention to the needed reformation. . . .

The thought of the equality of the sexes is no man's invention "but the rising of the general tide in the human soul." This idea is itself an epoch: that is so fully accepted by a few individuals as to stir them to remonstrance and to actions, to union and mutual communication of opinions, feelings and views is a commanding fact. "Revolutions go not backward. There is no good now enjoyed by society that was not once problematical." An idea built the wall of separation in education between the sexes and an idea will crumble it to dust. . . . One consideration I must place before the reader: the effect necessarily produced on girls and boys by the different prospects their future presents. The boy, as soon as he is capable of thinking, feels that he has to be a worker, that he is to stand on his own feet and exercise his talents in some profitable business. His self-respect, his love of independence, are at once healthfully excited. He feels himself an individual being, draws in with every breath, at home, at school, in the social circle, the idea of self-reliance and self-support. Hence his efforts to prepare himself for this unavoidable business of life are powerfully stimulated. His studies, though often irksome and ill-suited to his tastes, are pursued as a means to an end, and . . . he is constantly and urgently pushed onward in the career of learning. It is not so with girls. They study under the paralyzing idea that their acquirements cannot be brought into practical use. They may subserve the purposes of

promoting individual domestic pleasure and social enjoyment in conversation, but what are they in comparison with
the grand stimulation of independence and self-reliance, of
the capability of contributing to the comfort and happiness
of those whom they love as their own souls? Many a
talented and highly educated school girl feels no pleasure
in looking beyond her school life, because she sees no
bright and useful future beyond. Delighted as she is with
the acquisition of knowledge, she yet sends forth the plain-
tive inquiry, What shall I do? My learning can purchase for
me neither independence nor the ability to minister to the
wants of others. My food, my raiment are not the products of
my own industry. Shall this touching appeal meet with the
response in the heart of fathers, brothers, husbands and
sons? . . .

From the Essay "Sisters of Charity"

It cannot be denied that the present state of society needs
reformation. Various expedients have been tried, but as a
sensible writer remarks we have not yet tried the experiment of giving to Women the same political Rights as men
and throwing open to them all civil and ecclesiastical
offices—"In our hospitals, prisons, almhouses, lunatic
asylums, workhouses, reformatory schools, elementary
schools, Houses of Refuge—everywhere we want efficient
women." No one who has visited such institutions, where
by the way we are admitted as a favor, none of these institutions requiring in their by-laws that women should be associated with men as overseers etc. etc. but must perceive
the absolute need of women as coadjutors. Even those who
feel the importance of this union of the masculine and
feminine element regard it as a dernier resort to be tried,
rather than the carrying out of a law which has its foundation in the very nature of man, ignoring this fact vital to the
best welfare of society that without union of labor between
the sexes nothing can be well done, because there is noth-

ing done which does not affect the interests of both. . . .

It must be conceded that there is an absolute necessity for the industrial sphere of woman to be enlarged . . . Unless honest employment is found for women they must be driven by starvation and despair to dishonest and unworthy if not infamous means to preserve life. . . .

It is to the pale scholar over his midnight lamp not the successful general, that we look for the improvement of the human race, and when the leaders of the age are those whose physical frame is assimilated more especially to the feminine phase of life, why should idle prejudice any longer shut out women from taking their place wherever intellect rather than strength is required. It will not be till the business of the world is more equally distributed that either sex will thereby fulfill its vocation in life, or that we can hope for that harmonious cooperation which can alone make any great undertaking successful—at present women are depressed by the laws, depressed by a public opinion resulting from the laws, depressed by the prejudice of parents and guardians, till the greater part of the sex is ignorant of its own powers. . . .

Woman seeks to give to our laws an inward security and strength (and permanence) which is infinitely more important than any outward restraint, in fact the former is the only firm and durable basis of the latter. It is self evident that inequality of rights creates antagonisms and the assumption that we must continue in this state is productive of nothing but evil, because the privileged and the oppressed stand in opposition to each other, the latter yielding unwillingly the distinctions which the former demand and the former shutting themselves up in the self-made circle of their superiority and refusing even to examine the claims of the dependent class. How shall these two classes harmonize? The answer is simple. "Establish Justice" which will insure "domestic tranquillity, promote the general welfare and secure the blessings of liberty" to women and posterity. "The differences which exist between them in matters of small moment would readily disappear before their equality in those higher privileges on which they set supreme value." This state of things must be actualized, for it is impossible to lull the awakened soul into a belief that it is free when the galling fetters clank around it. It is impossible for any woman of lofty purpose and pure morality to accept the dogma that woman was made to be subservient to man.

Thus far woman has struggled through life with bandaged eyes, accepting the dogma of her weakness and inability to take care of herself not only physically but intellectually. She has held out a trembling hand and received gratefully the proffered aid. She has forgone her right to study, to know the laws and purposes of government to which she is subject. But there is now awakened in her a consciousness that she is defrauded of her legitimate Rights and that she never can fulfill her mission until she is placed in that position to which she feels herself called by the divinity within. Hitherto she has surrendered her person and her individuality to man, but she can no longer do this and not feel that she is outraging her nature and her God. There is now predominant in the minds of intelligent women to an extent never known before a struggling after freedom, an intense desire after a higher life. . . . Hitherto there has been at the root of her being darkness, inharmony, bondage and consequently the majesty of her being had been obscured, and the uprising of her nature is but the effort to give to her whole being the opportunity to expand into all its essential nobility.

Legislation can do much towards producing that harmonious cooperation of the sexes which be the establishment of equal rights to person and to property will release woman from the horrors of forced maternity and teach her partner to subject his passions to the control of reason. Oh how many mothers have I heard say I did not want this child, I am unable to do my duty to so many children and this feeling is a gangrene to my happiness. Think ye parents what a welcome awaits the helpless hapless being, the off-spring of lust, not of sanctified affection, who is thus ushered into existence. Do I plead for woman? No I plead for the race because I see then our endless curse hangs over humanity so long as marriage is thus misunderstood and desecrated. "Suffering," says Cousin, "is the most excellent of all things." I am inclined to think the philosopher is right, but for the suffering through which woman has passed as the mother of the race, she would not now feel so keenly the wrongs inflicted upon her, nor estimate as she now does how treasonable it would be to herself and humanity longer to keep silence. Woman by surrendering herself to the tutelage of man may in many cases live at her ease, but she will live the life of a slave, by asserting and claiming her natural Rights she assumes the perogative [!] which every free intelligence ought to assume, that she is the arbiter of her own destiny. . . . Self-reliance only can create true and exalted women. . . .

SOJOURNER TRUTH (C. 1797–1883)

88. "While the water is stirring I will step into the pool"

Sojourner Truth stands alone among black women in the nineteenth century in staunchly combining defense of her race with feminism. Her sense of self always centered on her awareness of her womanhood. She expressed this in her famous speech to the Akron, Ohio, women's rights convention in 1851, in which she built the refrain "and ain't I a woman?" into a poetic metaphor for the special plight of black women. Born a slave in Ulster County, N.Y., she was named Isabella Baumfree by her master. She saw her

Elizabeth C. Stanton, Susan B. Anthony, and Matilda J. Gage, *History of Woman Suffrage*, 6 vols. (New York: Fowler & Wells, 1881–1922) II:193–194.

brothers and sister sold off, and was herself sold as a child. Her master raped her and later married her to an older slave by whom she had five children. Freed by New York state law in 1827, she sued her master for the freedom of her child, who had been sold South, and rescued the boy. She was working as a domestic when, in 1843, a religious vision convinced her that she must become a preacher and change her name to Sojourner Truth "because I was to travel up and down the land showing the people their sins and being a sign unto them. . . . I was to declare the truth to the people."

It was as an itinerant preacher that Sojourner Truth reached fame and prominence in the North. She had a strong, almost mystical effect on audiences and frequently tamed hostile crowds by her fearless attitude and pithy comments. This illiterate woman spoke in metaphors of biblical richness, commenting shrewdly on politics, manners, mores, and prevalent values. She advocated abolition, women's rights, the protection of the poor, and her own brand of Christianity and brotherly love. She dictated her autobiography to a white friend and lived by selling it at her lectures. She bought a little house in Battle Creek, Mich., where she made her home in her old age.

During the Civil War she visited the Union troops, preaching to them and entertaining them. After the war she conceived the idea of resettling groups of freedmen in the West, lobbied and petitioned for this scheme, and continued to work for freedmen's relief. She died in 1883 at her home in Battle Creek.

The speech printed below was Sojourner's contribution to a heated debate during a meeting of the American Equal Rights Association held in New York City in 1867, which was the occasion for a rift between abolitionists and feminists, who had earlier been allied for passage of the Thirteenth Amendment, over the issue of woman suffrage. Abolitionists, struggling to get Negro suffrage, were unwilling to saddle their cause with the even less popular one of woman suffrage. Even so staunch a defender of woman's rights as Frederick Douglass declared that this was "the Negro's hour." No one, except Sojourner Truth, spoke for those doubly oppressed by race and sex—black women.

. . . I want women to have their rights. In the courts women have no right, no voice; nobody speaks for them. I wish woman to have her voice there among the pettifoggers. If it is not a fit place for women, it is unfit for men to be there.

I am above eighty years old; it is about time for me to be going. I have been forty years a slave and forty years free, and would be here forty years more to have equal rights for all. I suppose I am kept here because something remains for me to do; I suppose I am yet to help to break the chain. I have done a great deal of work; as much as a man, but did not get so much pay. I used to work in the field and bind grain, keeping up with the cradler; but men doing no more, got twice as much pay. . . . We do as much, we eat as much, we want as much. I suppose I am about the only colored woman that goes about to speak for the rights of the colored women. I want to keep the thing stirring, now that the ice is cracked. What we want is a little money. You men know that you get as much again as women, when you write, or for what you do. When we get our rights, we shall not have to come to you for money, for then we shall have money enough in our own pockets; and maybe you will ask us for money. But help us now until we get it. It is a good consolation to know that when we have got this battle once fought we shall not be coming to you any more. . . .

I am glad to see that men are getting their rights, but I want women to get theirs, and while the water is stirring I will step into the pool. Now that there is a great stir about colored men's getting their rights is the time for women to step in and have theirs. I am sometimes told that "Women ain't fit to vote. What, don't you know that a woman had seven devils in her: and do you suppose a woman is fit to rule the nation?" Seven devils aint no account; a man had a legion in him. The devils didn't know where to go; and so they asked that they might go into the swine. They thought that was as good a place as they came out from. They didn't ask to go into the sheep—no, into the hog; that was the selfish beast; and man is so selfish that he has got women's rights and his own too, and yet he won't give women their rights. He keeps them all to himself. . . .

ELIZABETH CADY STANTON

89. The solitude of self

On February 20, 1894, four women delivered speeches before a
Senate committee, arguing in favor of the woman suffrage amendment: Susan B. Anthony, Lucy Stone, Isabella Beecher Hooker,
and the seventy-six-year-old Elizabeth Cady Stanton. Mrs. Stanton's address, thereafter known as "The Solitude of Self" speech,
presented an altogether startling argument. Discarding practical
and pragmatic arguments and disregarding all the objections,
which prosuffrage speakers usually painstakingly tried to refute,
Stanton argued entirely from natural law. Her reasoning was fundamental and forceful in its simplicity. Whatever else fifty years of
agitation had brought forth in argument and refutation, the basic
truth remained: women were responsible individuals and as such
entitled to self-determination.

The speech was printed in the congressional record and circulated in a reprint by the *Woman's Tribune* in "many hundreds of
copies." It seems quite as appropriate today as it did then.

The point I wish plainly to bring before you on this occasion
is the individuality of each human soul—our Protestant
idea, the right of individual conscience and judgment—our
republican idea, individual citizenship. In discussing the
rights of woman, we are to consider, first, what belongs to
her as an individual, in a world of her own, the arbiter of her
own destiny, an imaginary Robinson Crusoe with her
woman Friday on a solitary island. Her rights under such
circumstances are to use all her faculties for her own safety
and happiness.

Secondly, if we consider her as a citizen, as a member of a
great nation, she must have the same rights as all other
members, according to the fundamental principles of our
Government.

Susan B. Anthony and Ida Husted Harper, eds., *The History of Woman
Suffrage*, 6 vols. (Indianapolis: Hollenbeck Press, 1902) IV: 189–191.

Thirdly, viewed as a woman, an equal factor in civilization, her rights and duties are still the same—individual happiness and development.

Fourthly, it is only the incidental relations of life, such as mother, wife, sister, daughter, which may involve some special duties and training. In the usual discussion in regard to woman's sphere, such men as Herbert Spencer, Frederick Harrison and Grant Allen uniformly subordinate her rights and duties as an individual, as a citizen, as a woman, to the necessities of these incidental relations, some of which a large class of women never assume. In discussing the sphere of man we do not decide his rights as an individual, as a citizen, as a man, by his duties as a father, a husband, a brother or a son, some of which he may never undertake. Moreover he would be better fitted for these very relations, and whatever special work he might choose to do to earn his bread, by the complete development of all his faculties as an individual. Just so with woman. The education which will fit her to discharge the duties in the largest sphere of human usefulness, will best fit her for whatever special work she may be compelled to do.

The isolation of every human soul and the necessity of self-dependence must give each individual the right to choose his own surroundings. The strongest reason for giving woman all the opportunities for higher education, for the full development of her faculties, her forces of mind and body; for giving her the most enlarged freedom of thought and action; a complete emancipation from all forms of bondage, of custom, dependence, superstition; from all the crippling influences of fear—is the solitude and personal responsibility of her own individual life. The strongest reason why we ask for woman a voice in the government under which she lives; in the religion she is asked to believe; equality in social life, where she is the chief factor; a place in the trades and professions, where she may earn her bread, is because of her birthright to self-sovereignty; because, as an individual, she must rely on herself. . . .

To throw obstacles in the way of a complete education is like putting out the eyes; to deny the rights of property is like cutting off the hands. To refuse political equality is like robbing the ostracized of all self-respect, of credit in the market place, of recompense in the world of work, of a voice in choosing those who make and administer the law, a choice in the jury before whom they are tried, and in the judge who decides their punishment. Shakespeare's play of Titus and Andronicus contains a terrible satire on woman's position in the nineteenth century—"Rude men seized the king's daughter, cut out her tongue, cut off her hands, and then bade her go call for water and wash her hands." What a picture of woman's position! Robbed of her natural rights, handicapped by law and custom at every turn, yet compelled to fight her own battles, and in the emergencies of life fall back on herself for protection. . . .

How the little courtesies of life on the surface of society, deemed so important from man towards woman, fade into utter insignificance in view of the deeper tragedies in which she must play her part alone, where no human aid is possible!

Nothing strengthens the judgment and quickens the conscience like individual responsibility. Nothing adds such dignity to character as the recognition of one's self-sovereignty; the right to an equal place, everywhere conceded—a place earned by personal merit, not an artificial attainment by inheritance, wealth, family and position. Conceding then that the responsibilities of life rest equally on man and woman, that their destiny is the same, they need the same preparation for time and eternity. The talk of sheltering woman from the fierce storms of life is the sheerest mockery, for they beat on her from every point of the compass, just as they do on man, and with more fatal results, for he has been trained to protect himself, to resist, to conquer. . . .

We see reason sufficient in the outer conditions of human

beings for individual liberty and development, but when we consider the self-dependence of every human soul, we see the need of courage, judgment and the exercise of every faculty of mind and body, strengthened and developed by use, in woman as well as man. . . .

90. Lucille Clifton (1936–   )

In the following thirteen superbly crafted lines, a modern black poet summarizes the essence of the experience of self-discovery expressed over and over again in the preceding documents. The poem gives voice to the sense of self-awareness ("turning on in/to my own self"), to the shedding of race and class barriers as defined by others, to the acceptance of a self created by one's own definition.

Lucille Clifton is a poet living in Baltimore. She participated in the 1961 YM-YWCA Poetry Center's Discovery Series. She has written three children's books. The poem below is from her third published volume of poetry.

TURNING

turning into my own
turning on in
to my own self
at last
turning out of the
white cage, turning out of the
lady cage
turning at last
on a stem like a black fruit
in my own season
at last

91. Muriel Rukeyser (1913–   )

From self-definition ("Announce your soul in discovery") comes strength, the strength of accepting one's sex, one's femaleness ("Know your own secrets . . . Go toward the essence, the impulse of creation"). Such acceptance leads to a new definition of humanity ("where power comes in music from the sex") which heals the ancient split imposed upon women by patriarchy. No longer walled off from self, from sisterhood and from that "spirit" by which civilized mankind defines itself in science, philosophy and artistic creation, woman is free to "seize structure. Correspond with the real. Fuse spirit and matter." Woman, no longer acted upon as man's "other," becomes free to act "on all things." She can pass, God-like and human "among . . . all things . . . moving the constellations of all things."

Muriel Rukeyser, poet, lecturer, and teacher, is a member of the National Institute of Arts and Letters and the recipient of many honors and awards. In addition to five volumes of prose and a number of children's books, she has published a dozen volumes of poetry.

THE SIX CANONS
(after Binyon)

Seize structure.
Correspond with the real.
Fuse spirit and matter.
Know your own secrets.
Announce your soul in discovery.
Go toward the essence, the impulse of creation,
    where power comes in music from the sex,
    where power comes in music from the spirit,
    where sex and spirit are one self
    passing among
    and acting on all things
    and their relationships,
    moving the constellations of all things.

Select Bibliography

The citations for the items referred to or quoted in this book can be found in the footnotes and source notes, and should first be consulted by those wishing further information.

Collateral Readings

Readers interested in seeking background and correlated readings in printed sources should consult one or more of the following major bibliographies in women's history:

Herstory, microfilm of content of International Women's History Periodical Archives (Berkeley, Calif.: Women's History Research Center); Sue-Ellen Jacobs, *Women in Perspective: A Guide to Cross-Cultural Studies* (Urbana: Univ. of Illinois Press, 1973); Edward and Janet James, eds., *Notable American Women: A Biographical Dictionary,* 3 vols. (Cambridge: Harvard Univ. Press, 1972), an invaluable reference work containing bibliographies on each of the 1,359 women listed and an introductory essay offering a useful overview of the field; Joan Kelly-Gadol, *Women's History: A Critically Selected Bibliography,* 4th ed. (Bronxville, N.Y.: Sarah Lawrence College, 1976); Albert Krichmar et al., *The Woman's Rights Movement in the United States, 1848–1970* (Metuchen, N.J.: Scarecrow Press, 1972); E. Leonard, S. Drinker, and M. Holden, eds., *The American Woman in Colonial and Revolutionary Times, 1565–1800; A Syllabus with Bibliography* (Philadelphia: Univ. of Pennsylvania Press, 1962); Gerda Lerner, *Bibliography in the History of American Women,* 2d ed. (Bronxville, N.Y.: Sarah Lawrence College, 1975); H. Carleton Marlow, *Bibliography of American Women,* microfilm ed. (Woodbridge, Conn.: Research Publications, Inc.); *Women and the Law: A Collection of Reading Lists* (Pittsburgh: Know, Inc., 1971); Women's History Research Center, *Bibliographies on Women—Indexed by Topic* (Berkeley, Calif., 1973).

Secondary sources on women's history have proliferated so greatly and range over so wide a field that their listing would far exceed the scope of this book. The following offer an introduction to the field:

Eleanor Flexner, *Century of Struggle*, rev. ed. (Cambridge: Belknap Press of Harvard Univ. Press, 1975); Alan Pendleton Grimes, *The Puritan Ethic and Woman Suffrage* (New York: Oxford Univ. Press, 1967); Aileen S. Kraditor, *Ideas of the Woman Suffrage Movement, 1890–1920* (New York: Columbia Univ. Press, 1965); Gerda Lerner, *The Woman in American History* (Reading, Mass.: Addison-Wesley Co., 1971); William O'Neill, *Everyone Was Brave* (Chicago: Quadrangle Books, 1969); Mary Ryan, *Womanhood in America: From Colonial Times to the Present* (New York: New Viewpoints/Franklin Watts, 1975).

The indispensable primary source for the history of the woman suffrage movement is Elizabeth C. Stanton, Susan B. Anthony, and Matilda J. Gage, *History of Woman Suffrage*, 6 vols. (New York: Fowler and Wells, 1881–1922). It can be usefully supplemented by the more recent, Anne F. and Andrew M. Scott, *One Half the People: The Fight for Woman's Suffrage* (Philadelphia: J. B. Lippincott, 1975).

The major specialized journals are *Feminist Studies* (Summer 1972 to date) 294 Riverside Drive, New York, N.Y., 10025; *Journal of Family History*, (September 1976 to date), National Council on Family Relations, 1219 University Ave., S.E., Minneapolis, Minn. 55414; *Signs: Journal of Women in Culture and Society* (September 1975 to date), Univ. of Chicago Press, 11030 Langley Ave., Chicago, Ill. 60628; *Women's Studies* (1972 to date), Gordon and Breach Science Publications, 440 Park Avenue, South, New York, N.Y., 10016.

PRIMARY SOURCES

The primary sources pertaining to women in history are varied, rich, little explored, and range over most fields of historical scholarship. They include the major collections of the papers of "notable women" and of the organized woman's movement. Any source pertaining to social history is likely to offer material concerning women.

Every state, and county historical society contains large numbers of primary sources pertaining to women. State and local government records, the records of health and welfare institutions, schools, school boards and committees, churches, voluntary associations, and other community institutions abound with source materials documenting the activities and concerns of women. Every collection of "family papers," regardless of how it is classified and indexed, encompasses women's history. The collections of reform organizations, from missionary to abolition societies, from literary circles to temperance organizations, from mothers' clubs to consumer organizations, reflect and document the history of women. Factory, business, and trade union records document the activities of working women, as do governmental investigation committees, legislative hearings, and the reports of specialized agencies. Even some sources in diplomatic and military history hold information about women's work, lives and concerns.

If the vastness and range of primary sources make it impractical to attempt a comprehensive listing of such sources within the scope of this book, the long neglect of the subject of women in history poses special problems of archival retrieval for the scholar in this field. With the exception of the few specialized collections and the manuscripts of famous women, most primary sources pertaining to women are hidden under male-oriented classifications. For example, family papers arranged under the names of male family heads tend to submerge sources by and about women. In many cases, women can only be identified through their husbands' names. In other cases, the categories of classification refer only to those activities in which men predominate.

Archivists have only very recently begun to develop and use categories of classification appropriate to women's history. Where they have done so, "hidden" sources of information about women have surfaced. Since the record of women and their activities is spread widely through most, if not all, historical sources, finding such information depends entirely on what questions are asked.

A major archival project, the Women's History Sources Survey, which will create a research guide to manuscripts and archival sources in the United States, is now under way at the University of Minnesota. A preliminary national questionnaire done in preparation for this project turned up over 2,000 "women's" collections scattered in various archives and libraries. This figure, which refers only to collections already classified, is by now considered outdated and far too low. The Women's History Sources Survey is already leading major historical archives to cataloging their holdings on women. Once completed, the project should make research on the subject as readily available as is that on any other historical subject. Until it does, the following brief account may be of some help to students and researchers. It obviously can merely highlight the most important sources and mention major collections of readily available primary sources in women's history.

The largest specialized collections of primary manuscripts and printed sources on the history of women are the Schlesinger Library at Radcliffe College and the Sophia Smith Collection at Smith College. Other important specialized collections are the Gerritsen Collection at the University of Kansas and the private collection of Miriam Y. Holden of New York City, both of which contain important sources of the history of European as well as American women; the Jane Addams Hull House library, which abounds in sources pertaining to the settlement house movement; the Galatea Collection of the Boston Public Library and the women's history collections at the Research Libraries of the New York Public Library. All these collections have recently been made available on microfilm.

The vast resources of the Library of Congress hold important manuscripts of individual women, records of the national and state suffrage organizations, and the papers of major reform and social welfare organizations in which women were active or in leadership. The National Archives hold a wealth of sources in official documents, in records of government agencies and departments, and in the massive records of both houses of Congress and their committees. Other major women's history collections may be found in the Henry E. Huntington Library, San Marino, Calif.; the Ida Rust McPherson Collection at Scripps College, Claremont, Calif.; and the Social Welfare History Archives Center and the Immigrant History Archives at the University of Minnesota Libraries. Outstanding among Southern collections are those at Atlanta University's Trevor Arnett Library; Duke University; and the University of Georgia, Athens. The Amistad Research Center at Dillard University, New Orleans, holds the large American Missionary Association Archives, which details the important work of women missionaries and educators. The Women's History Research Center, Berkeley, Calif., is the foremost archive of materials pertaining to the current women's movement, both here and abroad. The

Swarthmore College Peace Collection, Swarthmore, Pa., contains records of women's peace activities. Wayne State University Archives of Labor History contain important records of radical and trade union women.

The major collections of primary sources on black women are in the Schomburg Collection, New York Public Library; the Morehouse Collection, Howard University; and special collections at Fisk University and at the Library of Congress. For a more detailed discussion of these and other sources on black women see "Notes on Sources" in Gerda Lerner, *Black Women in White America* (New York: Pantheon, 1972).

Index